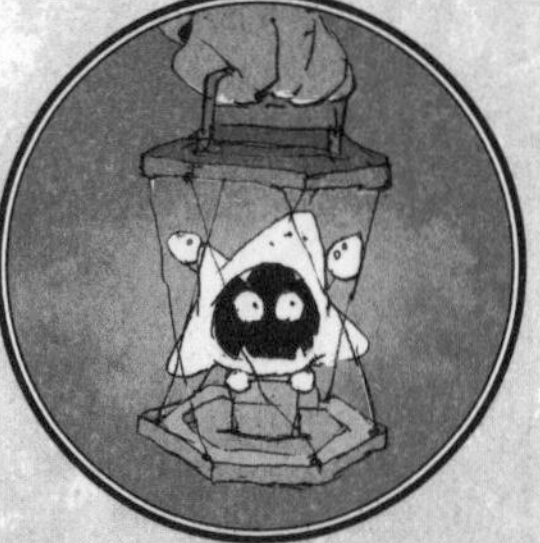

POSUKA DEMIZU

What if...there was no one,
not even a single person,
at that place?

What action would the kids take?
What would they regret?
What would they give up?

We say there are no what-ifs, but
we do have the freedom to
imagine.

Okay, we still can't take a
breather, but the story continues
in volume 7.

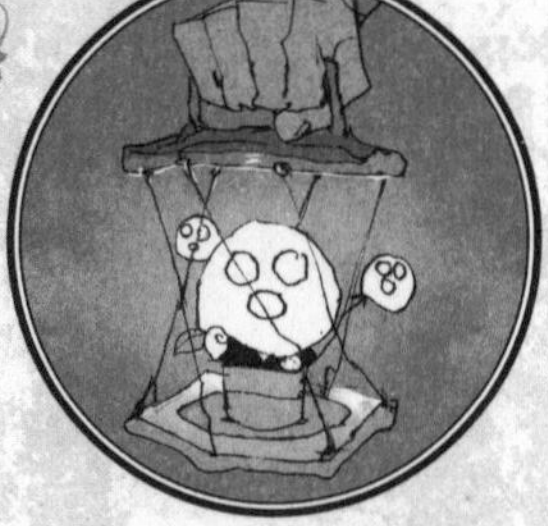

KAIU SHIRAI

Writer Shirai's personal
highlights for *The Promised
Neverland* fanatics, part 5:

1. Even the sticky notes are fun on the title page for chapter 45!

2. The straw hats in chapter 47! (There are other hats hidden within the chapter too. I think there are three more hidden hats, in various styles. The correct answer is...?)

3. There are clues to future plot points in the artwork! (Where? Some of it will be clear in the next volume.)

Okay, please enjoy this volume!

Posuka Demizu debuted as a manga artist with the 2013 *CoroCoro* series *Oreca Monster Bouken Retsuden*. A collection of illustrations, *The Art of Posuka Demizu*, was released in 2016 by PIE International.

Kaiu Shirai debuted in 2015 with *Ashley Gate no Yukue* on the *Shonen Jump+* website. Shirai first worked with Posuka Demizu on the two-shot *Poppy no Negai*, which was released in February 2016.

THE PROMISED NEVERLAND

VOLUME 6
SHONEN JUMP Manga Edition

STORY BY KAIU SHIRAI
ART BY POSUKA DEMIZU

Translation/Satsuki Yamashita
Touch-Up Art & Lettering/Mark McMurray
Design/Julian [JR] Robinson
Editor/Alexis Kirsch

Printed in Italy

Published by VIZ Media, LLC
P.O. Box 77010
San Francisco, CA 94107

10 9 8 7 6 5
First printing, October 2018
Fifth printing, April 2021

VIZ MEDIA
viz.com

ratings.viz.com RATED T+ OLDER TEEN

PARENTAL ADVISORY
THE PROMISED NEVERLAND is rated T+ and is recommended for ages 16 and up. This volume contains fantasy violence and adult themes.

SHONEN JUMP

THE PROMISED NEVERLAND

6

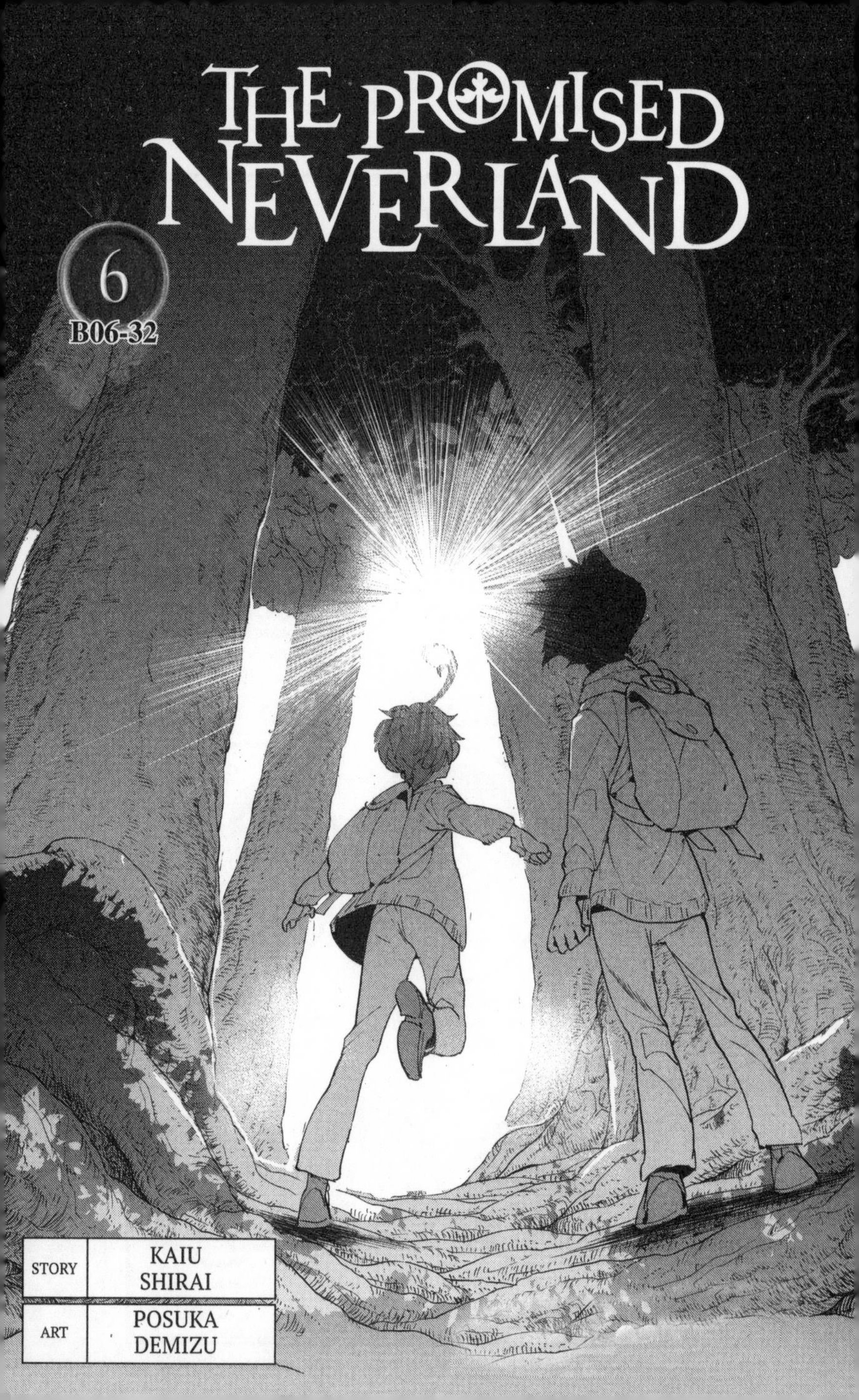

STORY	KAIU SHIRAI
ART	POSUKA DEMIZU

The Children of Grace Field House

They aim to free all of the children who are trapped in Grace Field House within two years.

CHARACTERS

EMMA

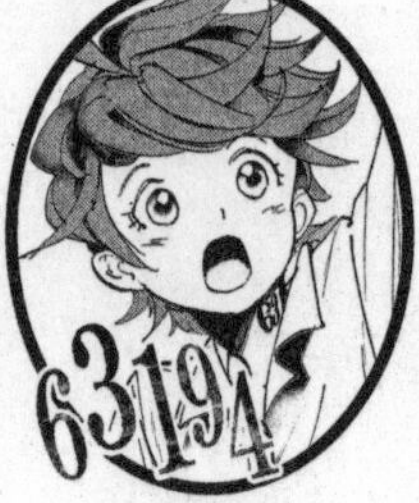
63194

An enthusiastic and optimistic girl with superb athletic and learning abilities.

RAY

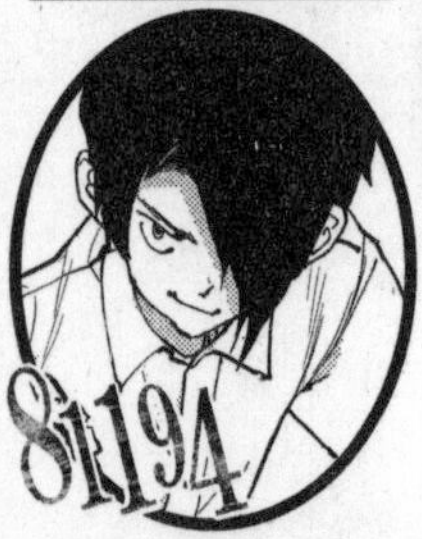
81194

The only one among the Grace Field House children who could match wits with Norman.

NORMAN

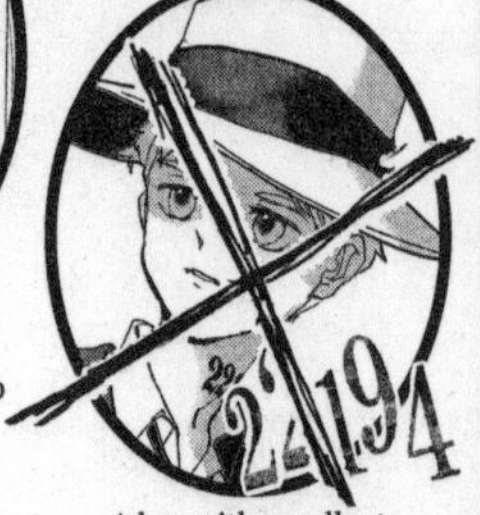
22194

A boy with excellent analytical and decision-making capabilities. He was the smartest child at Grace Field House.

PHIL

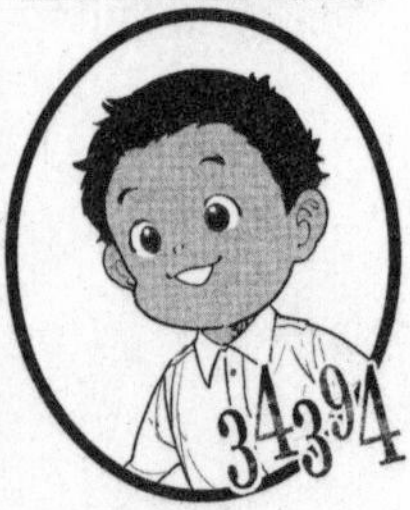
34394

A bighearted boy who loves Emma. He is always full of energy.

GILDA

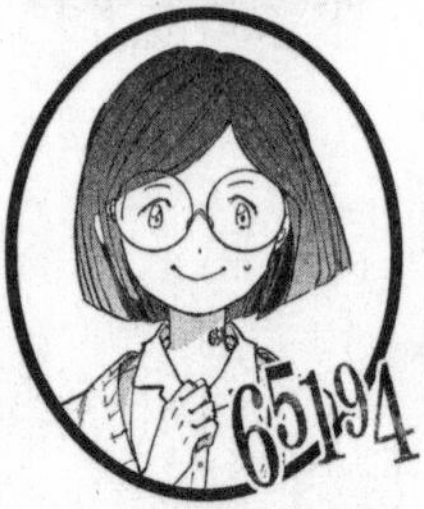
65194

A clever girl who has great insight and acts accordingly.

DON

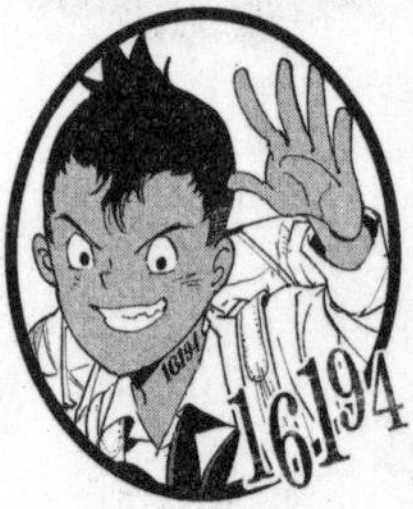
16194

A carefree boy who is cheerful but competitive.

LANNION

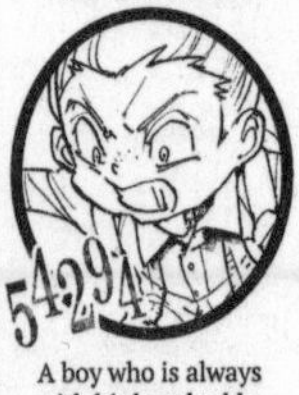
54294

A boy who is always with his best buddy, Thoma.

THOMA

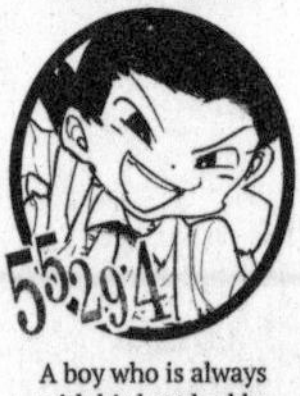
55294

A boy who is always with his best buddy, Lannion.

NAT

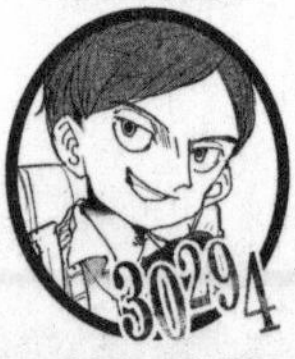
30294

A slightly narcissistic boy who is a bit of a scaredy-cat.

ANNA

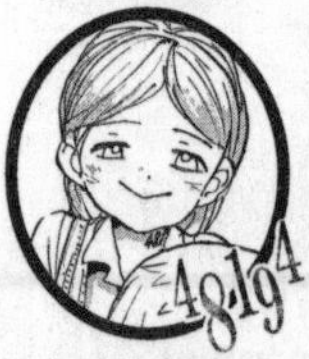
48194

A quiet but strong-willed girl who is kind to everyone.

The Adults of Grace Field House

They are kept alive to raise the children who will be presented to the demons.

KRONE

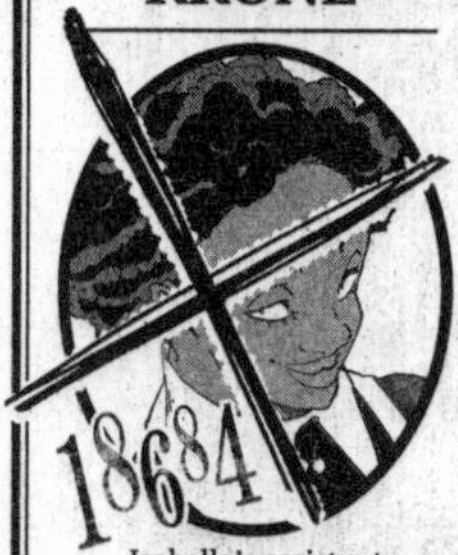
18684

Isabella's assistant and a subordinate of the demons.

GRANDMA

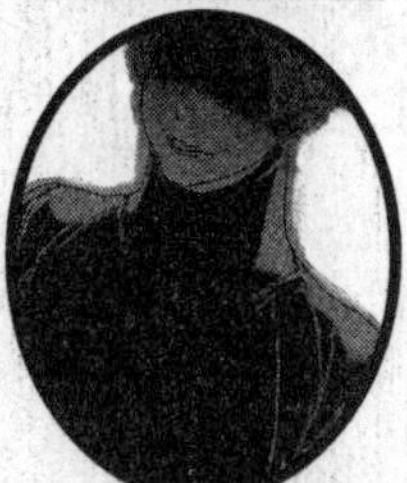

The supervisor of all the adults at Grace Field House.

ISABELLA

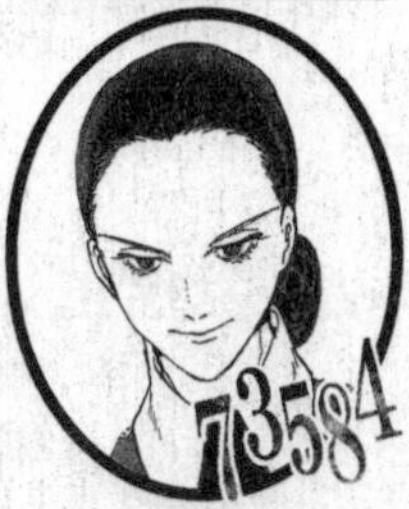
73584

A competent handler who raised Emma and the other children.

???

WILLIAM MINERVA

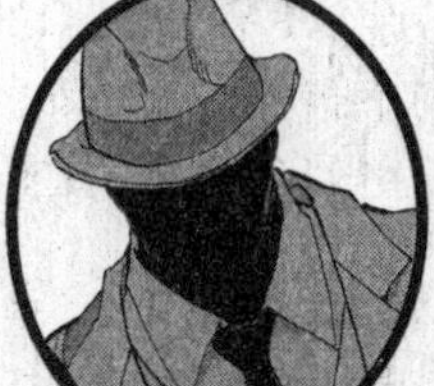

A mysterious figure who leaves various items that seem to help the children.

Demons of Grace Field House

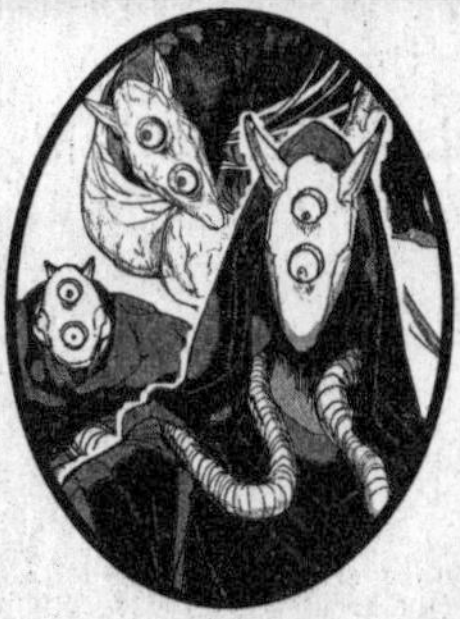

They raise human children to eat their developed brains.

The Story So Far

The 38 children of Grace Field House orphanage are all living happily with their "Mom," Isabella, treating her as if she were their real mother. One day, two of the oldest children, Emma and Norman, discover the existence of demons. They find out that Isabella is raising them to be food for the demons. The two reject their fate and decide to escape with the help of their closest friend, Ray. Eventually they bring Don and Gilda in on the plan. But before they can carry it out, Norman is shipped off. Emma and the others manage to pull off the escape anyway, but they leave the children four years and younger at the house for the time being as they head to point B06-32, a location indicated in Minerva's message.

THE PROMISED NEVERLAND 6

B06-32

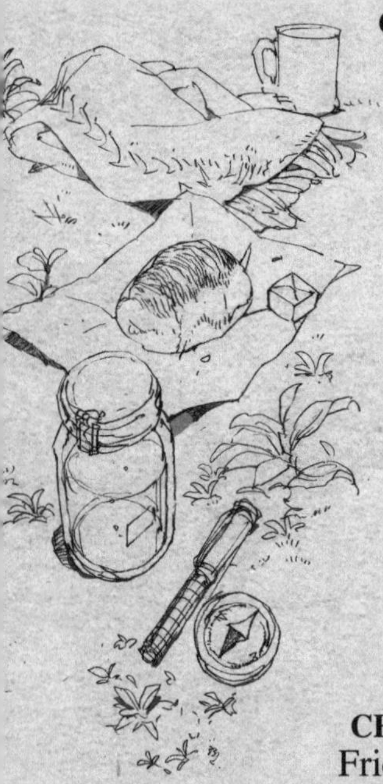

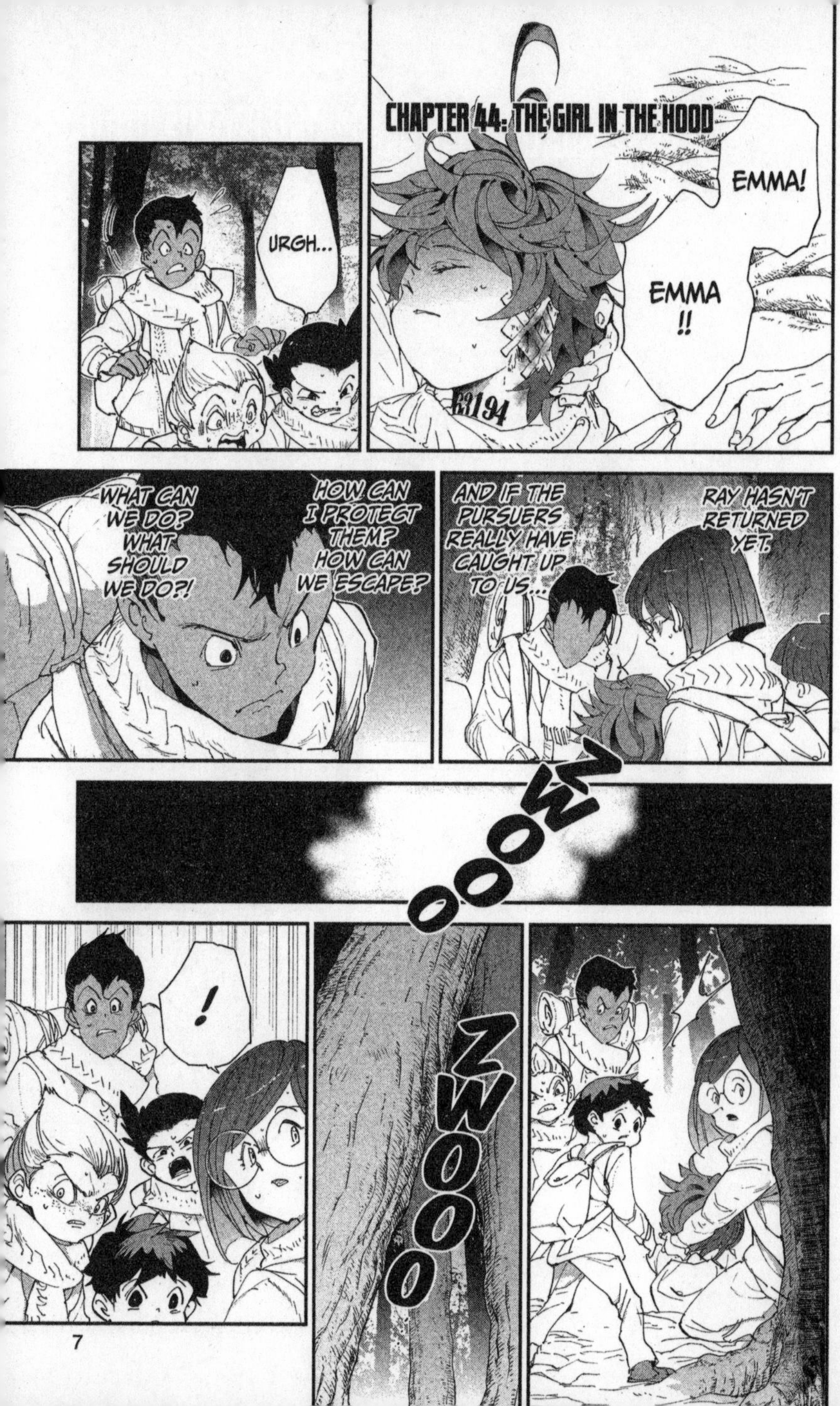
CHAPTER 44: THE GIRL IN THE HOOD
EMMA!
EMMA !!
URGH...
RAY HASN'T RETURNED YET.
AND IF THE PURSUERS REALLY HAVE CAUGHT UP TO US...
HOW CAN I PROTECT THEM? HOW CAN WE ESCAPE?
WHAT CAN WE DO? WHAT SHOULD WE DO?!
ZWOOOO
ZWOOOO
!

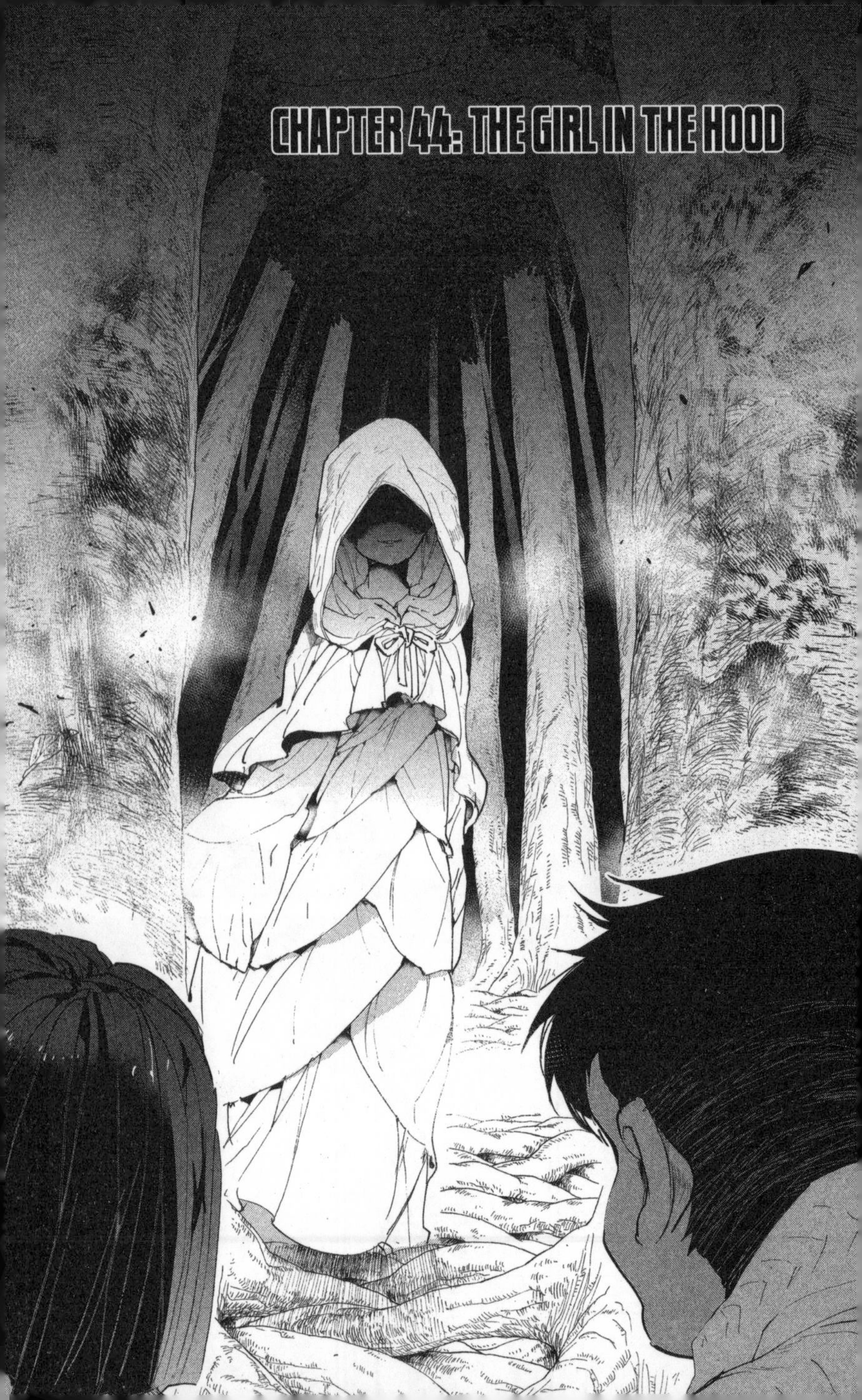
CHAPTER 44: THE GIRL IN THE HOOD

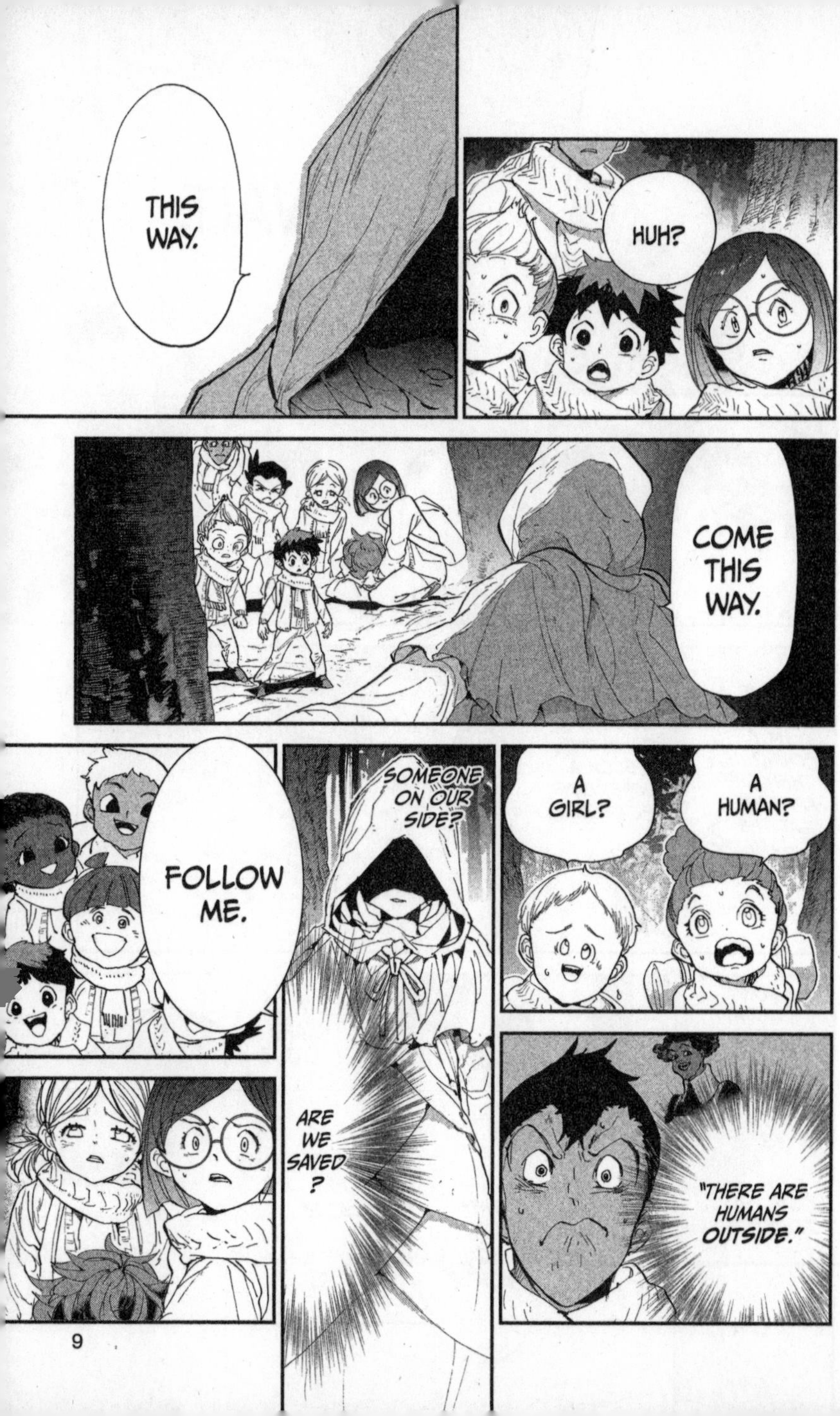
HUH?
THIS WAY.
COME THIS WAY.
A HUMAN?
A GIRL?
"THERE ARE HUMANS OUTSIDE."
SOMEONE ON OUR SIDE?
ARE WE SAVED?
FOLLOW ME.

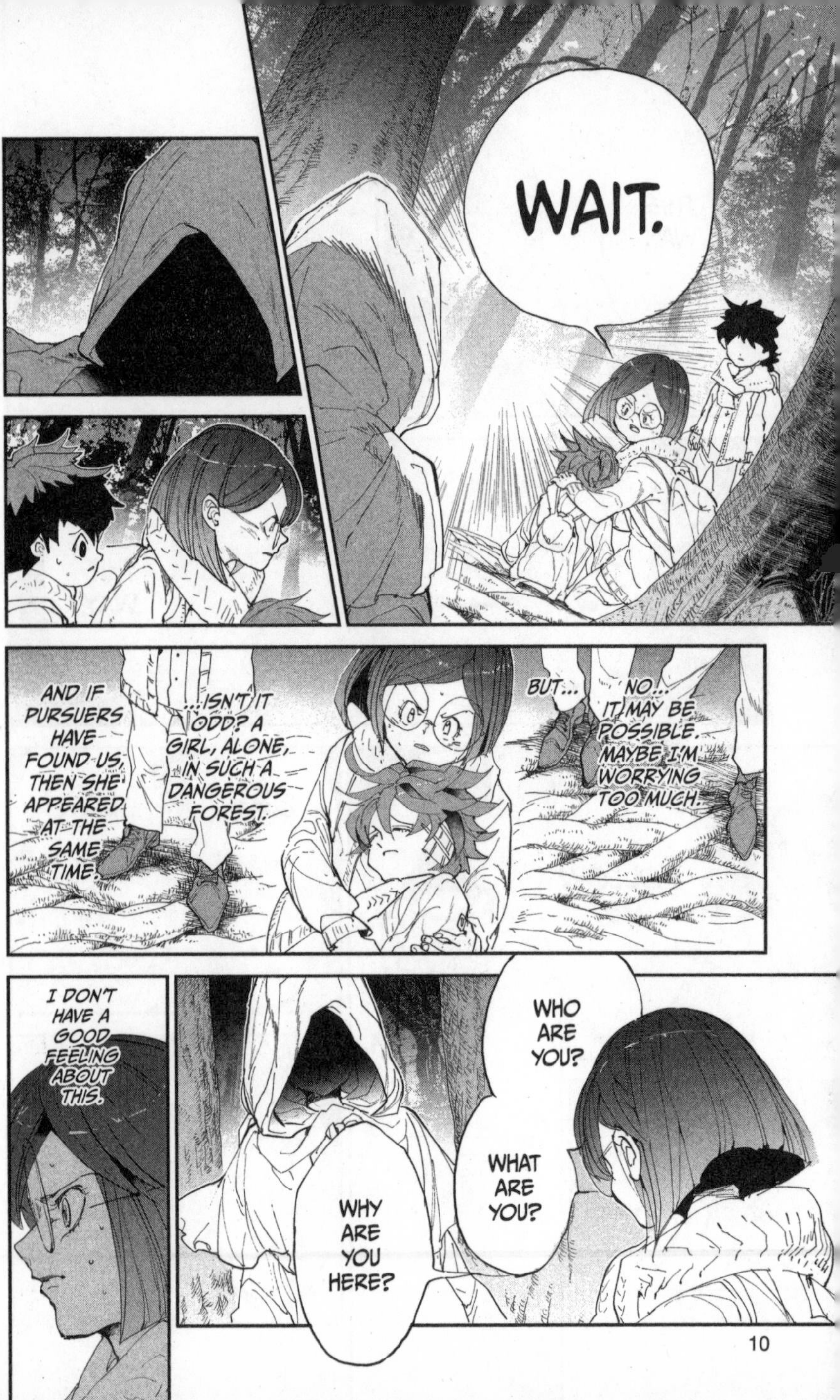
WAIT.
BUT... NO... IT MAY BE POSSIBLE. MAYBE I'M WORRYING TOO MUCH.
...ISN'T IT ODD? A GIRL, ALONE, IN SUCH A DANGEROUS FOREST.
AND IF PURSUERS HAVE FOUND US, THEN SHE APPEARED AT THE SAME TIME.
WHO ARE YOU?
WHAT ARE YOU?
WHY ARE YOU HERE?
I DON'T HAVE A GOOD FEELING ABOUT THIS.

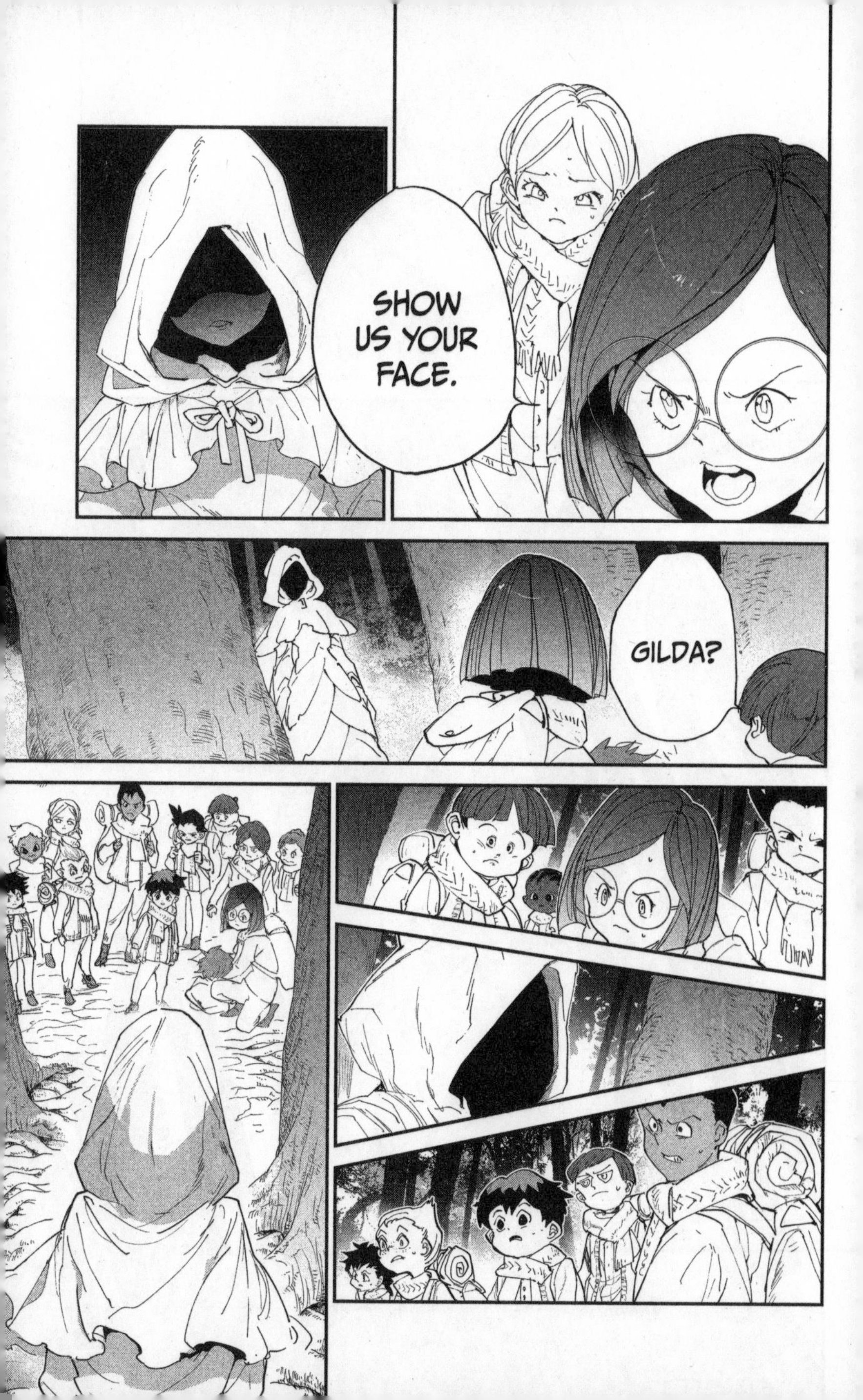
SHOW US YOUR FACE.
GILDA?

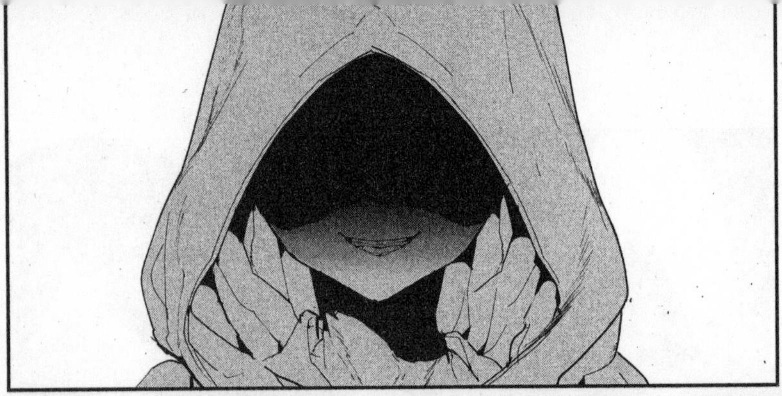

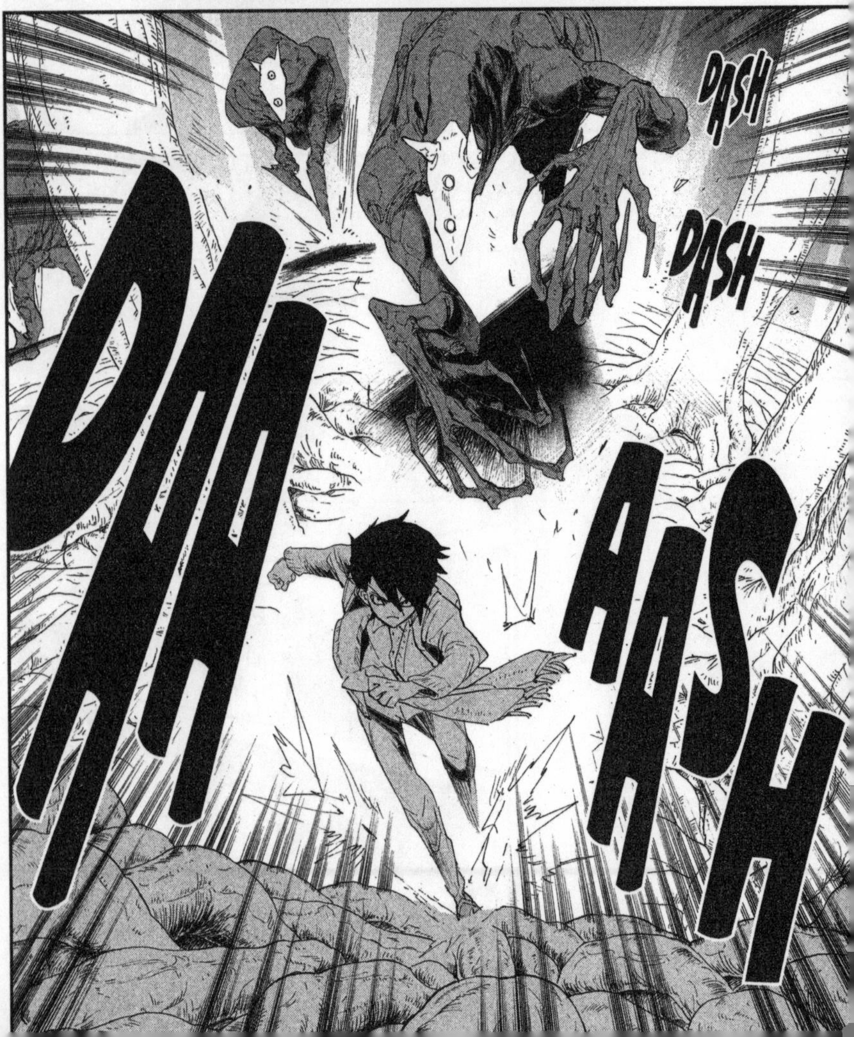
DASH
DASH
DAAAASH

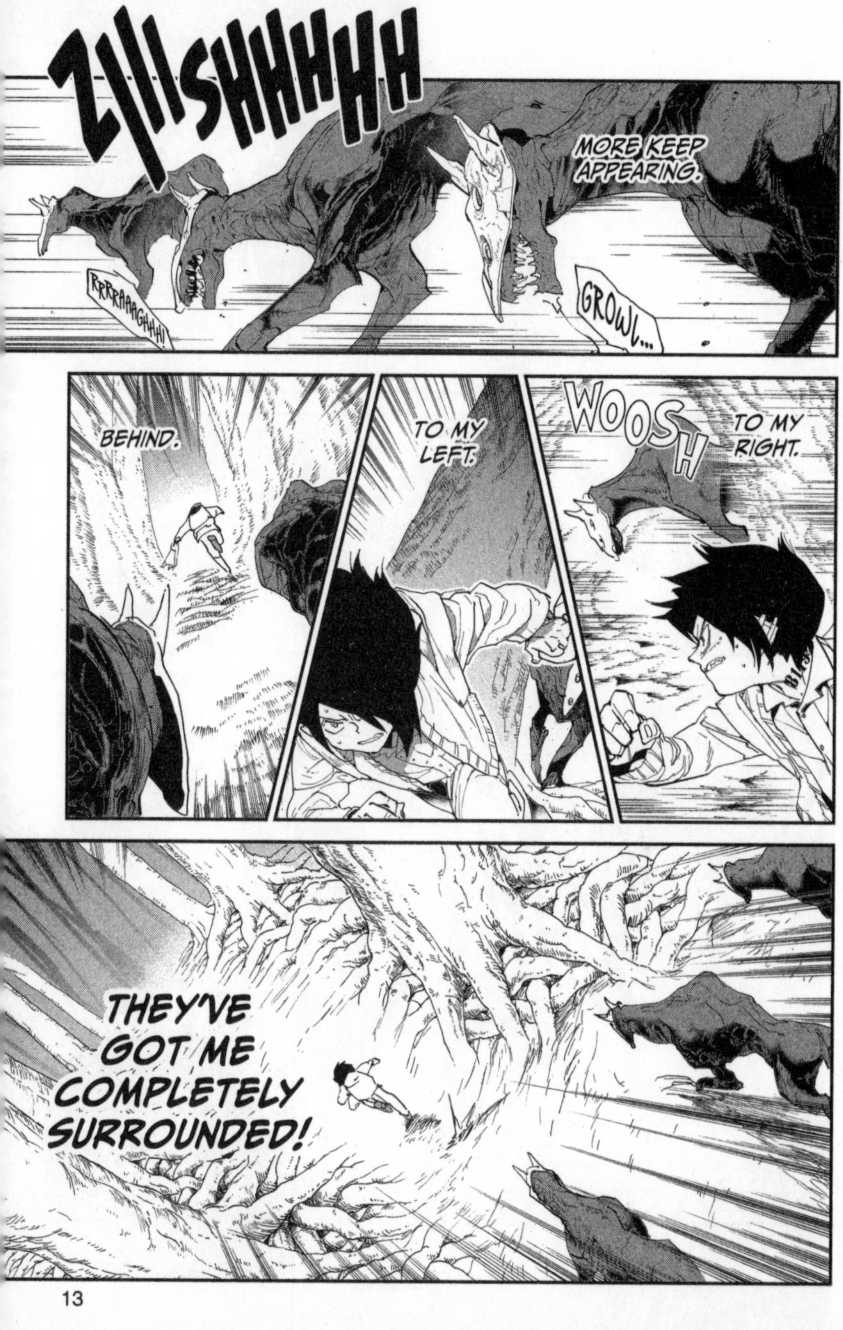
ZIIISHHHHHH
MORE KEEP APPEARING.
GROWL...
RRRRAAAGHHH!
WOOSH
TO MY RIGHT.
TO MY LEFT.
BEHIND.
THEY'VE GOT ME COMPLETELY SURROUNDED!

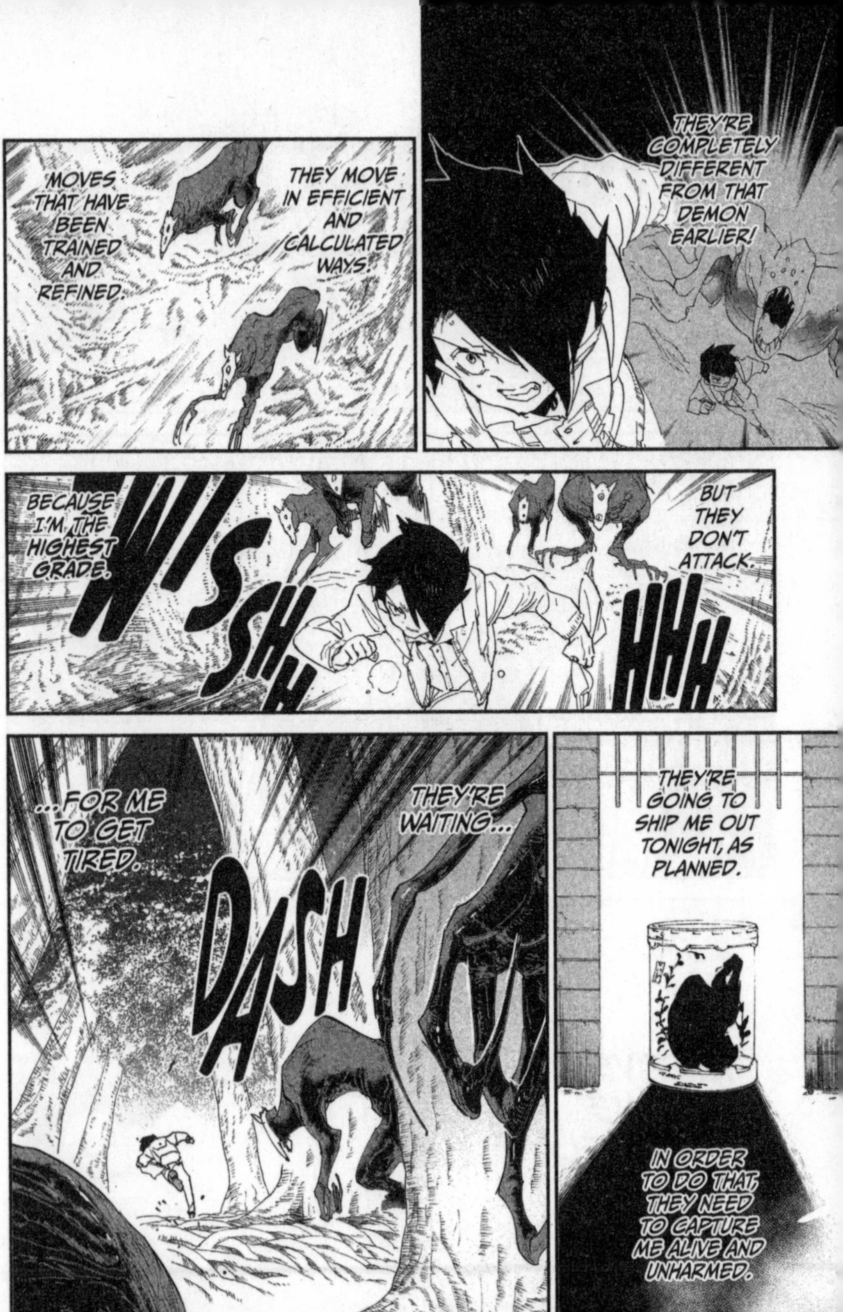
THEY'RE COMPLETELY DIFFERENT FROM THAT DEMON EARLIER!
THEY MOVE IN EFFICIENT AND CALCULATED WAYS.
MOVES THAT HAVE BEEN TRAINED AND REFINED.
BUT THEY DON'T ATTACK.
HHH
BECAUSE I'M THE HIGHEST GRADE.
WISHH
THEY'RE GOING TO SHIP ME OUT TONIGHT, AS PLANNED.
IN ORDER TO DO THAT, THEY NEED TO CAPTURE ME ALIVE AND UNHARMED.
THEY'RE WAITING...
...FOR ME TO GET TIRED.
DASH

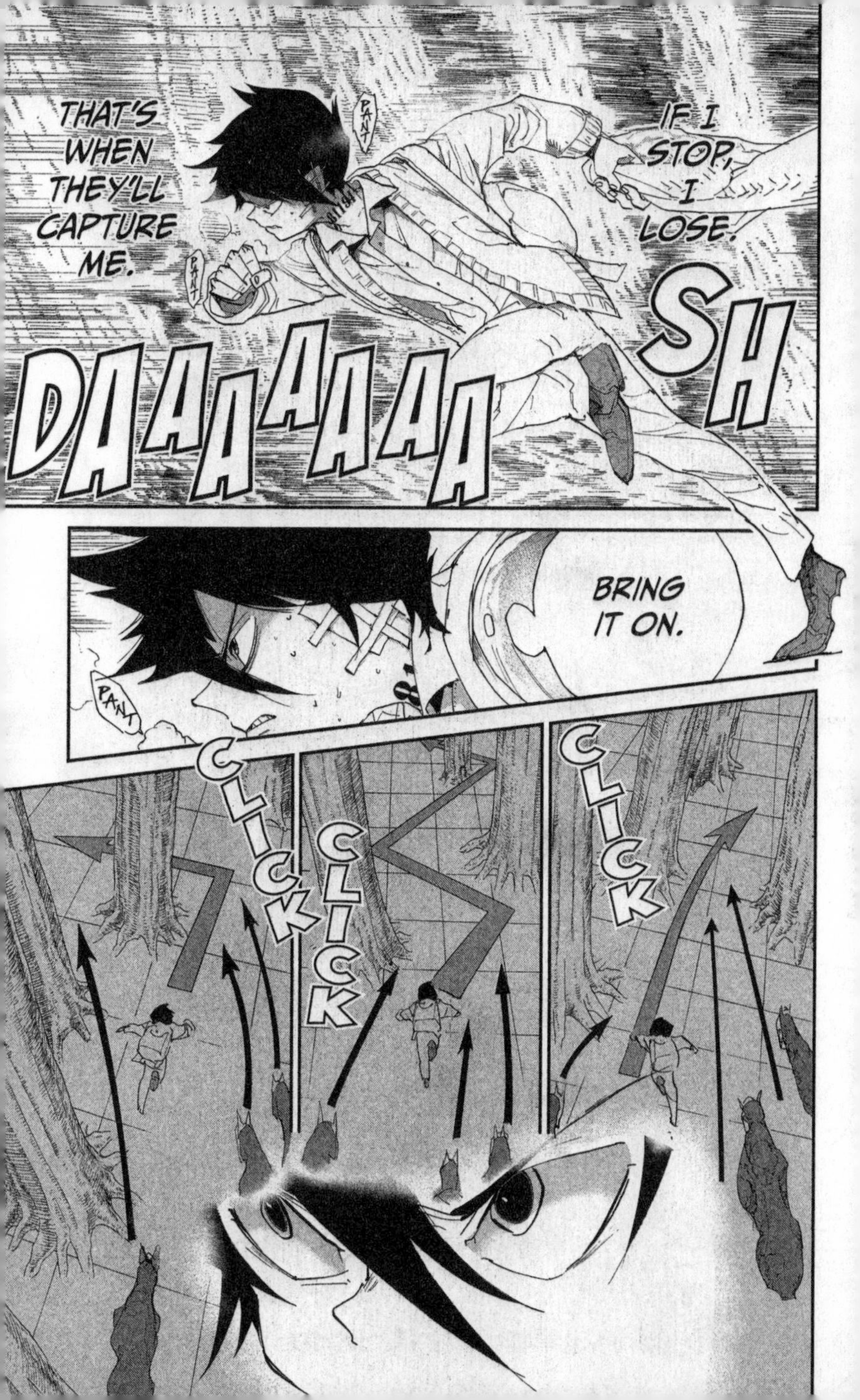
IF I STOP, I LOSE.
THAT'S WHEN THEY'LL CAPTURE ME.
PANT
PANT
DAAAAAAASH
BRING IT ON.
PANT
CLICK
CLICK
CLICK

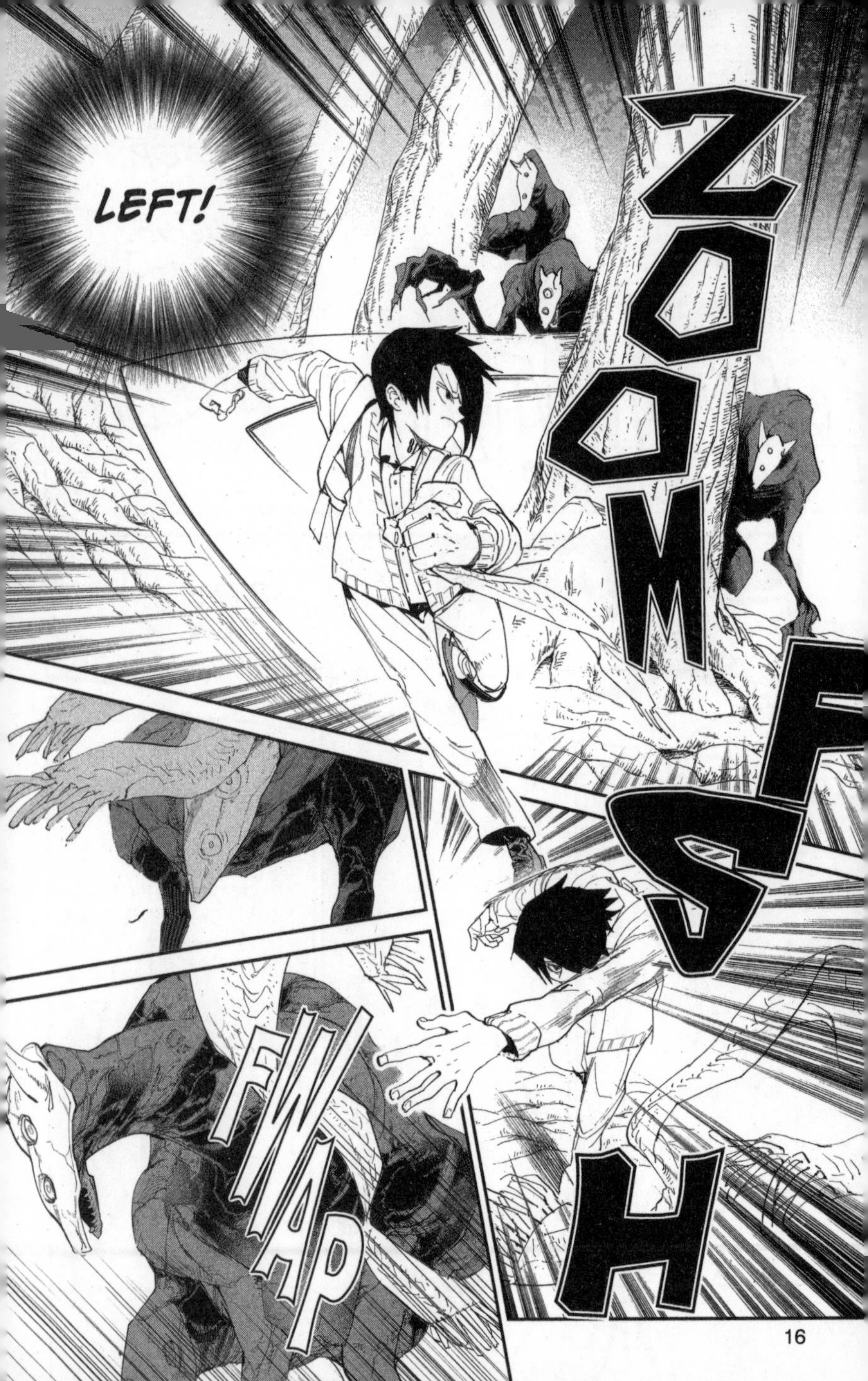
LEFT!
ZOOM
FSH
FWAP

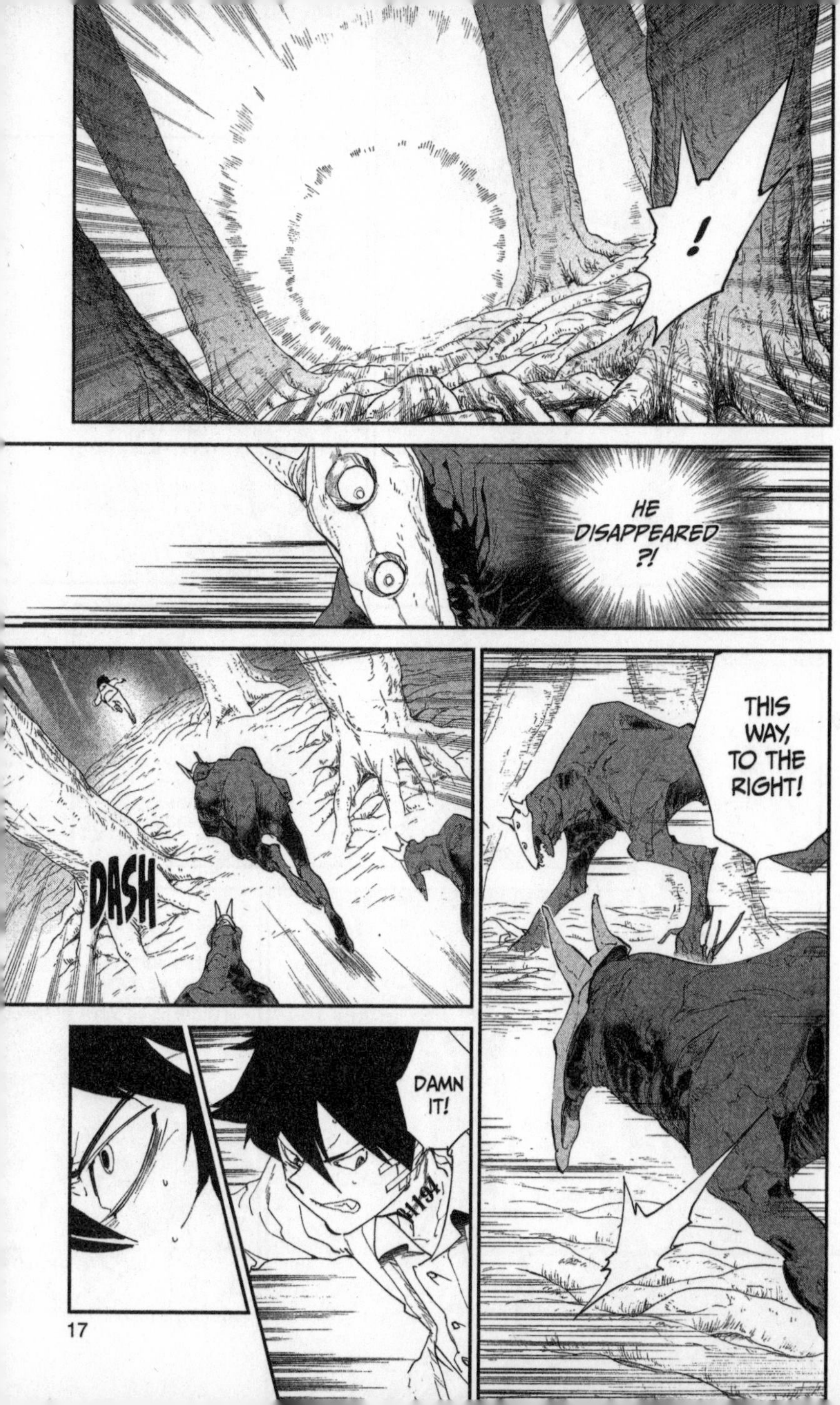
!
HE DISAPPEARED?!
THIS WAY, TO THE RIGHT!
DASH
DAMN IT!

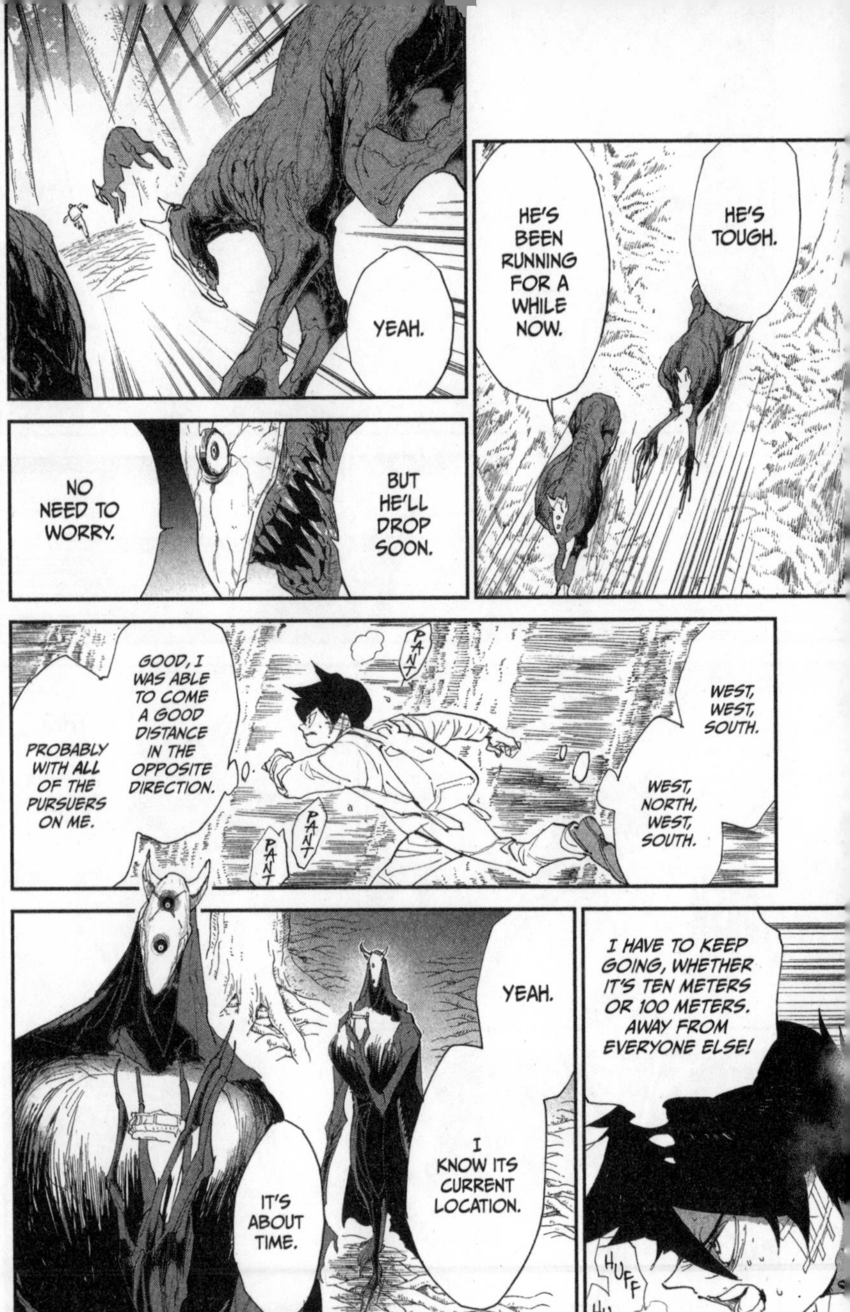
HE'S TOUGH.
HE'S BEEN RUNNING FOR A WHILE NOW.
YEAH.
BUT HE'LL DROP SOON.
NO NEED TO WORRY.
WEST, WEST, SOUTH.
WEST, NORTH, WEST, SOUTH.
PANT
GOOD, I WAS ABLE TO COME A GOOD DISTANCE IN THE OPPOSITE DIRECTION.
PROBABLY WITH ALL OF THE PURSUERS ON ME.
PANT
PANT
I HAVE TO KEEP GOING, WHETHER IT'S TEN METERS OR 100 METERS. AWAY FROM EVERYONE ELSE!
HUFF
HUFF
YEAH.
I KNOW ITS CURRENT LOCATION.
IT'S ABOUT TIME.

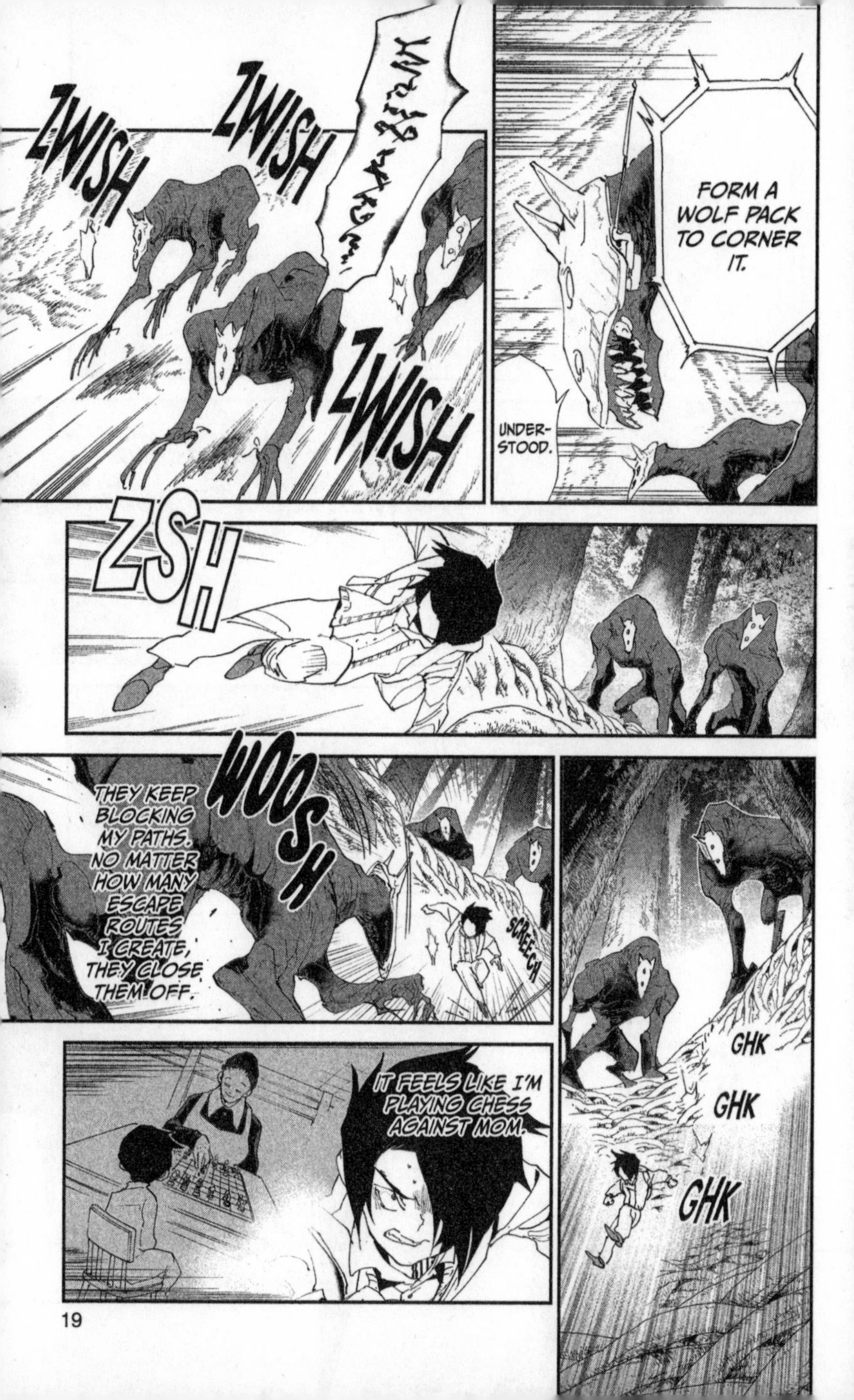
FORM A WOLF PACK TO CORNER IT.
UNDERSTOOD.
ZWISH
ZWISH
ZWISH
ZSH
GHK
GHK
GHK
WOOSH
THEY KEEP BLOCKING MY PATHS. NO MATTER HOW MANY ESCAPE ROUTES I CREATE, THEY CLOSE THEM OFF.
SCREECH
IT FEELS LIKE I'M PLAYING CHESS AGAINST MOM.

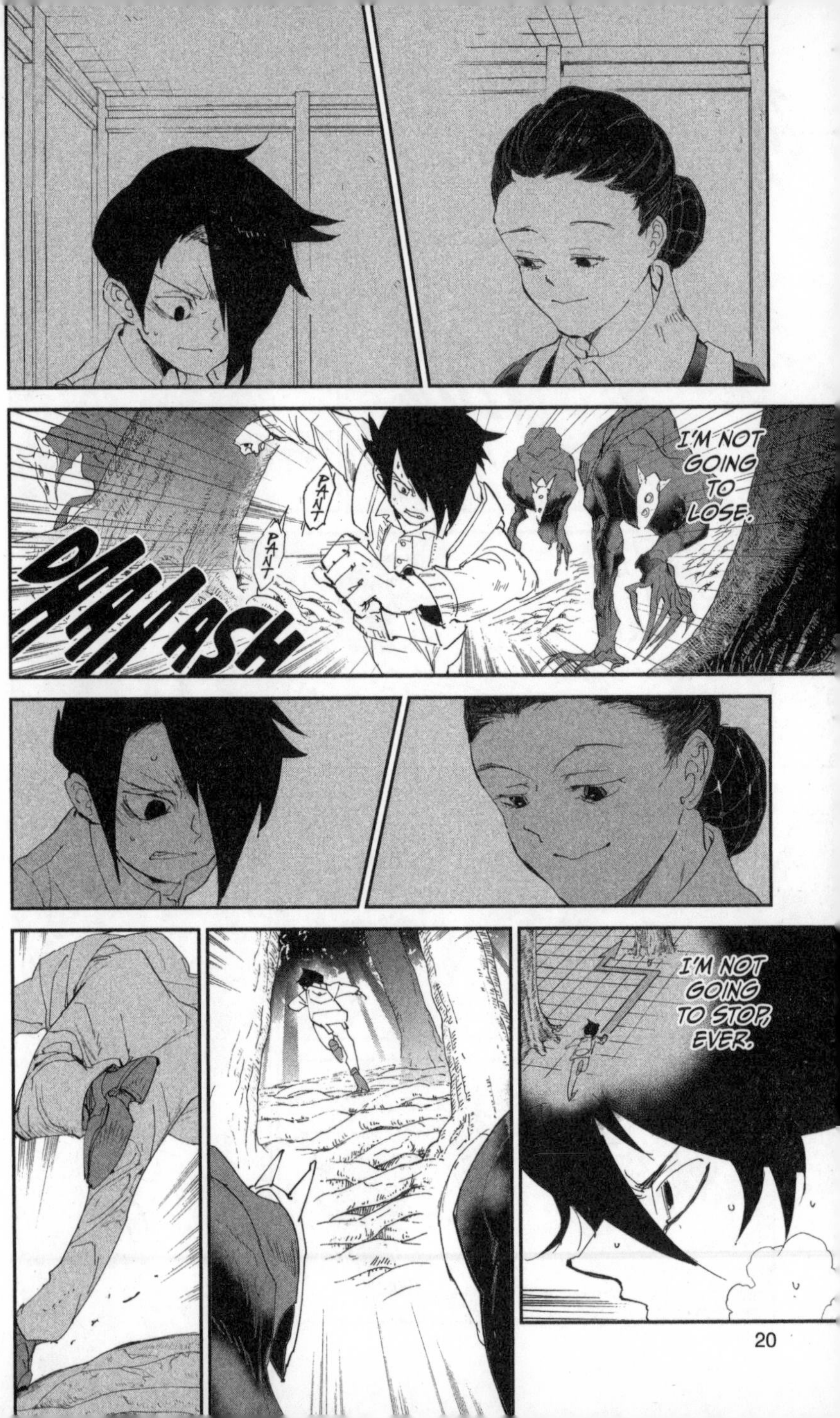
I'M NOT GOING TO LOSE.
PANT
PANT
DAAAASH
I'M NOT GOING TO STOP, EVER.

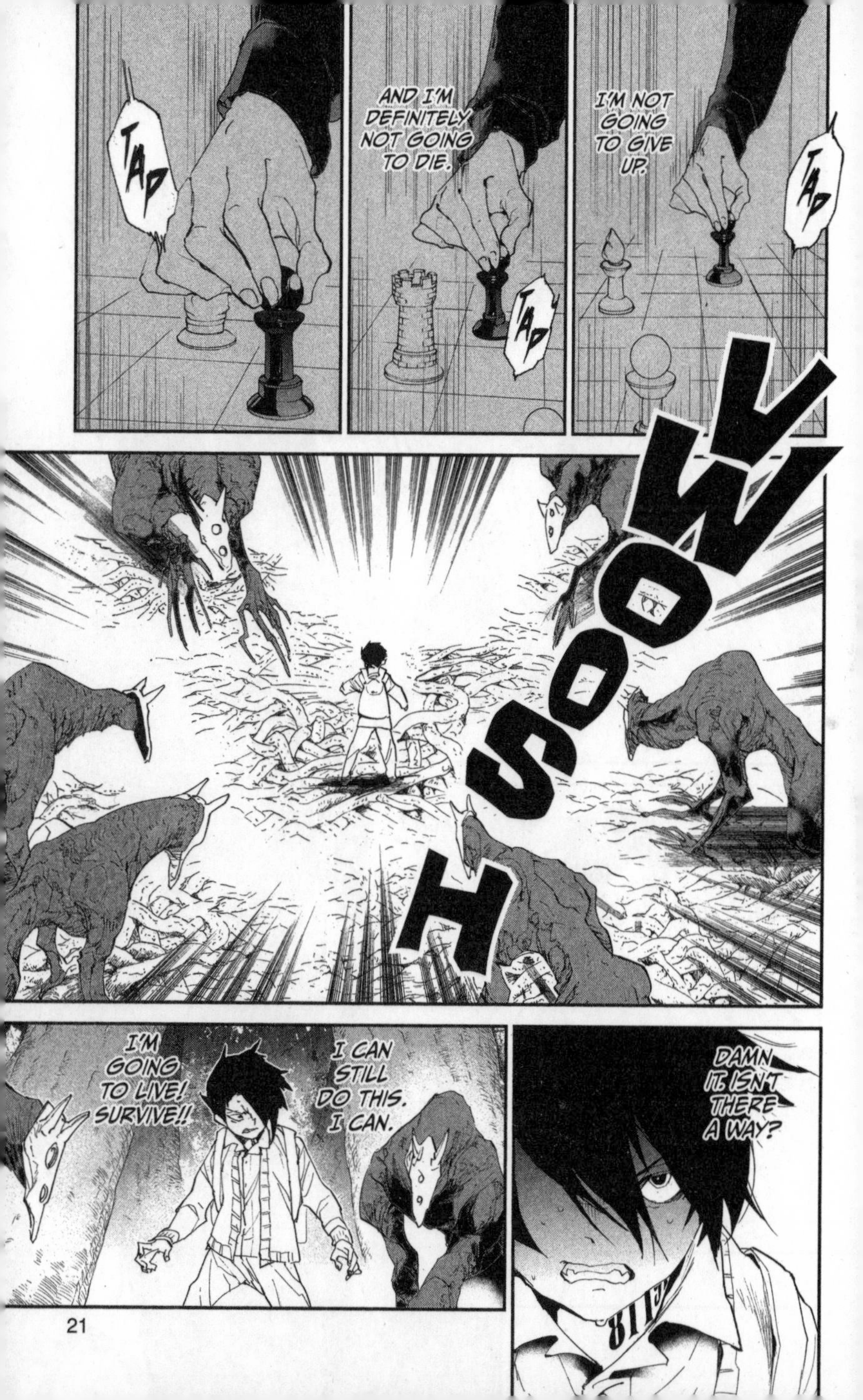
I'M NOT GOING TO GIVE UP.
TAP
AND I'M DEFINITELY NOT GOING TO DIE.
TAP
TAP
WHOOSH
DAMN IT. ISN'T THERE A WAY?
I CAN STILL DO THIS. I CAN.
I'M GOING TO LIVE! SURVIVE!!

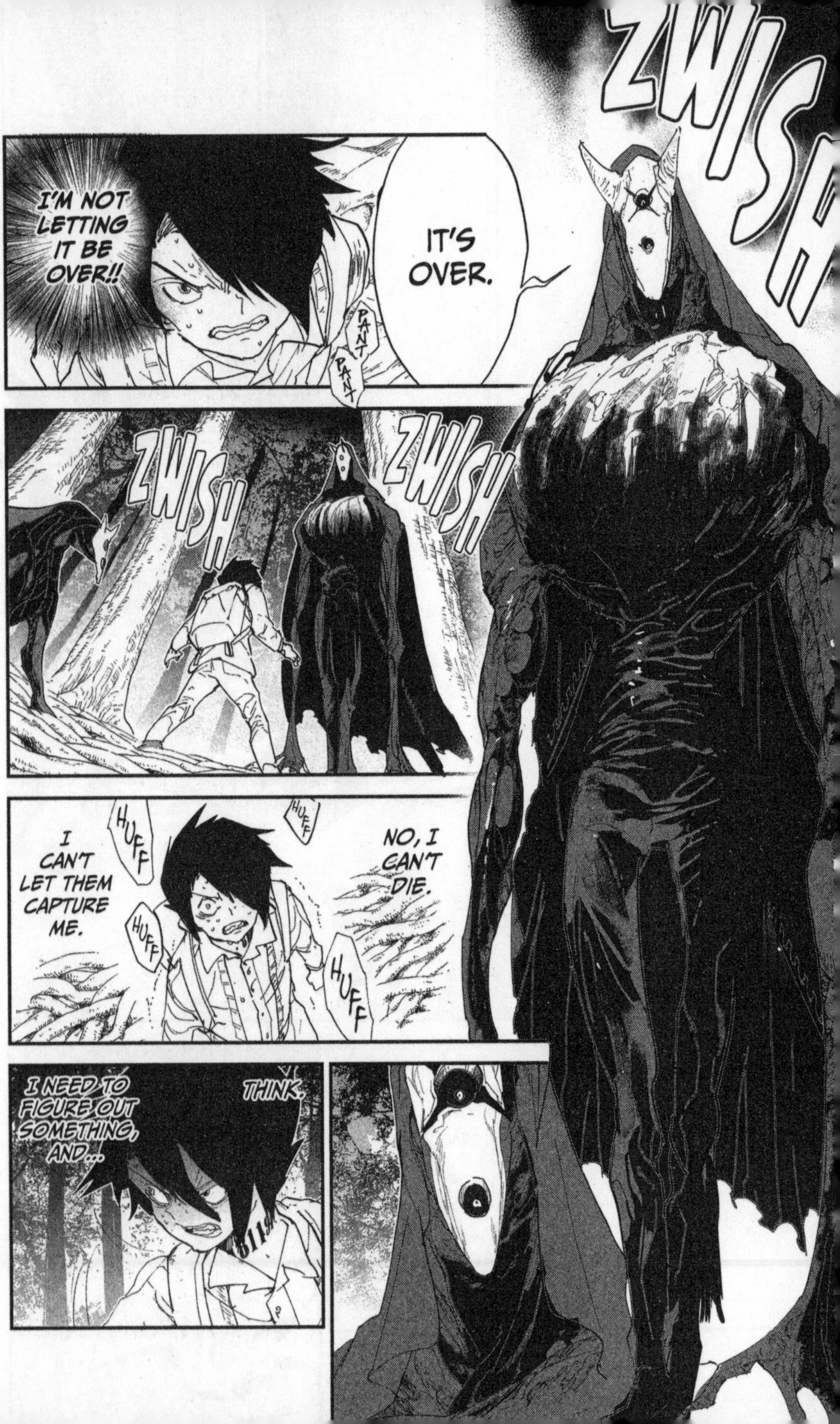
ZWISH
IT'S OVER.
PANT PANT
I'M NOT LETTING IT BE OVER!!
ZWISH
ZWISH
HUFF
NO, I CAN'T DIE.
HUFF
I CAN'T LET THEM CAPTURE ME.
HUFF
HUFF
THINK.
I NEED TO FIGURE OUT SOMETHING, AND...

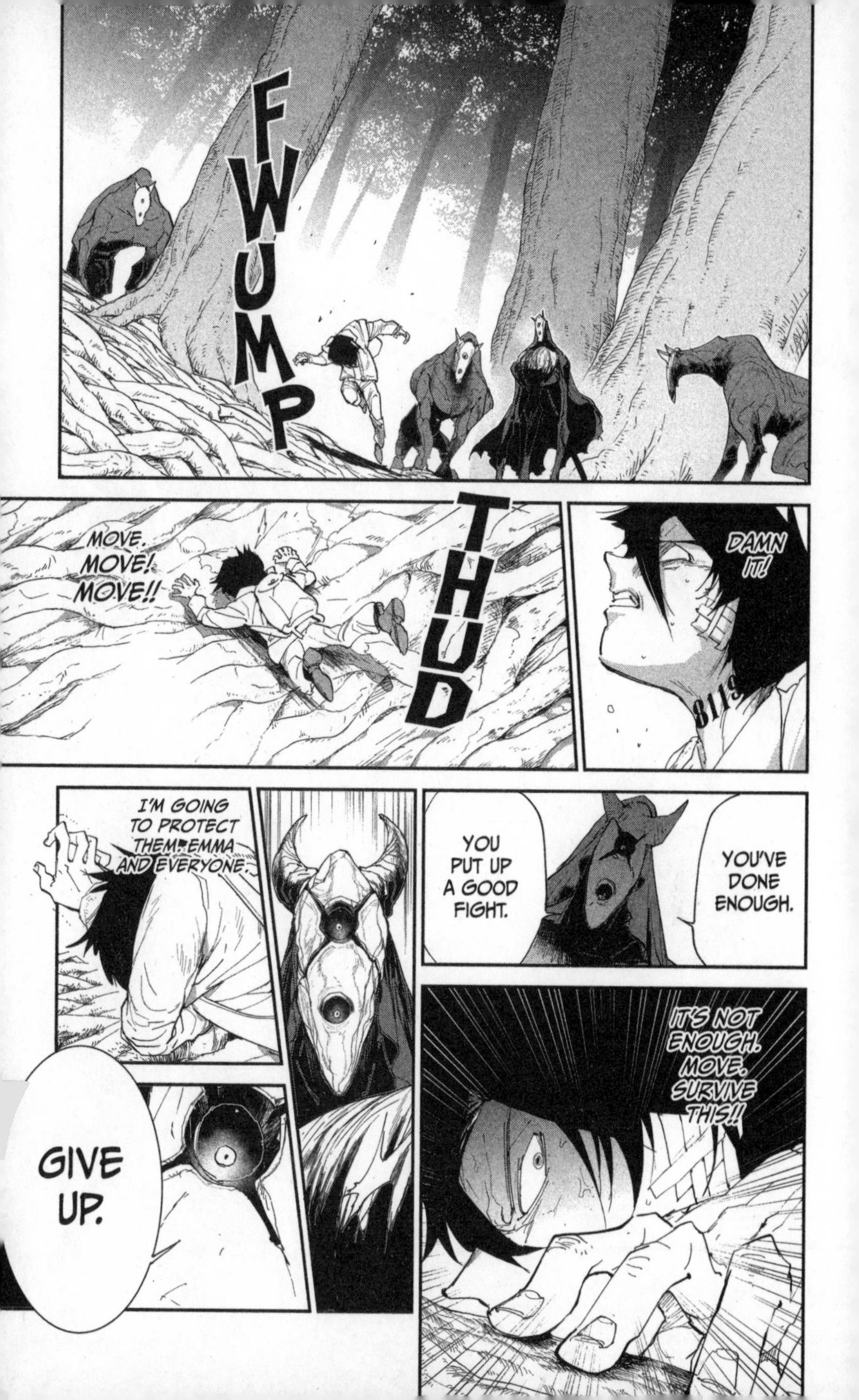
FWUMP
DAMN IT!
MOVE. MOVE! MOVE!!
THUD
YOU'VE DONE ENOUGH.
YOU PUT UP A GOOD FIGHT.
IT'S NOT ENOUGH. MOVE. SURVIVE THIS!!
I'M GOING TO PROTECT THEM. EMMA AND EVERYONE.
GIVE UP.

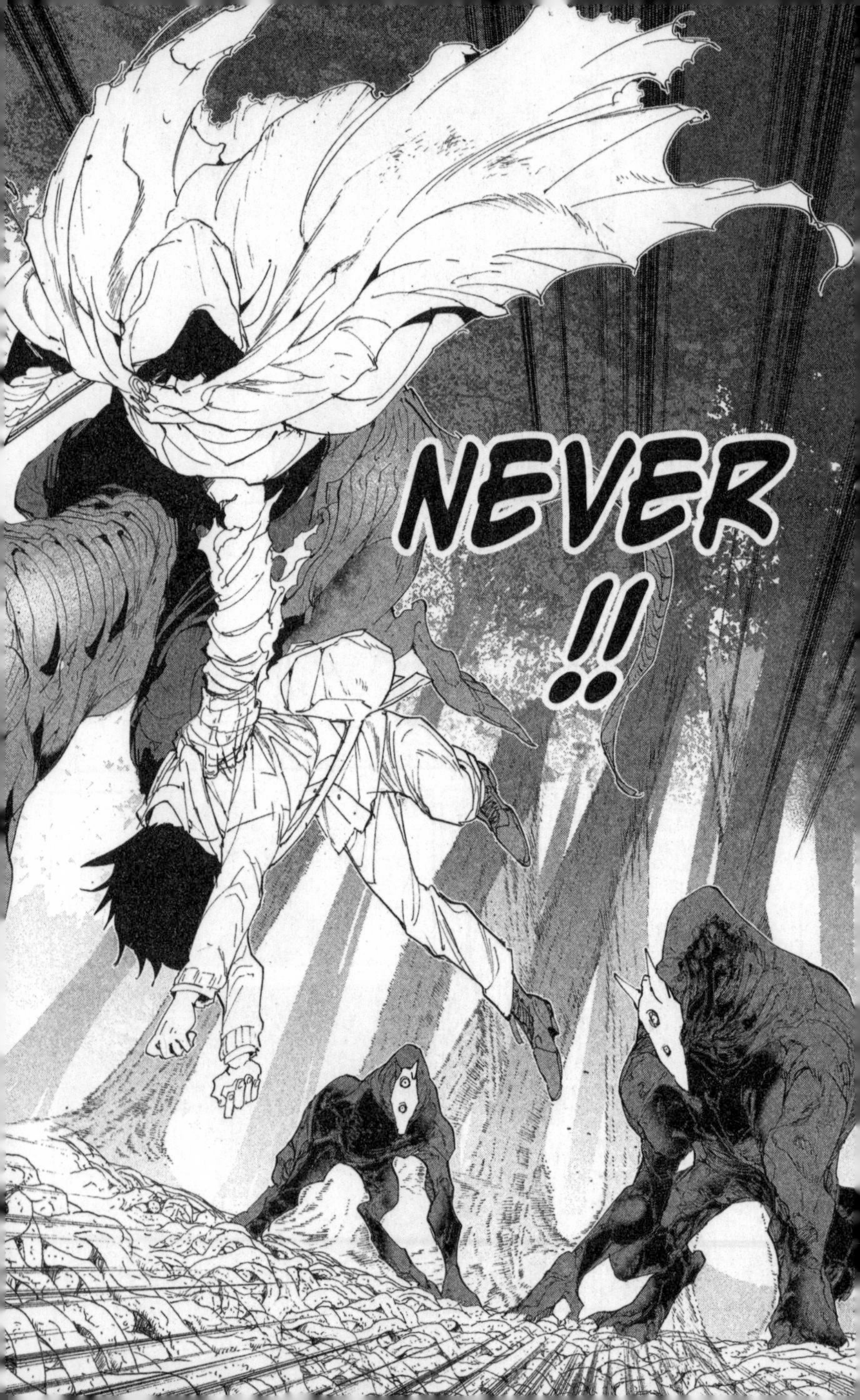
NEVER
!!

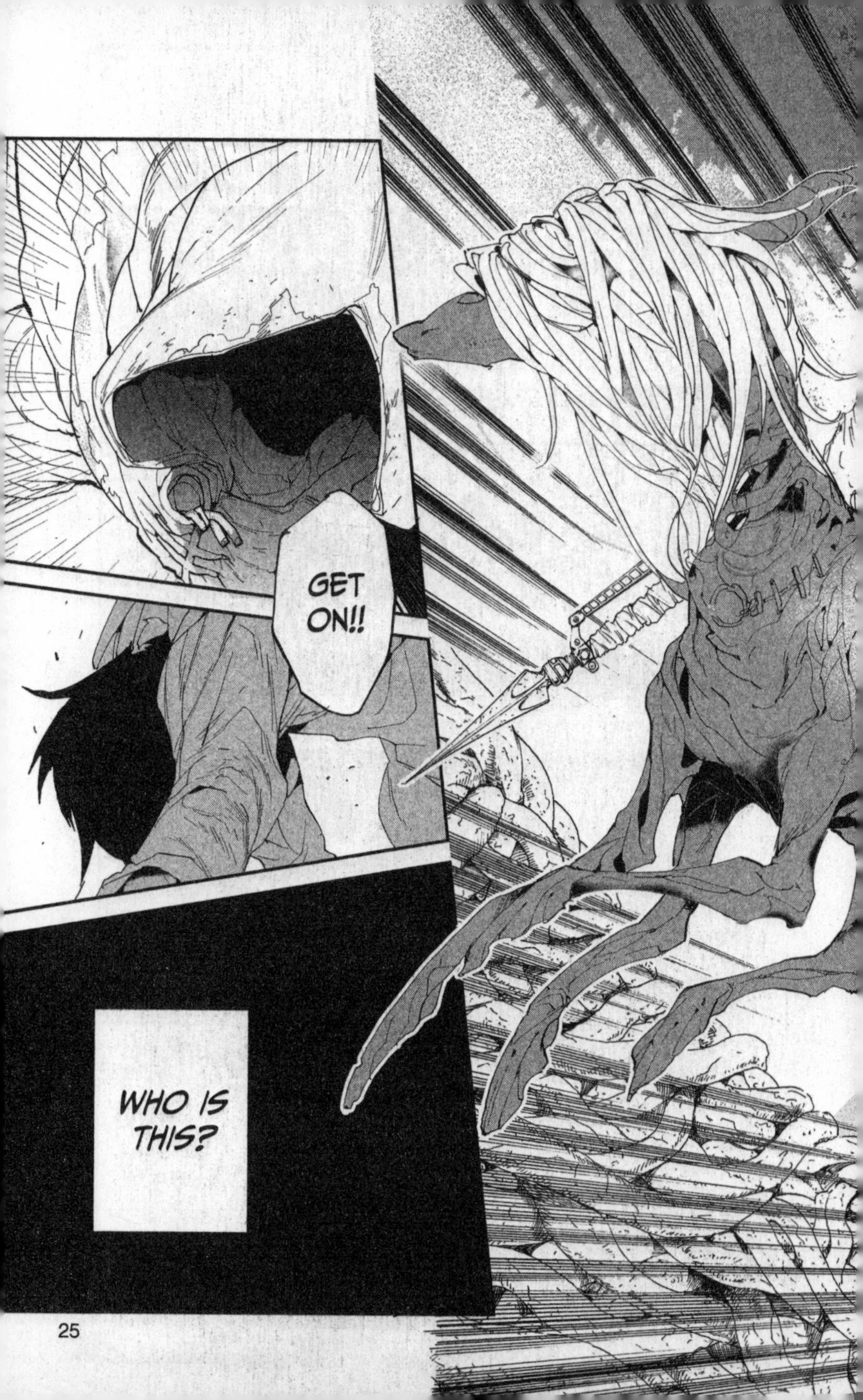
GET ON!!
WHO IS THIS?

CHRIS AND HIS SCARF

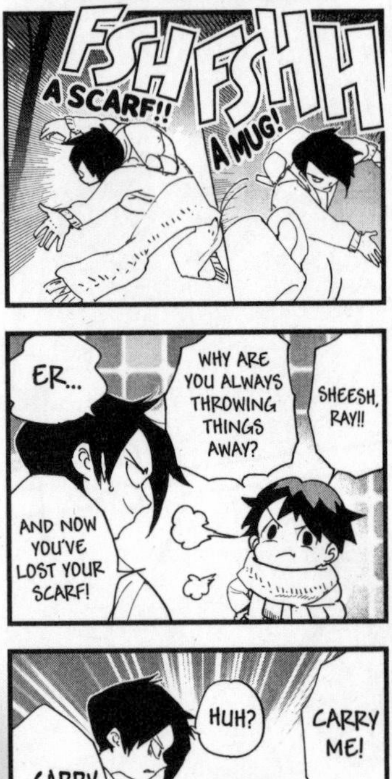
FSH FSHH
A SCARF!!
A MUG!
SHEESH, RAY!!
WHY ARE YOU ALWAYS THROWING THINGS AWAY?
ER...
AND NOW YOU'VE LOST YOUR SCARF!
CARRY ME!
HUH?
CARRY ME NOW, PLEASE!
NOW YOU'RE SET!

TO BE CONTINUED IN SIDE STORY 4-2

SIDE STORY 4-1

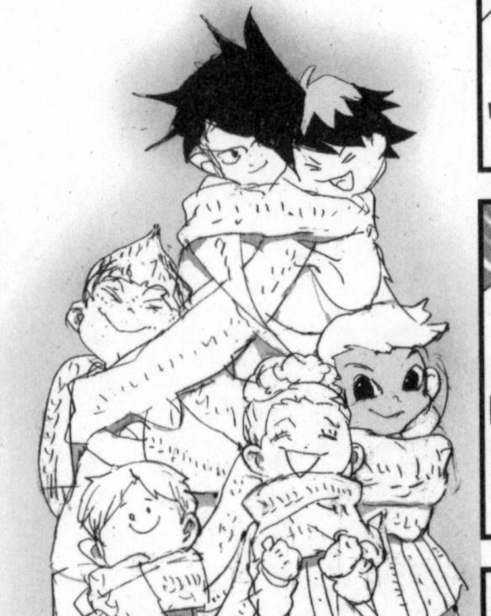

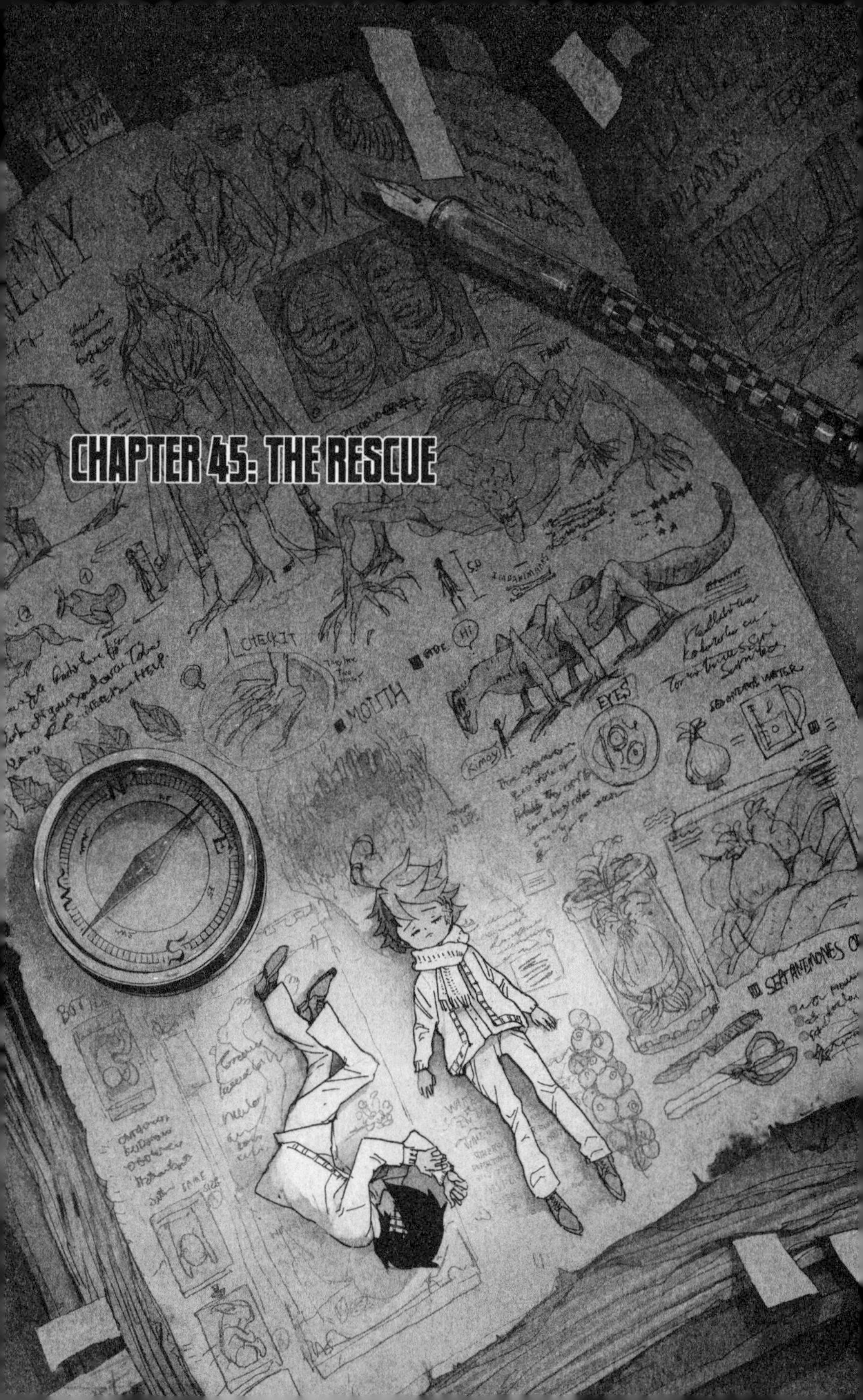
CHAPTER 45: THE RESCUE

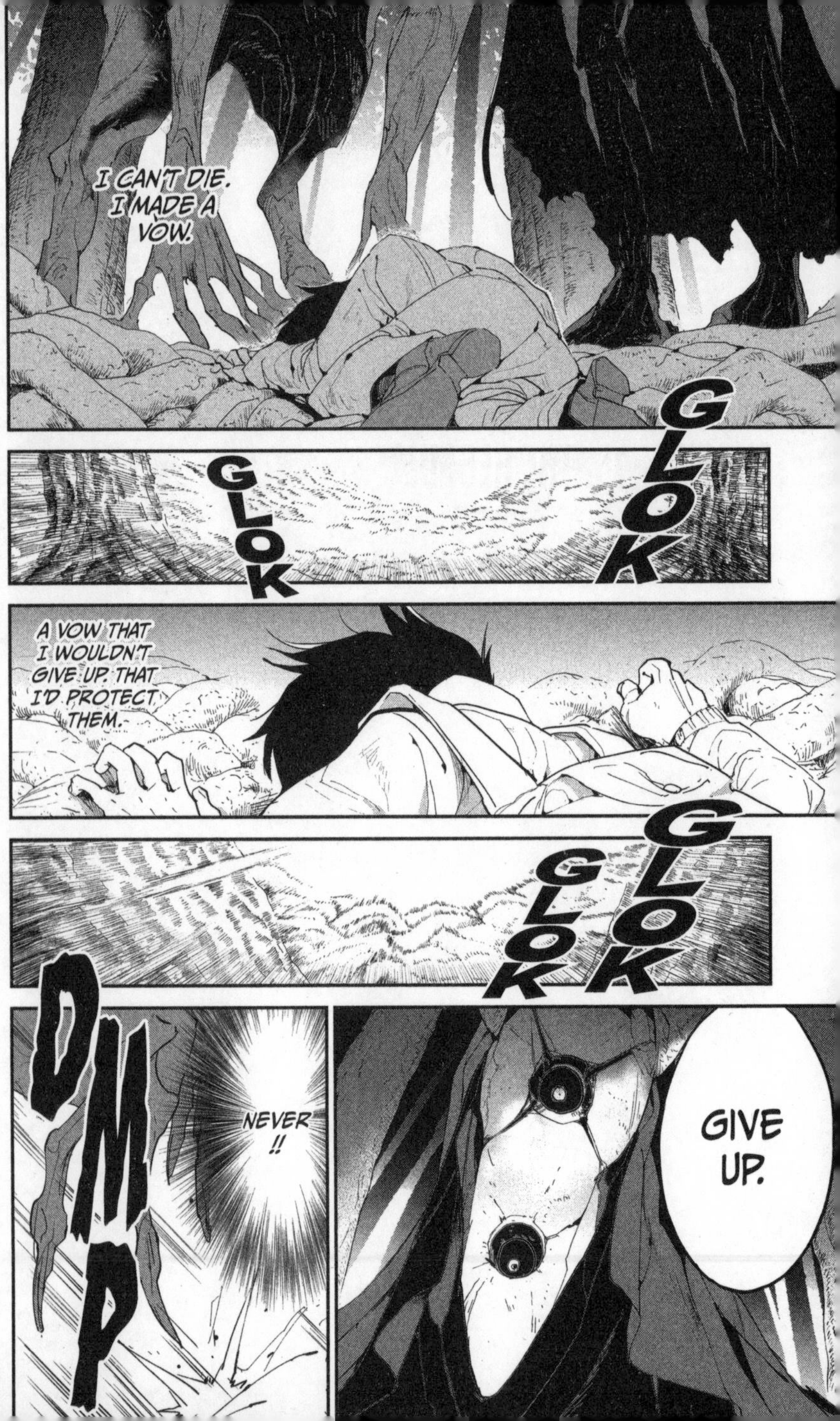
I CAN'T DIE. I MADE A VOW.
GLOK
GLOK
A VOW THAT I WOULDN'T GIVE UP. THAT I'D PROTECT THEM.
GLOK
GLOK
GIVE UP.
DMP
NEVER!!

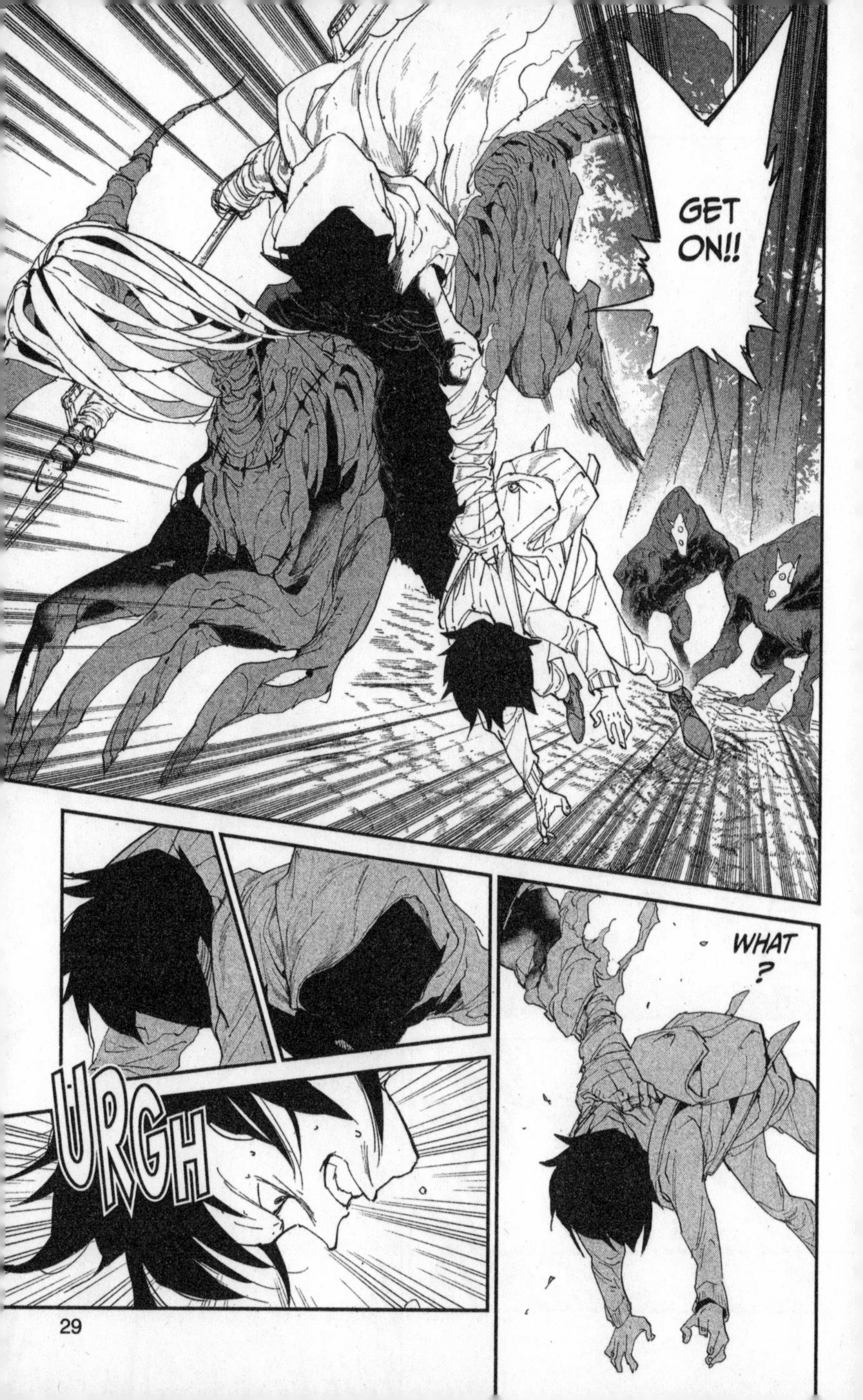
GET ON!!
WHAT ?
URGH

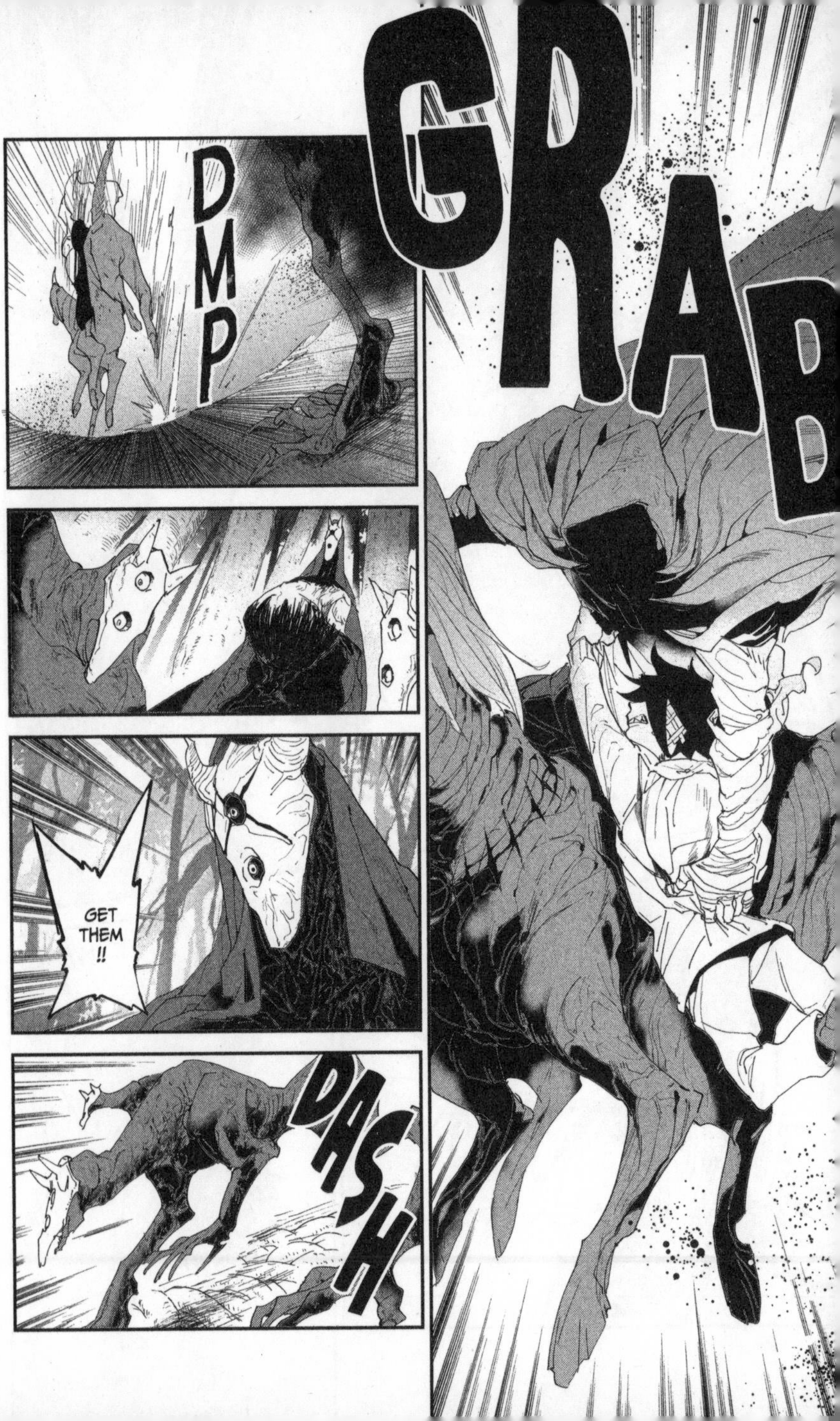
GRAB
DMP
GET THEM !!
DASH

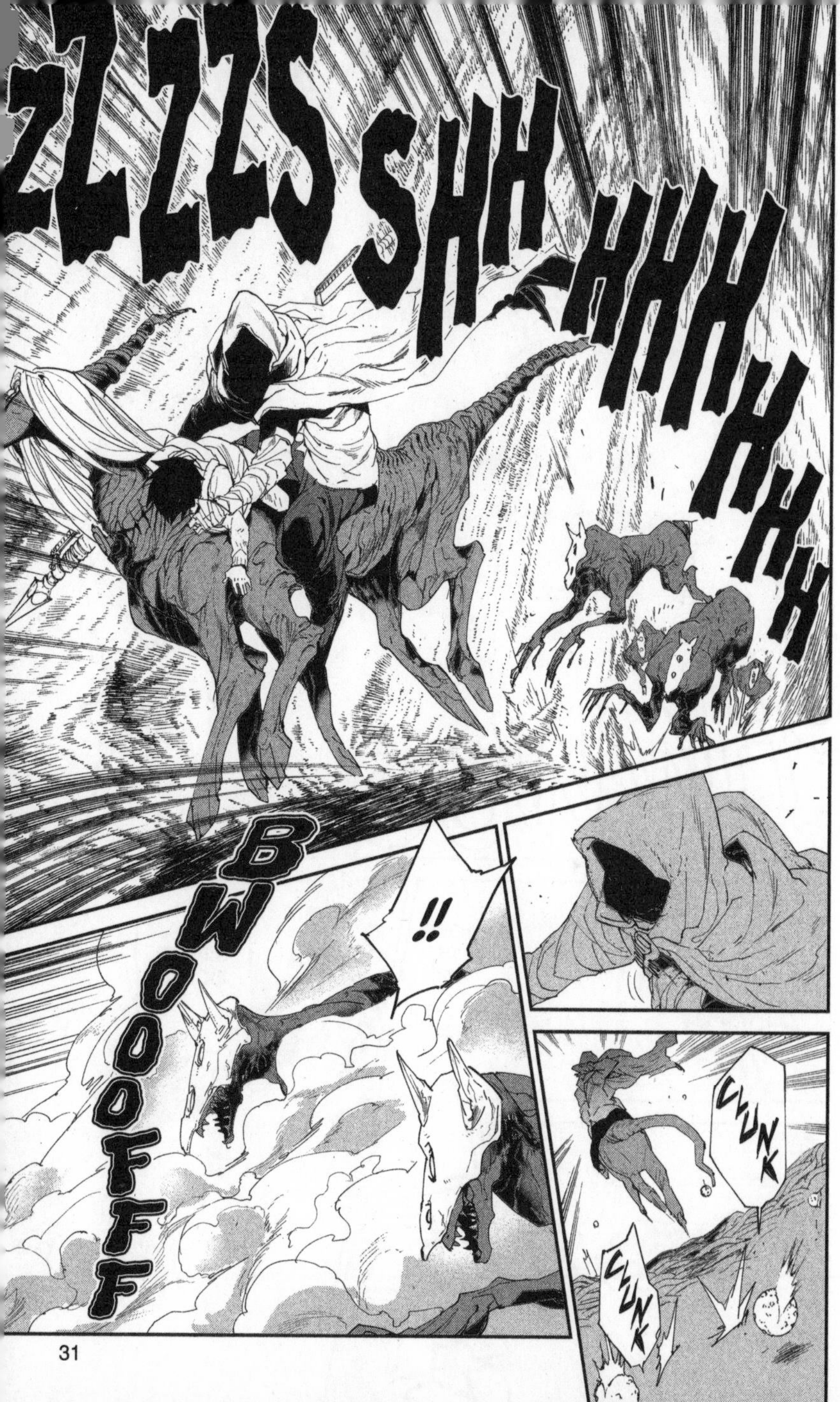
ZZZS SHHHHHHHH
CLUNK
CLUNK
BWOOOFFF
!!

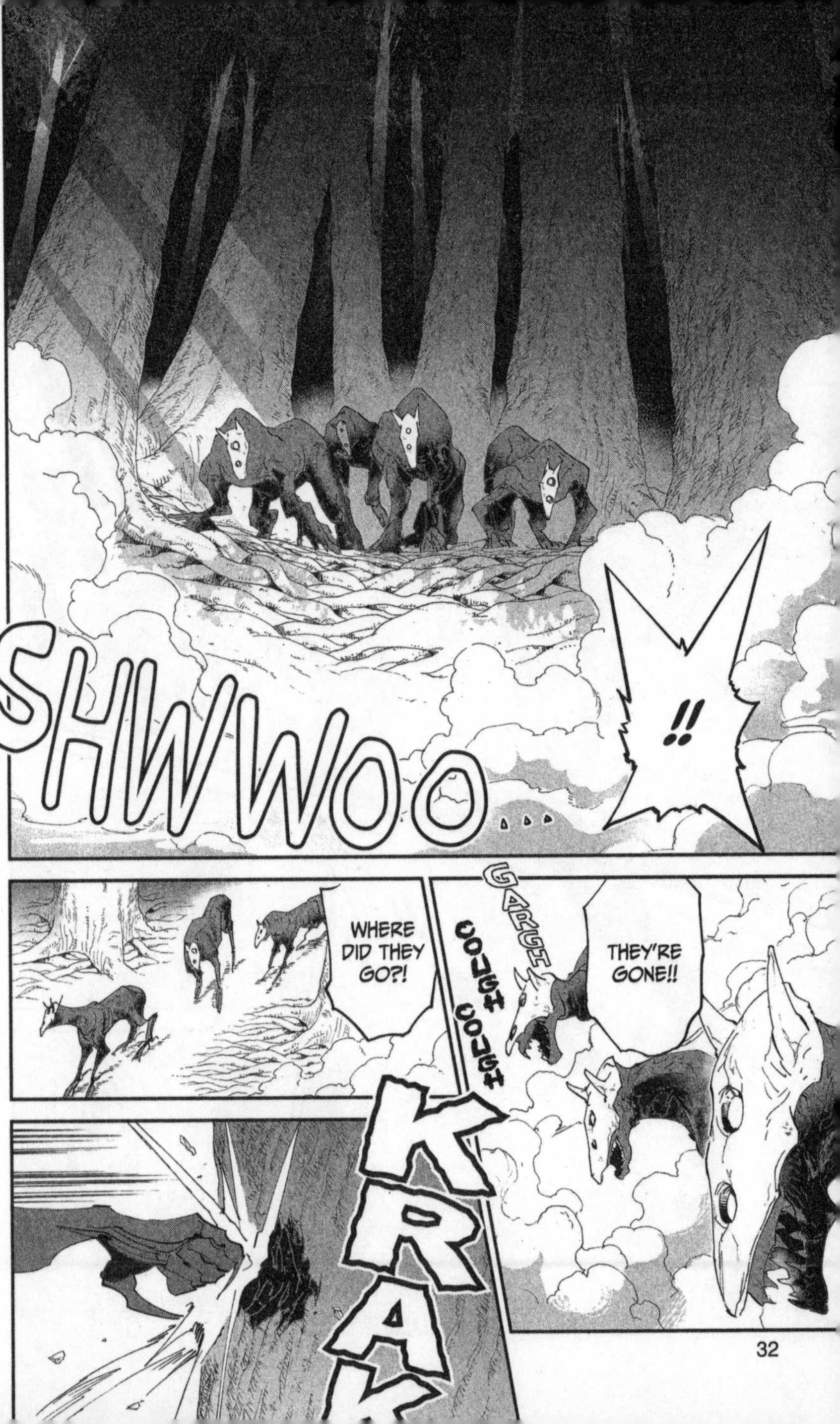
SHWWOO...
!!
THEY'RE GONE!!
GARGH
COUGH COUGH
WHERE DID THEY GO?!
KRA

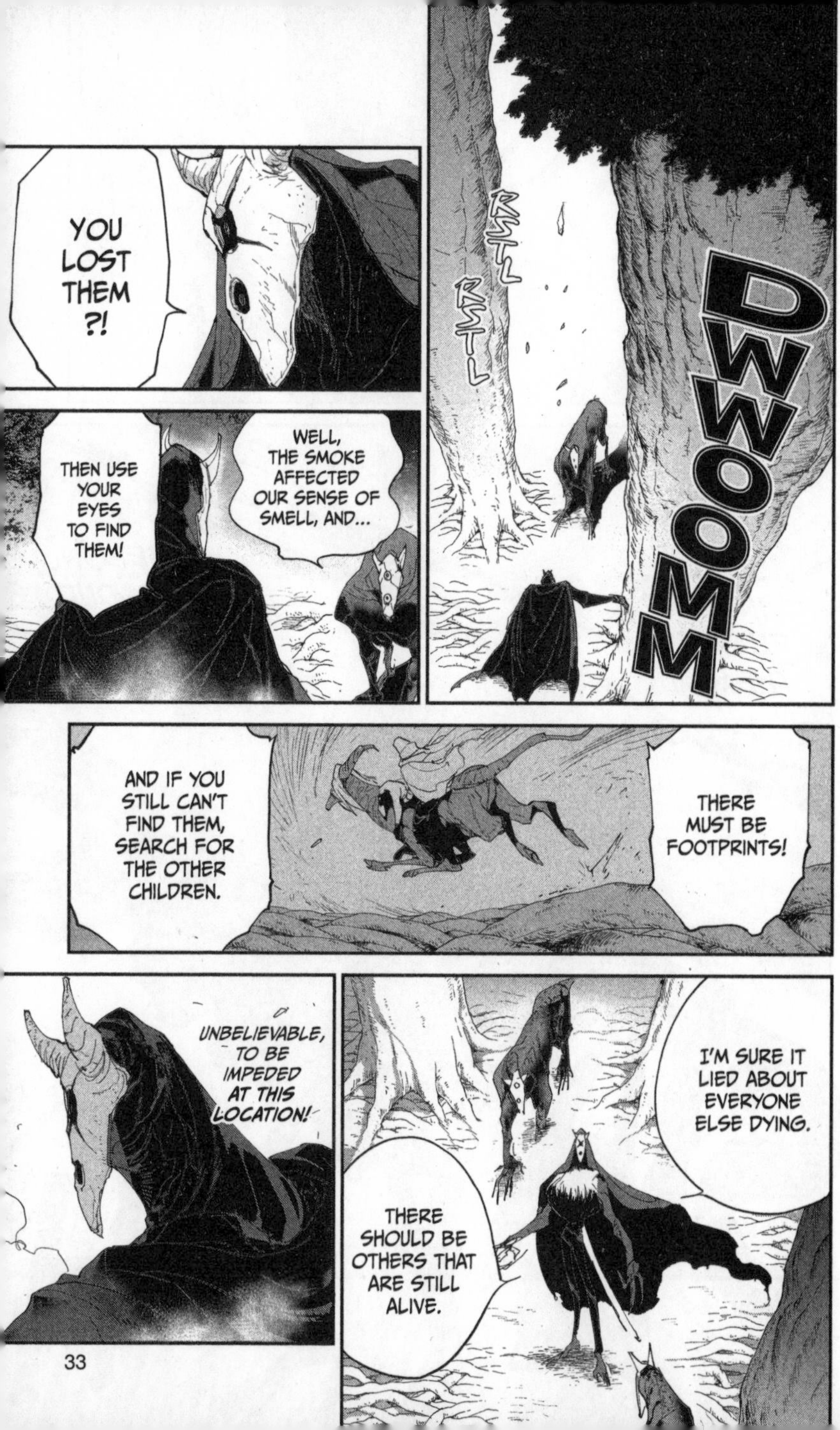
RSTL
RSTL
DWOOMM
YOU LOST THEM?!
WELL, THE SMOKE AFFECTED OUR SENSE OF SMELL, AND...
THEN USE YOUR EYES TO FIND THEM!
THERE MUST BE FOOTPRINTS!
AND IF YOU STILL CAN'T FIND THEM, SEARCH FOR THE OTHER CHILDREN.
I'M SURE IT LIED ABOUT EVERYONE ELSE DYING.
THERE SHOULD BE OTHERS THAT ARE STILL ALIVE.
UNBELIEVABLE, TO BE IMPEDED AT THIS LOCATION!

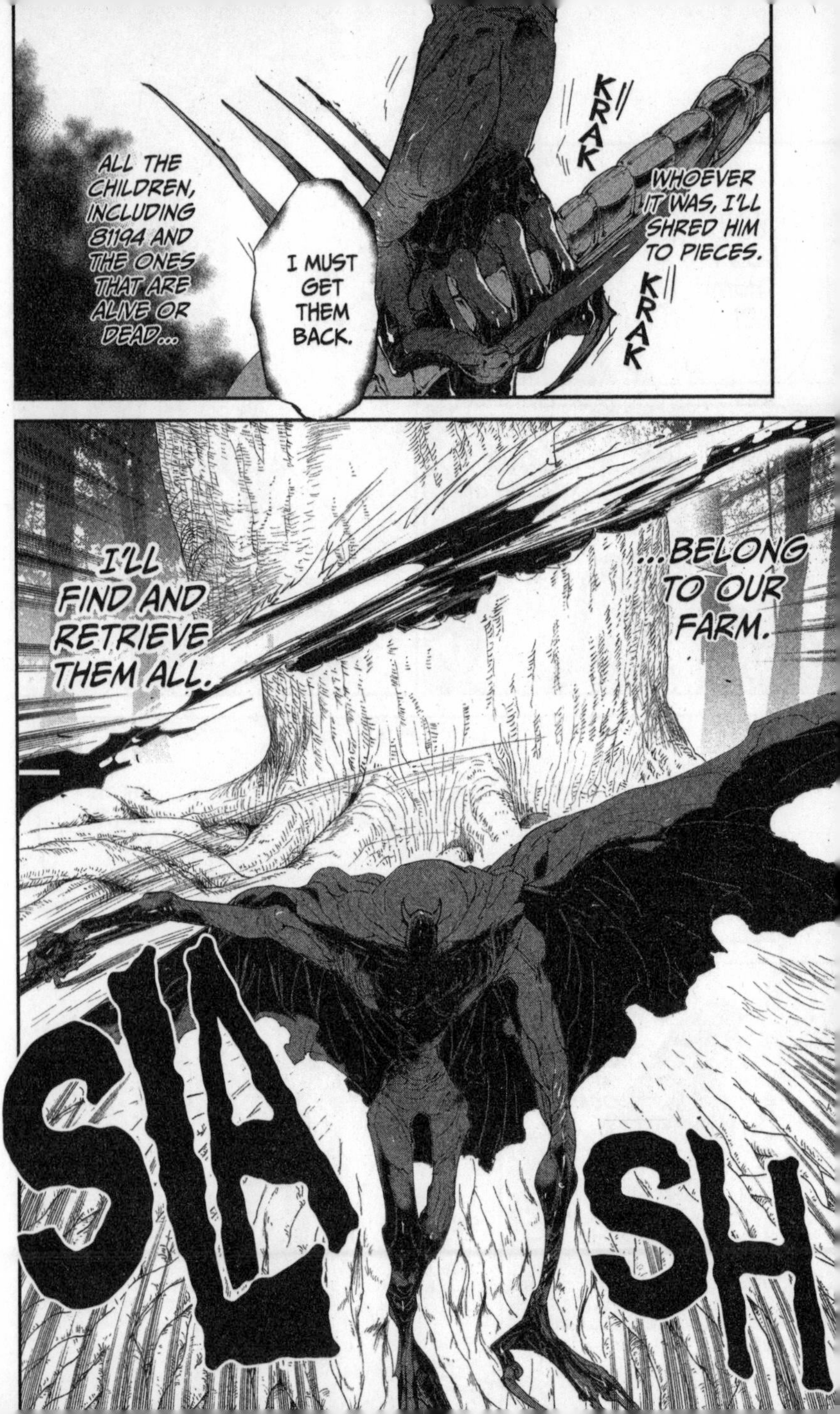
KRAK
WHOEVER IT WAS, I'LL SHRED HIM TO PIECES.
KRAK
I MUST GET THEM BACK.
ALL THE CHILDREN, INCLUDING 81194 AND THE ONES THAT ARE ALIVE OR DEAD...
...BELONG TO OUR FARM.
I'LL FIND AND RETRIEVE THEM ALL.
SLASH

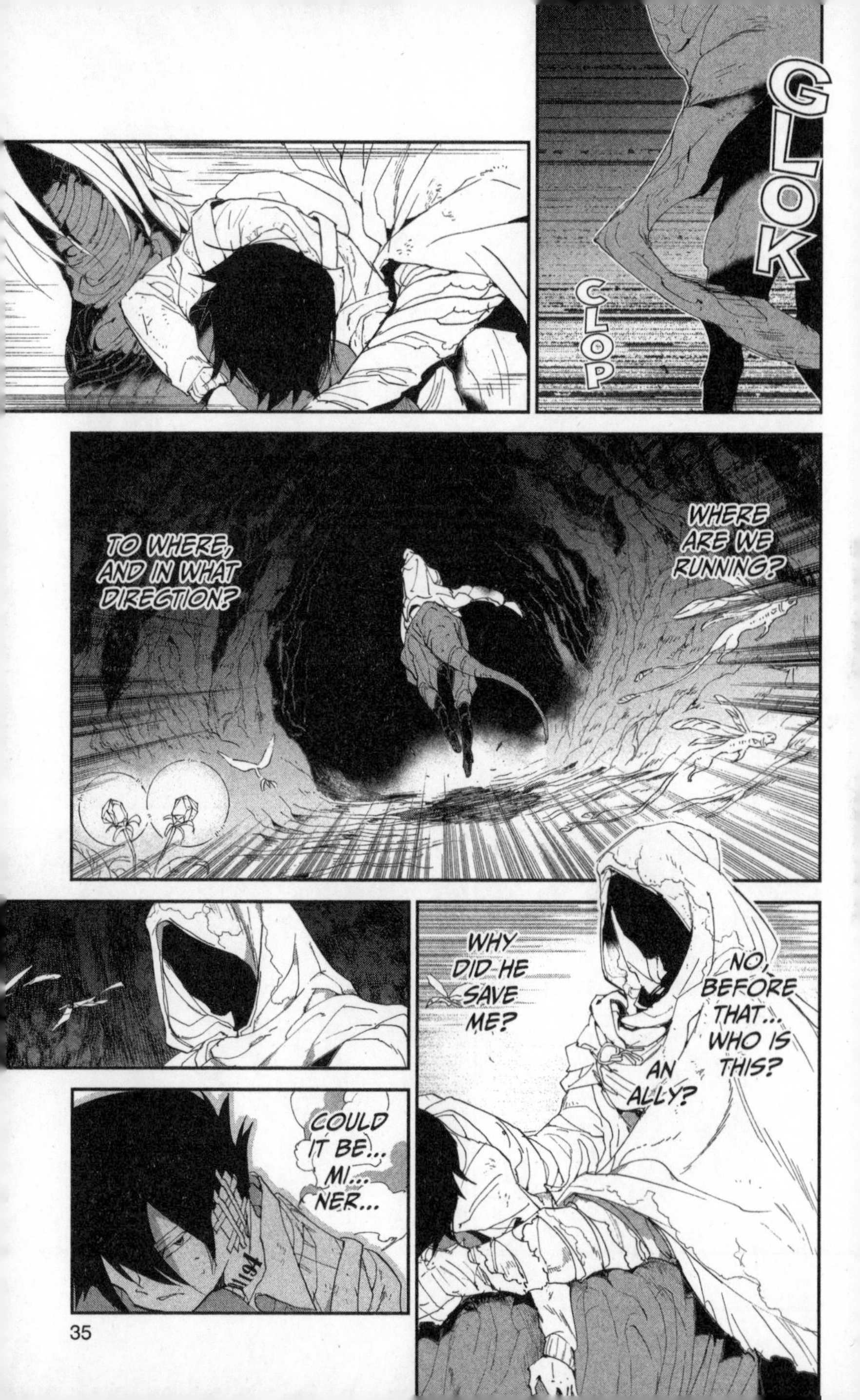
GLOK
CLOP
WHERE ARE WE RUNNING?
TO WHERE, AND IN WHAT DIRECTION?
WHY DID HE SAVE ME?
NO, BEFORE THAT... WHO IS THIS?
AN ALLY?
COULD IT BE... MI... NER...

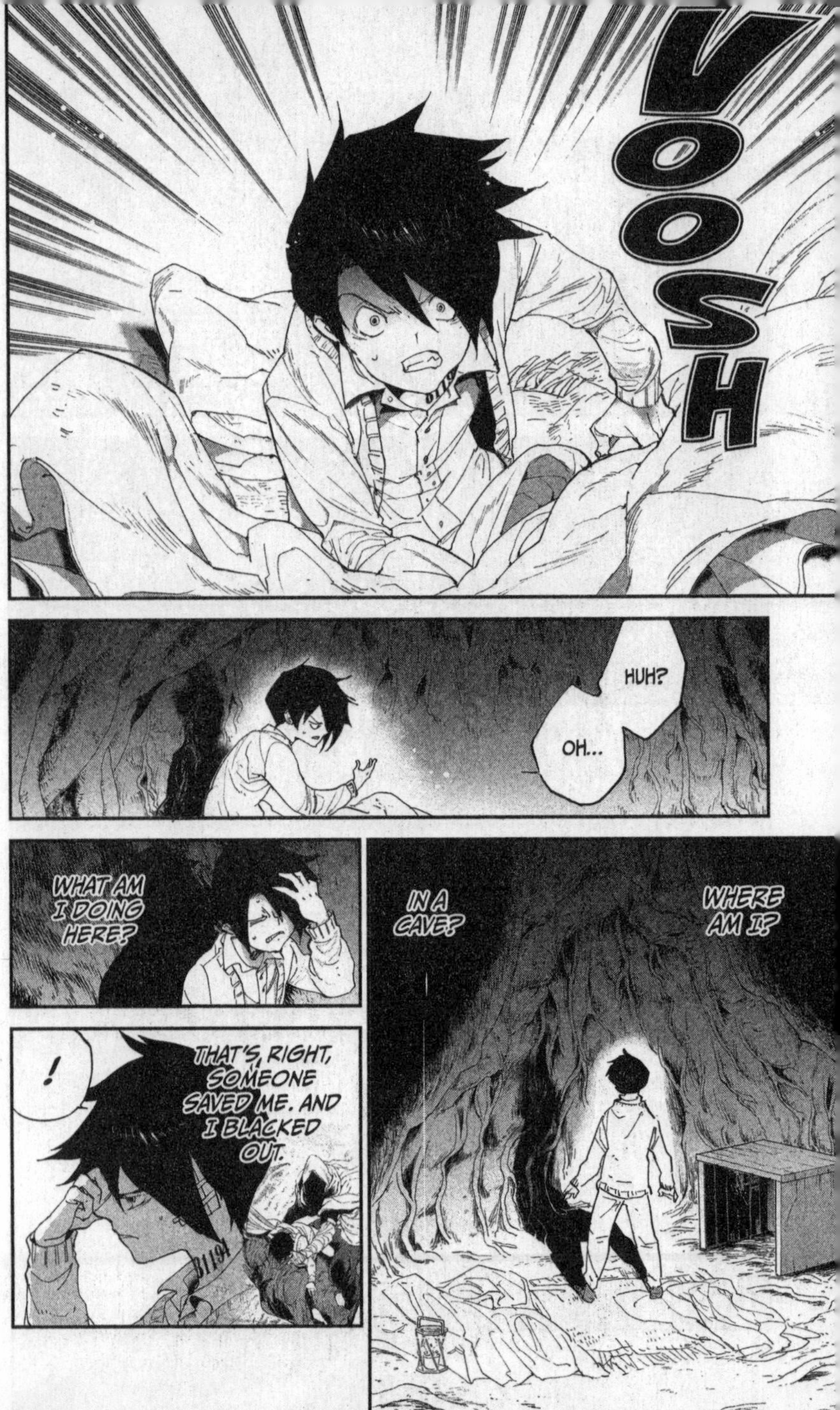
VOOSH
HUH?
OH...
WHERE AM I?
IN A CAVE?
WHAT AM I DOING HERE?
!
THAT'S RIGHT, SOMEONE SAVED ME. AND I BLACKED OUT.

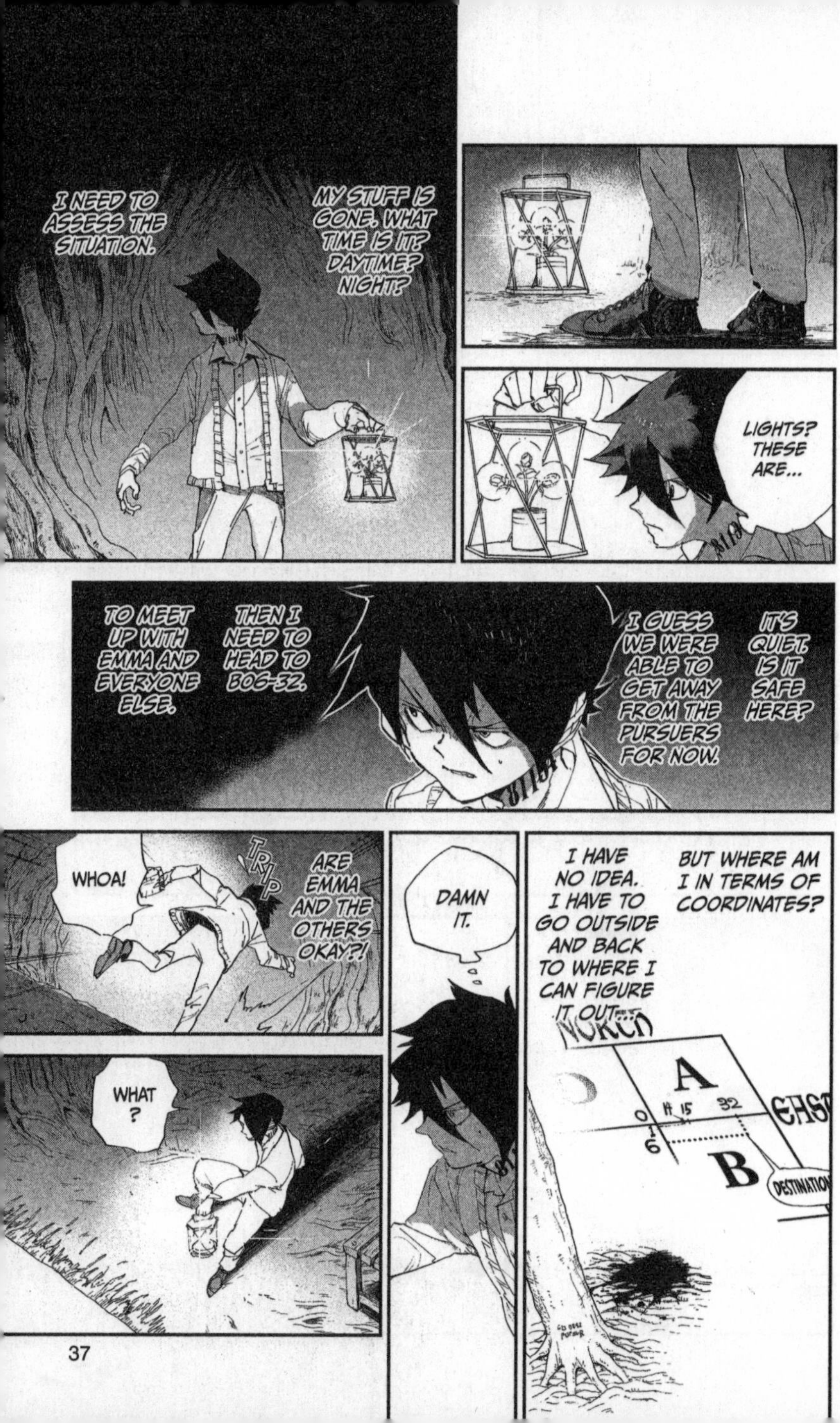
LIGHTS? THESE ARE...
MY STUFF IS GONE. WHAT TIME IS IT? DAYTIME? NIGHT?
I NEED TO ASSESS THE SITUATION.
IT'S QUIET. IS IT SAFE HERE?
I GUESS WE WERE ABLE TO GET AWAY FROM THE PURSUERS FOR NOW.
THEN I NEED TO HEAD TO B06-32.
TO MEET UP WITH EMMA AND EVERYONE ELSE.
BUT WHERE AM I IN TERMS OF COORDINATES?
I HAVE NO IDEA. I HAVE TO GO OUTSIDE AND BACK TO WHERE I CAN FIGURE IT OUT...
A
15
32
6
B
DAMN IT.
ARE EMMA AND THE OTHERS OKAY?!
TRIP
WHOA!
WHAT?

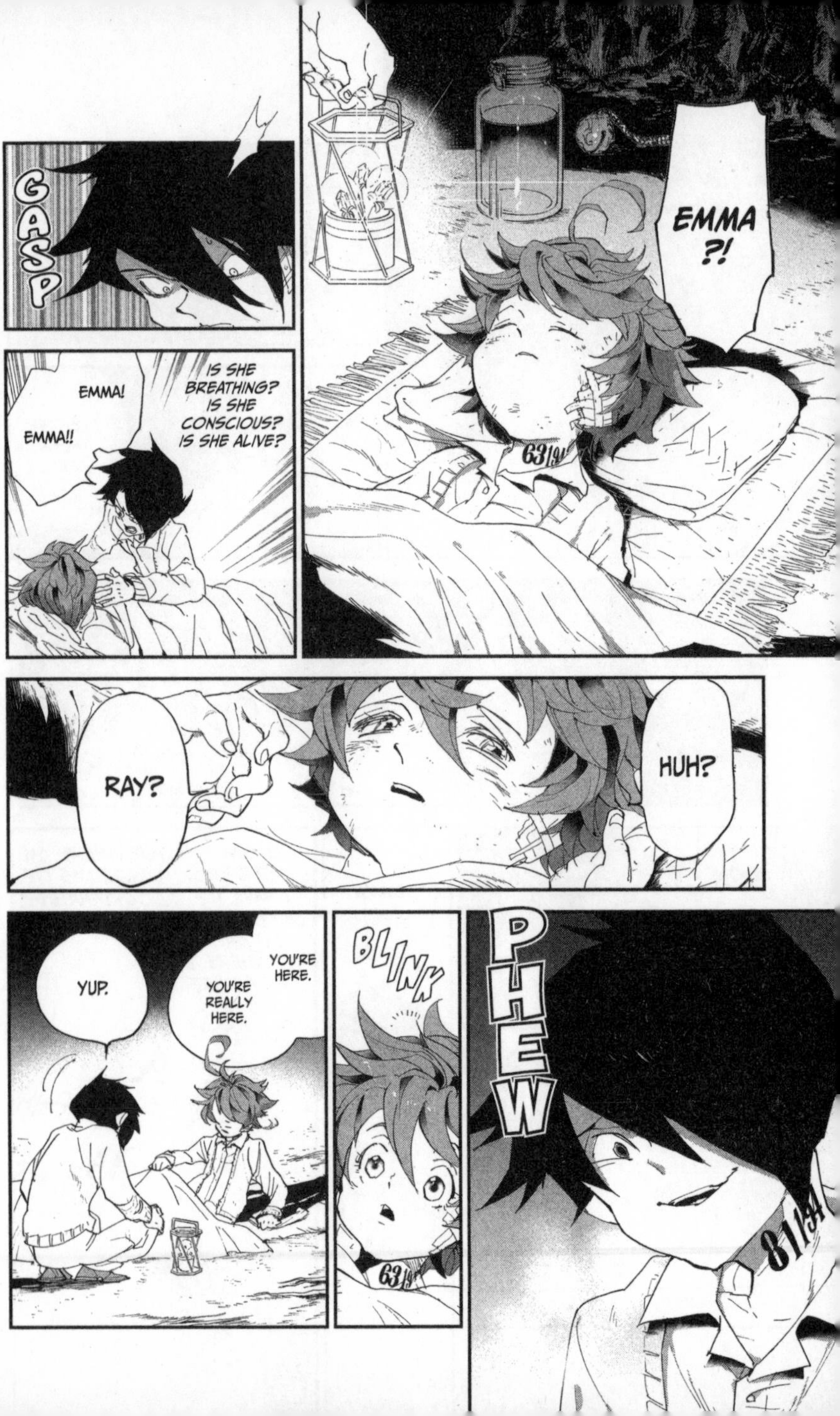
EMMA ?!
GASP
IS SHE BREATHING? IS SHE CONSCIOUS? IS SHE ALIVE?
EMMA!
EMMA!!
HUH?
RAY?
PHEW
BLINK
YOU'RE HERE.
YOU'RE REALLY HERE.
YUP.

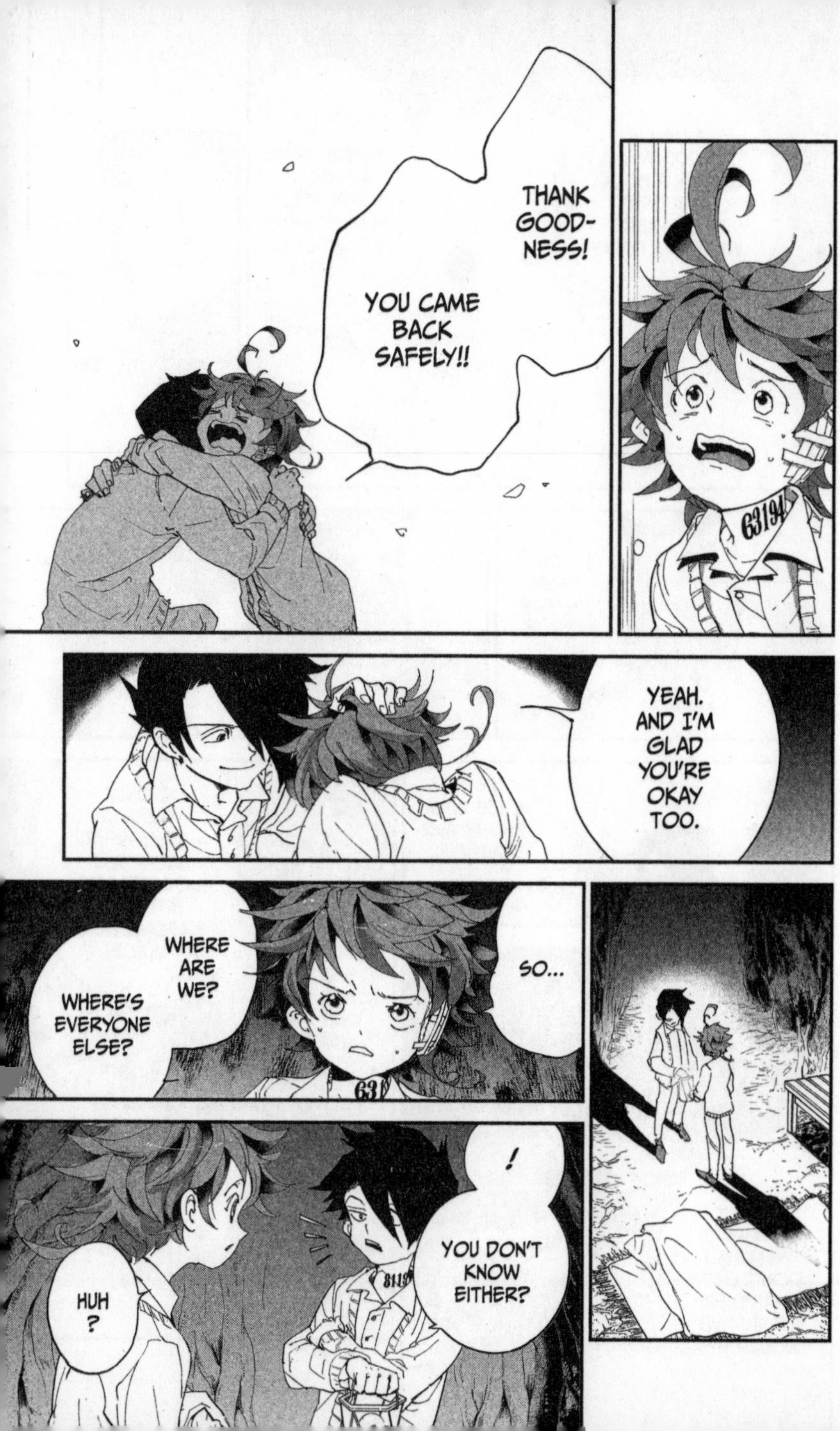
THANK GOODNESS!
YOU CAME BACK SAFELY!!
YEAH. AND I'M GLAD YOU'RE OKAY TOO.
SO...
WHERE ARE WE?
WHERE'S EVERYONE ELSE?
!
YOU DON'T KNOW EITHER?
HUH?

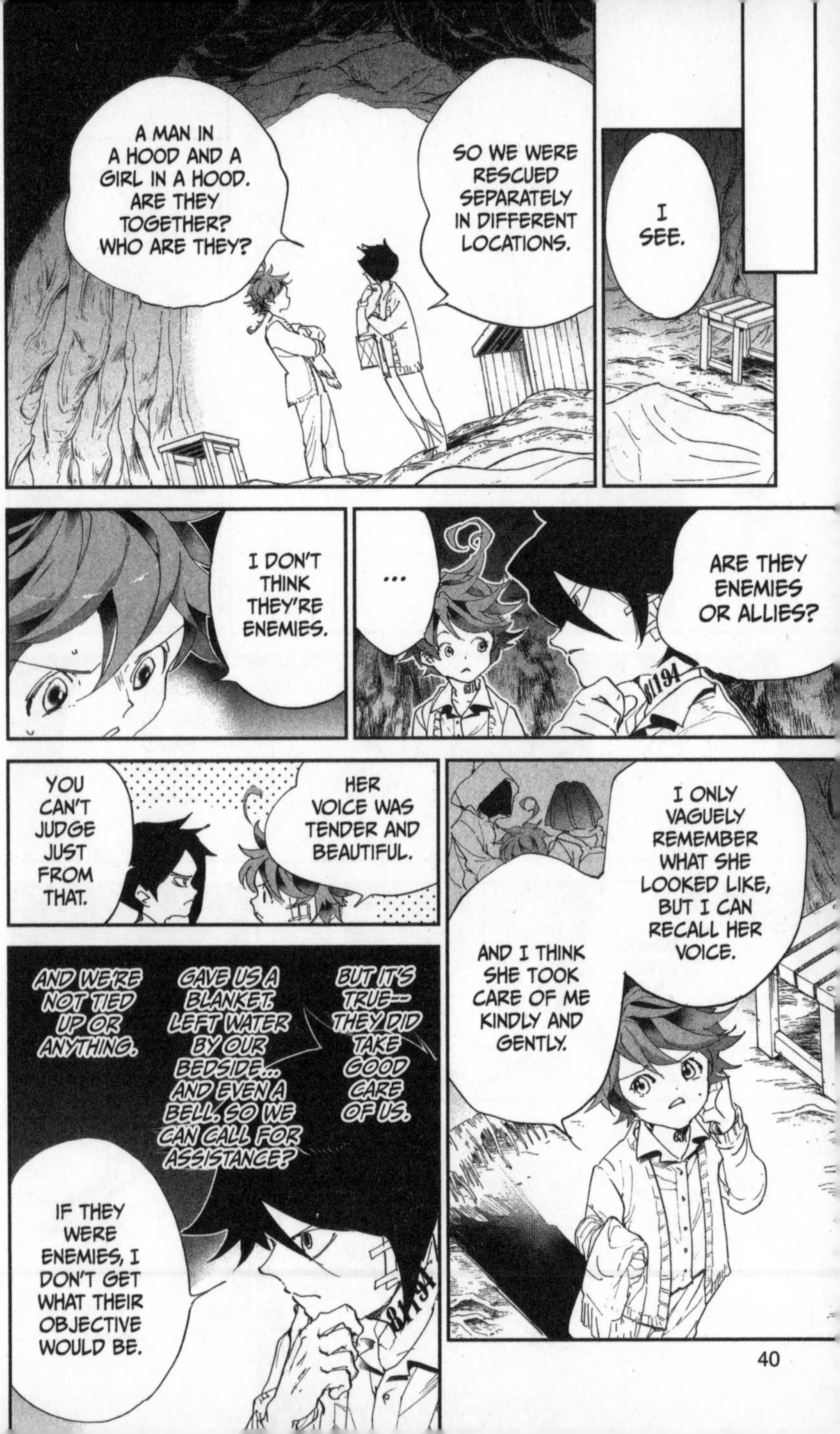
I SEE.
SO WE WERE RESCUED SEPARATELY IN DIFFERENT LOCATIONS.
A MAN IN A HOOD AND A GIRL IN A HOOD. ARE THEY TOGETHER? WHO ARE THEY?
ARE THEY ENEMIES OR ALLIES?
...
I DON'T THINK THEY'RE ENEMIES.
I ONLY VAGUELY REMEMBER WHAT SHE LOOKED LIKE, BUT I CAN RECALL HER VOICE.
AND I THINK SHE TOOK CARE OF ME KINDLY AND GENTLY.
HER VOICE WAS TENDER AND BEAUTIFUL.
YOU CAN'T JUDGE JUST FROM THAT.
BUT IT'S TRUE-- THEY DID TAKE GOOD CARE OF US.
GAVE US A BLANKET. LEFT WATER BY OUR BEDSIDE... AND EVEN A BELL, SO WE CAN CALL FOR ASSISTANCE?
AND WE'RE NOT TIED UP OR ANYTHING.
IF THEY WERE ENEMIES, I DON'T GET WHAT THEIR OBJECTIVE WOULD BE.

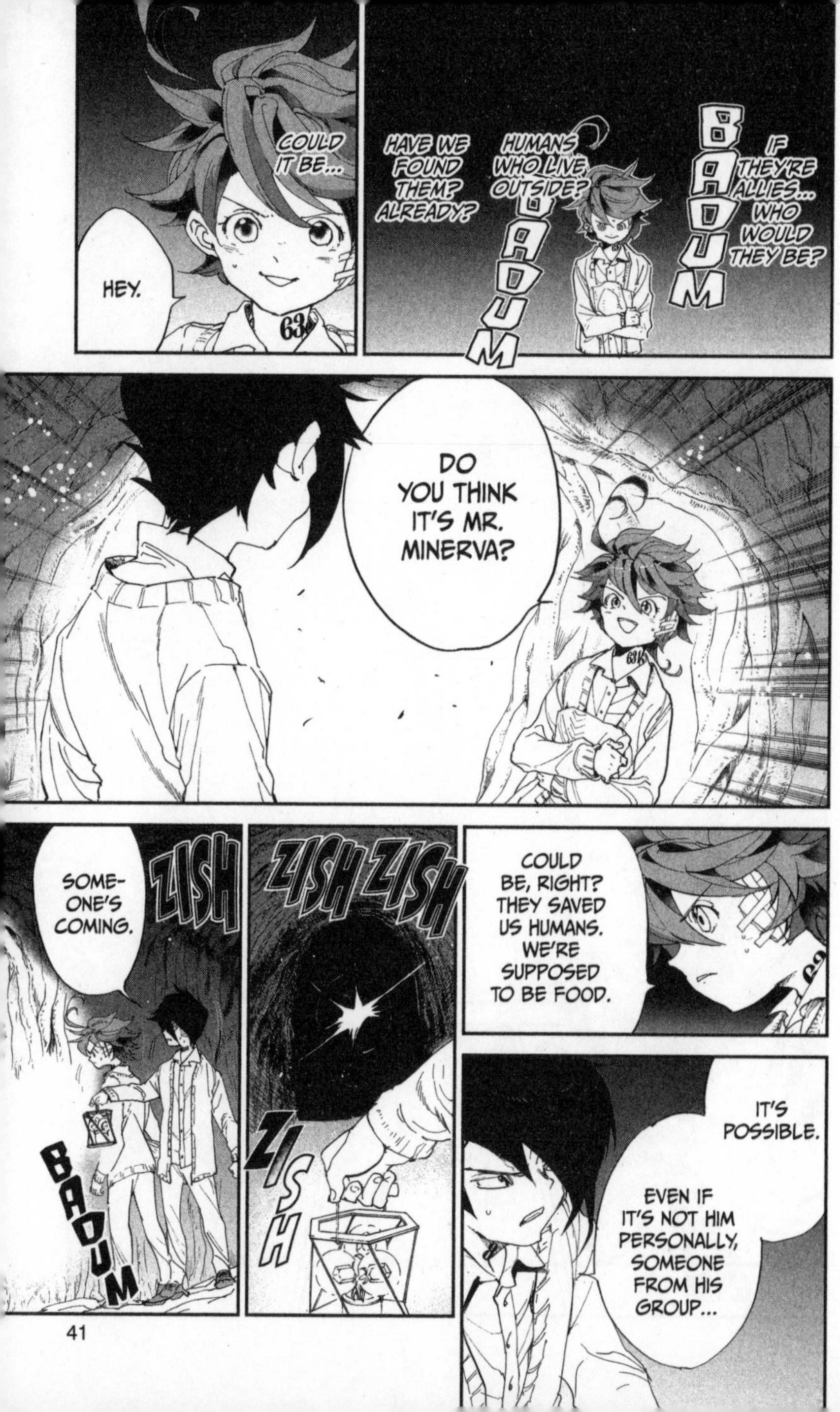

BADUM
IF THEY'RE ALLIES... WHO WOULD THEY BE?
HUMANS WHO LIVE OUTSIDE?
HAVE WE FOUND THEM? ALREADY?
BADUM
COULD IT BE...
HEY.
DO YOU THINK IT'S MR. MINERVA?
COULD BE, RIGHT? THEY SAVED US HUMANS. WE'RE SUPPOSED TO BE FOOD.
IT'S POSSIBLE.
EVEN IF IT'S NOT HIM PERSONALLY, SOMEONE FROM HIS GROUP...
ZISH ZISH
ZISH
ZISH
SOME-ONE'S COMING.
BADUM

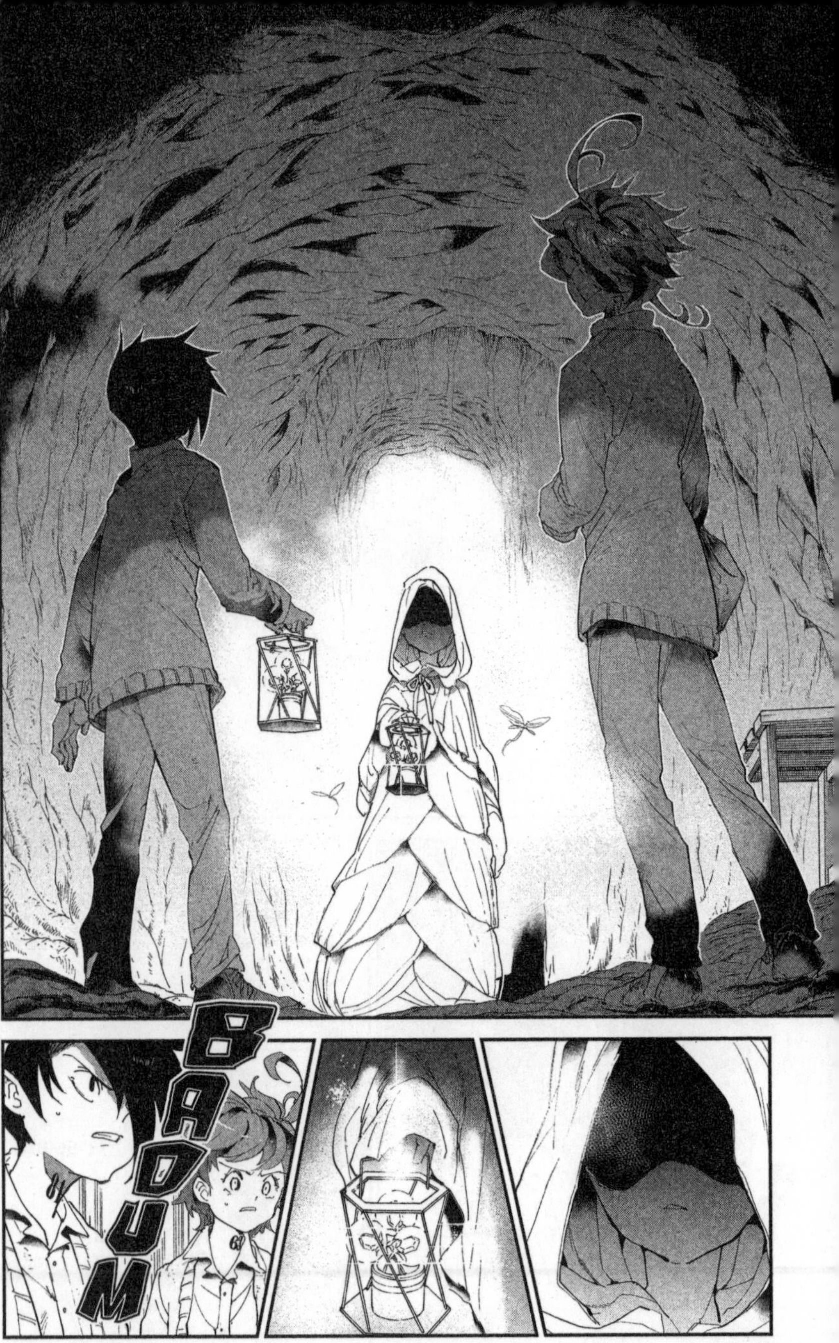
BADUM

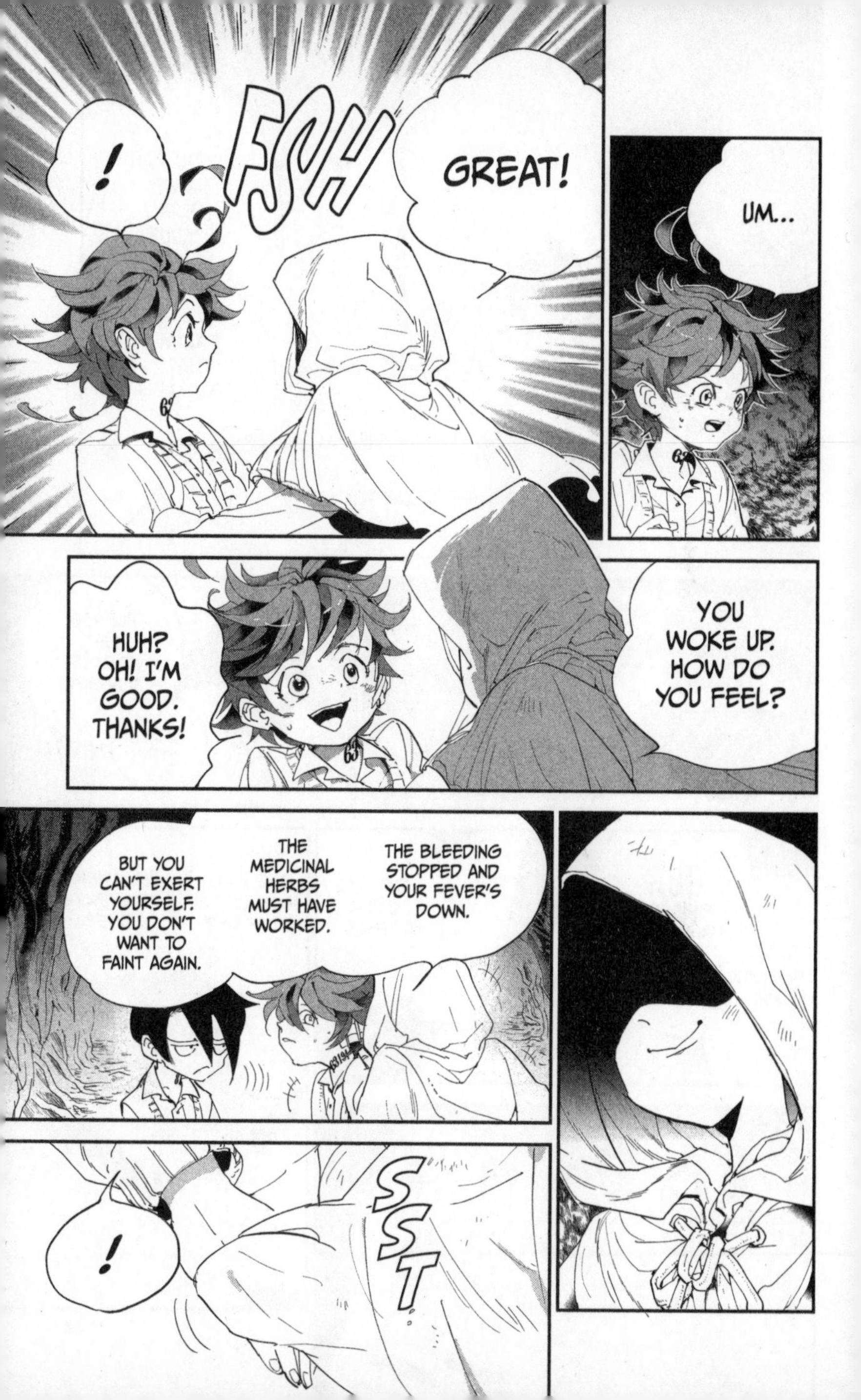
UM...
GREAT!
FSH
!
YOU WOKE UP. HOW DO YOU FEEL?
HUH? OH! I'M GOOD. THANKS!
THE BLEEDING STOPPED AND YOUR FEVER'S DOWN.
THE MEDICINAL HERBS MUST HAVE WORKED.
BUT YOU CAN'T EXERT YOURSELF. YOU DON'T WANT TO FAINT AGAIN.
SST
!

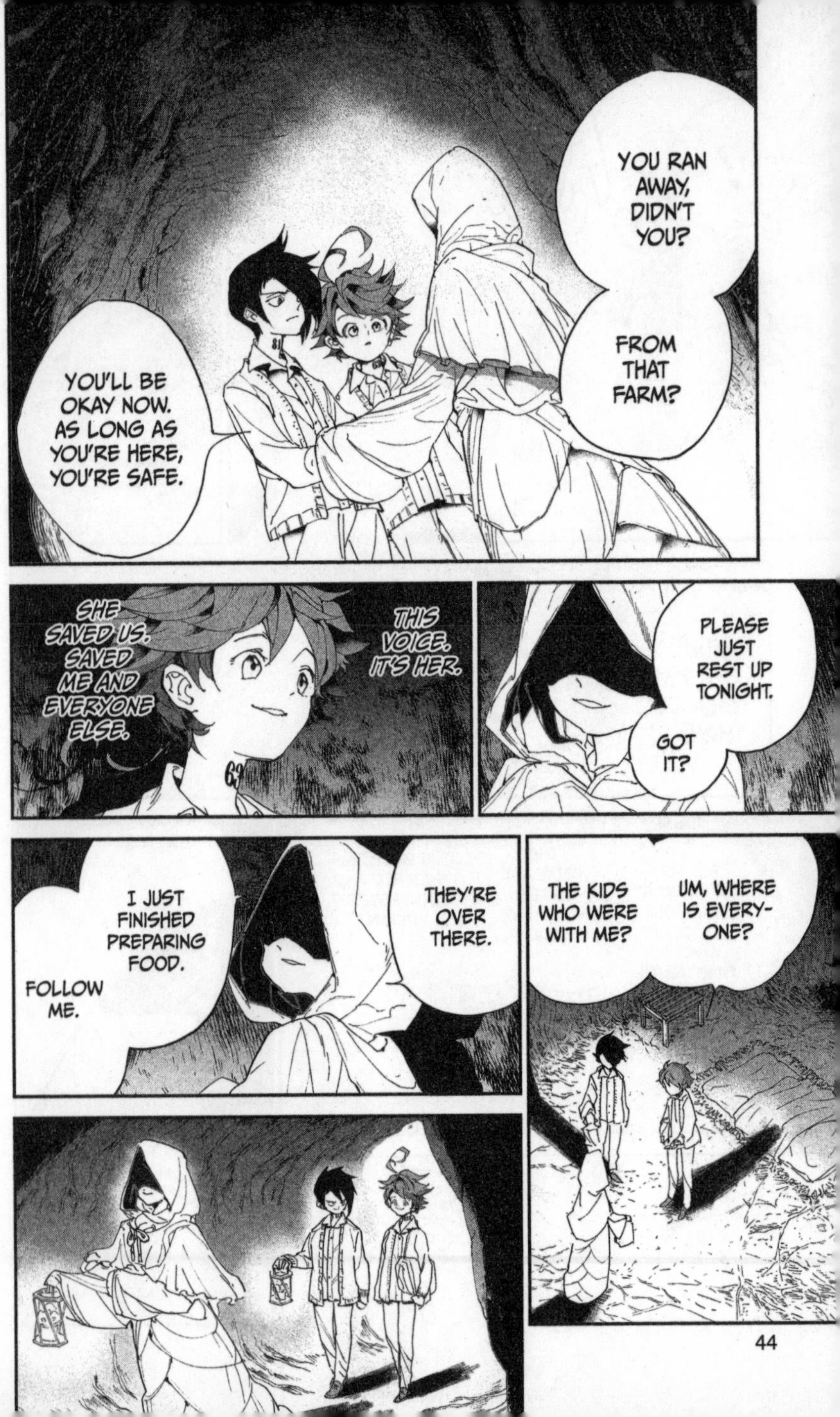
YOU RAN AWAY, DIDN'T YOU?
FROM THAT FARM?
YOU'LL BE OKAY NOW. AS LONG AS YOU'RE HERE, YOU'RE SAFE.
PLEASE JUST REST UP TONIGHT.
GOT IT?
THIS VOICE. IT'S HER.
SHE SAVED US. SAVED ME AND EVERYONE ELSE.
UM, WHERE IS EVERY-ONE?
THE KIDS WHO WERE WITH ME?
THEY'RE OVER THERE.
I JUST FINISHED PREPARING FOOD.
FOLLOW ME.

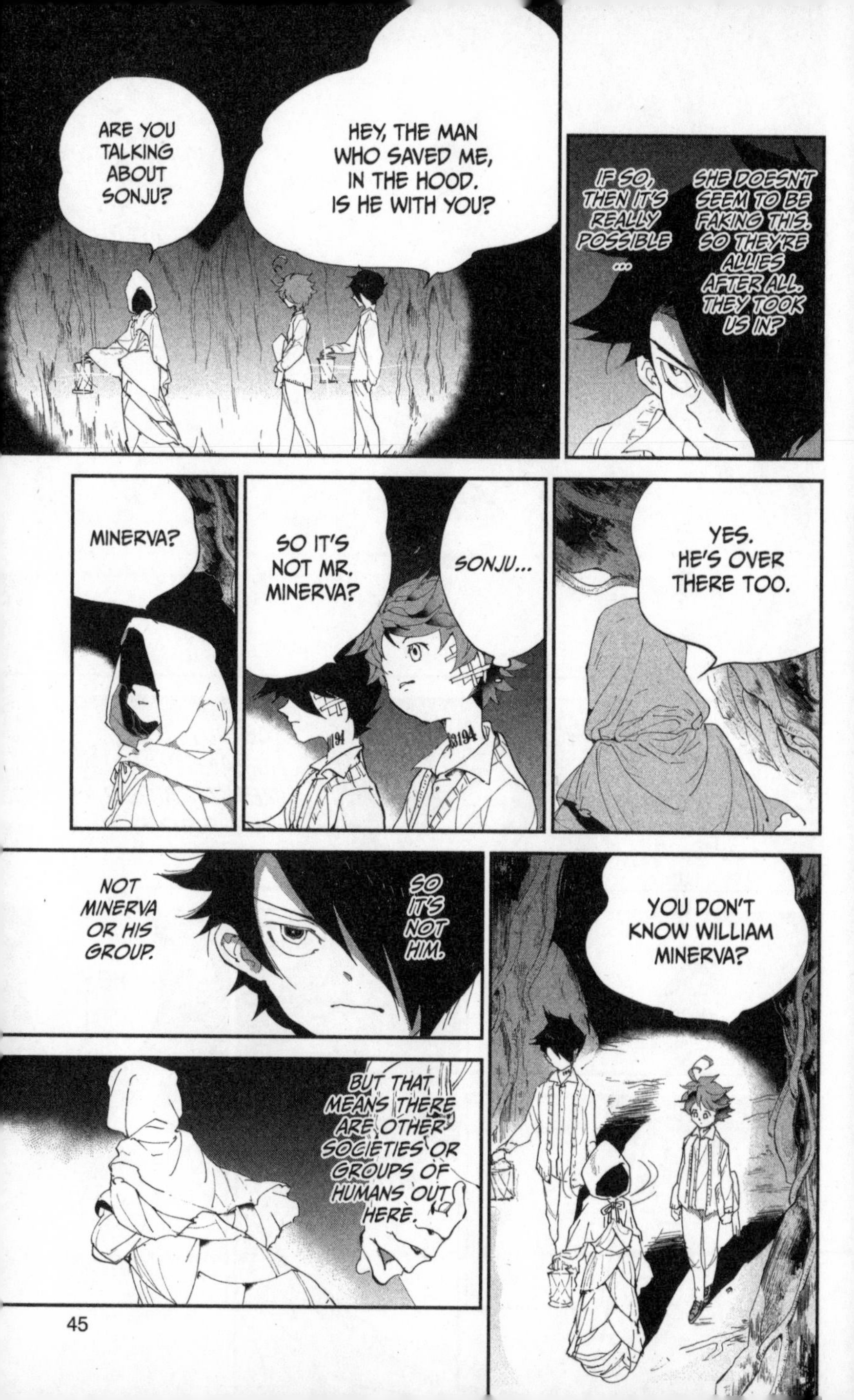
SHE DOESN'T SEEM TO BE FAKING THIS. SO THEY'RE ALLIES AFTER ALL. THEY TOOK US IN?
IF SO, THEN IT'S REALLY POSSIBLE...
HEY, THE MAN WHO SAVED ME, IN THE HOOD. IS HE WITH YOU?
ARE YOU TALKING ABOUT SONJU?
YES. HE'S OVER THERE TOO.
SONJU...
SO IT'S NOT MR. MINERVA?
MINERVA?
YOU DON'T KNOW WILLIAM MINERVA?
SO IT'S NOT HIM.
NOT MINERVA OR HIS GROUP.
BUT THAT MEANS THERE ARE OTHER SOCIETIES OR GROUPS OF HUMANS OUT HERE.

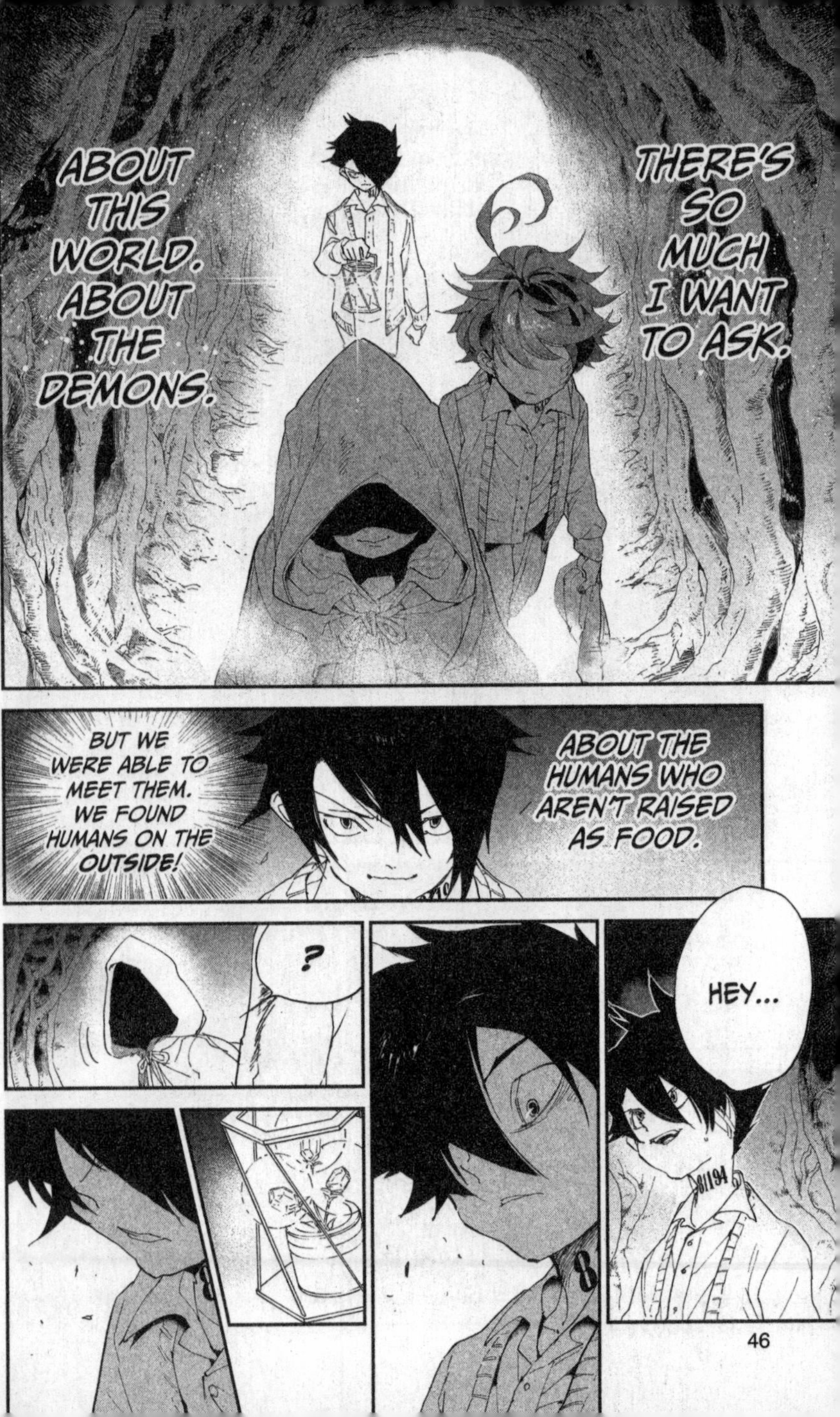
THERE'S SO MUCH I WANT TO ASK.
ABOUT THIS WORLD. ABOUT THE DEMONS.
ABOUT THE HUMANS WHO AREN'T RAISED AS FOOD.
BUT WE WERE ABLE TO MEET THEM. WE FOUND HUMANS ON THE OUTSIDE!
HEY...
?
81194

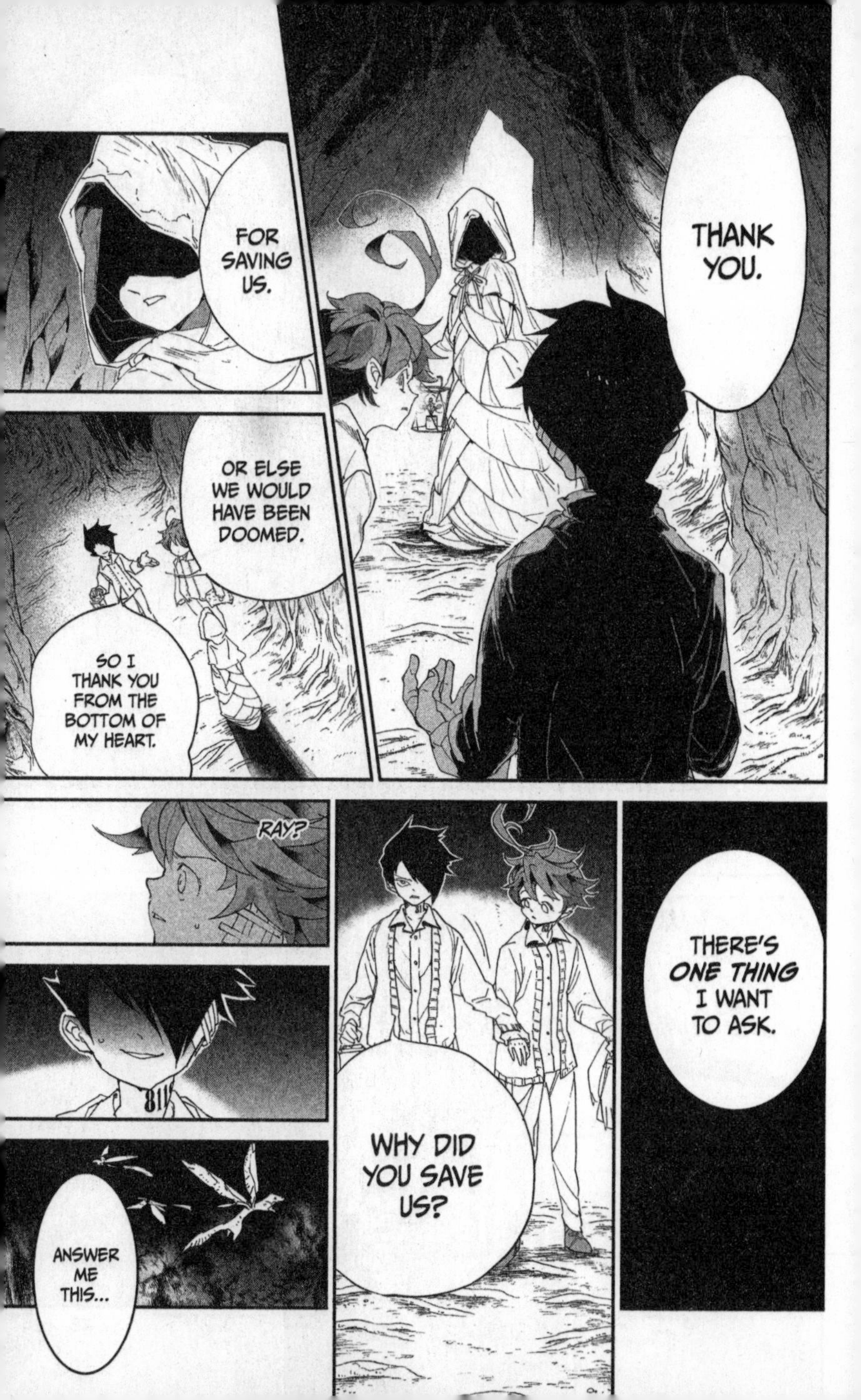
THANK YOU.
FOR SAVING US.
OR ELSE WE WOULD HAVE BEEN DOOMED.
SO I THANK YOU FROM THE BOTTOM OF MY HEART.
THERE'S *ONE THING* I WANT TO ASK.
WHY DID YOU SAVE US?
RAY?
ANSWER ME THIS...

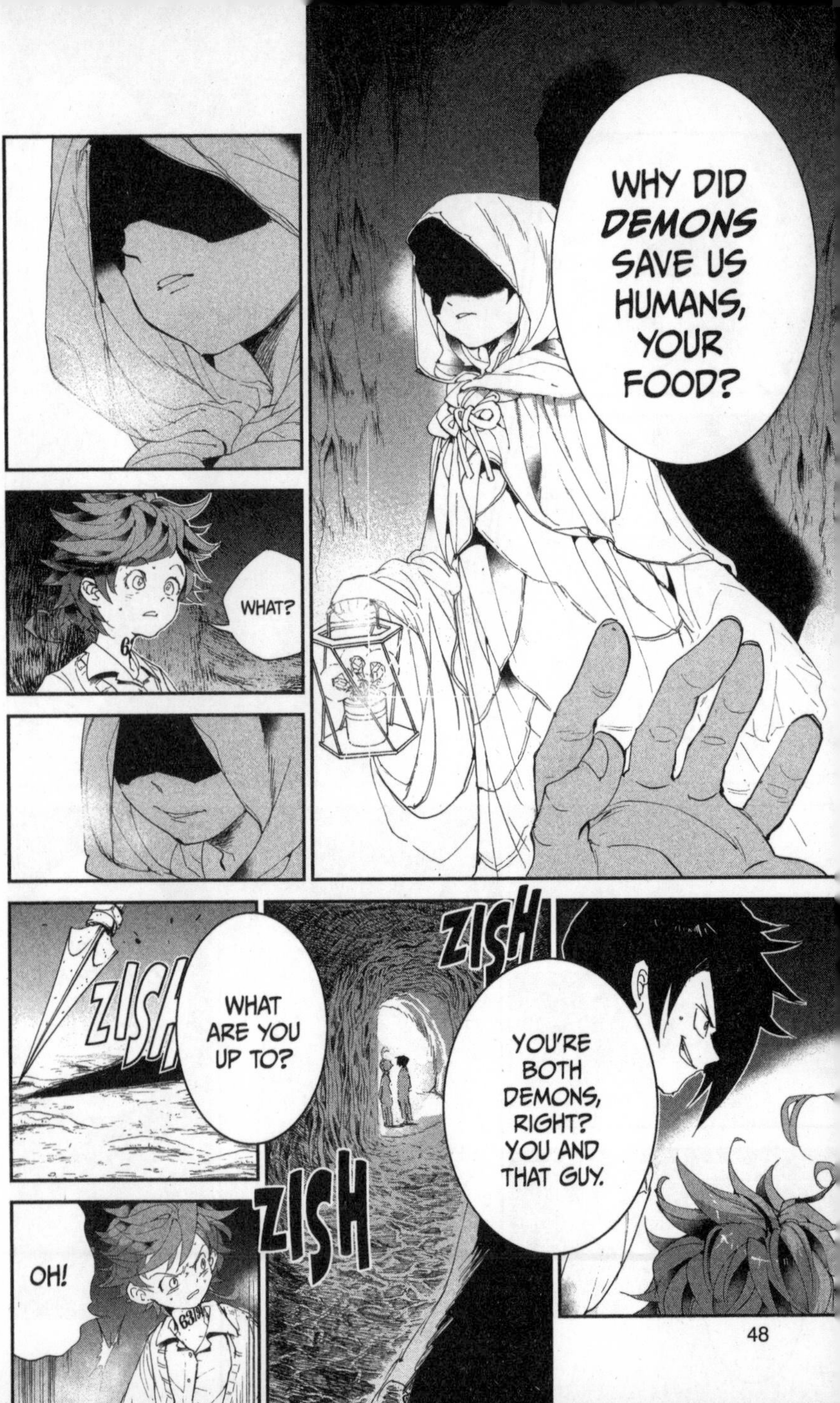
WHY DID *DEMONS* SAVE US HUMANS, YOUR FOOD?
WHAT?
ZISH
YOU'RE BOTH DEMONS, RIGHT? YOU AND THAT GUY.
WHAT ARE YOU UP TO?
ZISH
ZISH
OH!

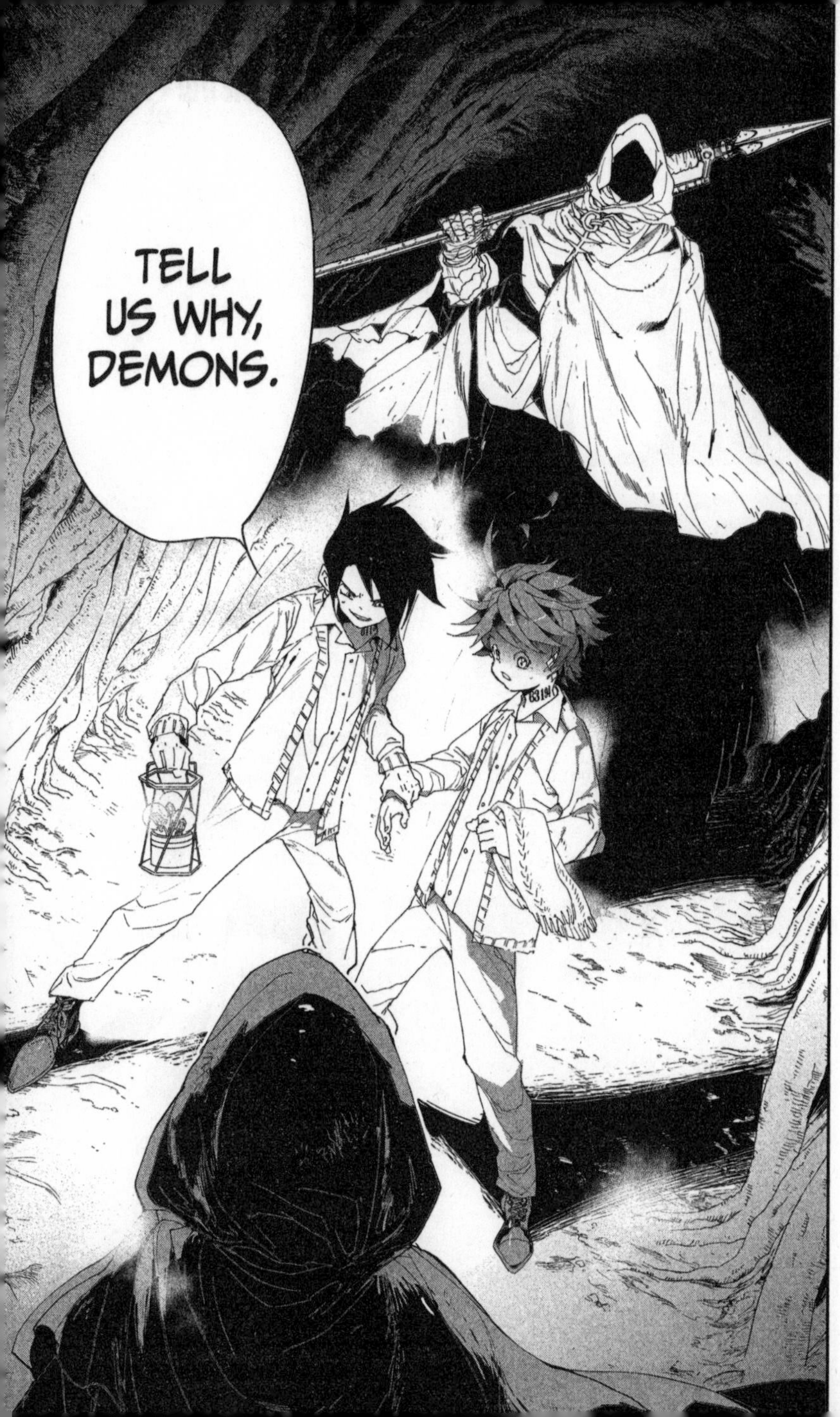
TELL US WHY, DEMONS.

THE PROMISED NEVERLAND SIDE STORY SCENE 010

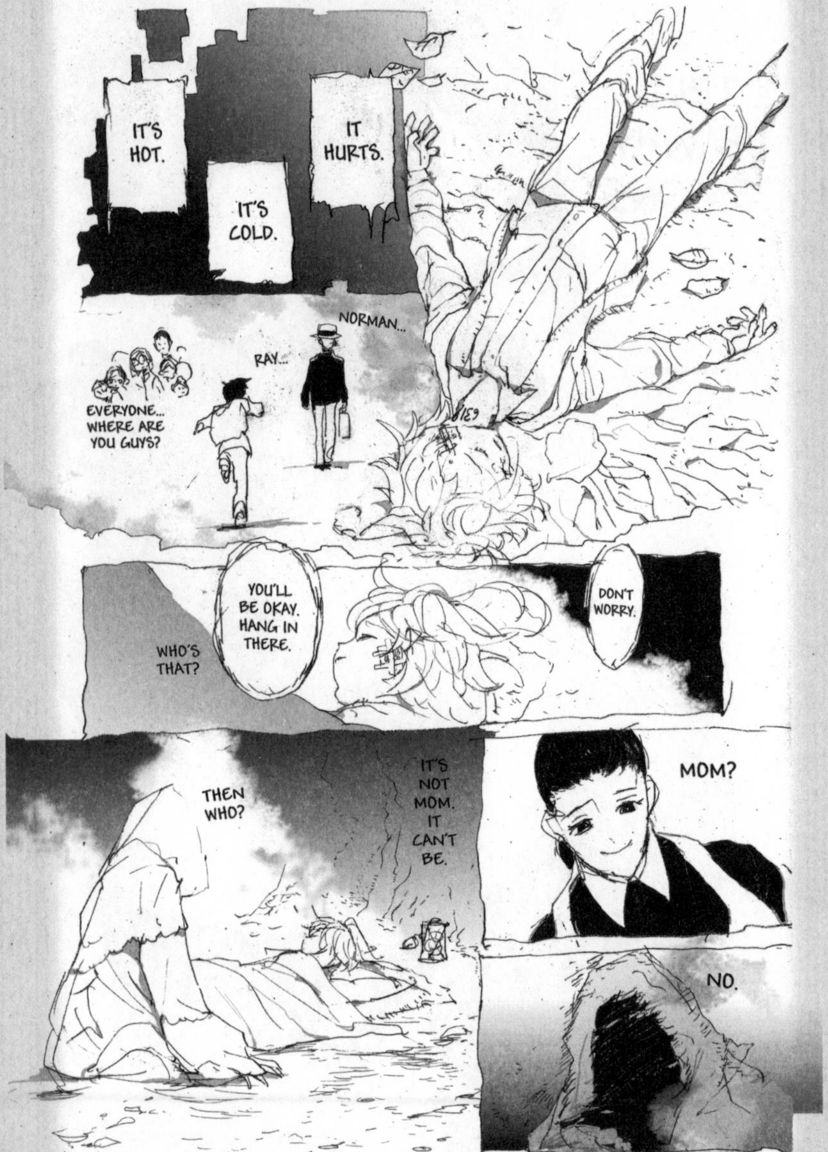
IT HURTS.
IT'S COLD.
IT'S HOT.
NORMAN...
RAY...
EVERYONE... WHERE ARE YOU GUYS?
DON'T WORRY.
YOU'LL BE OKAY. HANG IN THERE.
WHO'S THAT?
MOM?
NO.
IT'S NOT MOM. IT CAN'T BE.
THEN WHO?

CHAPTER 46: SONJU AND MUJIKA

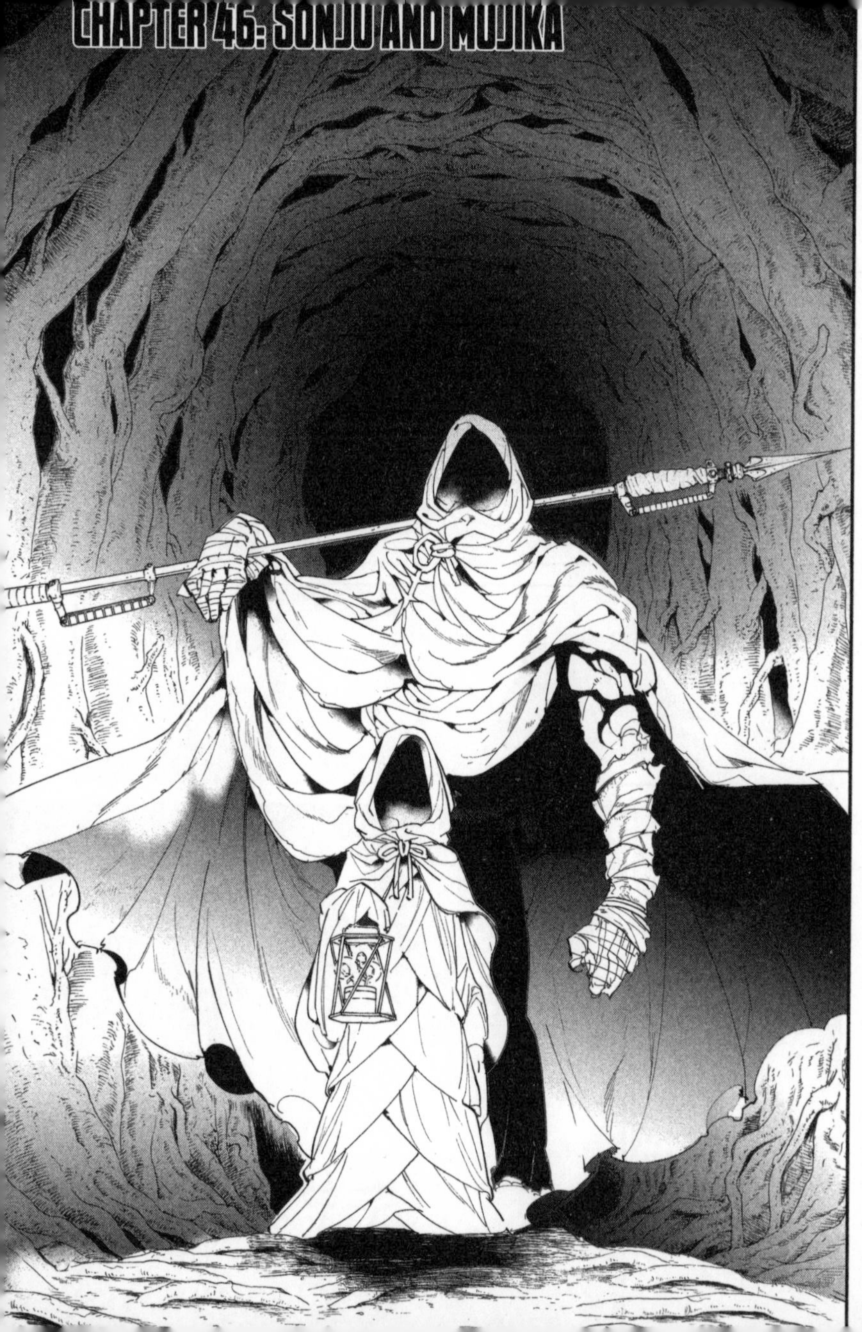

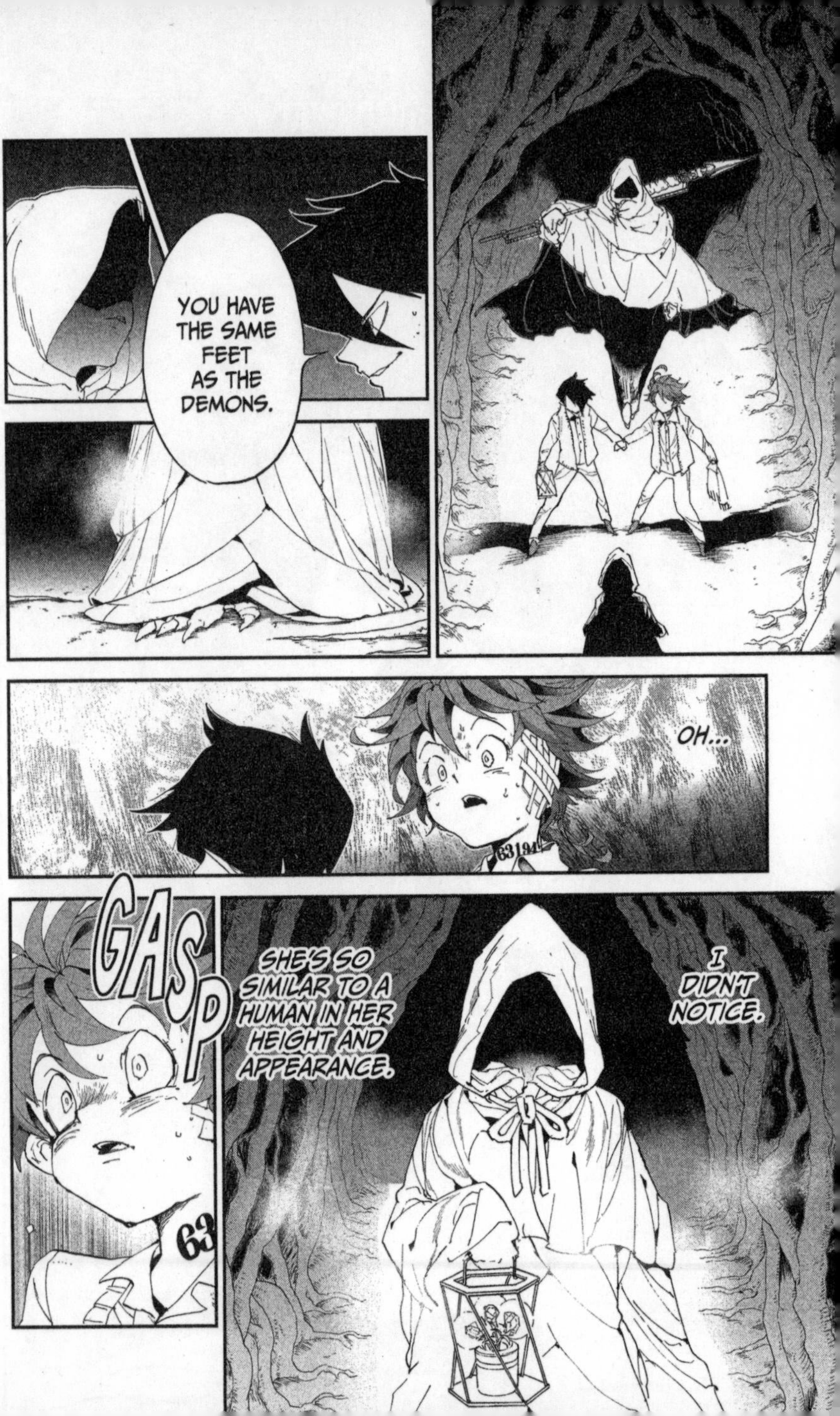
YOU HAVE THE SAME FEET AS THE DEMONS.
OH...
I DIDN'T NOTICE.
SHE'S SO SIMILAR TO A HUMAN IN HER HEIGHT AND APPEARANCE.
GASP

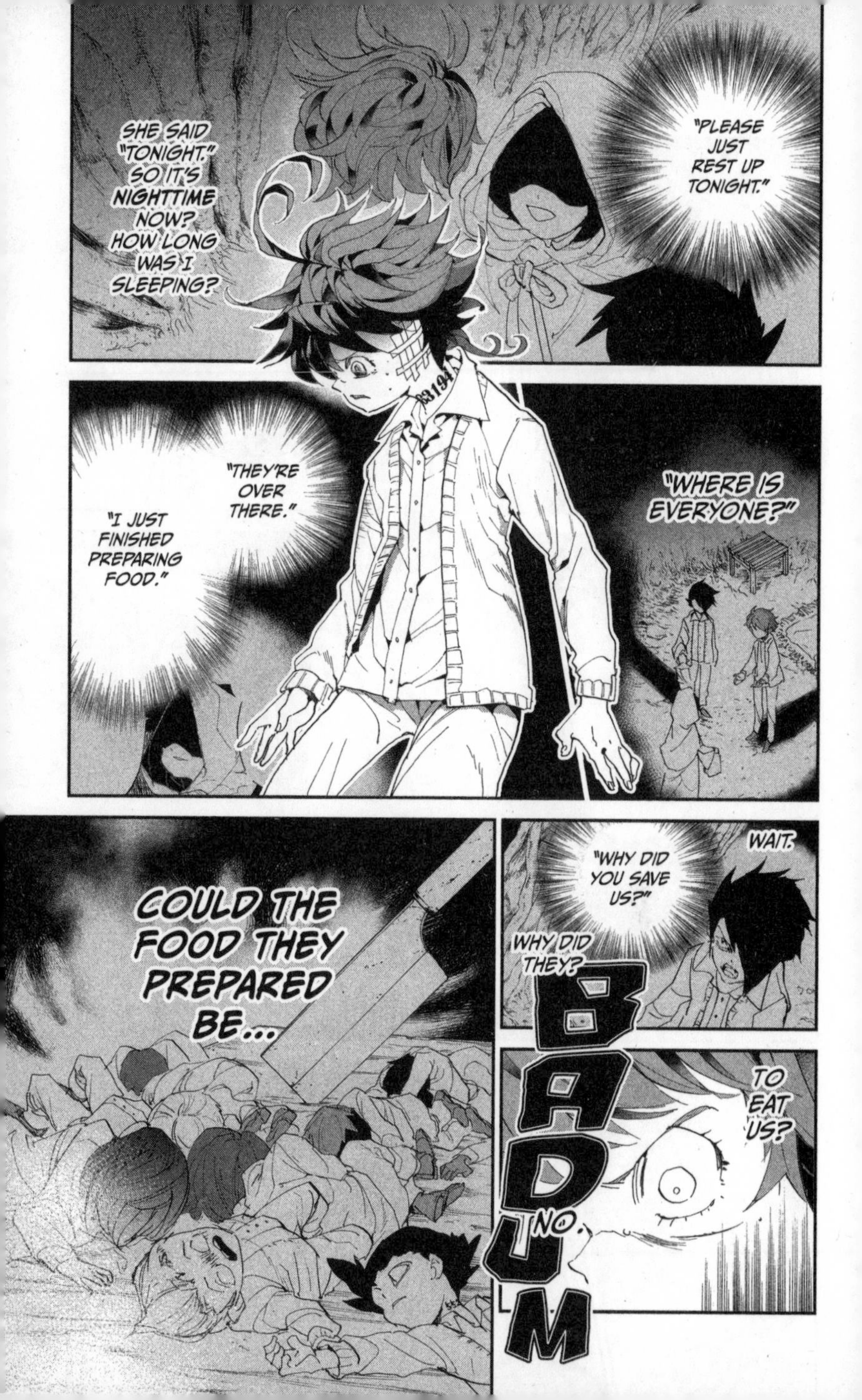
"PLEASE JUST REST UP TONIGHT."
SHE SAID "TONIGHT." SO IT'S NIGHTTIME NOW? HOW LONG WAS I SLEEPING?
"WHERE IS EVERYONE?"
"THEY'RE OVER THERE."
"I JUST FINISHED PREPARING FOOD."
WAIT.
"WHY DID YOU SAVE US?"
WHY DID THEY?
TO EAT US?
NO.
BADUM
COULD THE FOOD THEY PREPARED BE...

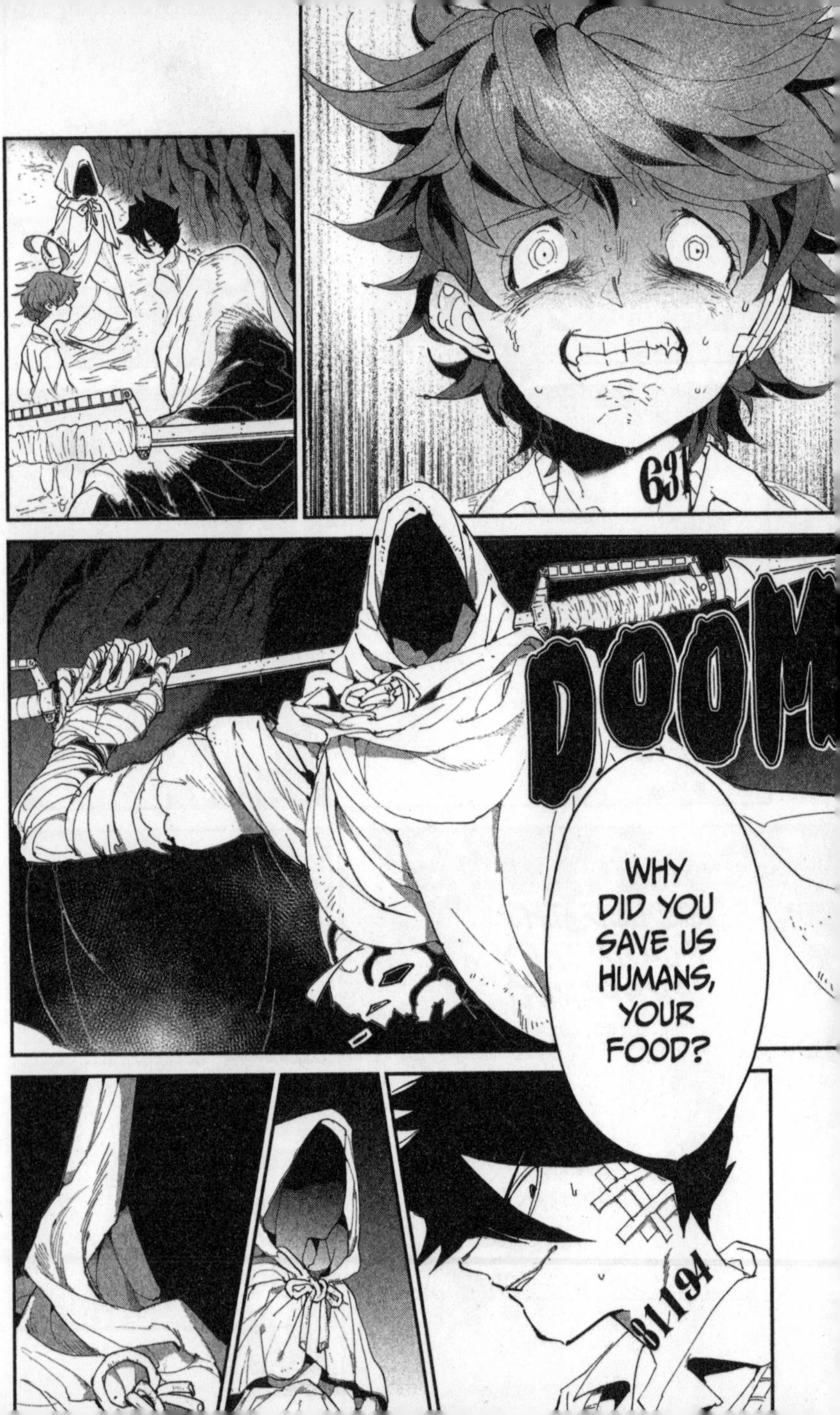
631
DOOM
WHY DID YOU SAVE US HUMANS, YOUR FOOD?
81194

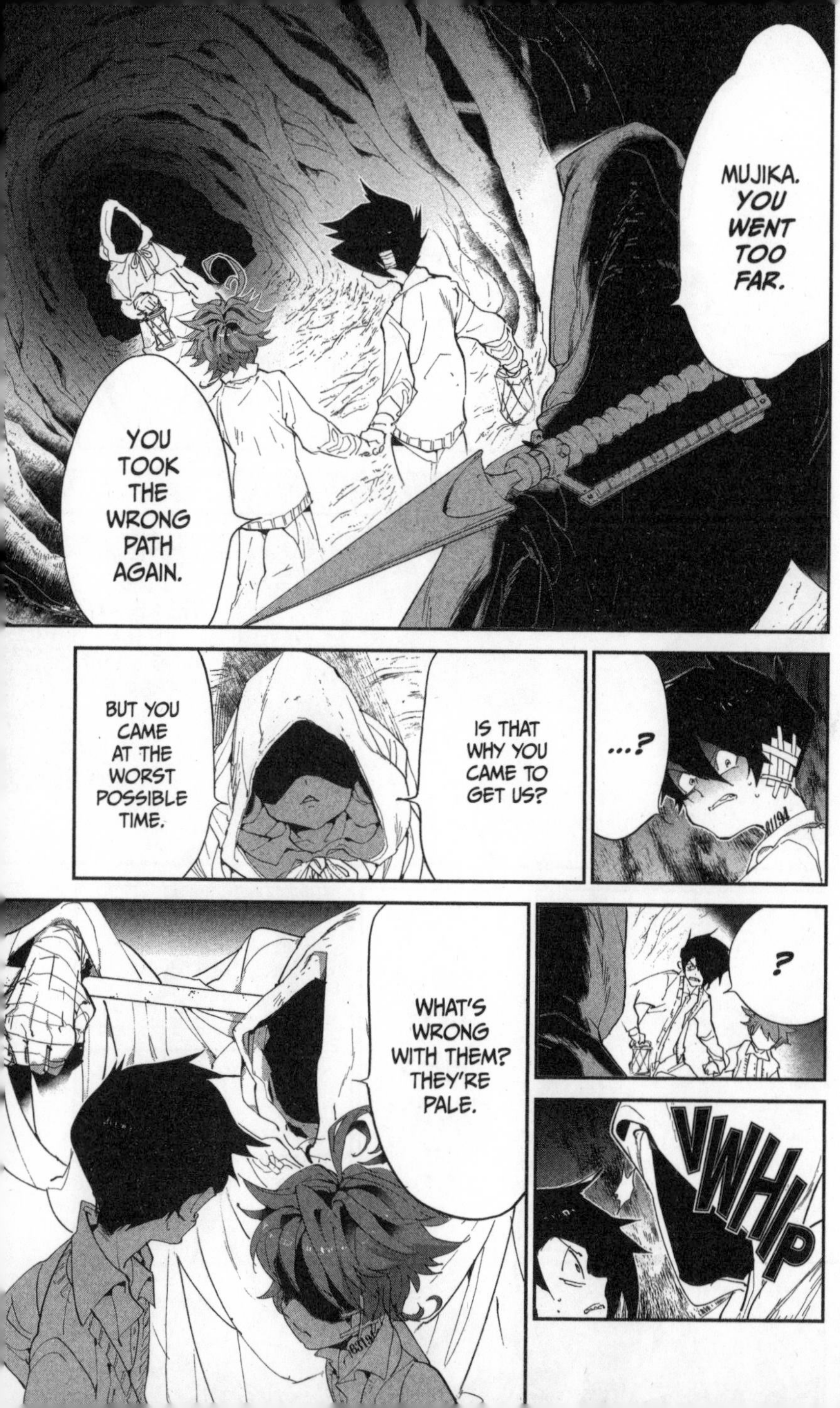
MUJIKA. YOU WENT TOO FAR.
YOU TOOK THE WRONG PATH AGAIN.
...?
IS THAT WHY YOU CAME TO GET US?
BUT YOU CAME AT THE WORST POSSIBLE TIME.
?
VWHIP
WHAT'S WRONG WITH THEM? THEY'RE PALE.

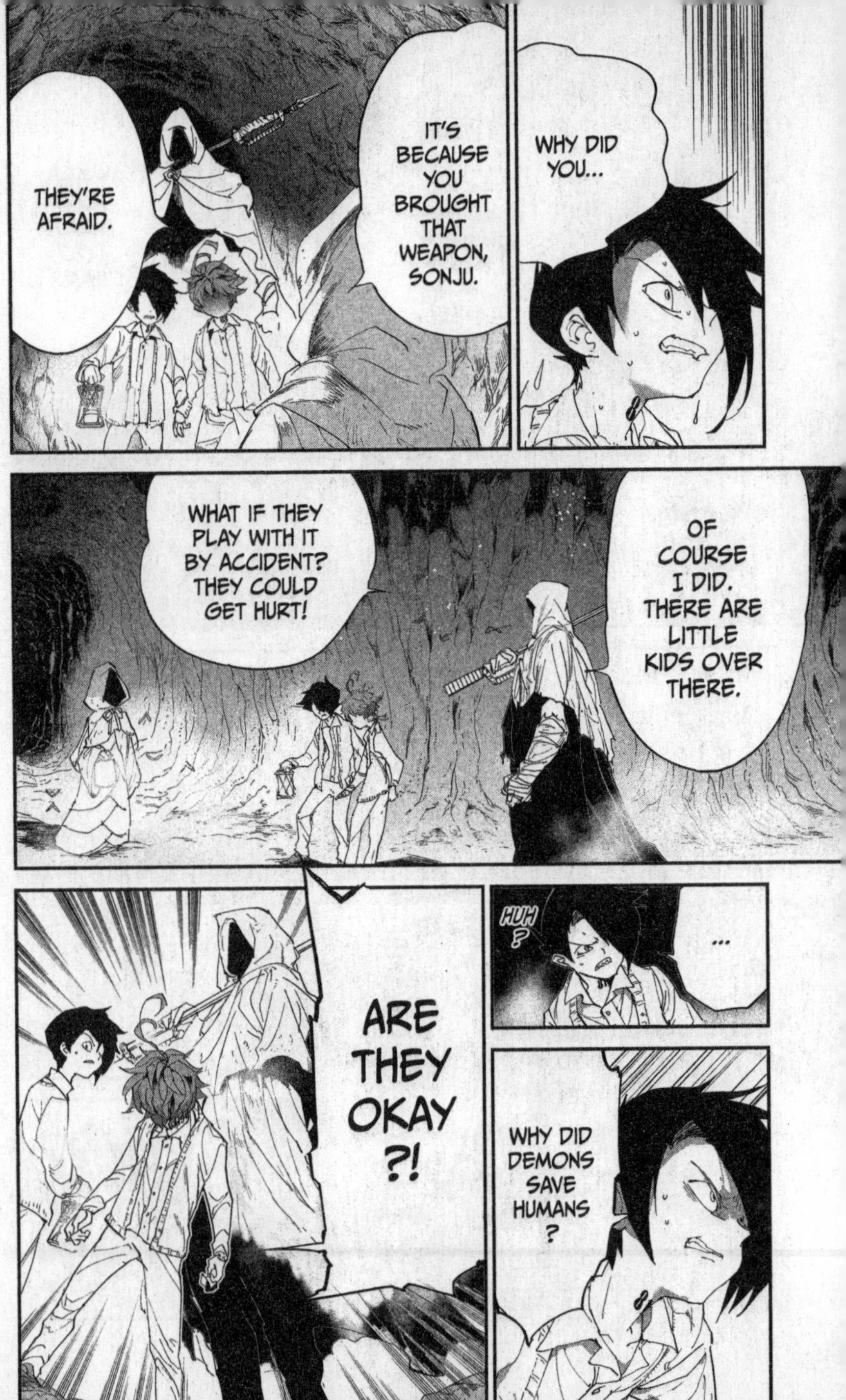
WHY DID YOU...
IT'S BECAUSE YOU BROUGHT THAT WEAPON, SONJU.
THEY'RE AFRAID.
OF COURSE I DID. THERE ARE LITTLE KIDS OVER THERE.
WHAT IF THEY PLAY WITH IT BY ACCIDENT? THEY COULD GET HURT!
HUH?
...
WHY DID DEMONS SAVE HUMANS?
ARE THEY OKAY?!

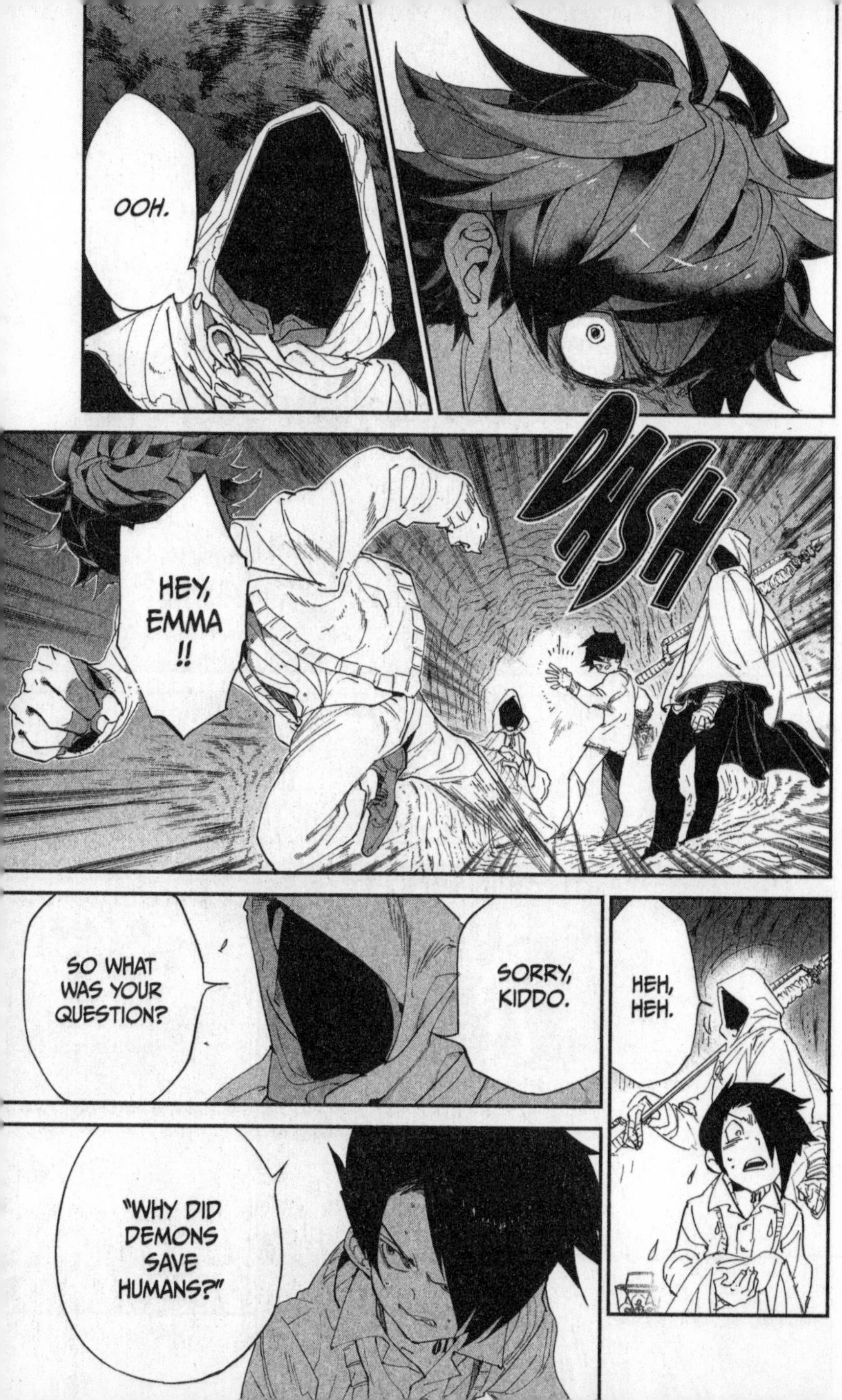
OOH.
DASH
HEY, EMMA!!
HEH, HEH.
SORRY, KIDDO.
SO WHAT WAS YOUR QUESTION?
"WHY DID DEMONS SAVE HUMANS?"

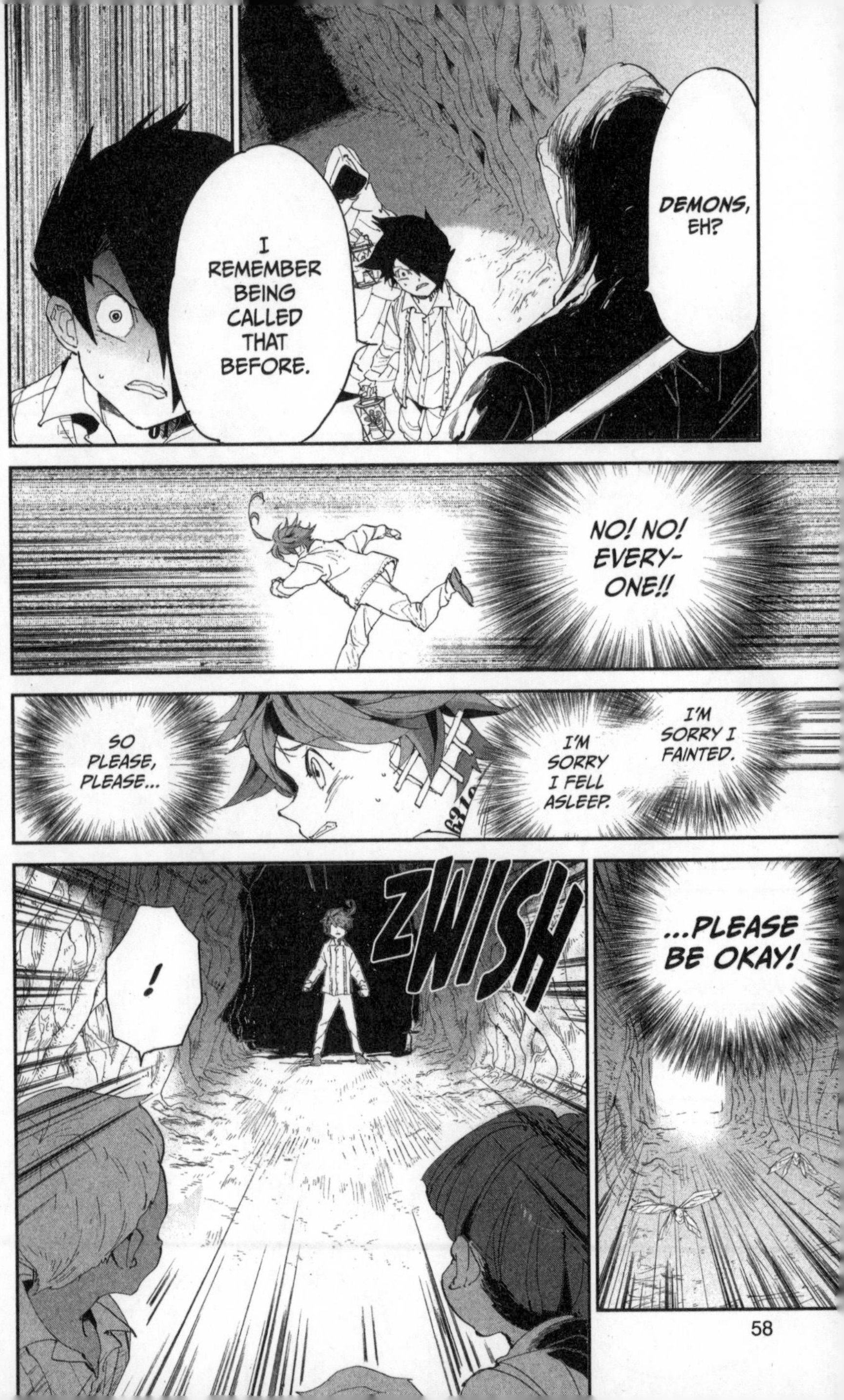
DEMONS, EH?
I REMEMBER BEING CALLED THAT BEFORE.
NO! NO! EVERYONE!!
I'M SORRY I FAINTED.
I'M SORRY I FELL ASLEEP.
SO PLEASE, PLEASE...
...PLEASE BE OKAY!
ZWISH
!

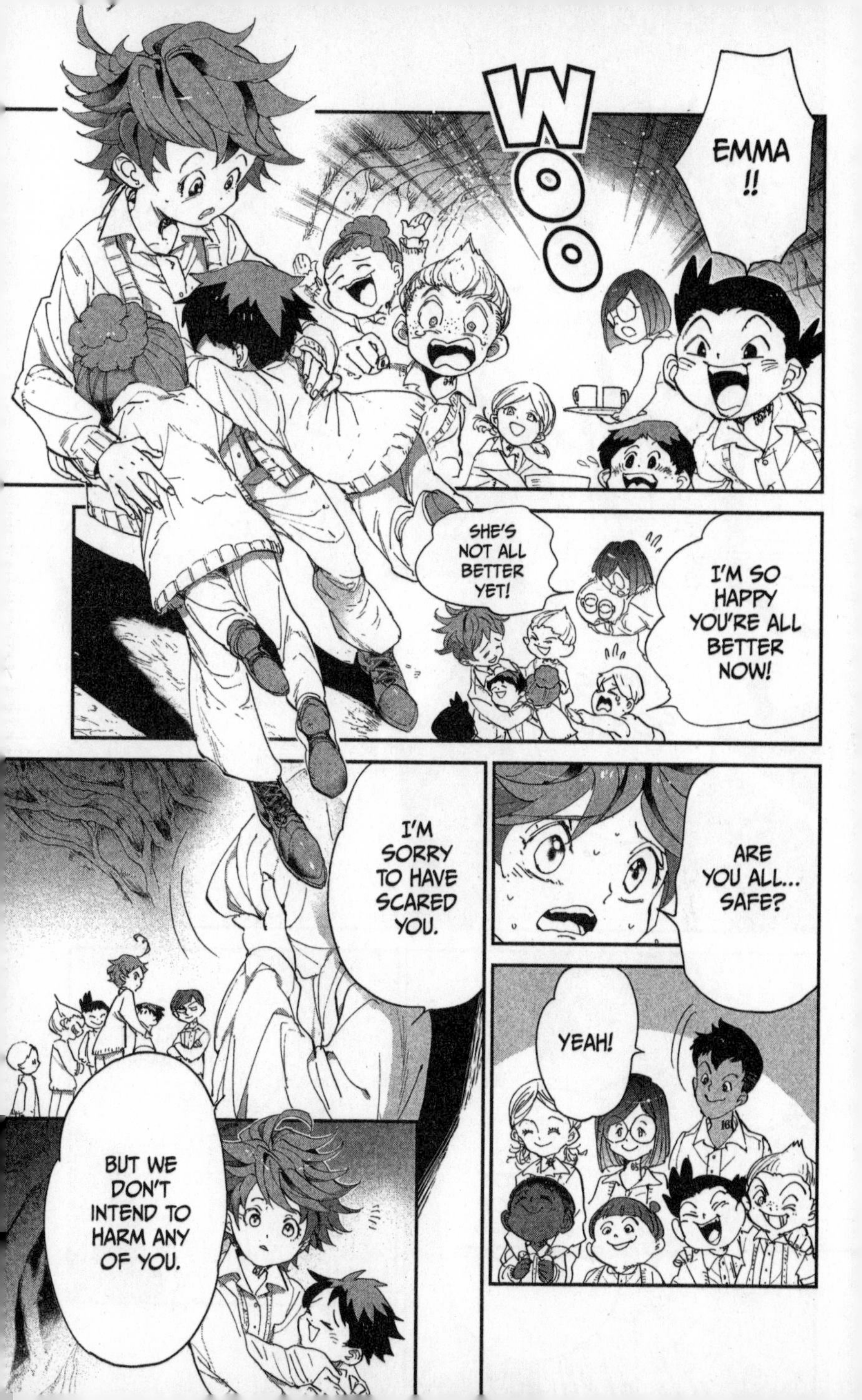
EMMA !!
WOOO
I'M SO HAPPY YOU'RE ALL BETTER NOW!
SHE'S NOT ALL BETTER YET!
ARE YOU ALL... SAFE?
YEAH!
I'M SORRY TO HAVE SCARED YOU.
BUT WE DON'T INTEND TO HARM ANY OF YOU.

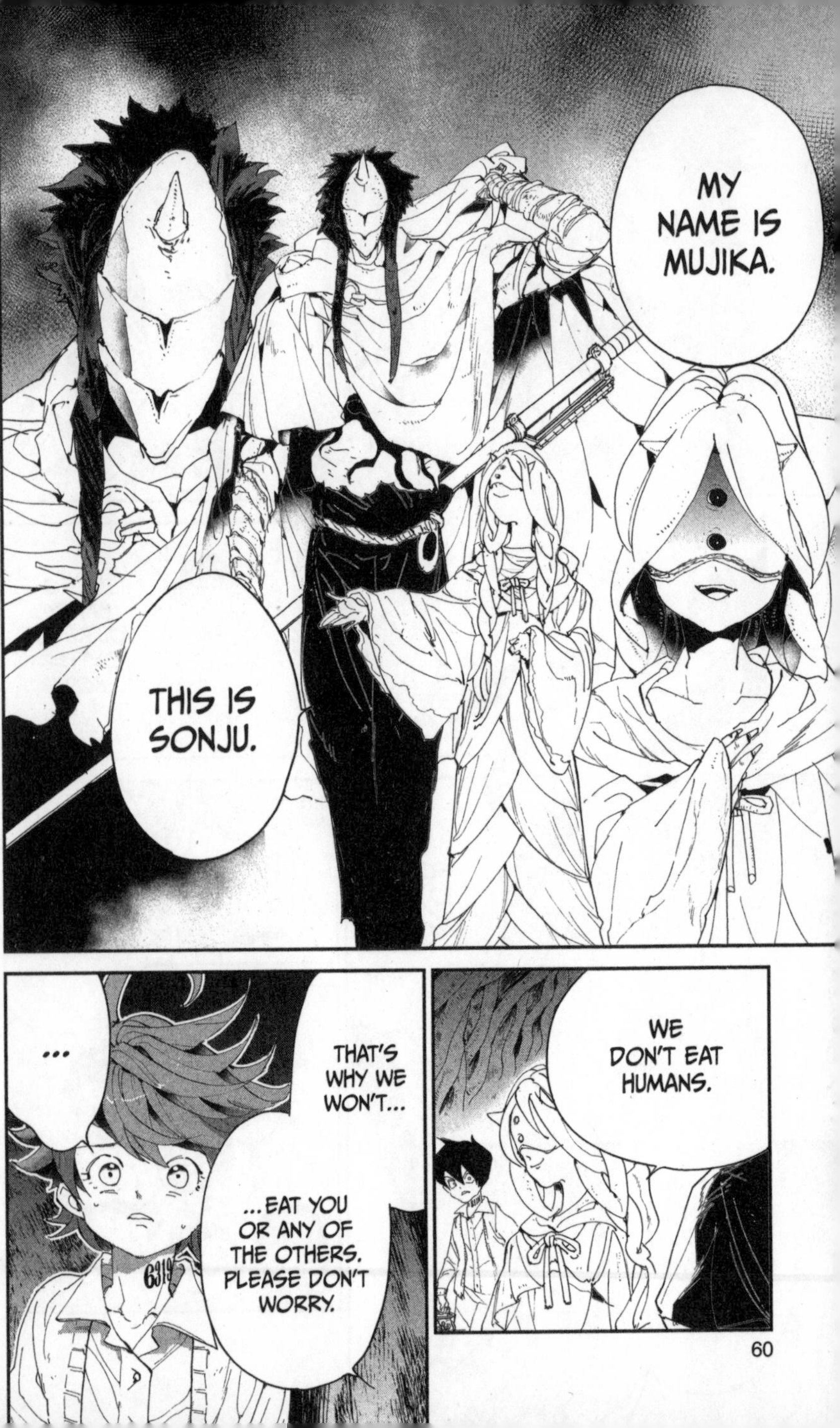

MY NAME IS MUJIKA.
THIS IS SONJU.
WE DON'T EAT HUMANS.
THAT'S WHY WE WON'T...
...
...EAT YOU OR ANY OF THE OTHERS. PLEASE DON'T WORRY.
6319

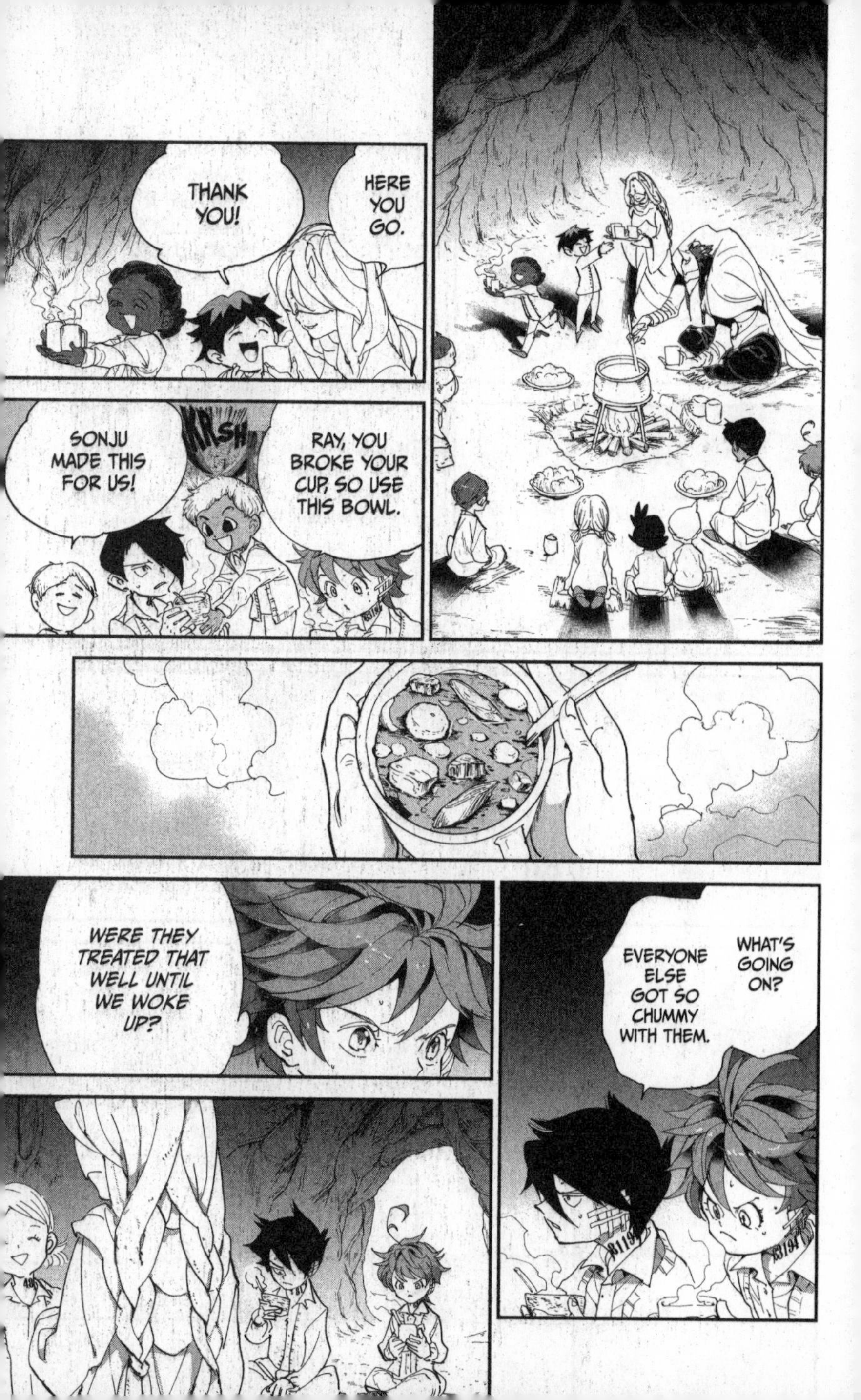
HERE YOU GO.
THANK YOU!
RAY, YOU BROKE YOUR CUP, SO USE THIS BOWL.
KRSH
SONJU MADE THIS FOR US!
WHAT'S GOING ON?
EVERYONE ELSE GOT SO CHUMMY WITH THEM.
WERE THEY TREATED THAT WELL UNTIL WE WOKE UP?

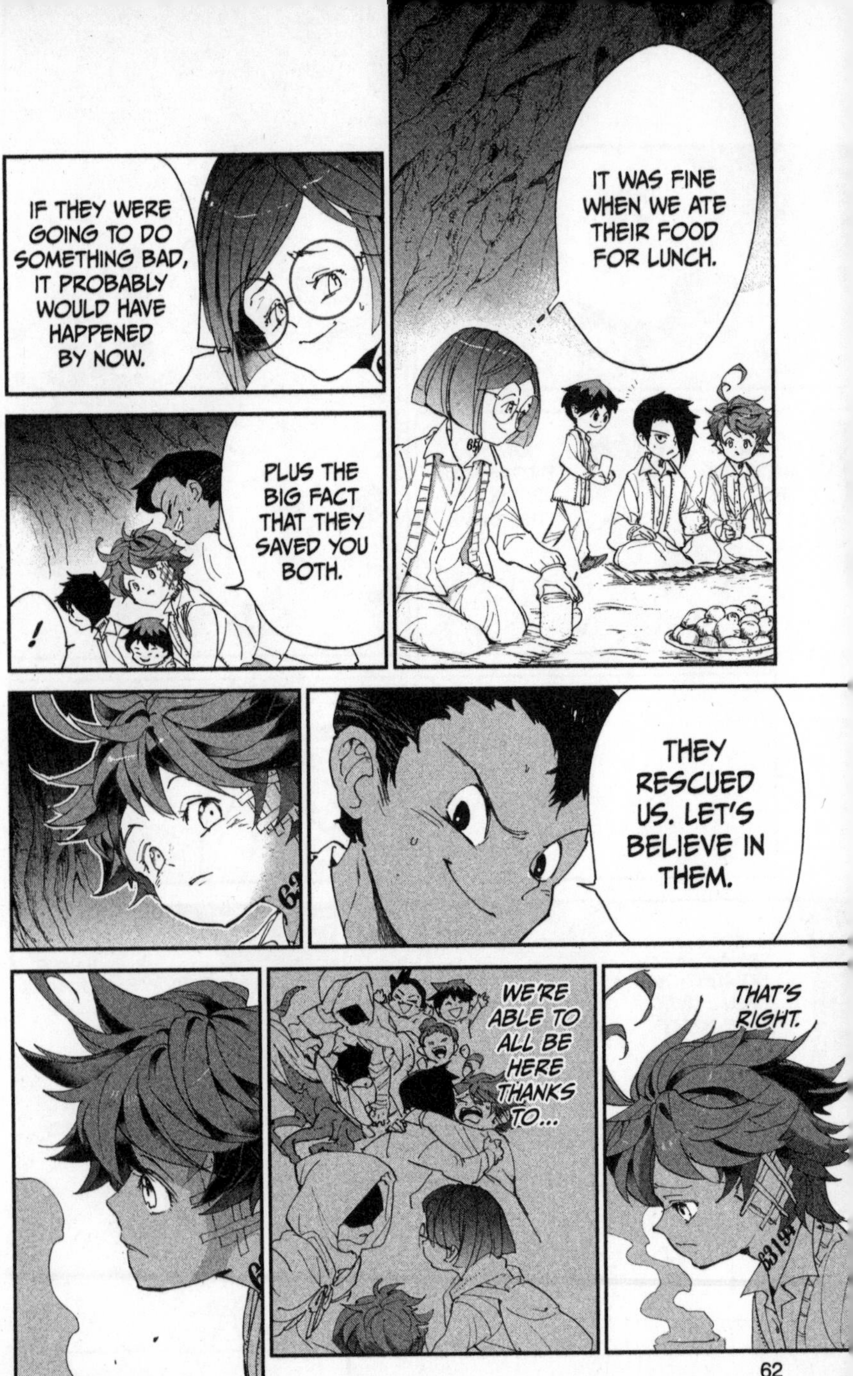
IT WAS FINE WHEN WE ATE THEIR FOOD FOR LUNCH.
IF THEY WERE GOING TO DO SOMETHING BAD, IT PROBABLY WOULD HAVE HAPPENED BY NOW.
PLUS THE BIG FACT THAT THEY SAVED YOU BOTH.
!
THEY RESCUED US. LET'S BELIEVE IN THEM.
THAT'S RIGHT.
WE'RE ABLE TO ALL BE HERE THANKS TO...

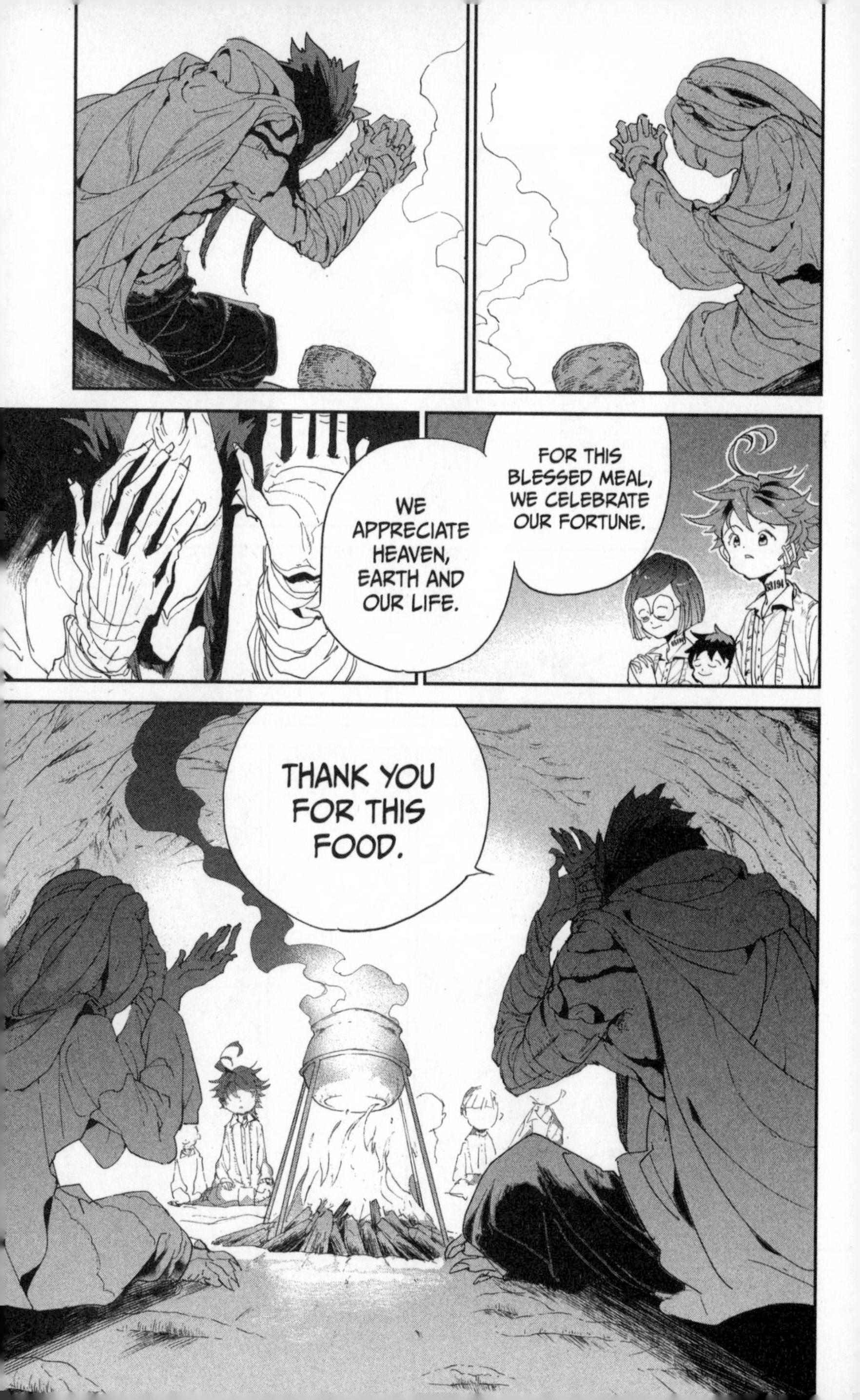
FOR THIS BLESSED MEAL, WE CELEBRATE OUR FORTUNE.
WE APPRECIATE HEAVEN, EARTH AND OUR LIFE.
THANK YOU FOR THIS FOOD.

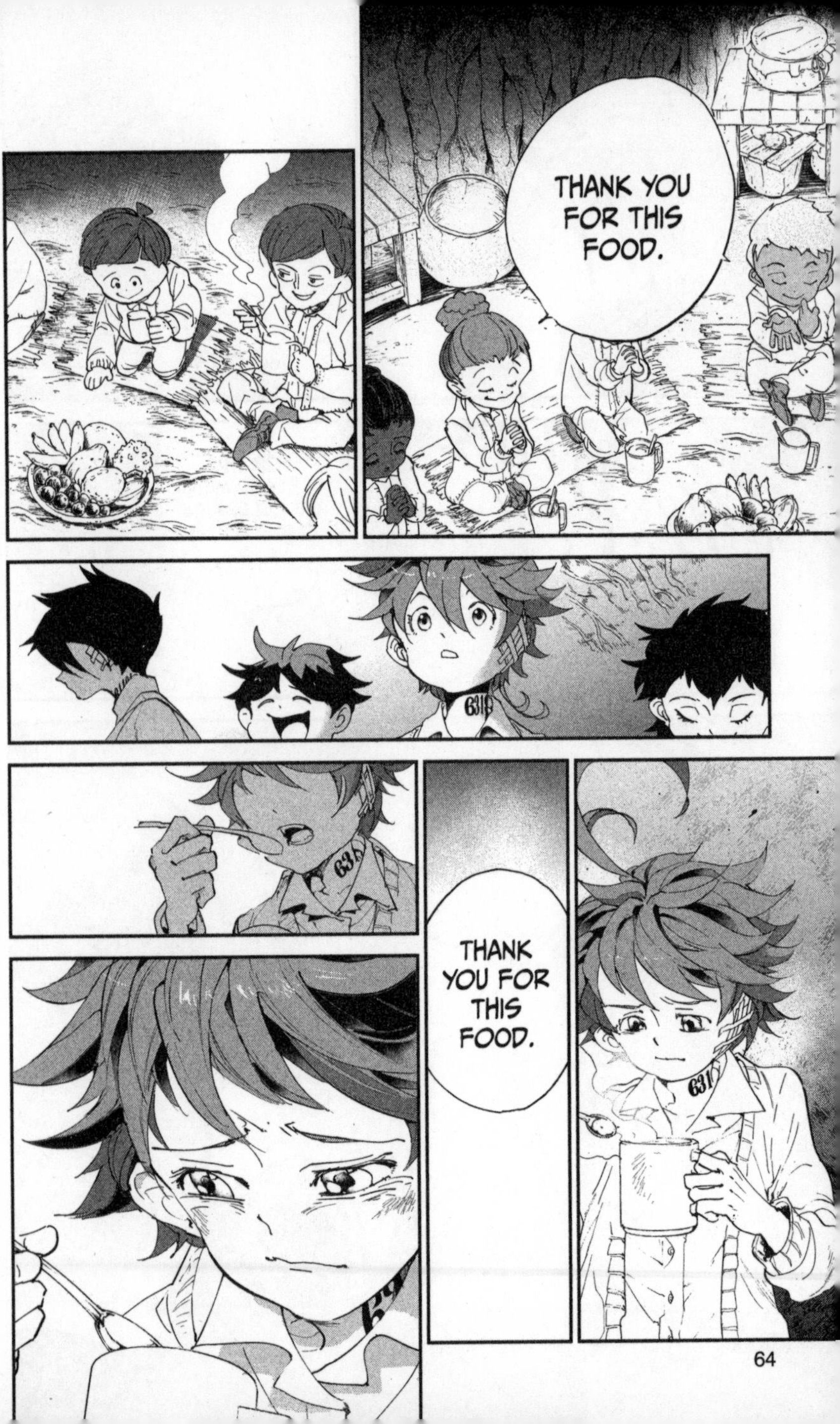
THANK YOU FOR THIS FOOD.
THANK YOU FOR THIS FOOD.

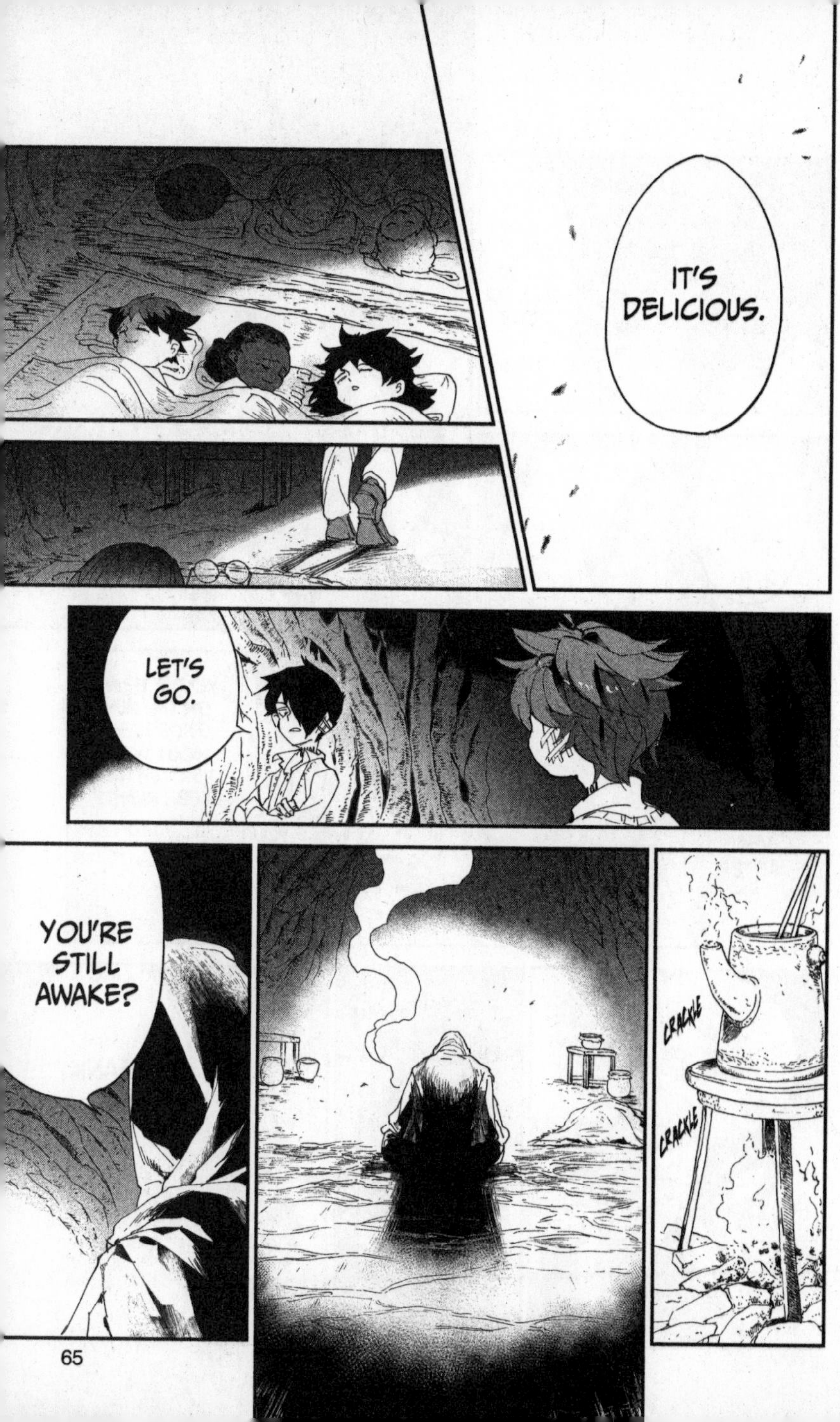
IT'S DELICIOUS.
LET'S GO.
CRACKLE
CRACKLE
YOU'RE STILL AWAKE?

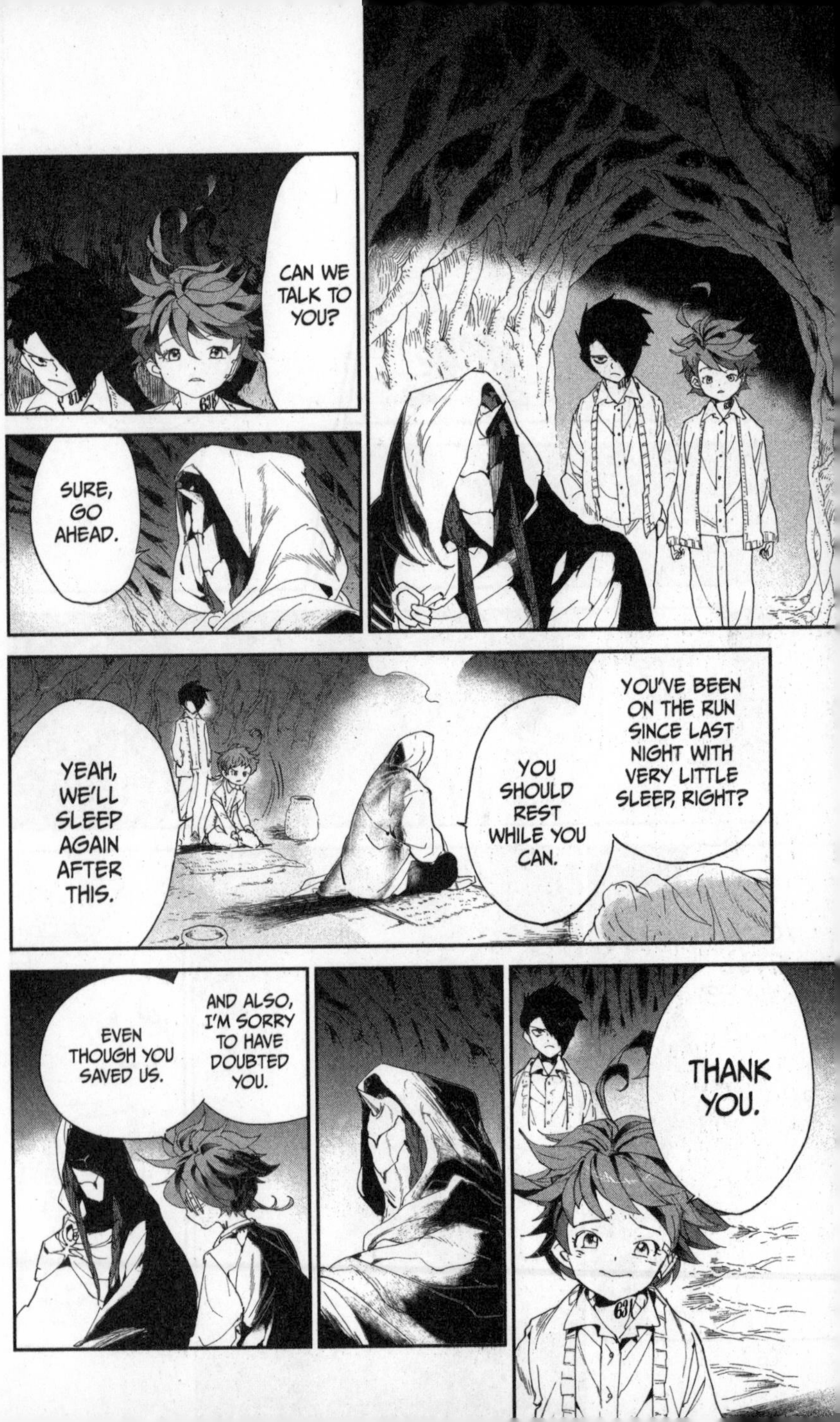
CAN WE TALK TO YOU?
SURE, GO AHEAD.
YOU'VE BEEN ON THE RUN SINCE LAST NIGHT WITH VERY LITTLE SLEEP, RIGHT?
YOU SHOULD REST WHILE YOU CAN.
YEAH, WE'LL SLEEP AGAIN AFTER THIS.
THANK YOU.
AND ALSO, I'M SORRY TO HAVE DOUBTED YOU.
EVEN THOUGH YOU SAVED US.

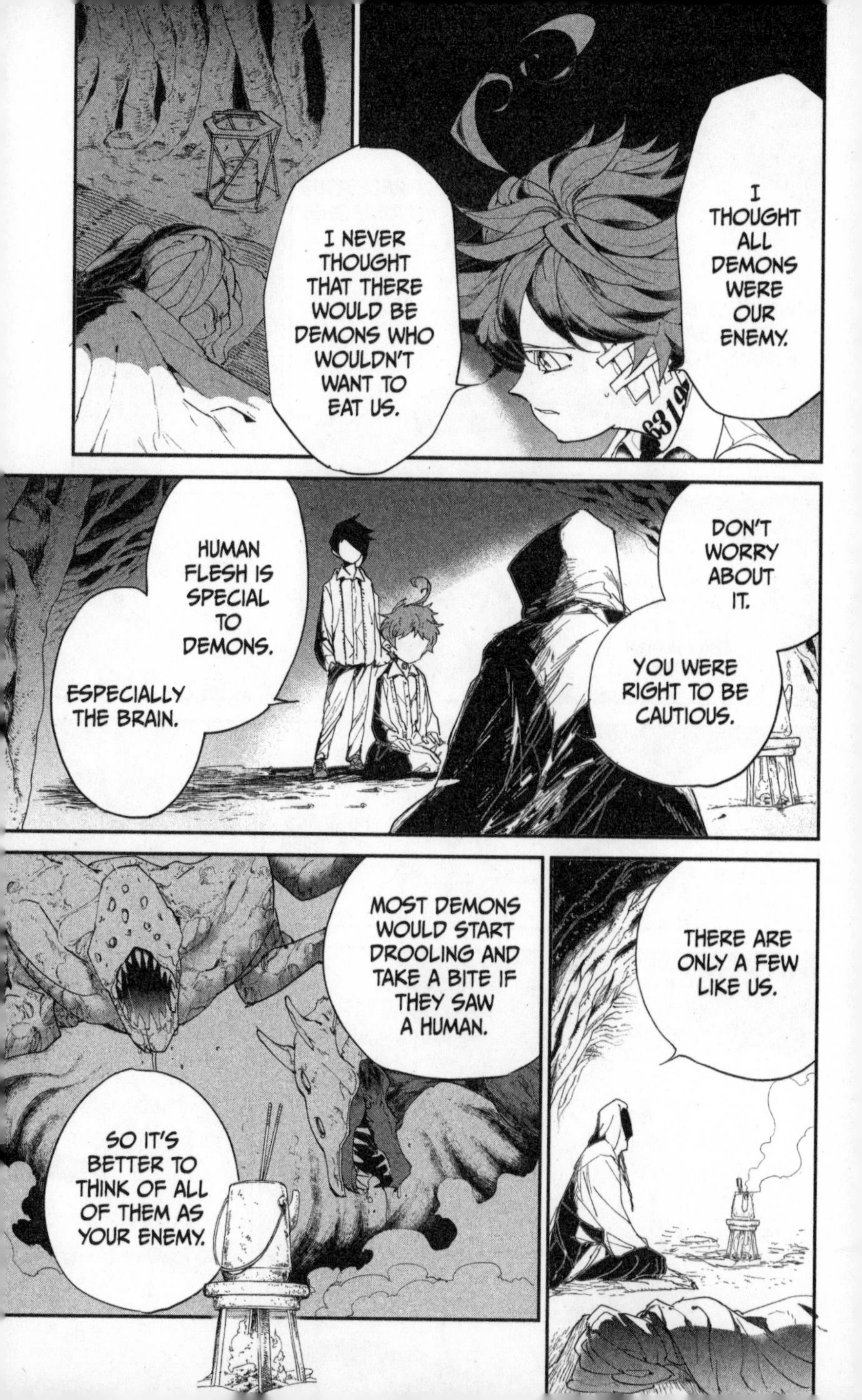
I THOUGHT ALL DEMONS WERE OUR ENEMY.
I NEVER THOUGHT THAT THERE WOULD BE DEMONS WHO WOULDN'T WANT TO EAT US.
DON'T WORRY ABOUT IT.
YOU WERE RIGHT TO BE CAUTIOUS.
HUMAN FLESH IS SPECIAL TO DEMONS.
ESPECIALLY THE BRAIN.
THERE ARE ONLY A FEW LIKE US.
MOST DEMONS WOULD START DROOLING AND TAKE A BITE IF THEY SAW A HUMAN.
SO IT'S BETTER TO THINK OF ALL OF THEM AS YOUR ENEMY.

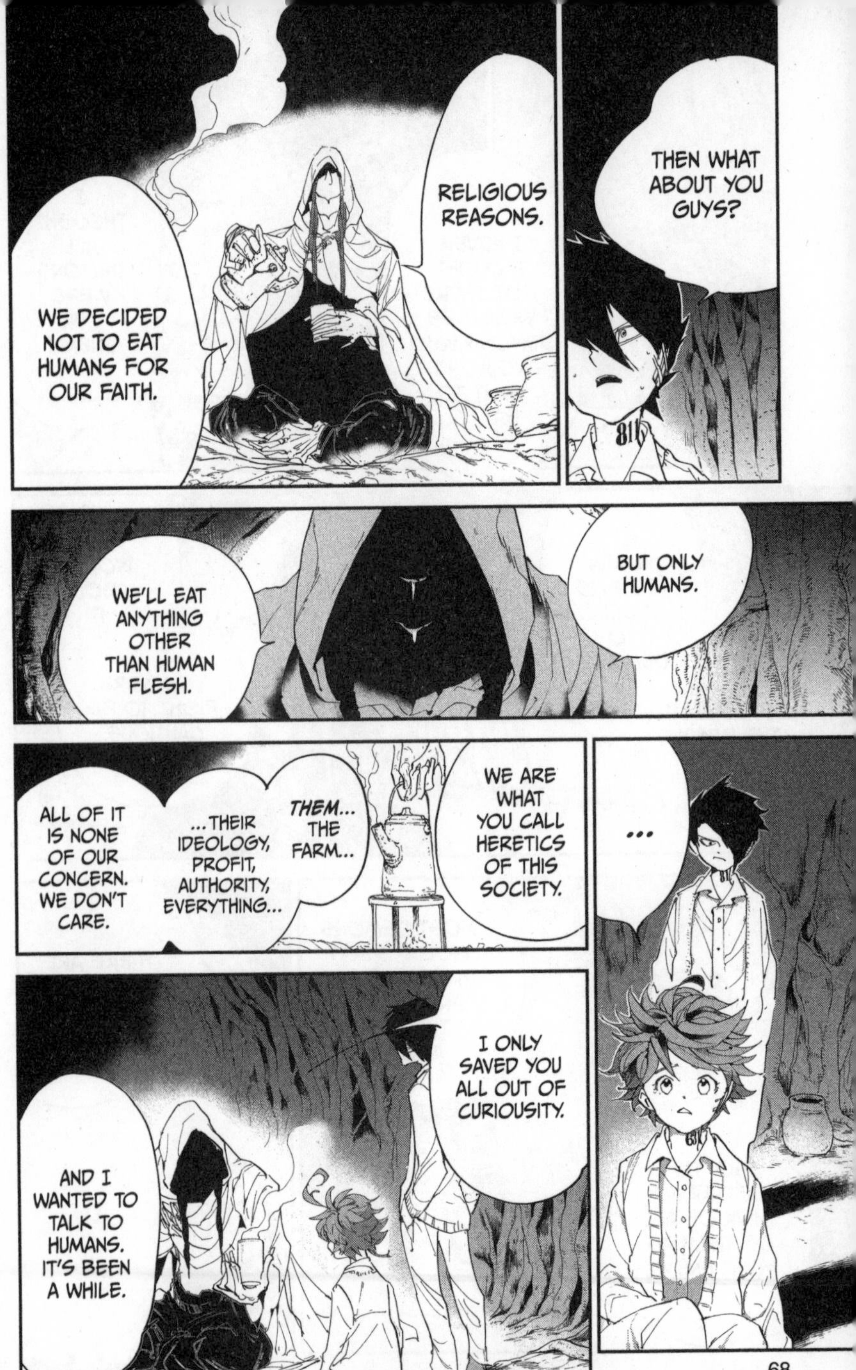
THEN WHAT ABOUT YOU GUYS?
RELIGIOUS REASONS.
WE DECIDED NOT TO EAT HUMANS FOR OUR FAITH.
BUT ONLY HUMANS.
WE'LL EAT ANYTHING OTHER THAN HUMAN FLESH.
...
WE ARE WHAT YOU CALL HERETICS OF THIS SOCIETY.
THEM... THE FARM...
...THEIR IDEOLOGY, PROFIT, AUTHORITY, EVERYTHING...
ALL OF IT IS NONE OF OUR CONCERN. WE DON'T CARE.
I ONLY SAVED YOU ALL OUT OF CURIOUSITY.
AND I WANTED TO TALK TO HUMANS. IT'S BEEN A WHILE.

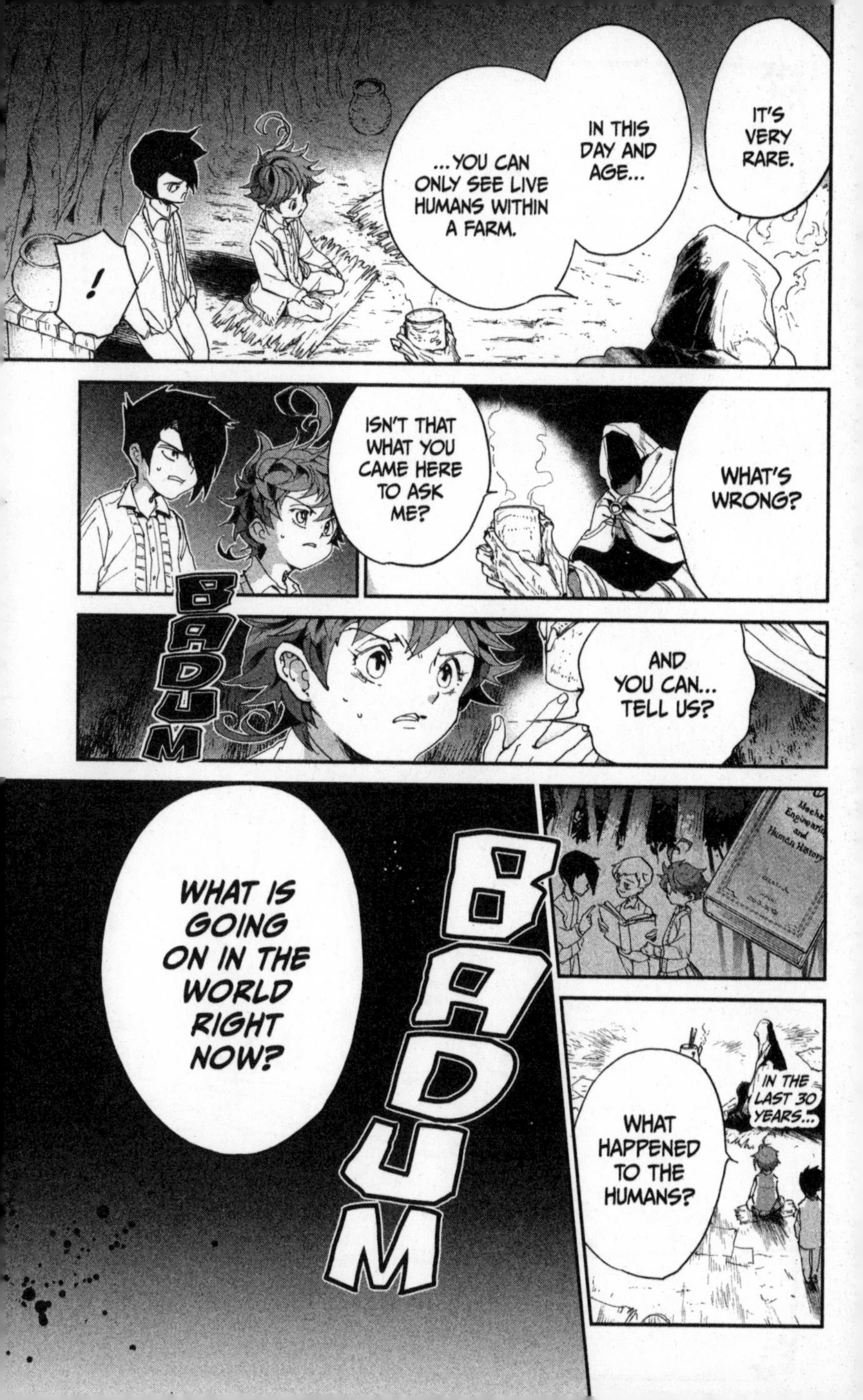
IT'S VERY RARE.
IN THIS DAY AND AGE...
...YOU CAN ONLY SEE LIVE HUMANS WITHIN A FARM.
!
WHAT'S WRONG?
ISN'T THAT WHAT YOU CAME HERE TO ASK ME?
BADUM
AND YOU CAN... TELL US?
BADUM
IN THE LAST 30 YEARS...
WHAT HAPPENED TO THE HUMANS?
BADUM
WHAT IS GOING ON IN THE WORLD RIGHT NOW?

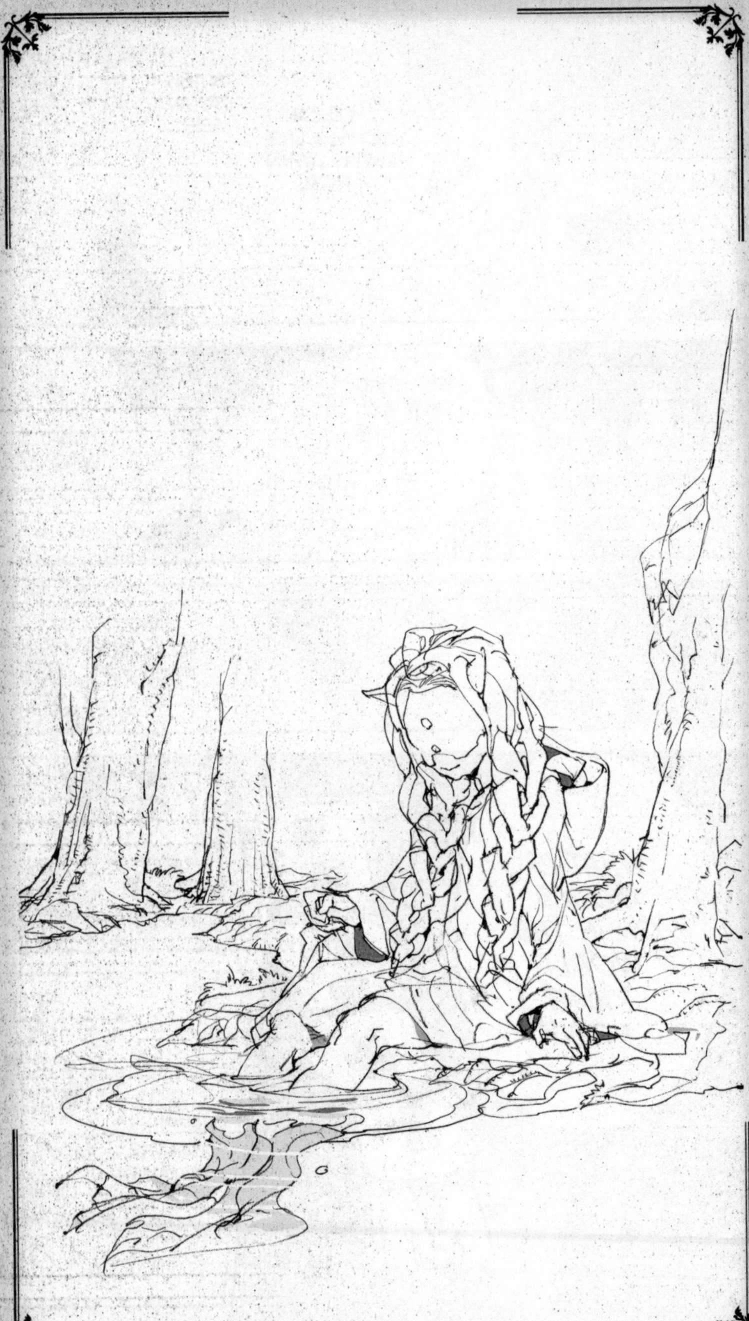

CHAPTER 47: AN OLD TALE

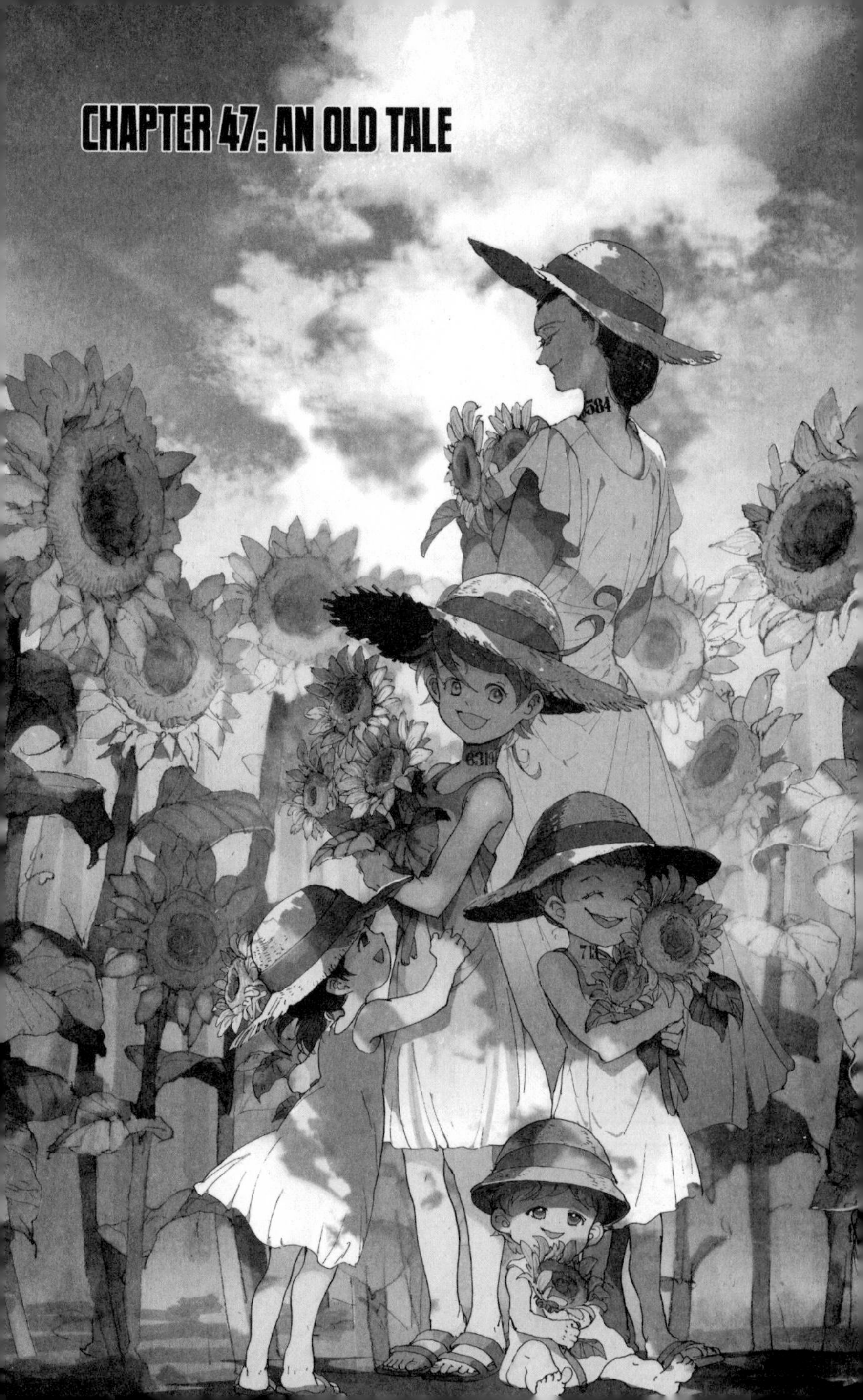

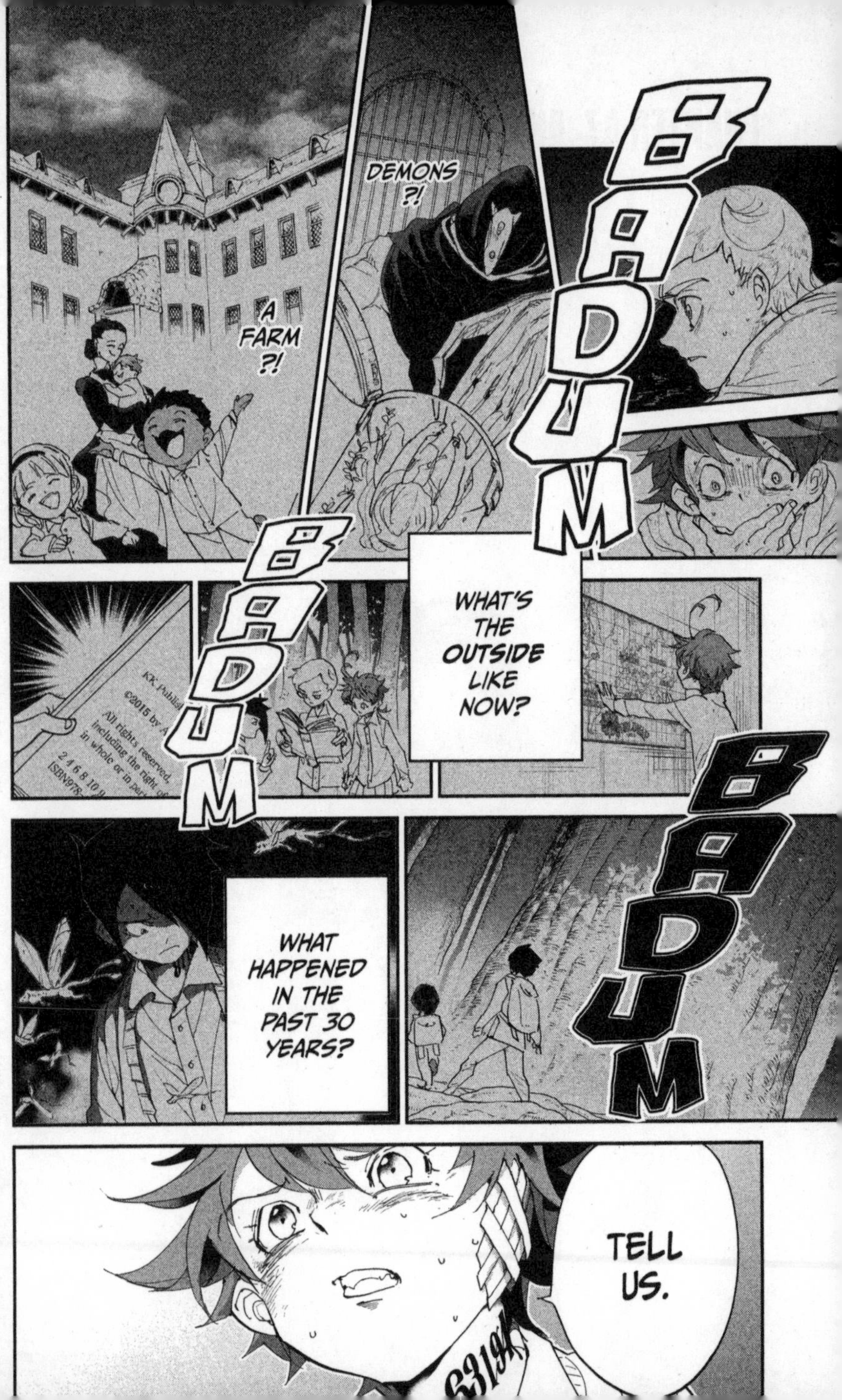
BADUM
DEMONS ?!
A FARM ?!
WHAT'S THE OUTSIDE LIKE NOW?
BADUM
BADUM
WHAT HAPPENED IN THE PAST 30 YEARS?
TELL US.

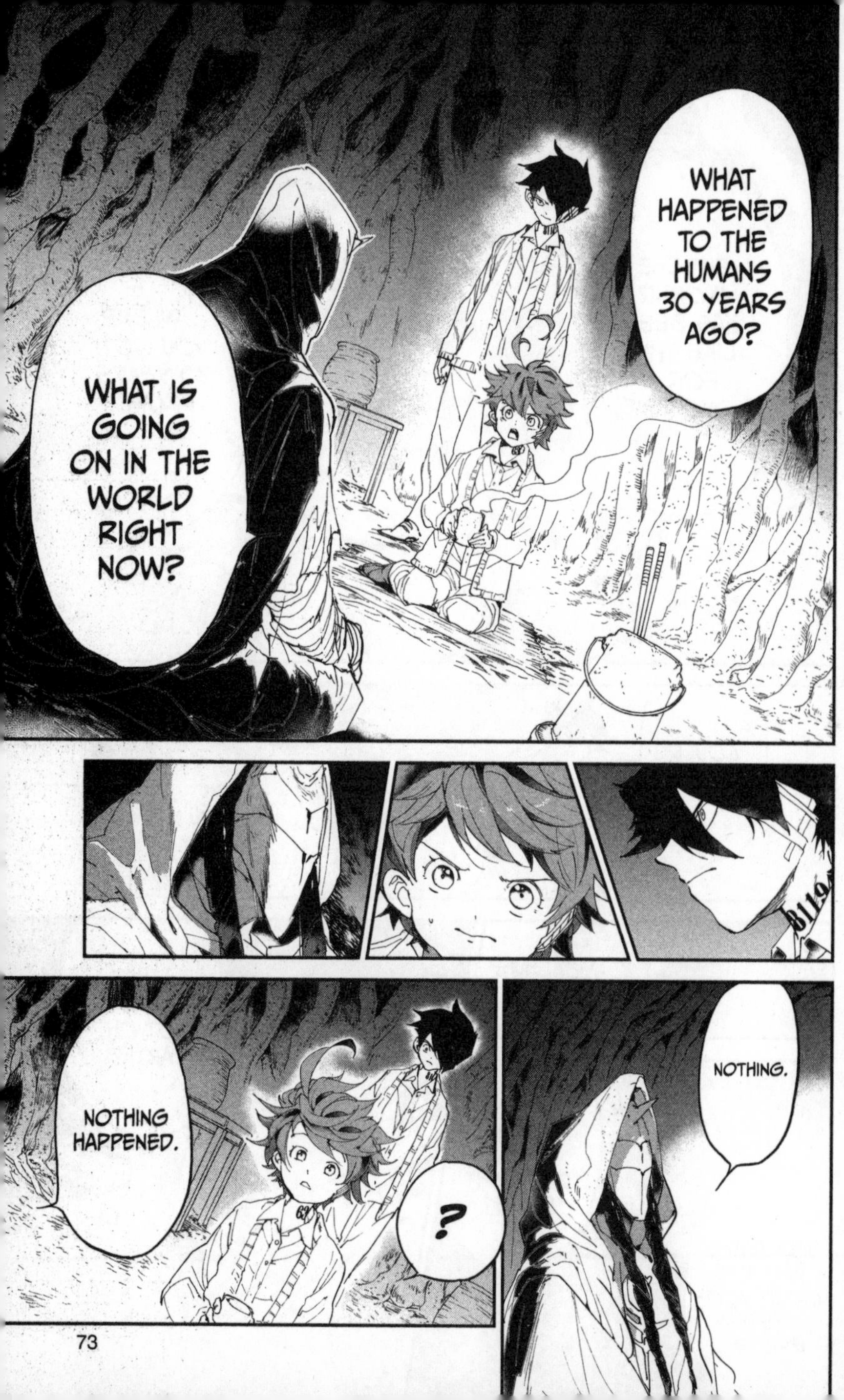
WHAT HAPPENED TO THE HUMANS 30 YEARS AGO?
WHAT IS GOING ON IN THE WORLD RIGHT NOW?
NOTHING.
NOTHING HAPPENED.
?

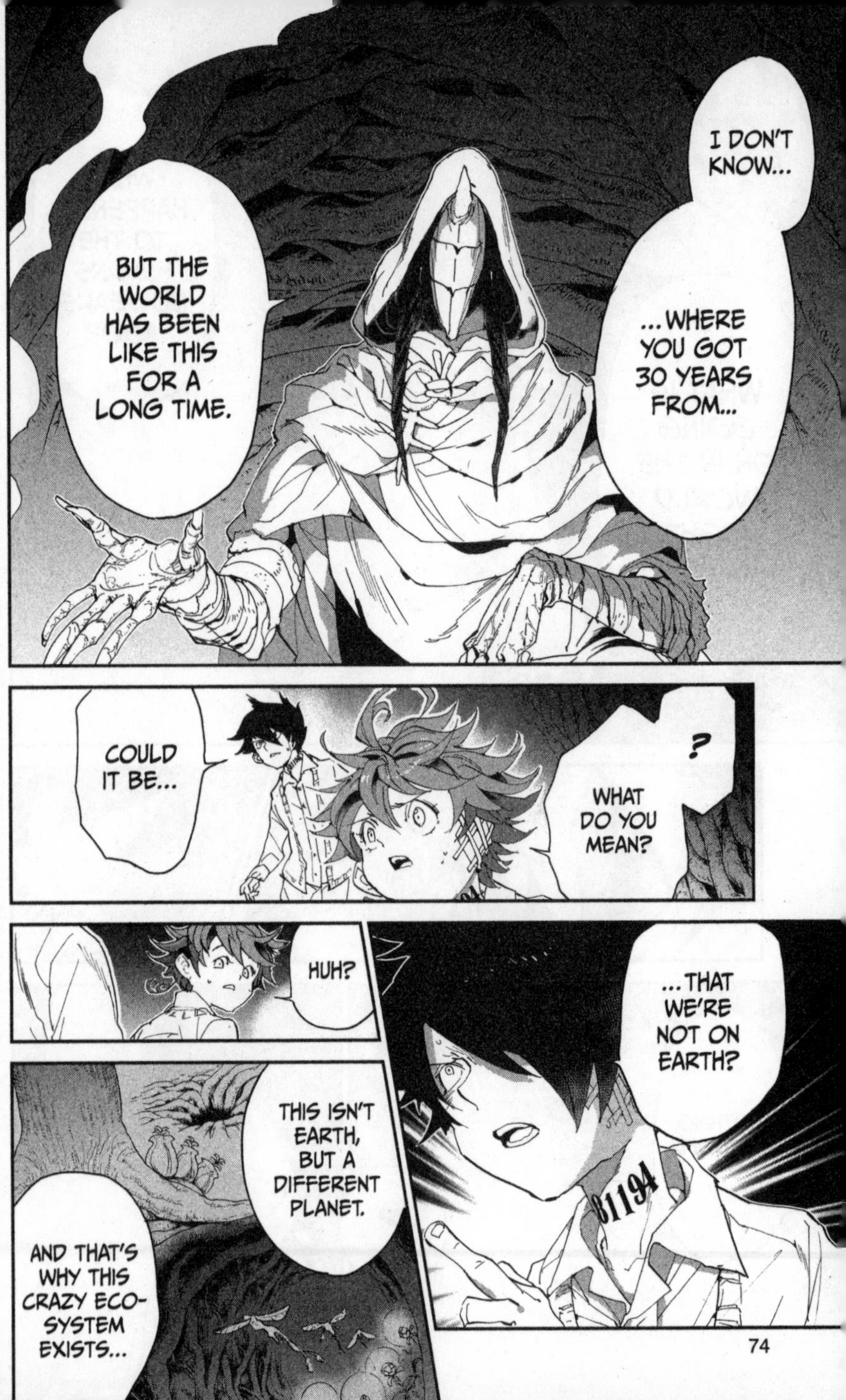
I DON'T KNOW...
...WHERE YOU GOT 30 YEARS FROM...
BUT THE WORLD HAS BEEN LIKE THIS FOR A LONG TIME.
?
WHAT DO YOU MEAN?
COULD IT BE...
...THAT WE'RE NOT ON EARTH?
HUH?
THIS ISN'T EARTH, BUT A DIFFERENT PLANET.
AND THAT'S WHY THIS CRAZY ECO-SYSTEM EXISTS...
81194

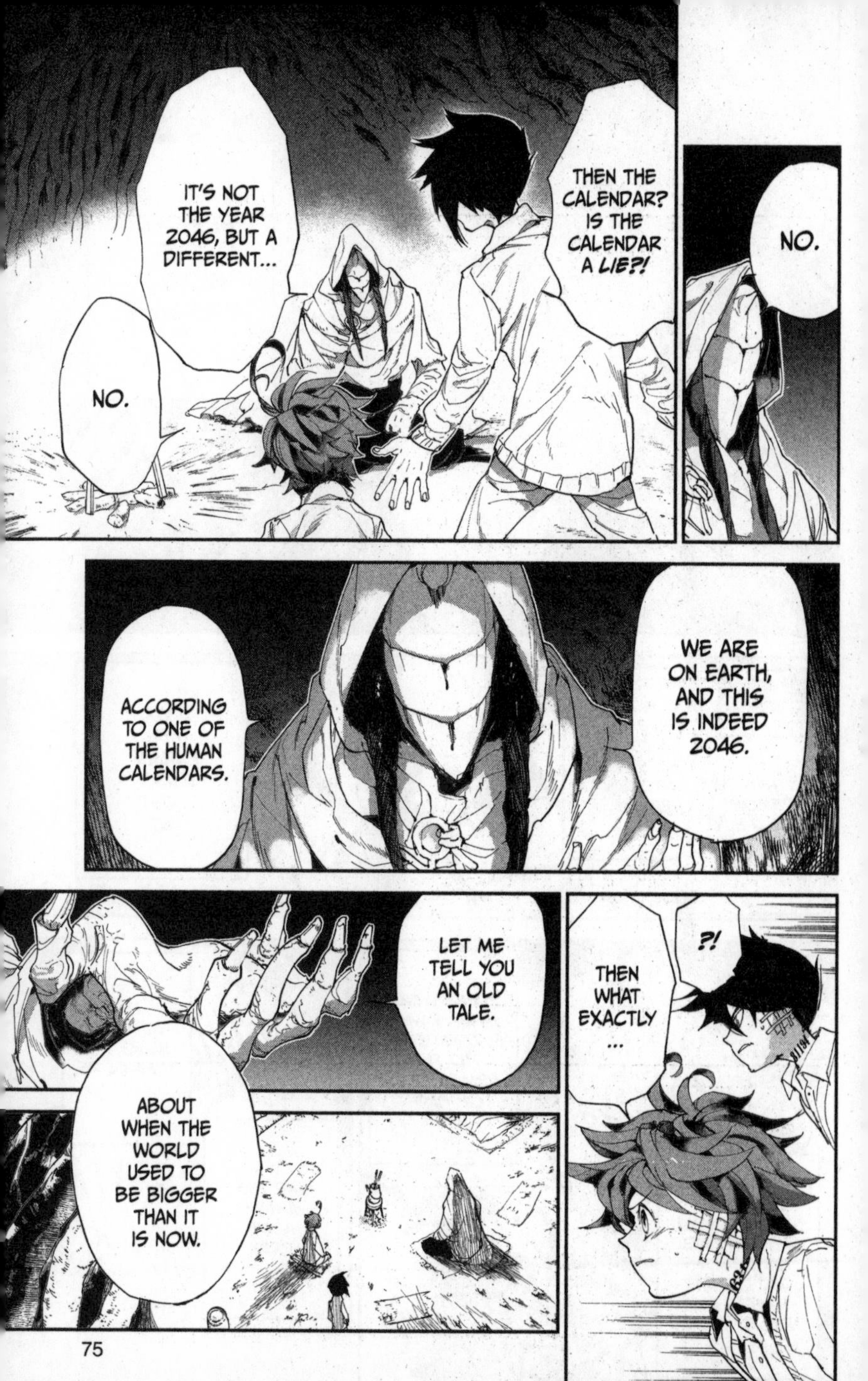
IT'S NOT THE YEAR 2046, BUT A DIFFERENT...
NO.
THEN THE CALENDAR? IS THE CALENDAR A *LIE?!*
NO.
WE ARE ON EARTH, AND THIS IS INDEED 2046.
ACCORDING TO ONE OF THE HUMAN CALENDARS.
?!
THEN WHAT EXACTLY ...
LET ME TELL YOU AN OLD TALE.
ABOUT WHEN THE WORLD USED TO BE BIGGER THAN IT IS NOW.

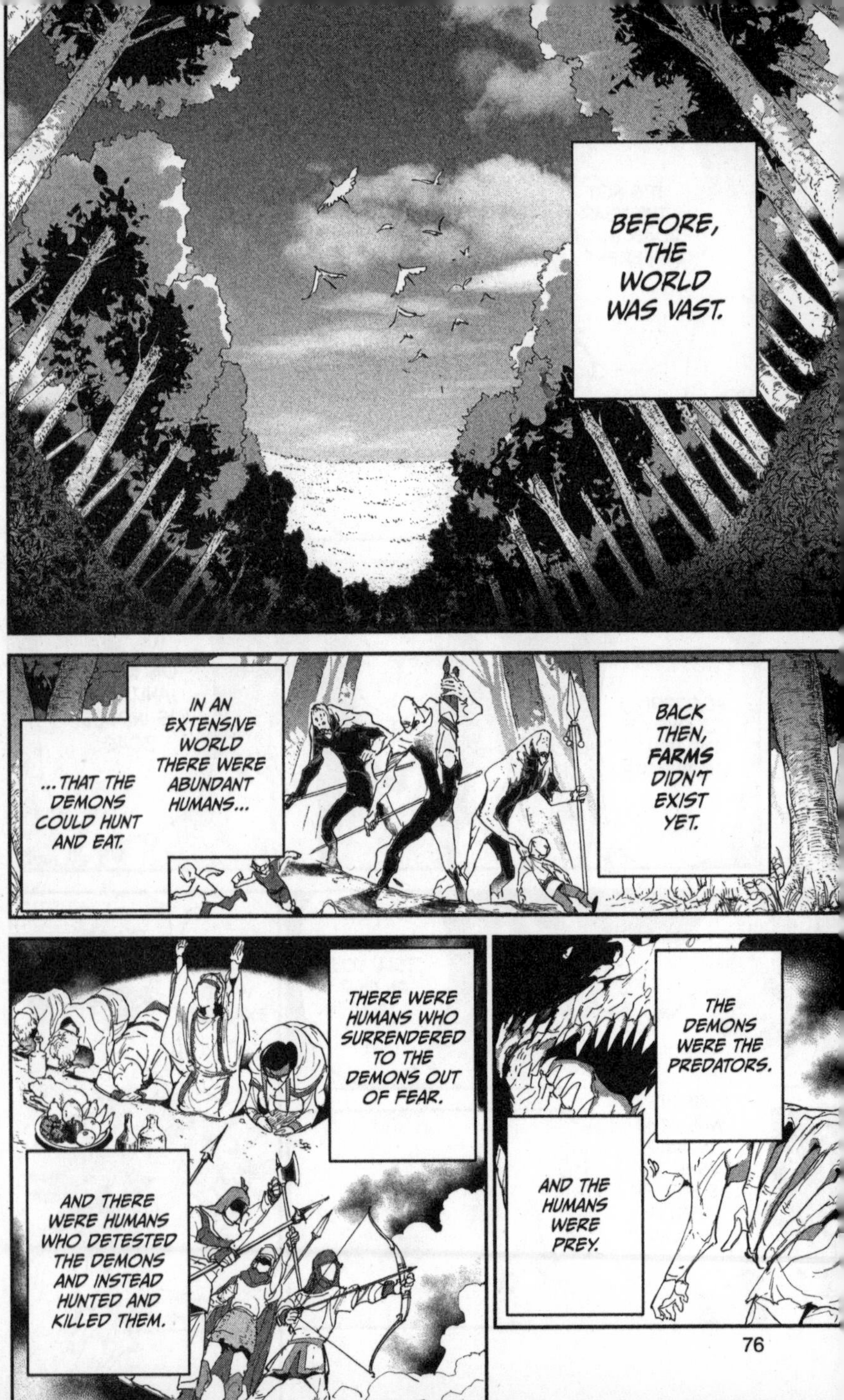
BEFORE, THE WORLD WAS VAST.
BACK THEN, FARMS DIDN'T EXIST YET.
IN AN EXTENSIVE WORLD THERE WERE ABUNDANT HUMANS...
...THAT THE DEMONS COULD HUNT AND EAT.
THE DEMONS WERE THE PREDATORS.
AND THE HUMANS WERE PREY.
THERE WERE HUMANS WHO SURRENDERED TO THE DEMONS OUT OF FEAR.
AND THERE WERE HUMANS WHO DETESTED THE DEMONS AND INSTEAD HUNTED AND KILLED THEM.

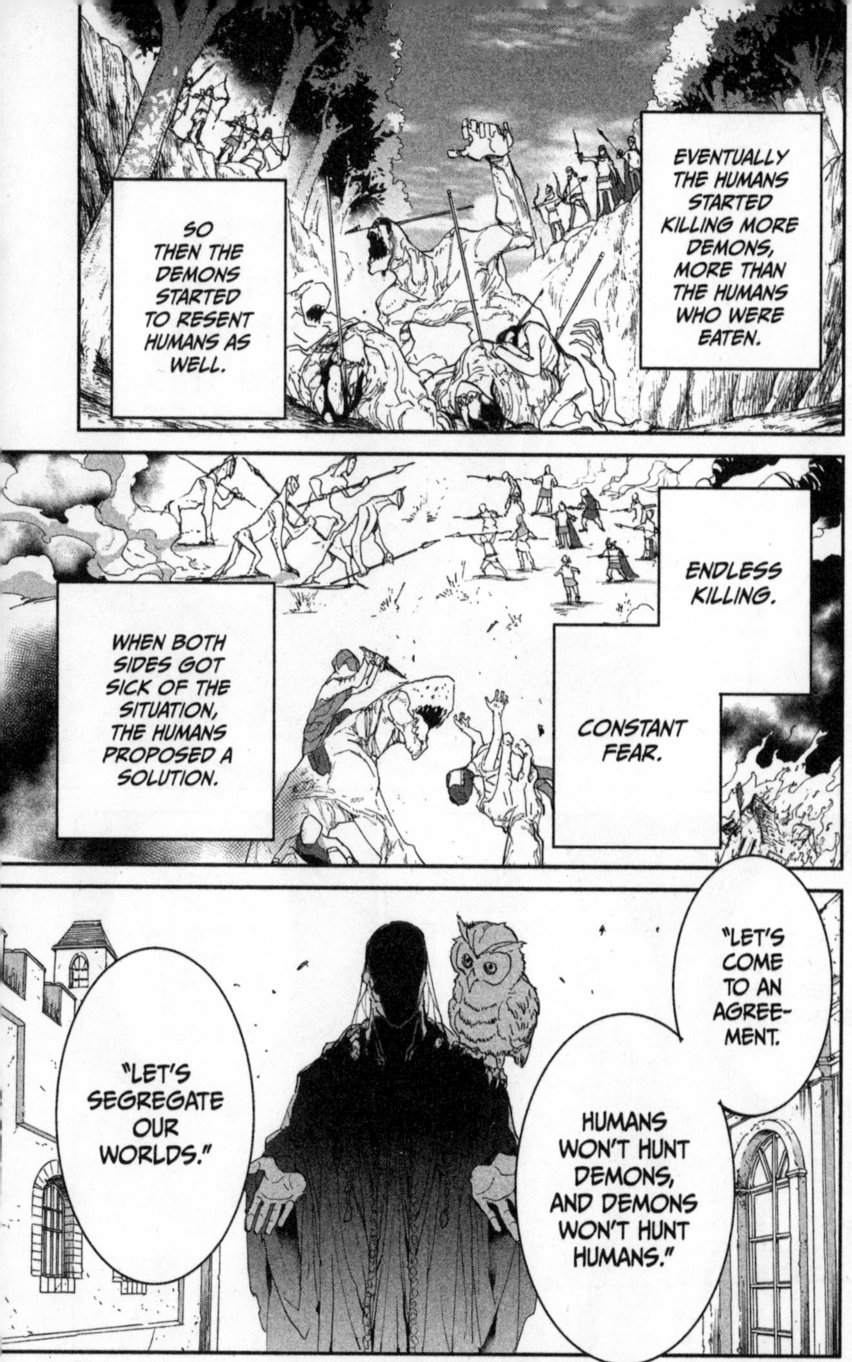
EVENTUALLY THE HUMANS STARTED KILLING MORE DEMONS, MORE THAN THE HUMANS WHO WERE EATEN.
SO THEN THE DEMONS STARTED TO RESENT HUMANS AS WELL.
ENDLESS KILLING.
CONSTANT FEAR.
WHEN BOTH SIDES GOT SICK OF THE SITUATION, THE HUMANS PROPOSED A SOLUTION.
"LET'S COME TO AN AGREE-MENT.
HUMANS WON'T HUNT DEMONS, AND DEMONS WON'T HUNT HUMANS."
"LET'S SEGREGATE OUR WORLDS."

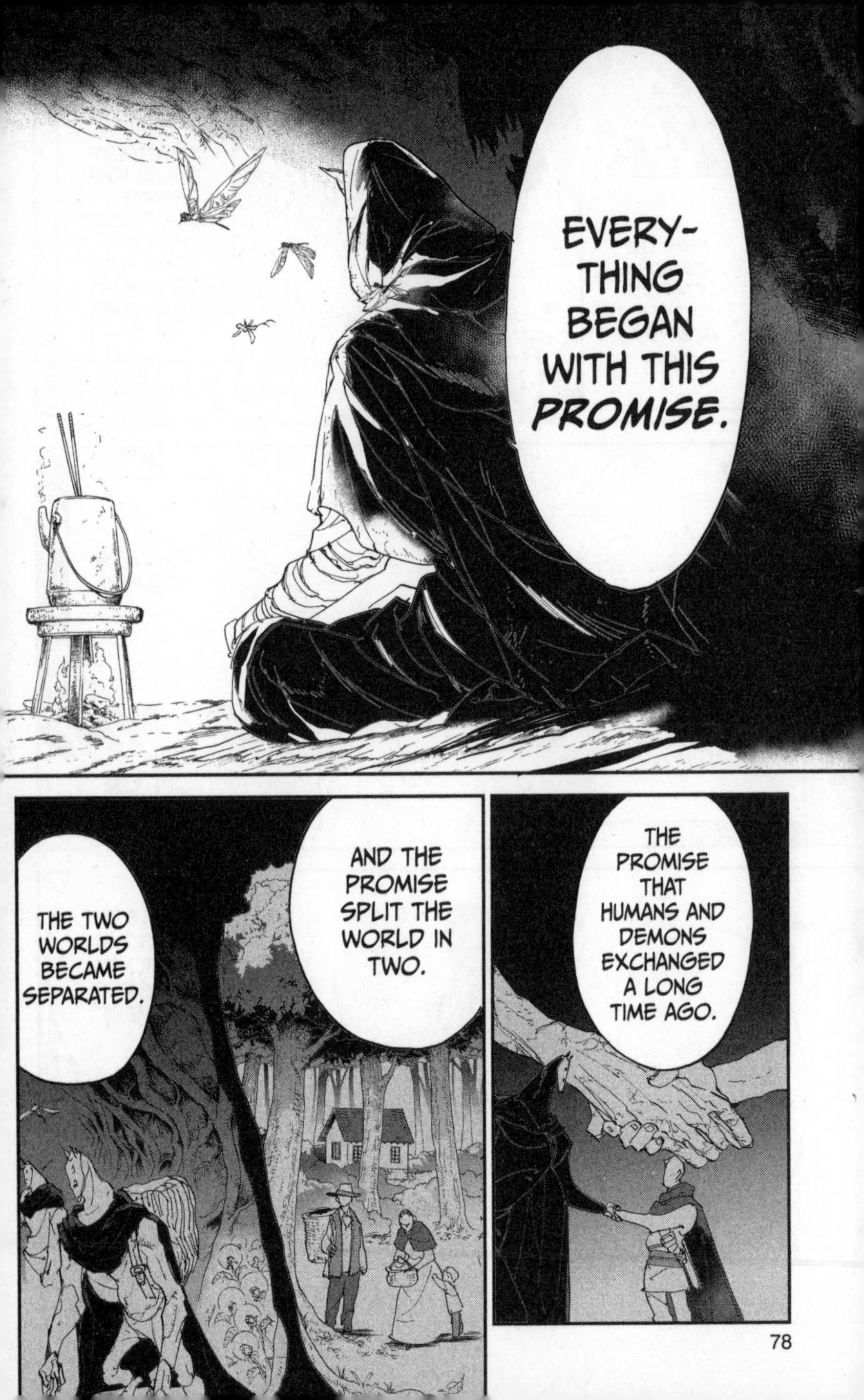
EVERYTHING BEGAN WITH THIS *PROMISE.*
THE PROMISE THAT HUMANS AND DEMONS EXCHANGED A LONG TIME AGO.
AND THE PROMISE SPLIT THE WORLD IN TWO.
THE TWO WORLDS BECAME SEPARATED.

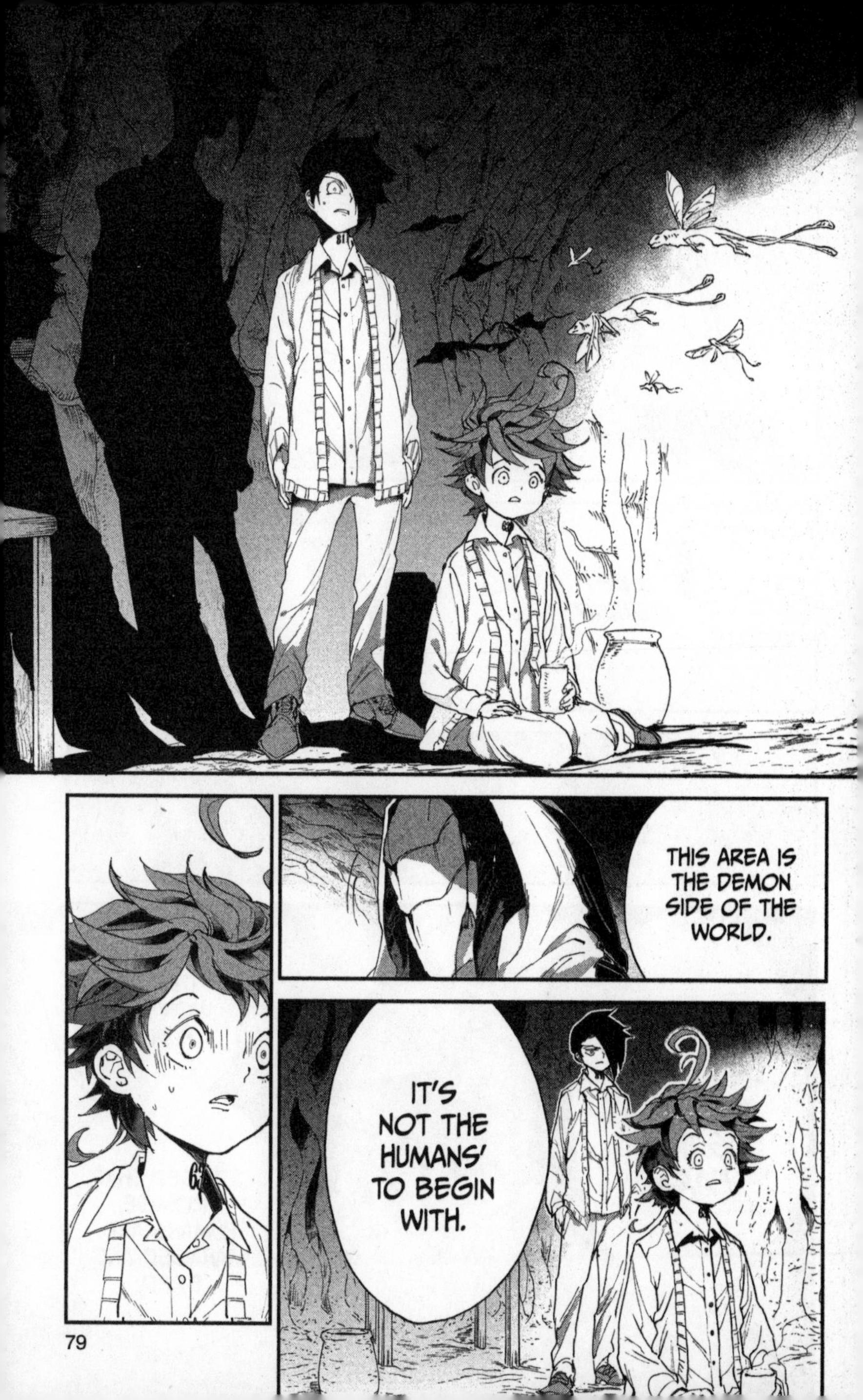
THIS AREA IS THE DEMON SIDE OF THE WORLD.
IT'S NOT THE HUMANS' TO BEGIN WITH.

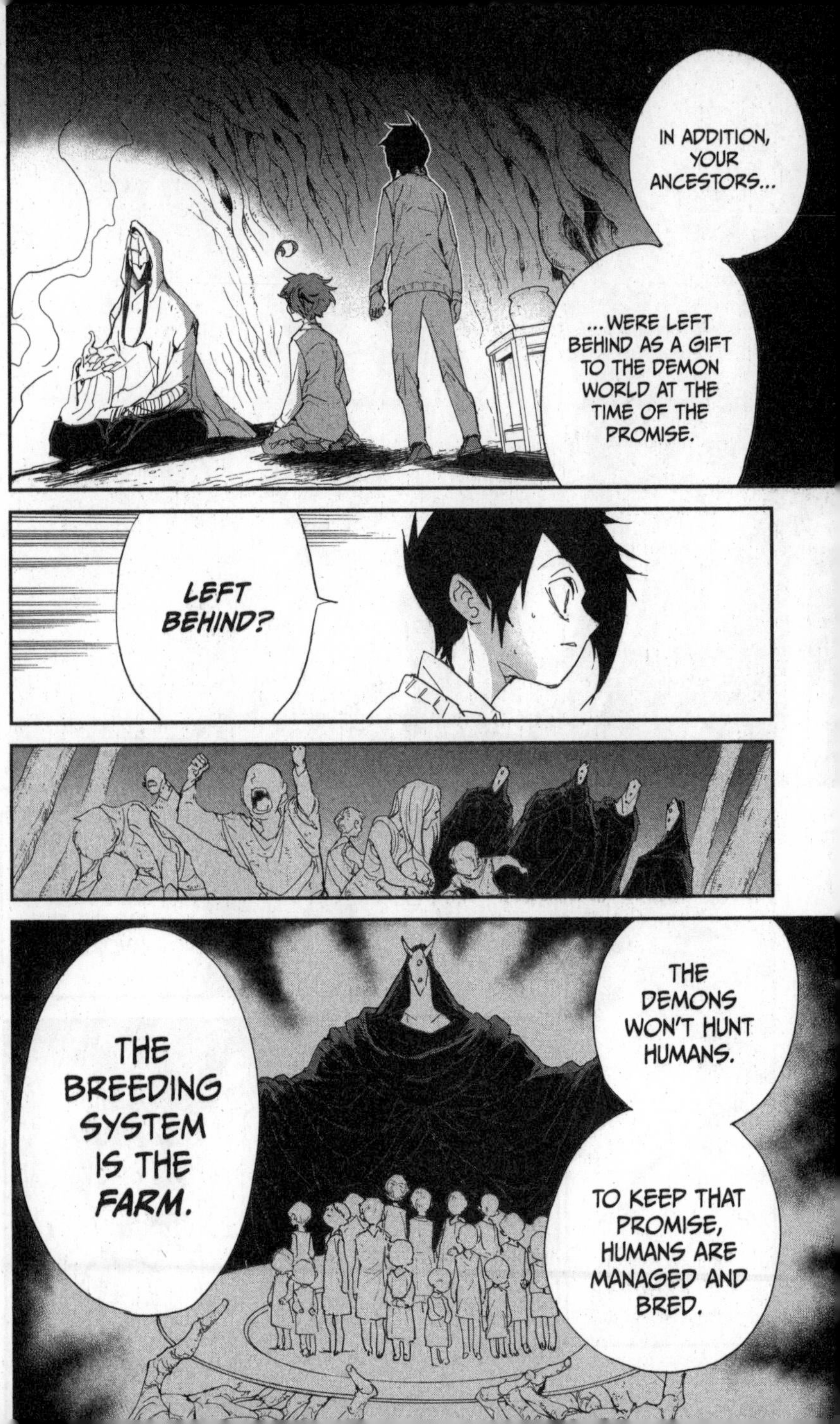
IN ADDITION, YOUR ANCESTORS...
...WERE LEFT BEHIND AS A GIFT TO THE DEMON WORLD AT THE TIME OF THE PROMISE.
LEFT BEHIND?
THE DEMONS WON'T HUNT HUMANS.
TO KEEP THAT PROMISE, HUMANS ARE MANAGED AND BRED.
THE BREEDING SYSTEM IS THE FARM.

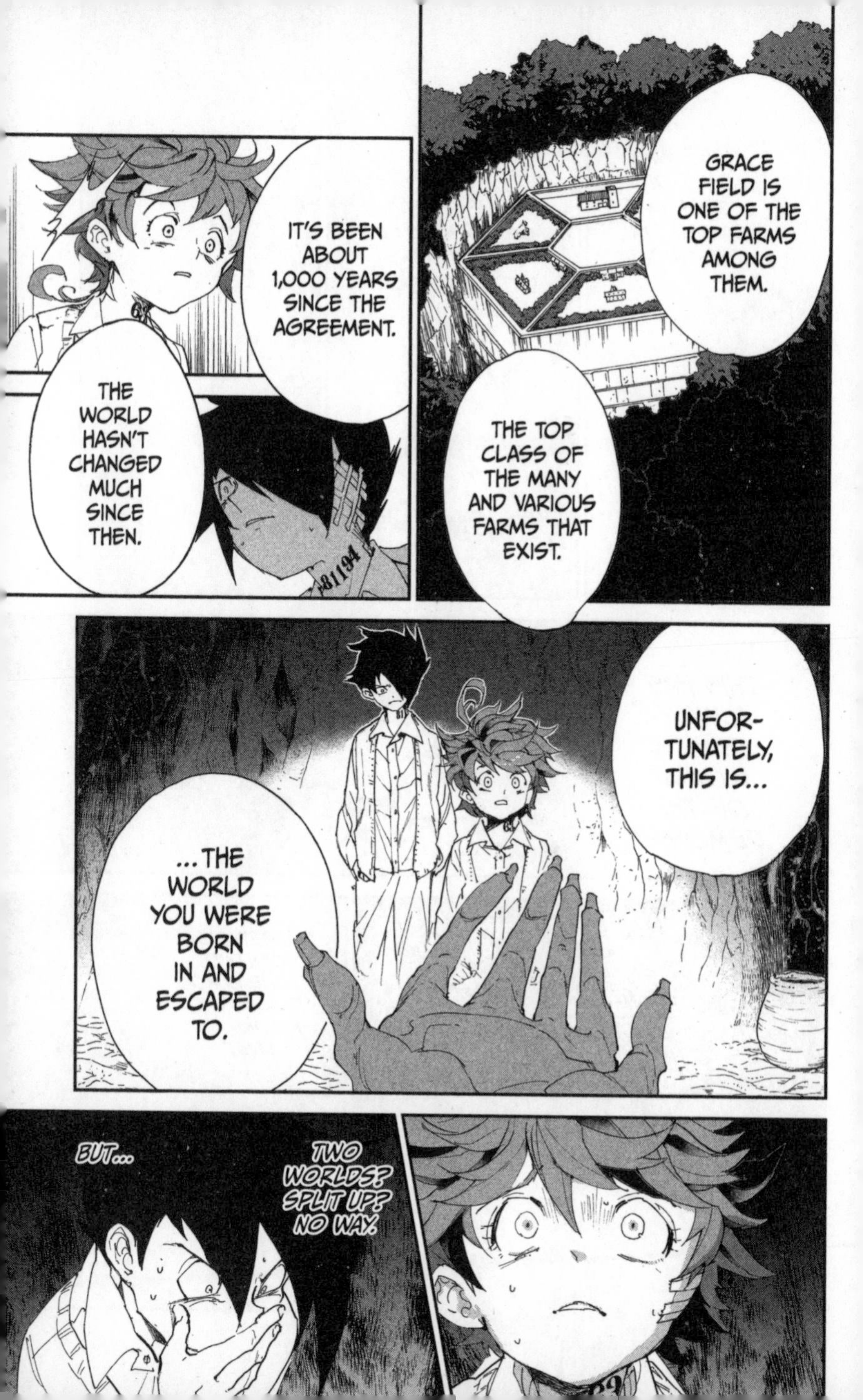
GRACE FIELD IS ONE OF THE TOP FARMS AMONG THEM.
THE TOP CLASS OF THE MANY AND VARIOUS FARMS THAT EXIST.
IT'S BEEN ABOUT 1,000 YEARS SINCE THE AGREEMENT.
THE WORLD HASN'T CHANGED MUCH SINCE THEN.
UNFOR-TUNATELY, THIS IS...
...THE WORLD YOU WERE BORN IN AND ESCAPED TO.
TWO WORLDS? SPLIT UP? NO WAY.
BUT...

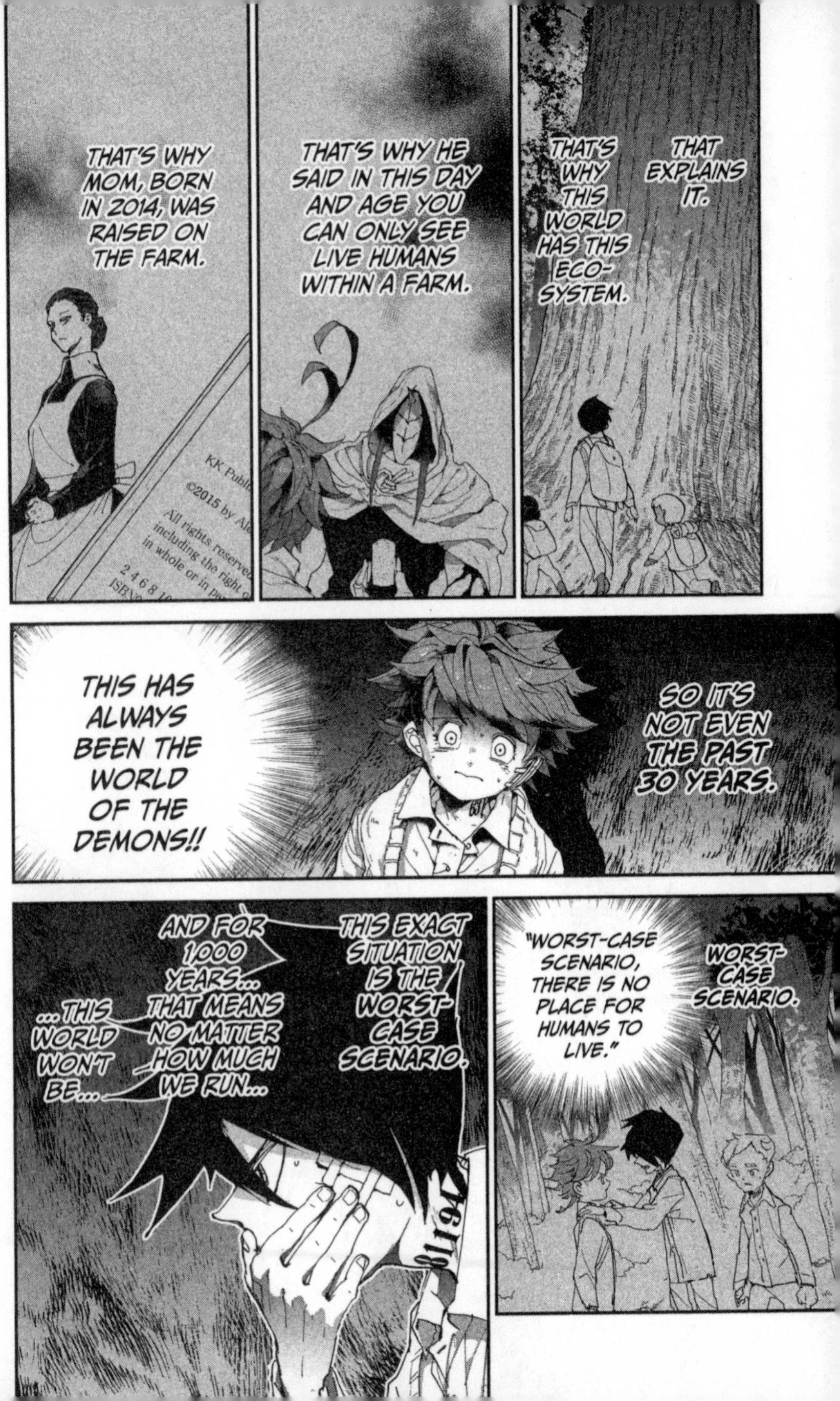
THAT EXPLAINS IT.
THAT'S WHY THIS WORLD HAS THIS ECO-SYSTEM.
THAT'S WHY HE SAID IN THIS DAY AND AGE YOU CAN ONLY SEE LIVE HUMANS WITHIN A FARM.
THAT'S WHY MOM, BORN IN 2014, WAS RAISED ON THE FARM.
KK Publi
©2015 by Al
All rights reserve
including the right of
in whole or in pa
SO IT'S NOT EVEN THE PAST 30 YEARS.
THIS HAS ALWAYS BEEN THE WORLD OF THE DEMONS!!
WORST-CASE SCENARIO.
"WORST-CASE SCENARIO, THERE IS NO PLACE FOR HUMANS TO LIVE."
THIS EXACT SITUATION IS THE WORST-CASE SCENARIO.
AND FOR 1,000 YEARS...
THAT MEANS NO MATTER HOW MUCH WE RUN...
...THIS WORLD WON'T BE...

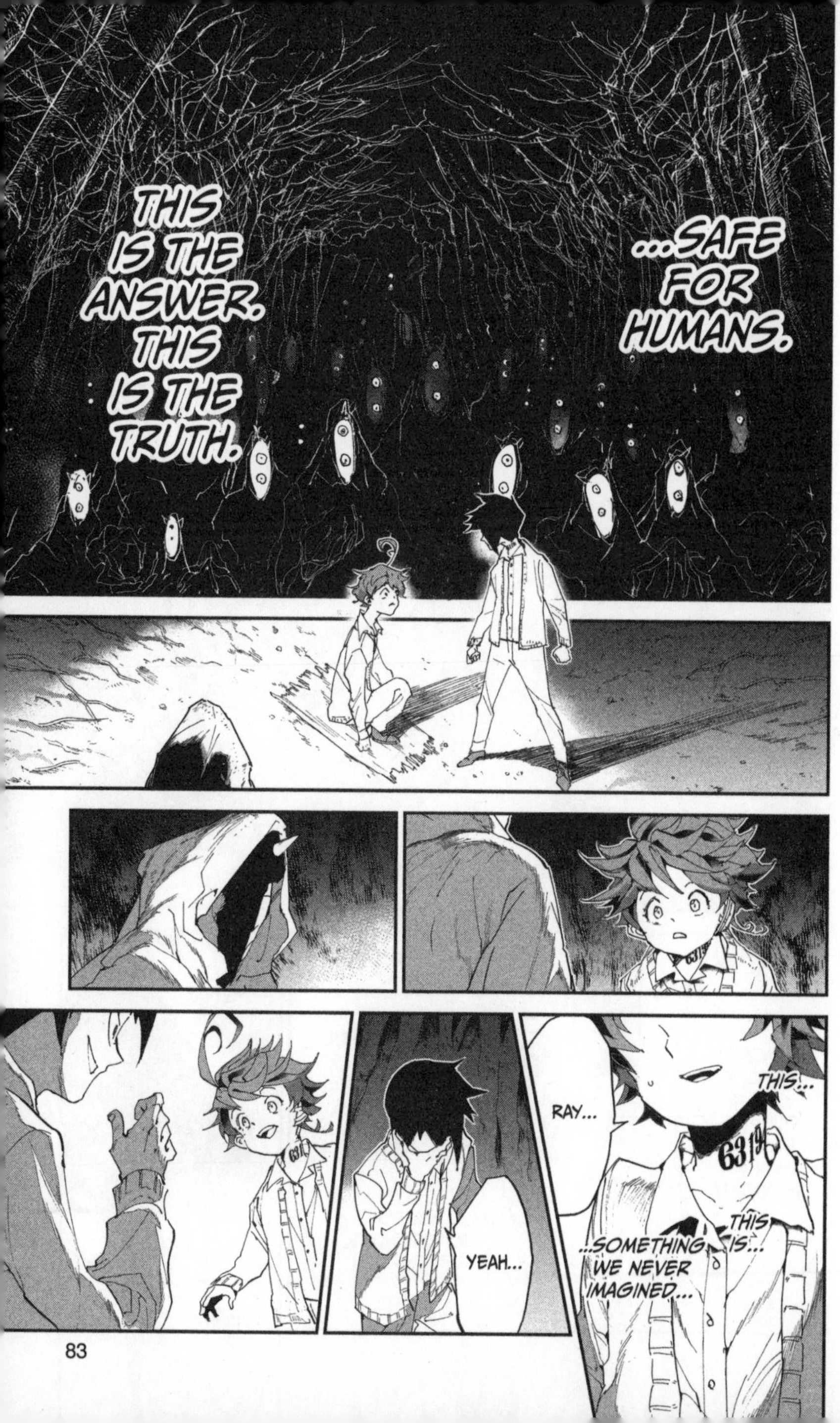
...SAFE FOR HUMANS.
THIS IS THE ANSWER. THIS IS THE TRUTH.
THIS...
RAY...
THIS IS...
...SOMETHING WE NEVER IMAGINED...
YEAH...

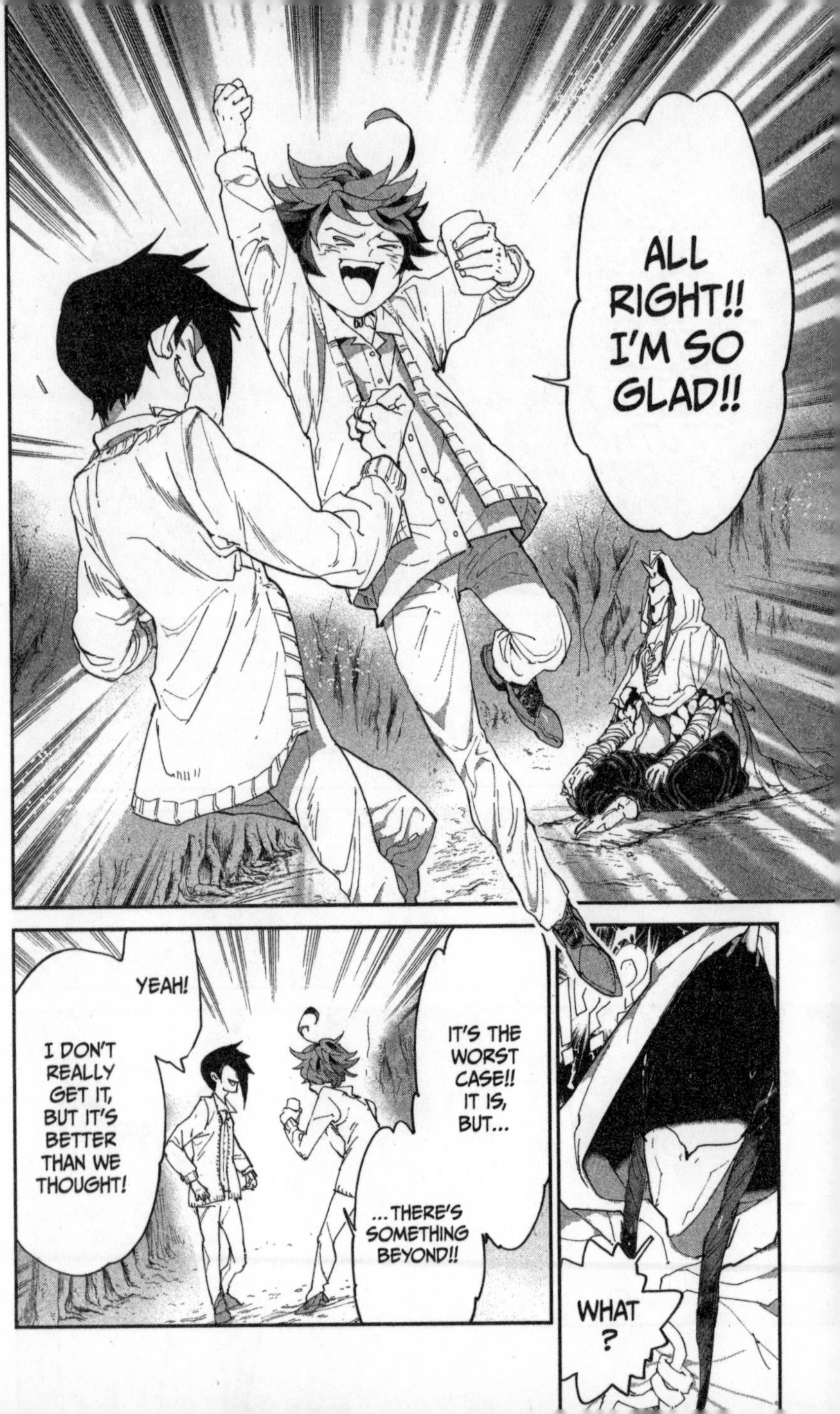
ALL RIGHT!! I'M SO GLAD!!
WHAT ?
IT'S THE WORST CASE!! IT IS, BUT...
...THERE'S SOMETHING BEYOND!!
YEAH!
I DON'T REALLY GET IT, BUT IT'S BETTER THAN WE THOUGHT!

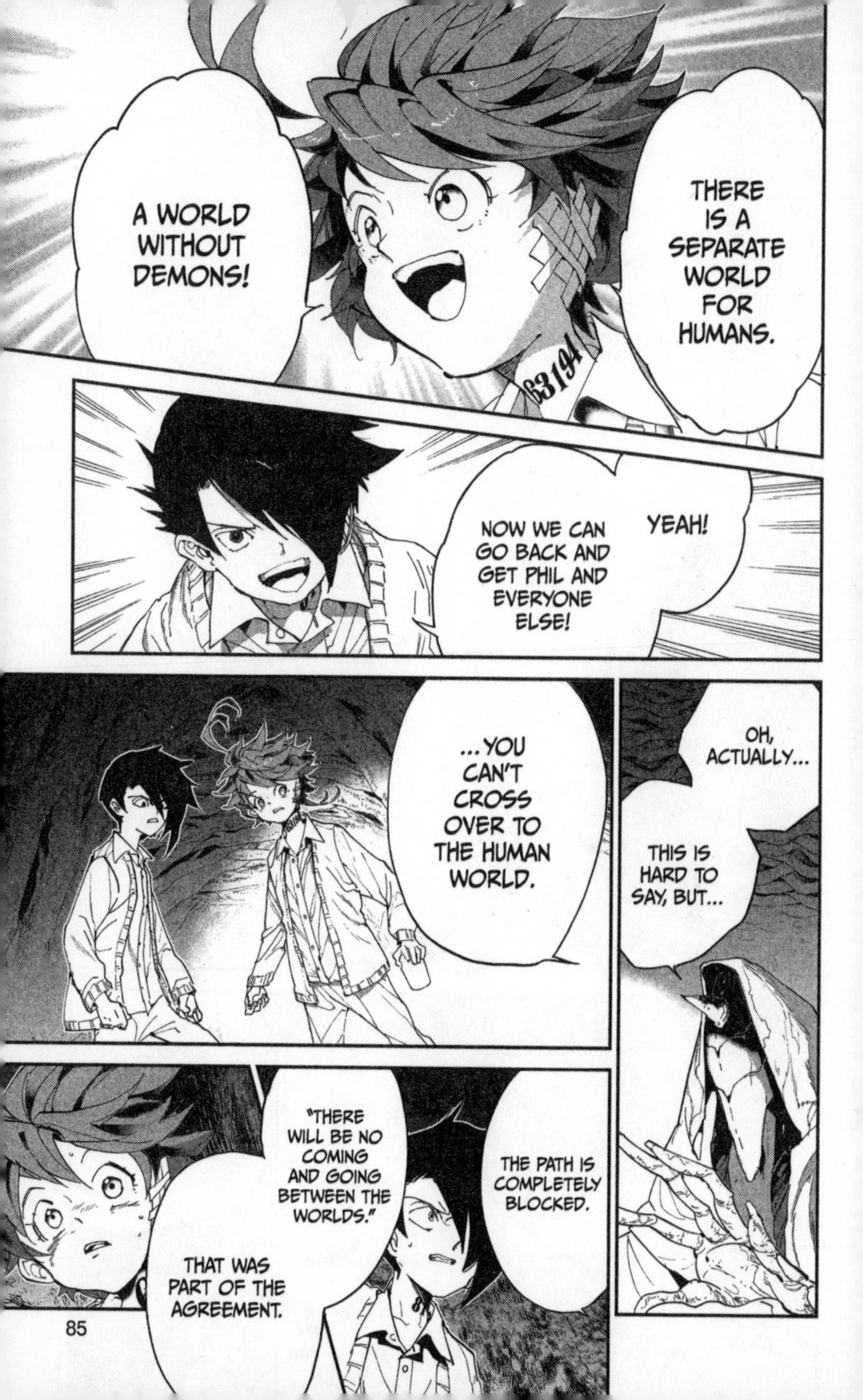
THERE IS A SEPARATE WORLD FOR HUMANS.
A WORLD WITHOUT DEMONS!
YEAH!
NOW WE CAN GO BACK AND GET PHIL AND EVERYONE ELSE!
OH, ACTUALLY...
THIS IS HARD TO SAY, BUT...
...YOU CAN'T CROSS OVER TO THE HUMAN WORLD.
THE PATH IS COMPLETELY BLOCKED.
"THERE WILL BE NO COMING AND GOING BETWEEN THE WORLDS."
THAT WAS PART OF THE AGREEMENT.

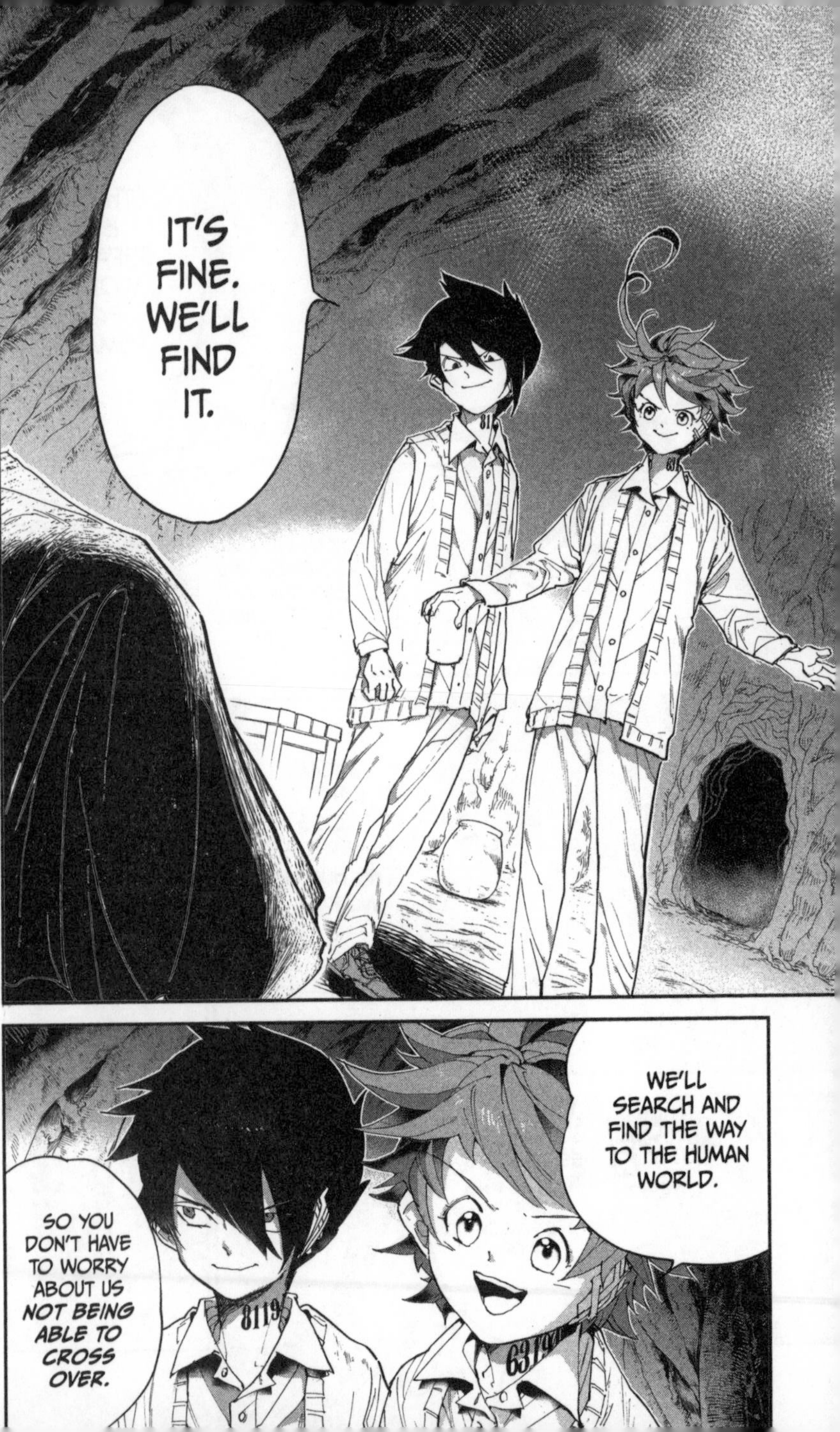
IT'S FINE. WE'LL FIND IT.
WE'LL SEARCH AND FIND THE WAY TO THE HUMAN WORLD.
SO YOU DON'T HAVE TO WORRY ABOUT US ***NOT BEING ABLE TO CROSS OVER.***

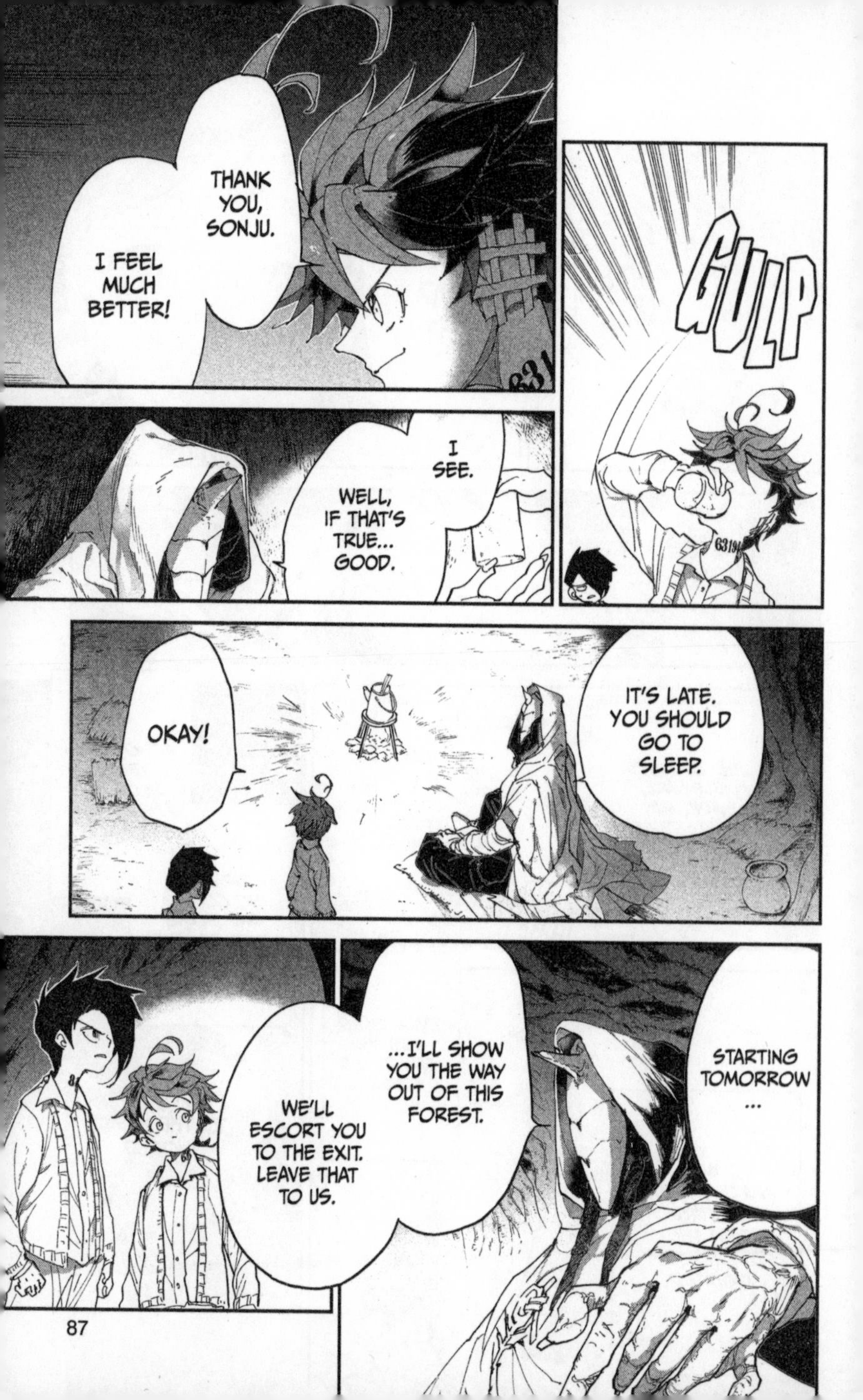
GULP
THANK YOU, SONJU.
I FEEL MUCH BETTER!
I SEE.
WELL, IF THAT'S TRUE... GOOD.
IT'S LATE. YOU SHOULD GO TO SLEEP.
OKAY!
STARTING TOMORROW ...
...I'LL SHOW YOU THE WAY OUT OF THIS FOREST.
WE'LL ESCORT YOU TO THE EXIT. LEAVE THAT TO US.

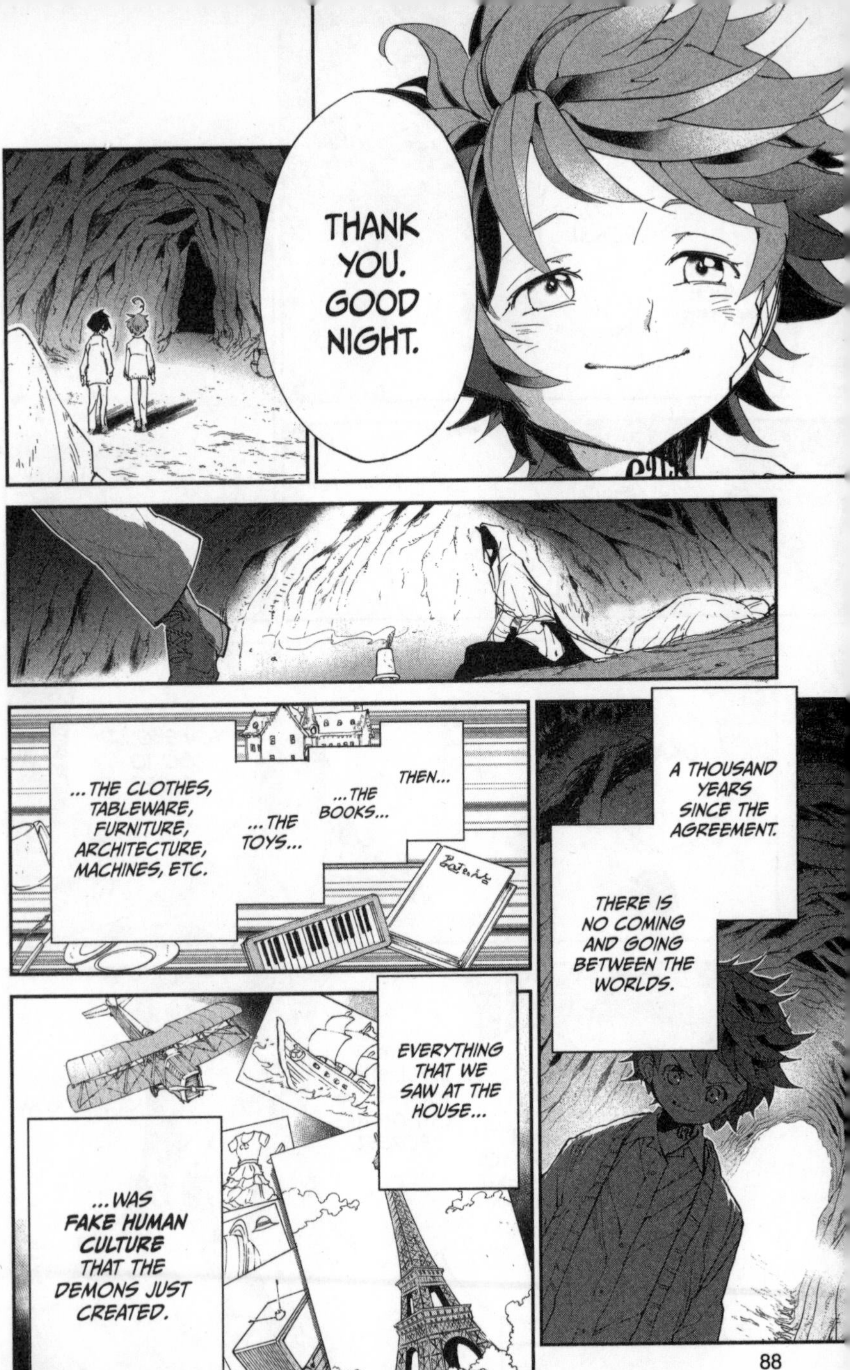
THANK YOU. GOOD NIGHT.
A THOUSAND YEARS SINCE THE AGREEMENT.
THERE IS NO COMING AND GOING BETWEEN THE WORLDS.
THEN...
...THE BOOKS...
...THE TOYS...
...THE CLOTHES, TABLEWARE, FURNITURE, ARCHITECTURE, MACHINES, ETC.
EVERYTHING THAT WE SAW AT THE HOUSE...
...WAS FAKE HUMAN CULTURE THAT THE DEMONS JUST CREATED.

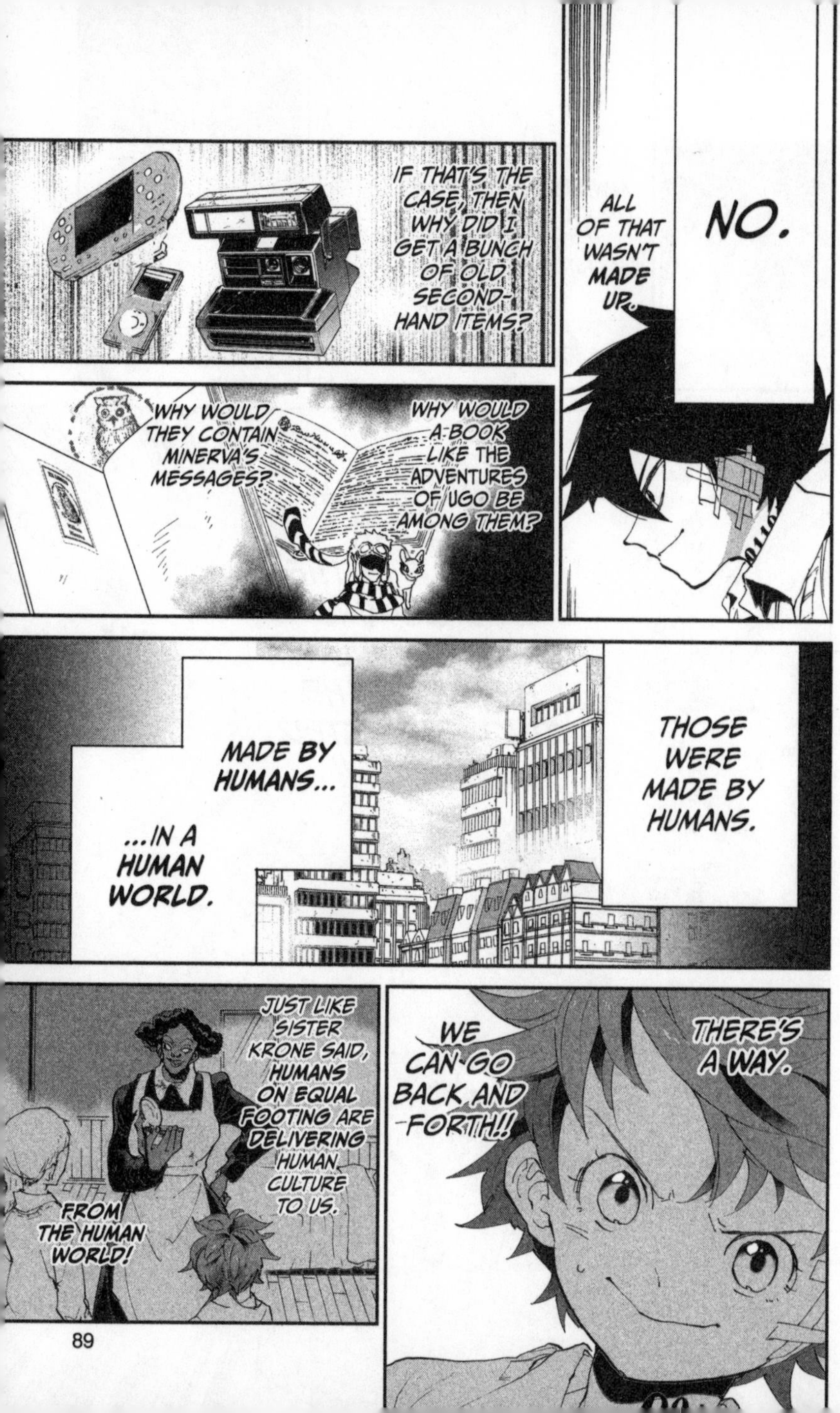
NO.
ALL OF THAT WASN'T MADE UP.
IF THAT'S THE CASE, THEN WHY DID I GET A BUNCH OF OLD SECOND-HAND ITEMS?
WHY WOULD A BOOK LIKE THE ADVENTURES OF UGO BE AMONG THEM?
WHY WOULD THEY CONTAIN MINERVA'S MESSAGES?
THOSE WERE MADE BY HUMANS.
MADE BY HUMANS...
...IN A HUMAN WORLD.
THERE'S A WAY.
WE CAN GO BACK AND FORTH!!
JUST LIKE SISTER KRONE SAID, HUMANS ON EQUAL FOOTING ARE DELIVERING HUMAN CULTURE TO US.
FROM THE HUMAN WORLD!

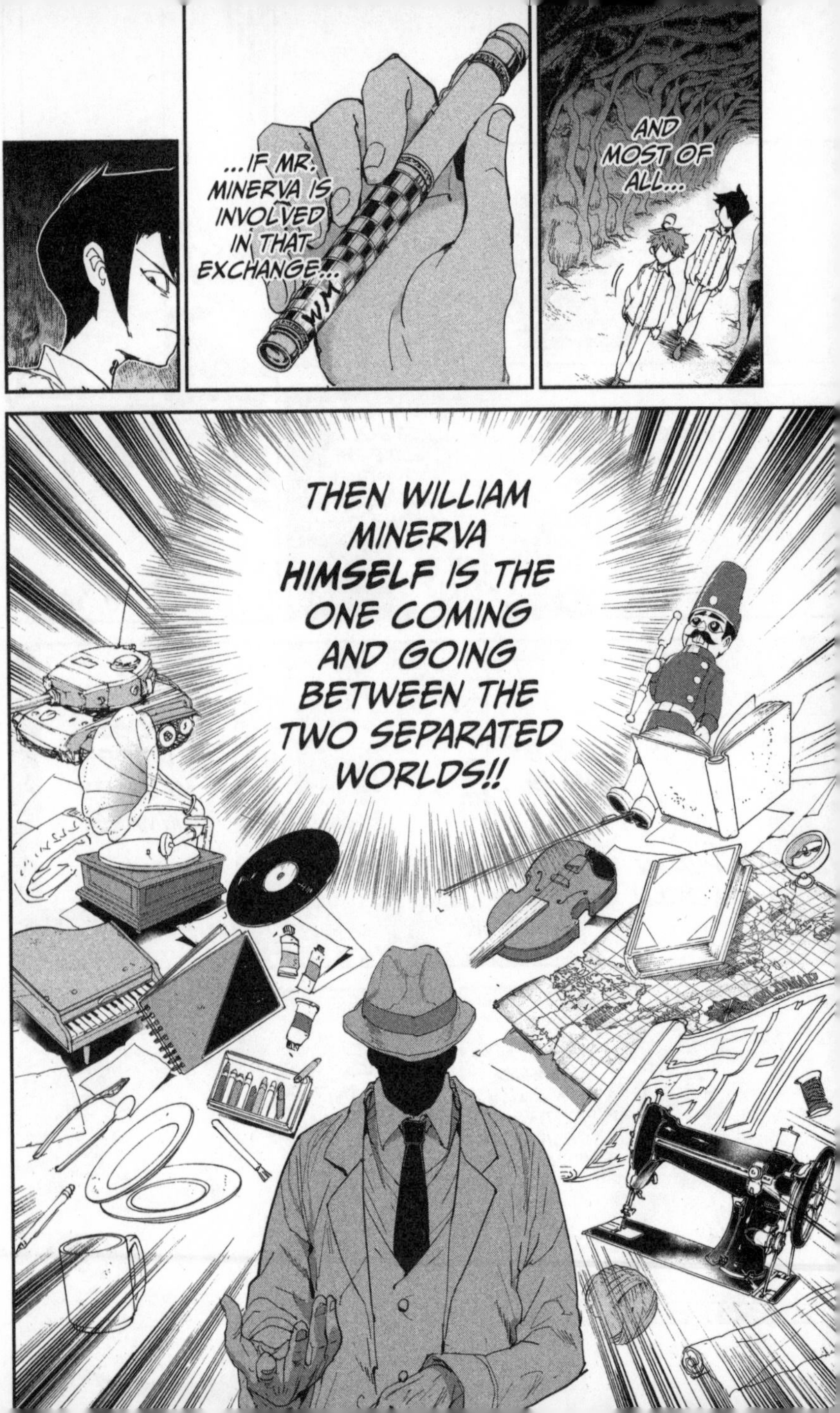
AND MOST OF ALL...
...IF MR. MINERVA IS INVOLVED IN THAT EXCHANGE...
W.M
THEN WILLIAM MINERVA HIMSELF IS THE ONE COMING AND GOING BETWEEN THE TWO SEPARATED WORLDS!!

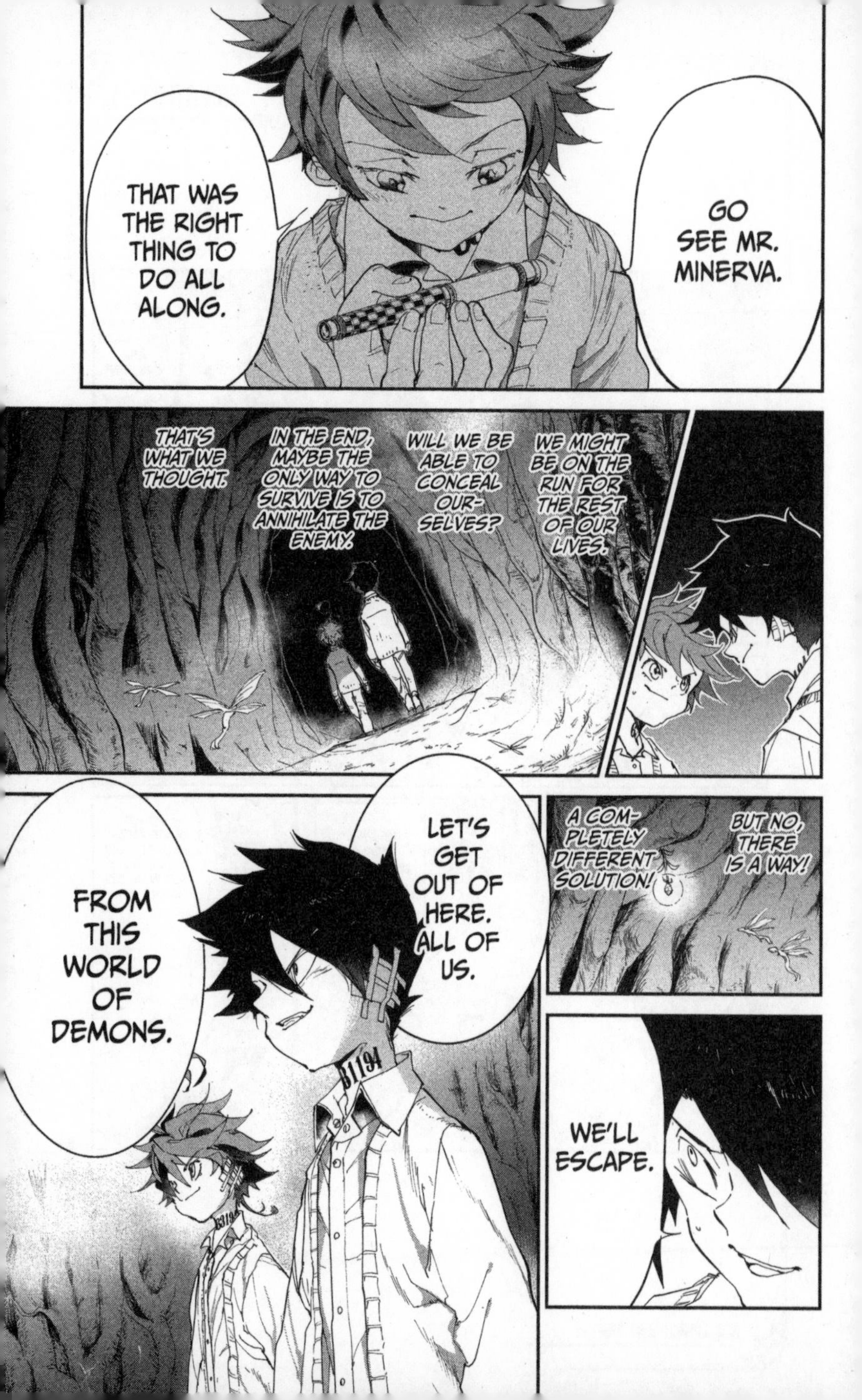
GO SEE MR. MINERVA.
THAT WAS THE RIGHT THING TO DO ALL ALONG.
WE MIGHT BE ON THE RUN FOR THE REST OF OUR LIVES.
WILL WE BE ABLE TO CONCEAL OUR-SELVES?
IN THE END, MAYBE THE ONLY WAY TO SURVIVE IS TO ANNIHILATE THE ENEMY.
THAT'S WHAT WE THOUGHT.
BUT NO, THERE IS A WAY!
A COM-PLETELY DIFFERENT SOLUTION!
WE'LL ESCAPE.
LET'S GET OUT OF HERE. ALL OF US.
FROM THIS WORLD OF DEMONS.
B1194

CHILDREN'S DAY

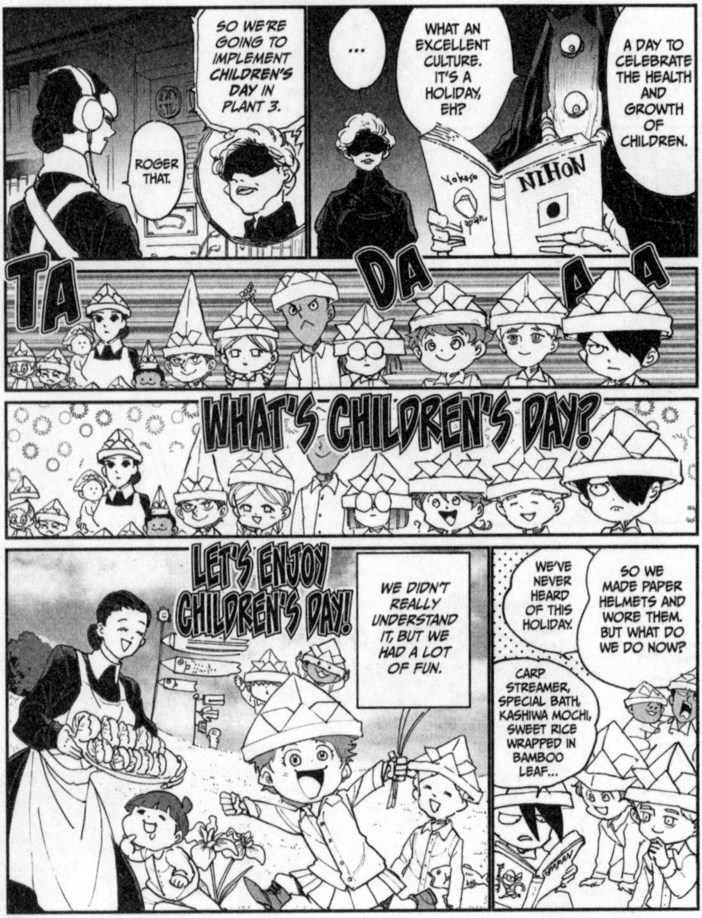
A DAY TO CELEBRATE THE HEALTH AND GROWTH OF CHILDREN.
WHAT AN EXCELLENT CULTURE. IT'S A HOLIDAY, EH?
NIHON
...
SO WE'RE GOING TO IMPLEMENT CHILDREN'S DAY IN PLANT 3.
ROGER THAT.
TA DA A A
WHAT'S CHILDREN'S DAY?
SO WE MADE PAPER HELMETS AND WORE THEM. BUT WHAT DO WE DO NOW?
WE'VE NEVER HEARD OF THIS HOLIDAY.
CARP STREAMER, SPECIAL BATH, KASHIWA MOCHI, SWEET RICE WRAPPED IN BAMBOO LEAF...
LET'S ENJOY CHILDREN'S DAY!
WE DIDN'T REALLY UNDERSTAND IT, BUT WE HAD A LOT OF FUN.

TO BE CONTINUED IN SIDE STORY 5-2

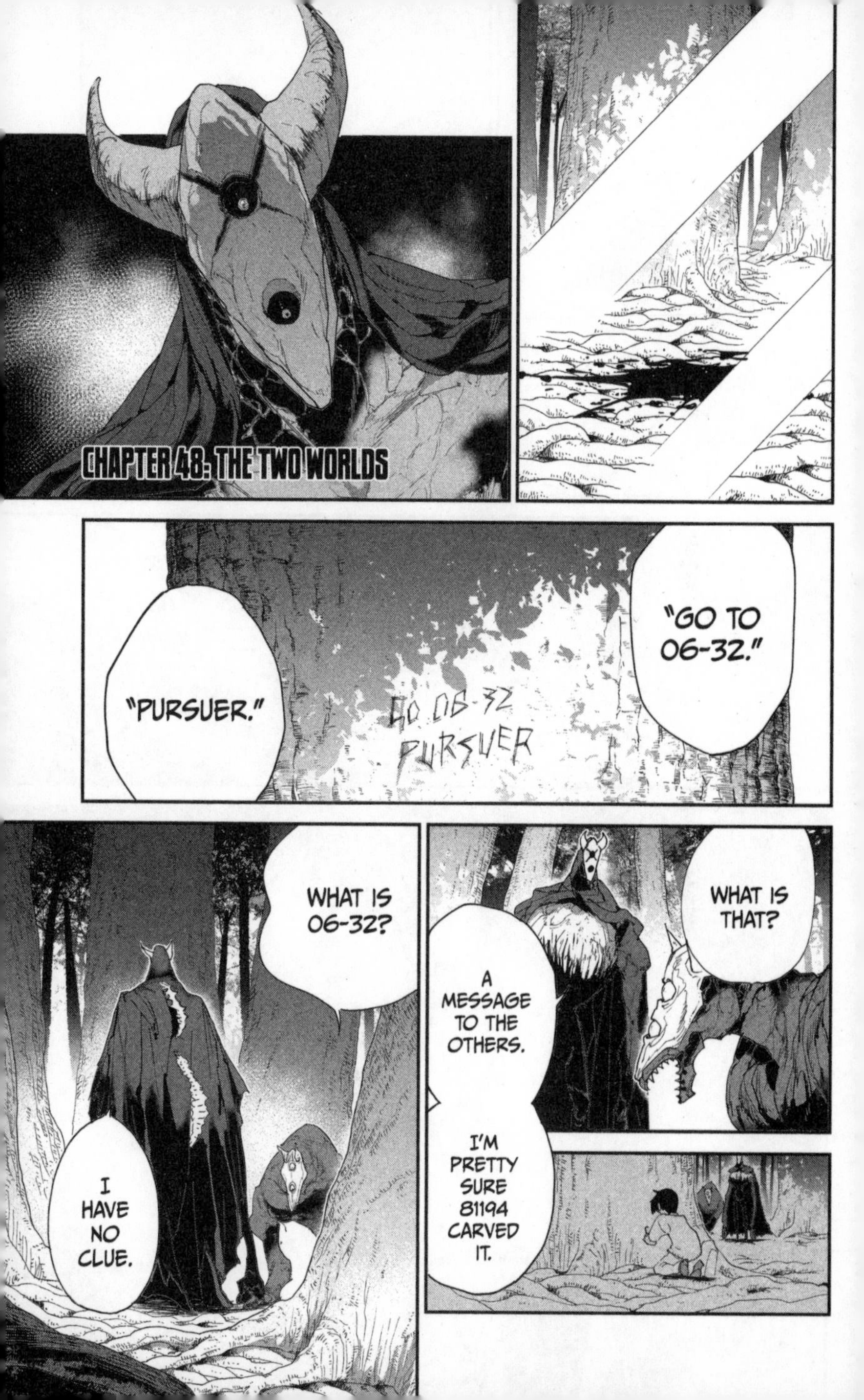
CHAPTER 48: THE TWO WORLDS
"GO TO 06-32."
GO 06-32
PURSUER
"PURSUER."
WHAT IS THAT?
A MESSAGE TO THE OTHERS.
I'M PRETTY SURE 81194 CARVED IT.
WHAT IS 06-32?
I HAVE NO CLUE.

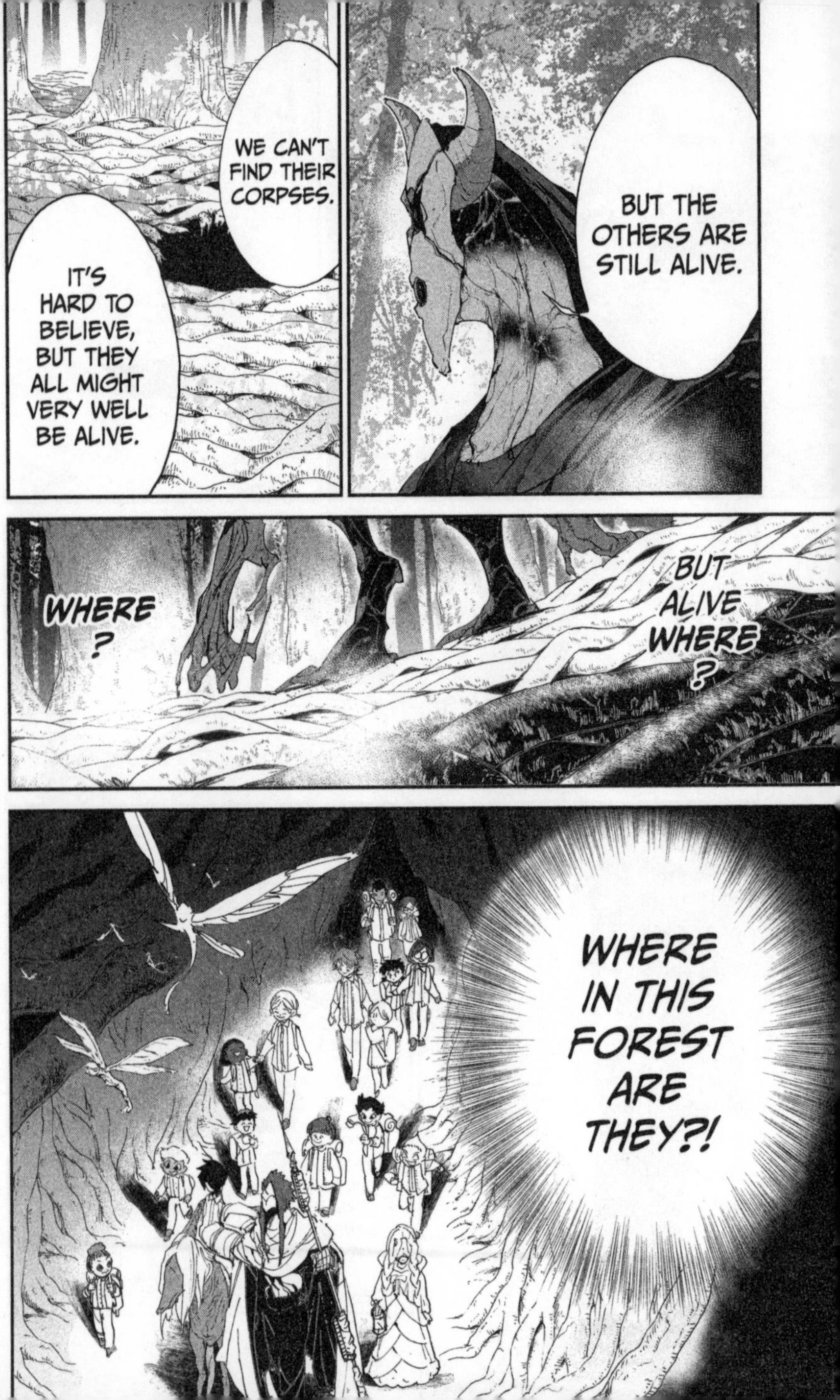
BUT THE OTHERS ARE STILL ALIVE.
WE CAN'T FIND THEIR CORPSES.
IT'S HARD TO BELIEVE, BUT THEY ALL MIGHT VERY WELL BE ALIVE.
BUT ALIVE WHERE?
WHERE?
WHERE IN THIS FOREST ARE THEY?!

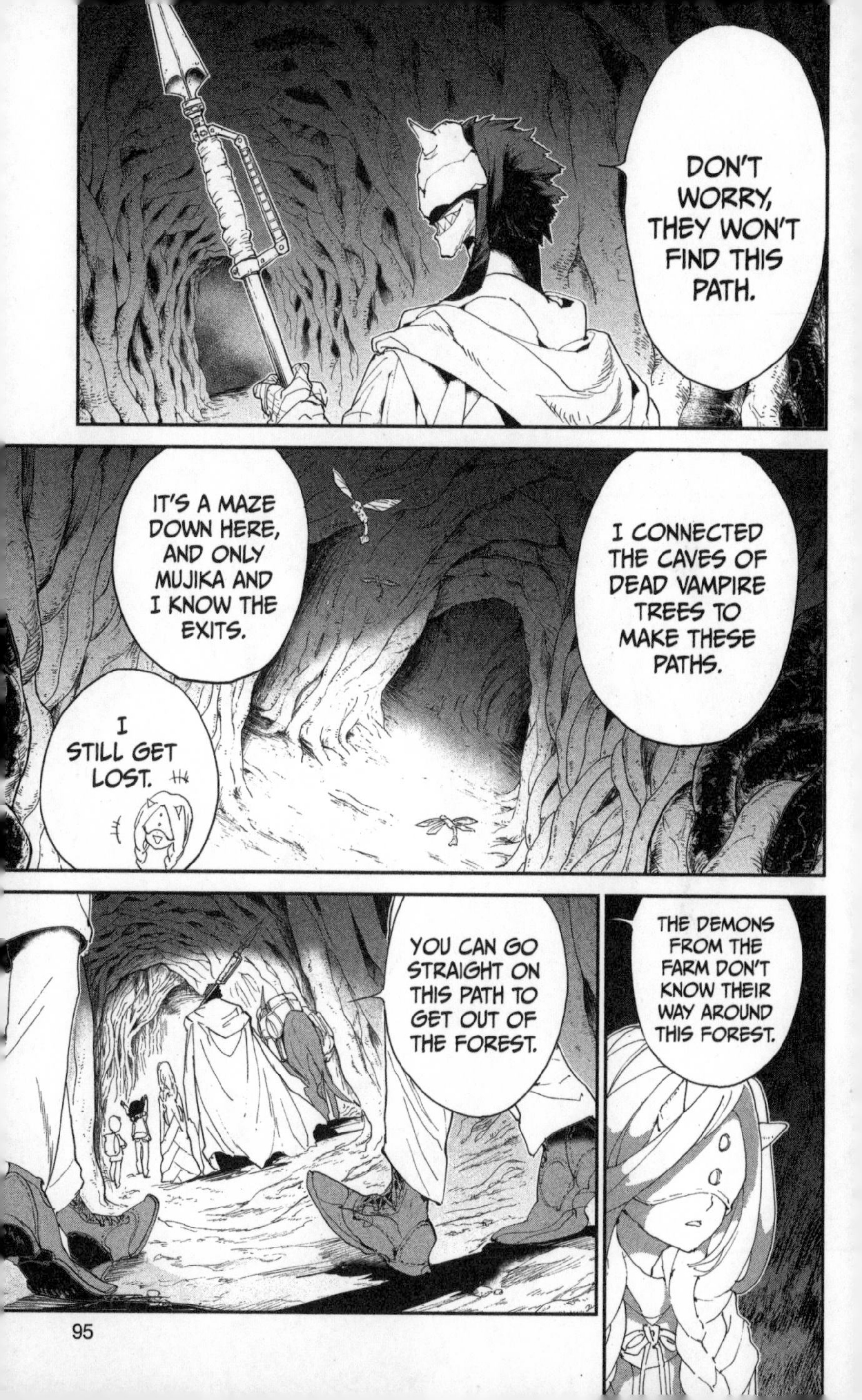
DON'T WORRY, THEY WON'T FIND THIS PATH.
I CONNECTED THE CAVES OF DEAD VAMPIRE TREES TO MAKE THESE PATHS.
IT'S A MAZE DOWN HERE, AND ONLY MUJIKA AND I KNOW THE EXITS.
I STILL GET LOST.
THE DEMONS FROM THE FARM DON'T KNOW THEIR WAY AROUND THIS FOREST.
YOU CAN GO STRAIGHT ON THIS PATH TO GET OUT OF THE FOREST.

CHAPTER 48: THE TWO WORLDS

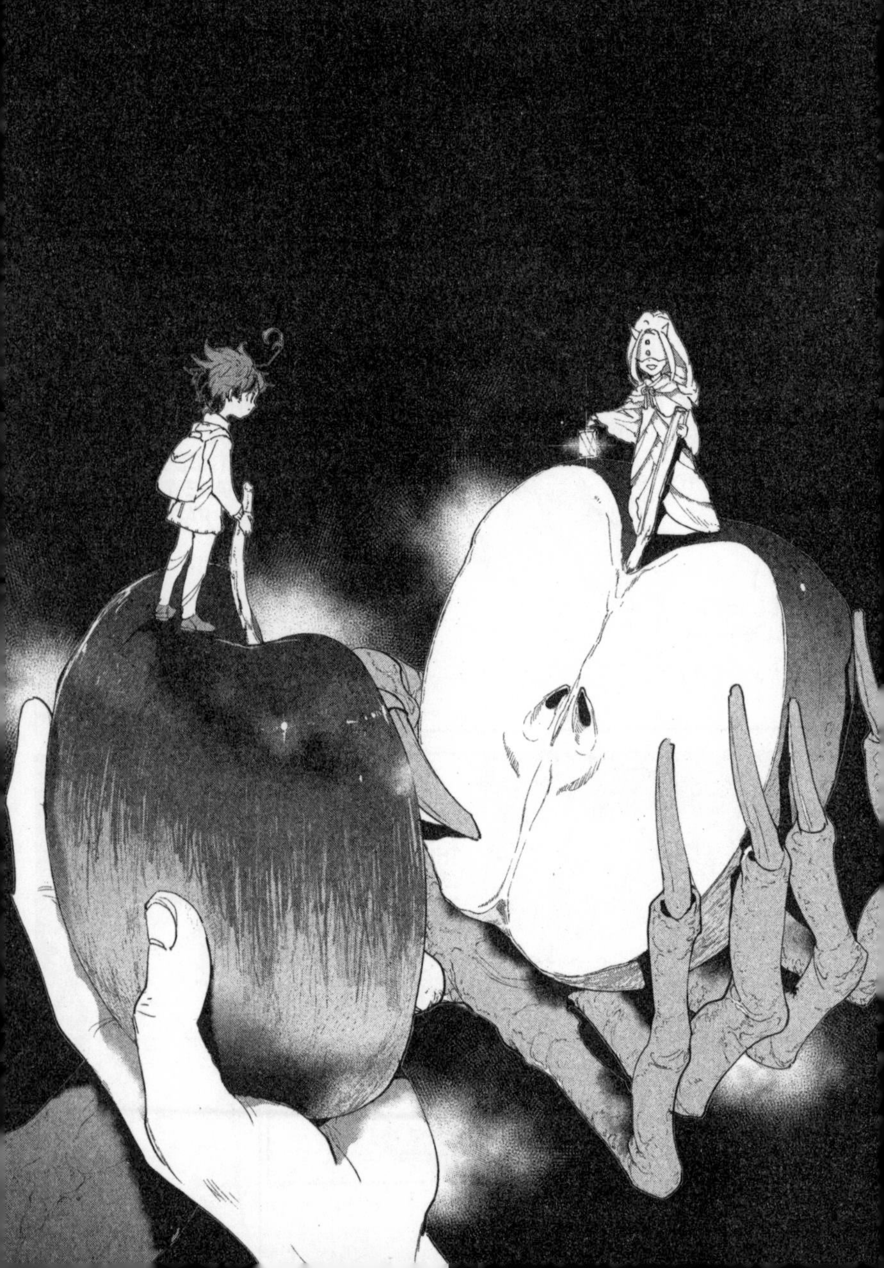

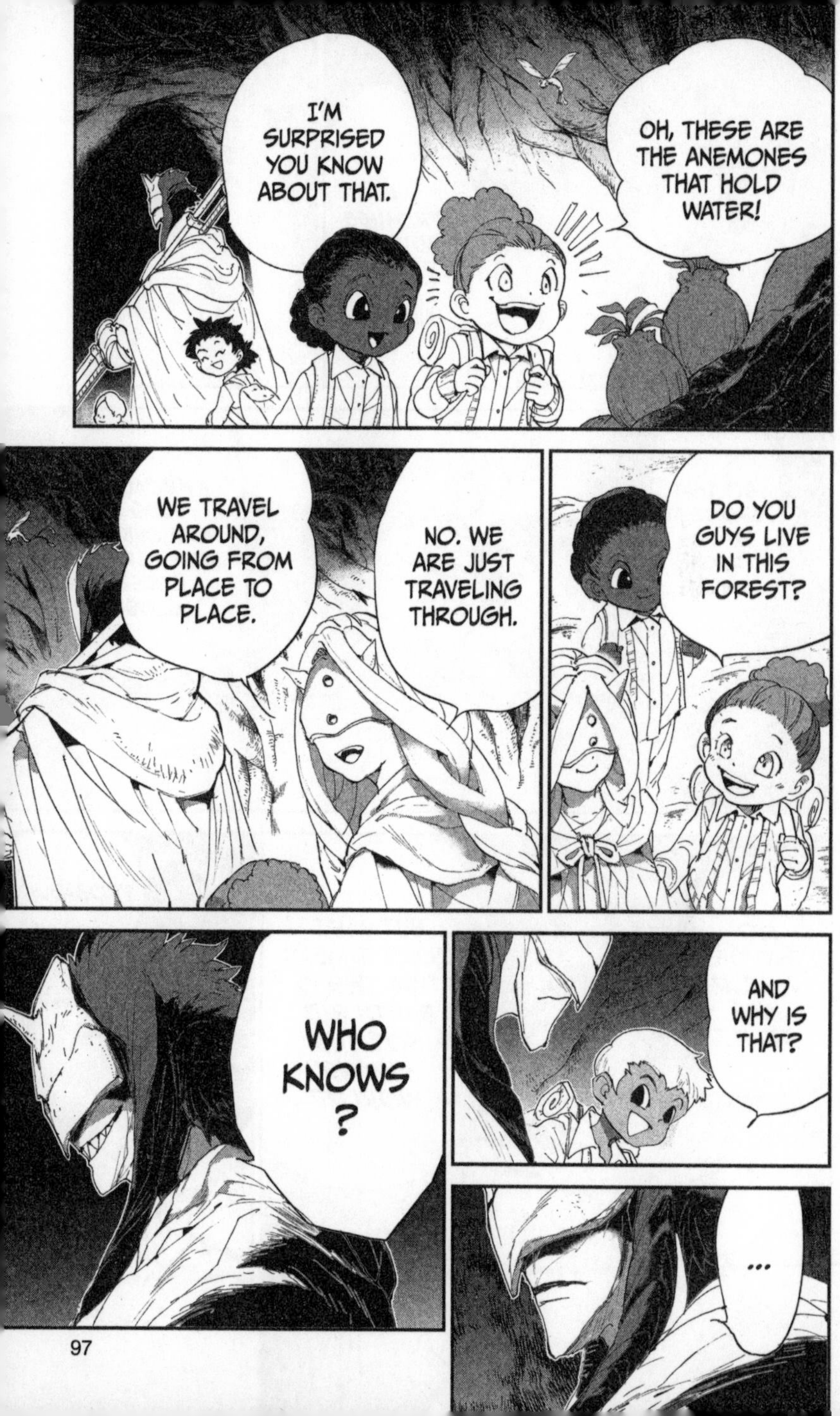
OH, THESE ARE THE ANEMONES THAT HOLD WATER!
I'M SURPRISED YOU KNOW ABOUT THAT.
DO YOU GUYS LIVE IN THIS FOREST?
NO. WE ARE JUST TRAVELING THROUGH.
WE TRAVEL AROUND, GOING FROM PLACE TO PLACE.
AND WHY IS THAT?
...
WHO KNOWS?

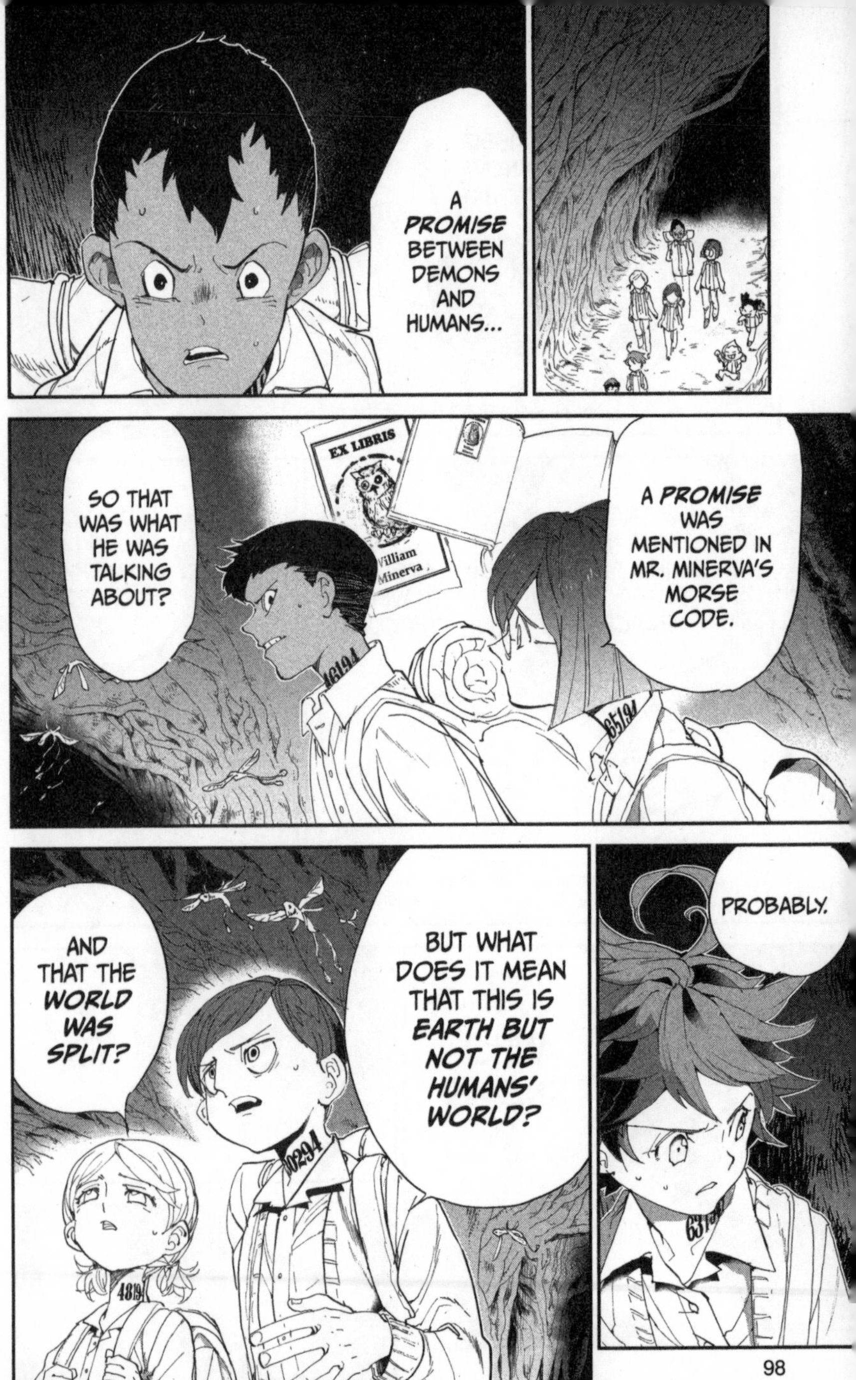
A *PROMISE* BETWEEN DEMONS AND HUMANS...
A *PROMISE* WAS MENTIONED IN MR. MINERVA'S MORSE CODE.
EX LIBRIS
William Minerva
SO THAT WAS WHAT HE WAS TALKING ABOUT?
PROBABLY.
BUT WHAT DOES IT MEAN THAT THIS IS *EARTH BUT NOT THE HUMANS' WORLD?*
AND THAT THE *WORLD WAS SPLIT?*

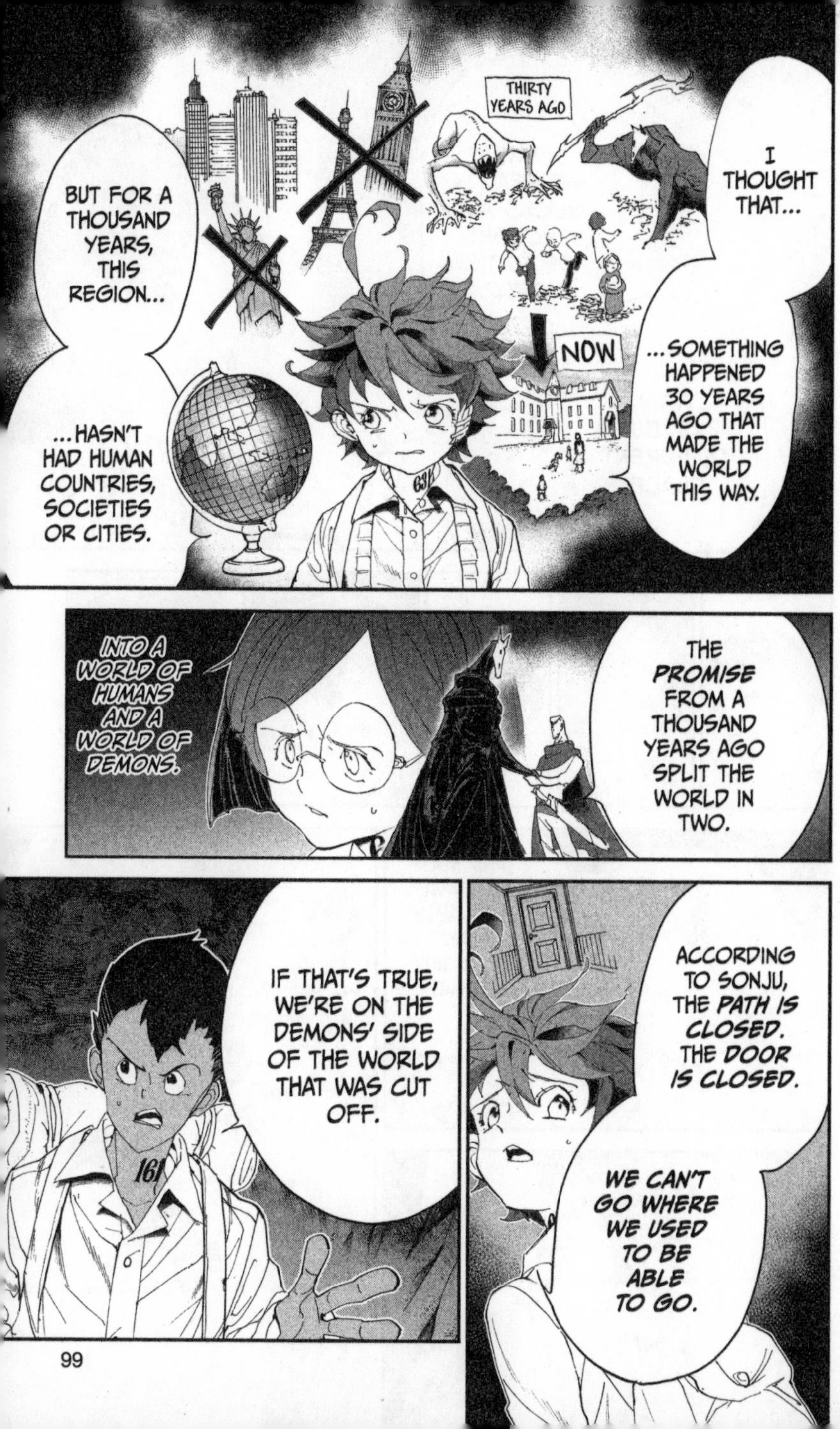
I THOUGHT THAT...
THIRTY YEARS AGO
...SOMETHING HAPPENED 30 YEARS AGO THAT MADE THE WORLD THIS WAY.
NOW
BUT FOR A THOUSAND YEARS, THIS REGION...
...HASN'T HAD HUMAN COUNTRIES, SOCIETIES OR CITIES.
THE *PROMISE* FROM A THOUSAND YEARS AGO SPLIT THE WORLD IN TWO.
INTO A WORLD OF HUMANS AND A WORLD OF DEMONS.
ACCORDING TO SONJU, THE *PATH IS CLOSED*. THE *DOOR IS CLOSED*.
WE CAN'T GO WHERE WE USED TO BE ABLE TO GO.
IF THAT'S TRUE, WE'RE ON THE DEMONS' SIDE OF THE WORLD THAT WAS CUT OFF.

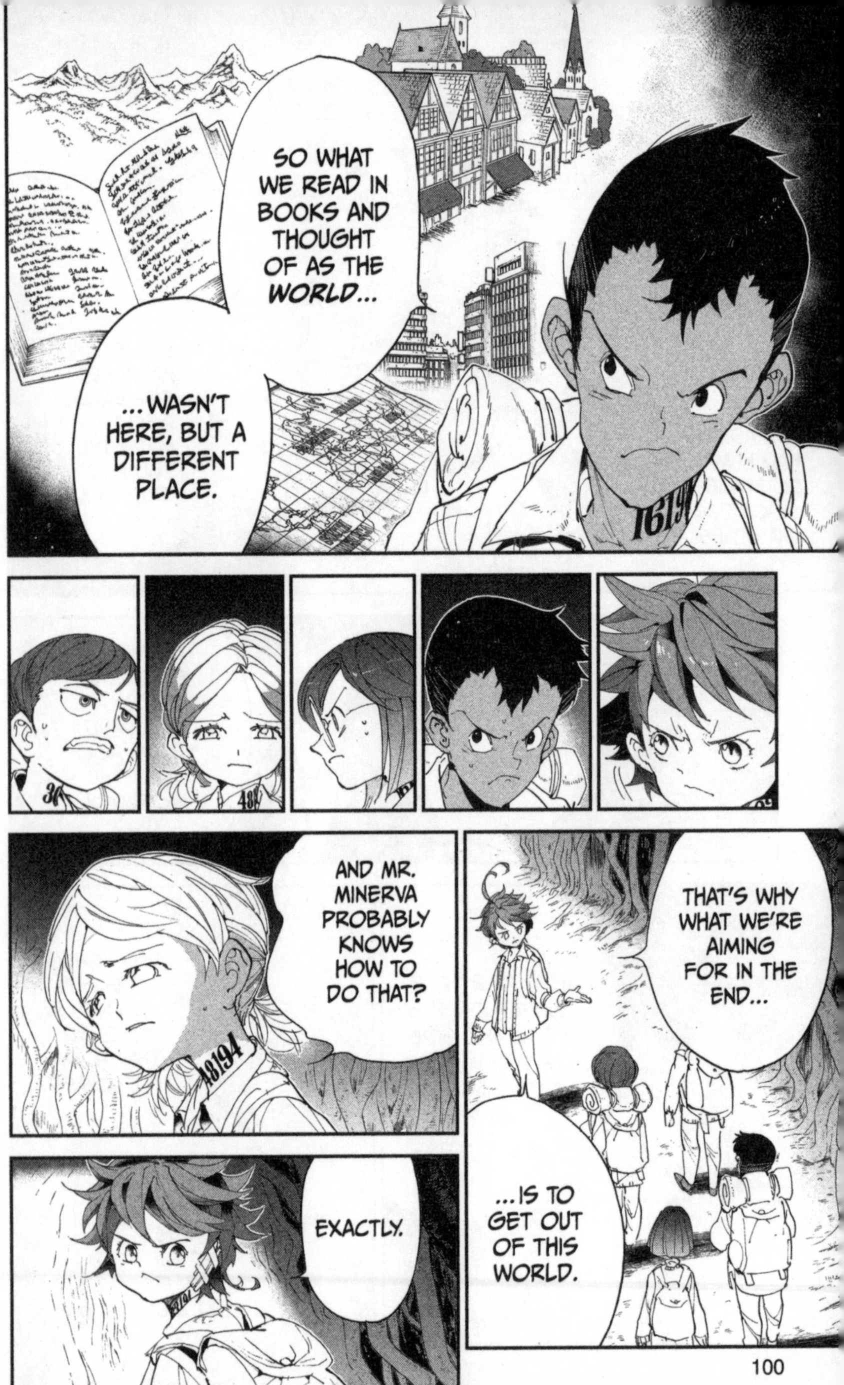
SO WHAT WE READ IN BOOKS AND THOUGHT OF AS THE *WORLD*...
...WASN'T HERE, BUT A DIFFERENT PLACE.
THAT'S WHY WHAT WE'RE AIMING FOR IN THE END...
...IS TO GET OUT OF THIS WORLD.
AND MR. MINERVA PROBABLY KNOWS HOW TO DO THAT?
EXACTLY.

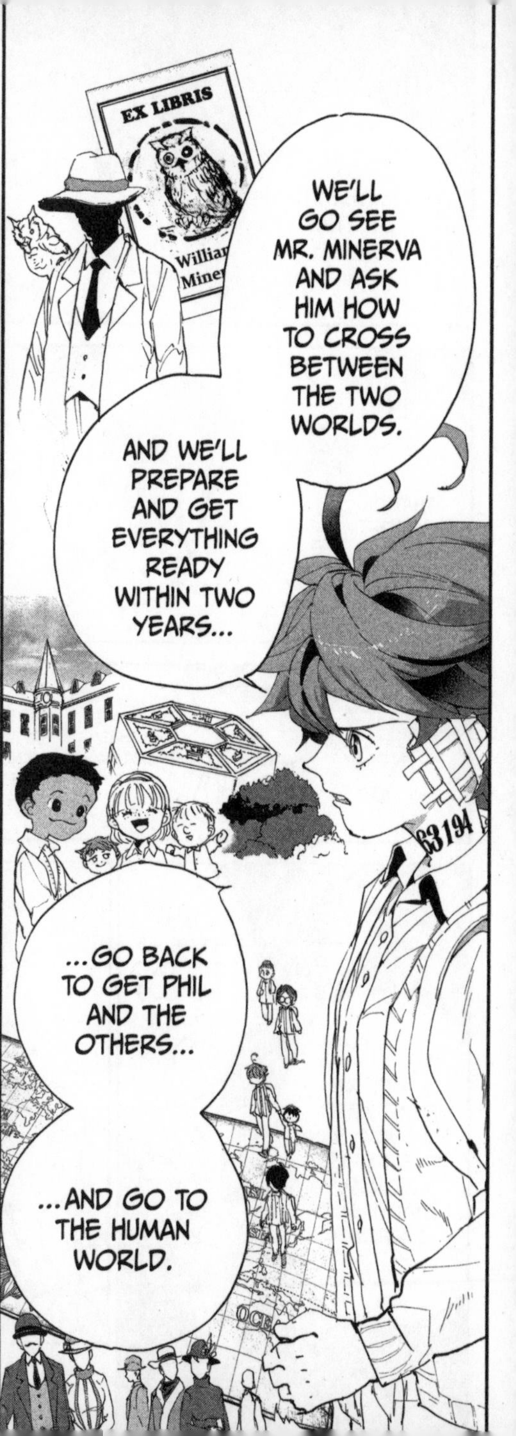
EX LIBRIS
WE'LL GO SEE MR. MINERVA AND ASK HIM HOW TO CROSS BETWEEN THE TWO WORLDS.
AND WE'LL PREPARE AND GET EVERYTHING READY WITHIN TWO YEARS...
...GO BACK TO GET PHIL AND THE OTHERS...
...AND GO TO THE HUMAN WORLD.

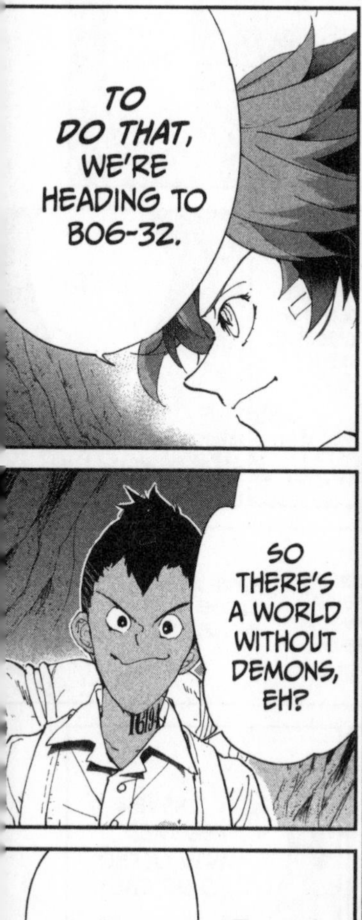
TO DO THAT, WE'RE HEADING TO B06-32.
SO THERE'S A WORLD WITHOUT DEMONS, EH?
AN UN-EXPECTED HOPE.

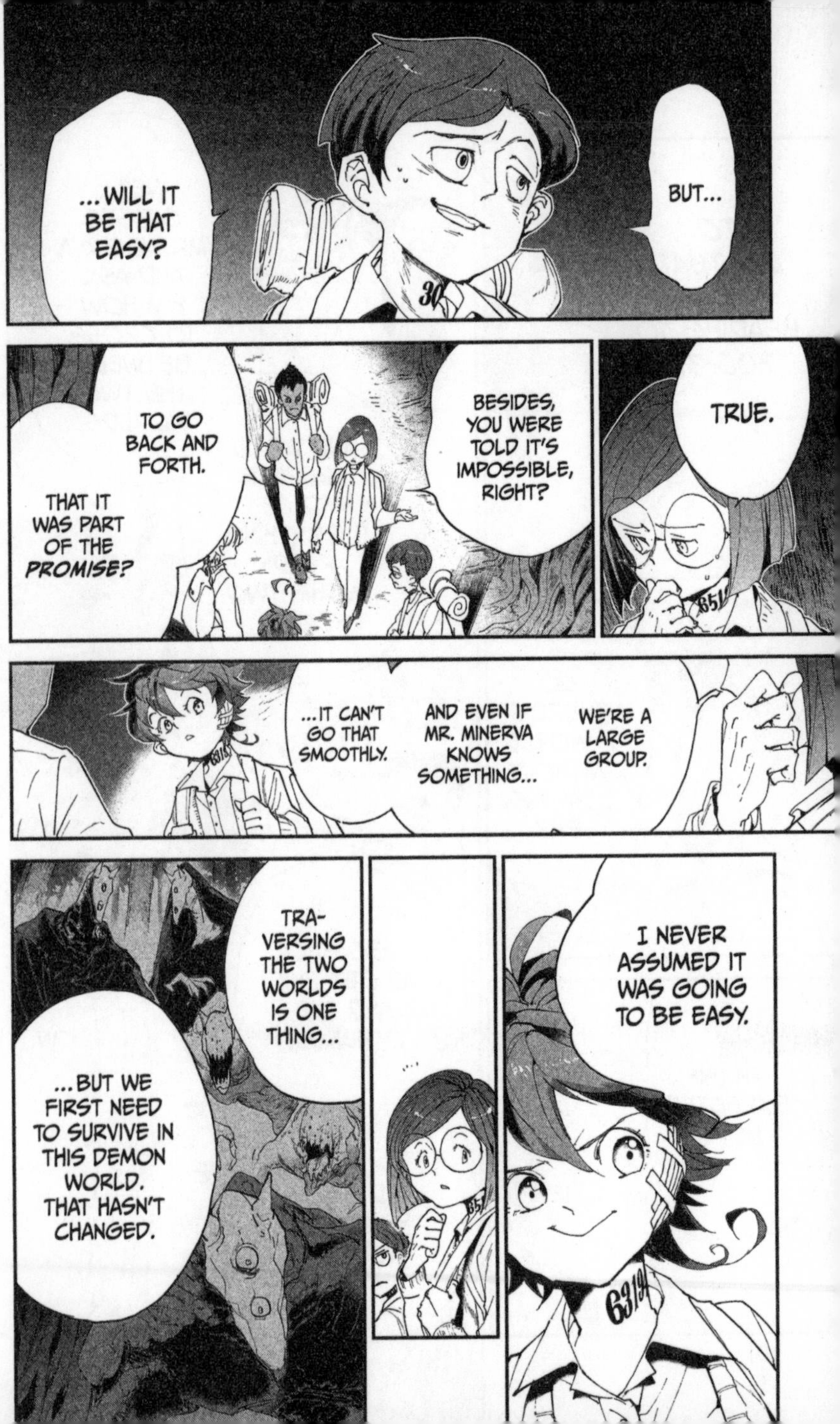
BUT...
...WILL IT BE THAT EASY?
TRUE.
BESIDES, YOU WERE TOLD IT'S IMPOSSIBLE, RIGHT?
TO GO BACK AND FORTH.
THAT IT WAS PART OF THE *PROMISE?*
WE'RE A LARGE GROUP.
AND EVEN IF MR. MINERVA KNOWS SOMETHING...
...IT CAN'T GO THAT SMOOTHLY.
I NEVER ASSUMED IT WAS GOING TO BE EASY.
...
TRAVERSING THE TWO WORLDS IS ONE THING...
...BUT WE FIRST NEED TO SURVIVE IN THIS DEMON WORLD. THAT HASN'T CHANGED.

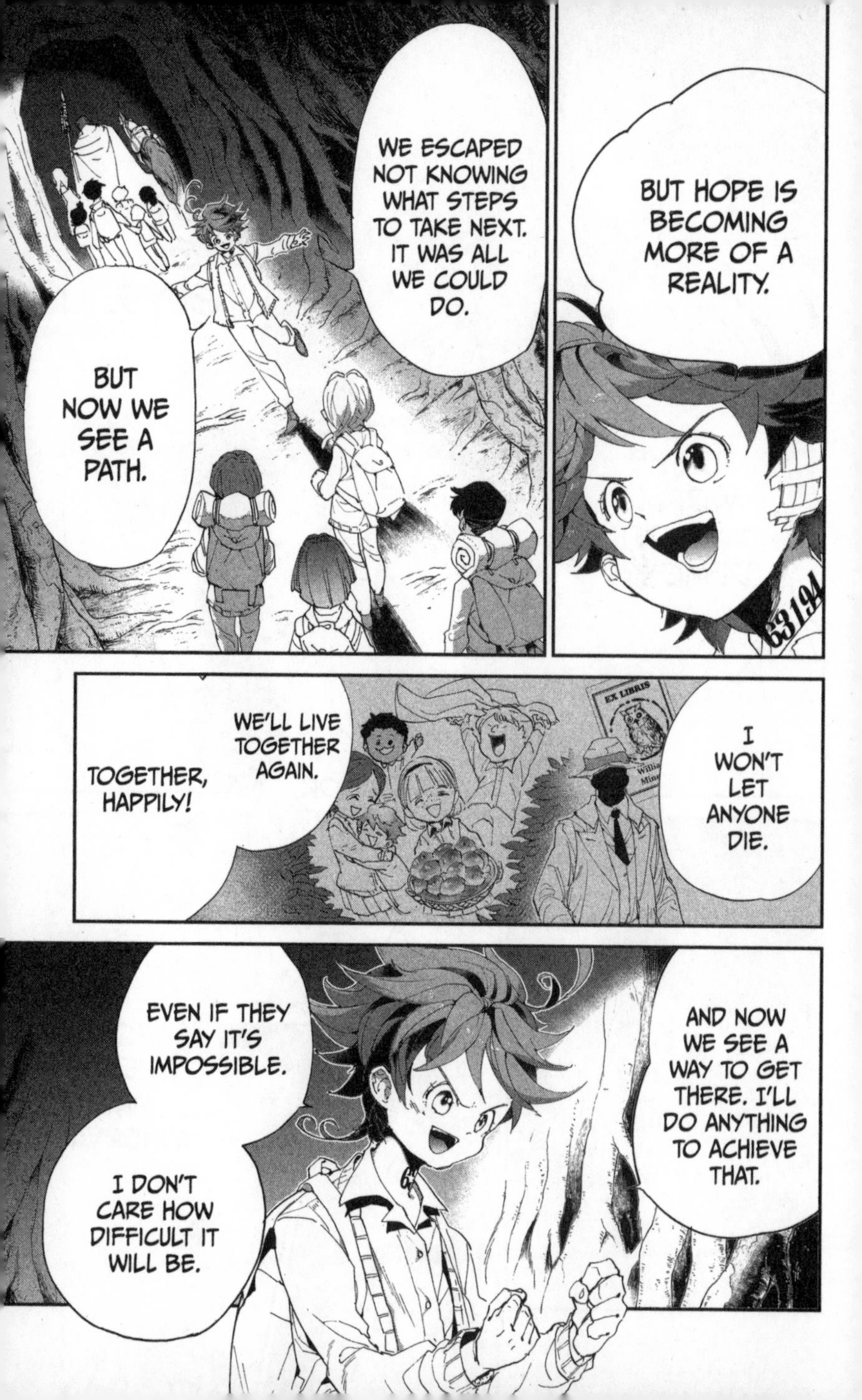

BUT HOPE IS BECOMING MORE OF A REALITY.
63194
WE ESCAPED NOT KNOWING WHAT STEPS TO TAKE NEXT. IT WAS ALL WE COULD DO.
BUT NOW WE SEE A PATH.
I WON'T LET ANYONE DIE.
EX LIBRIS
WE'LL LIVE TOGETHER AGAIN.
TOGETHER, HAPPILY!
AND NOW WE SEE A WAY TO GET THERE. I'LL DO ANYTHING TO ACHIEVE THAT.
EVEN IF THEY SAY IT'S IMPOSSIBLE.
I DON'T CARE HOW DIFFICULT IT WILL BE.

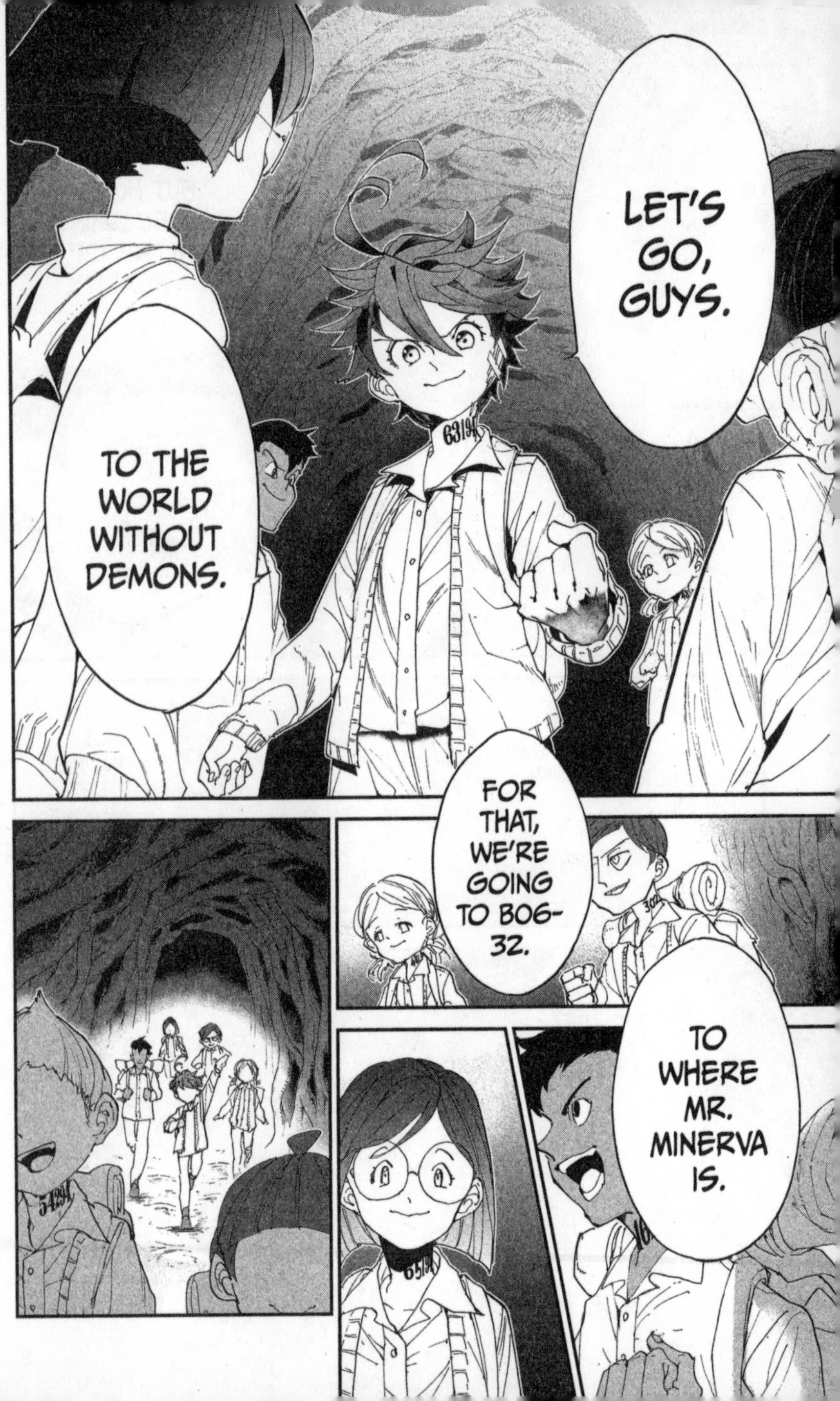
LET'S GO, GUYS.
TO THE WORLD WITHOUT DEMONS.
FOR THAT, WE'RE GOING TO B06-32.
TO WHERE MR. MINERVA IS.

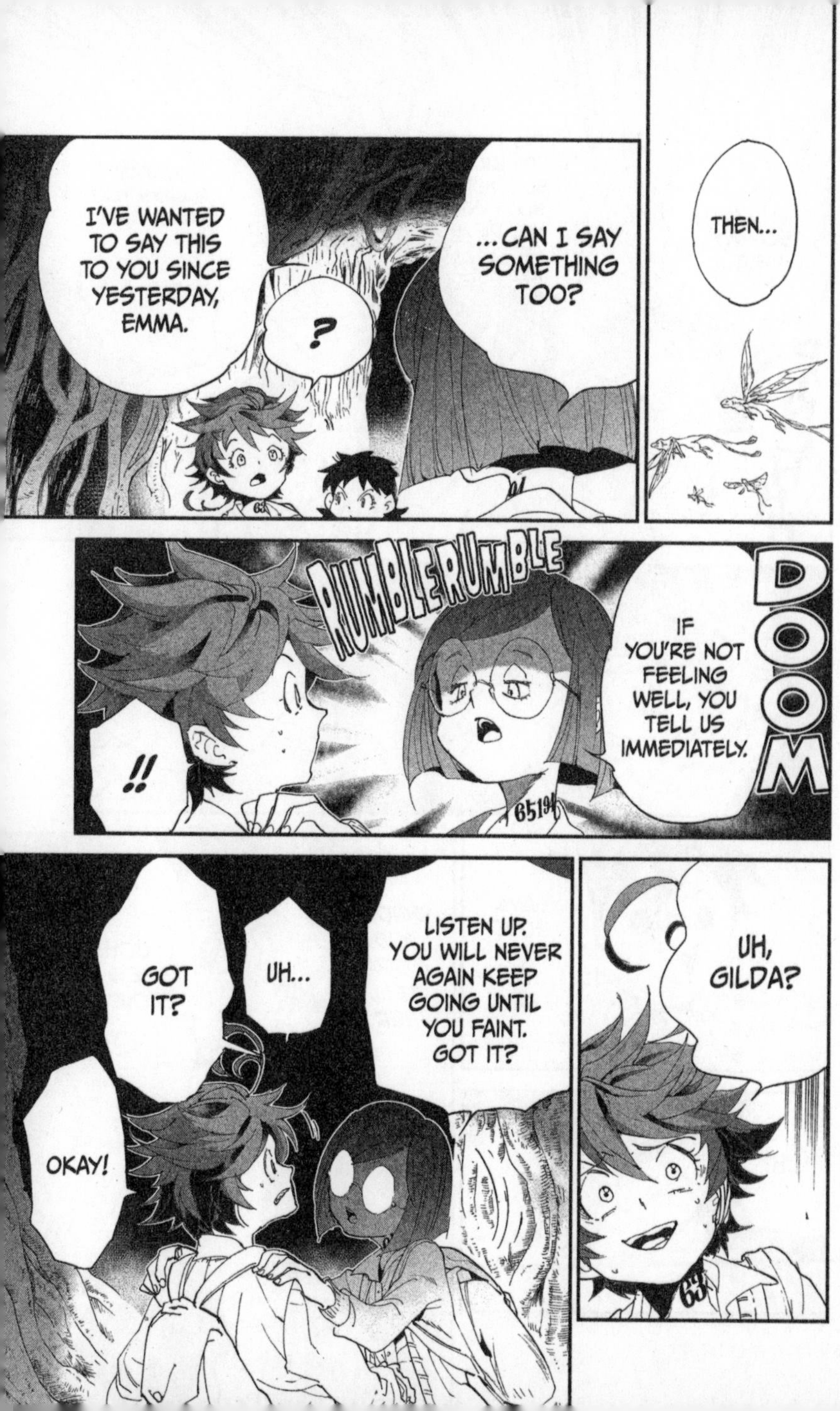
THEN...
...CAN I SAY SOMETHING TOO?
I'VE WANTED TO SAY THIS TO YOU SINCE YESTERDAY, EMMA.
?
DOOM
IF YOU'RE NOT FEELING WELL, YOU TELL US IMMEDIATELY.
RUMBLE RUMBLE
!!
UH, GILDA?
LISTEN UP. YOU WILL NEVER AGAIN KEEP GOING UNTIL YOU FAINT. GOT IT?
UH...
GOT IT?
OKAY!

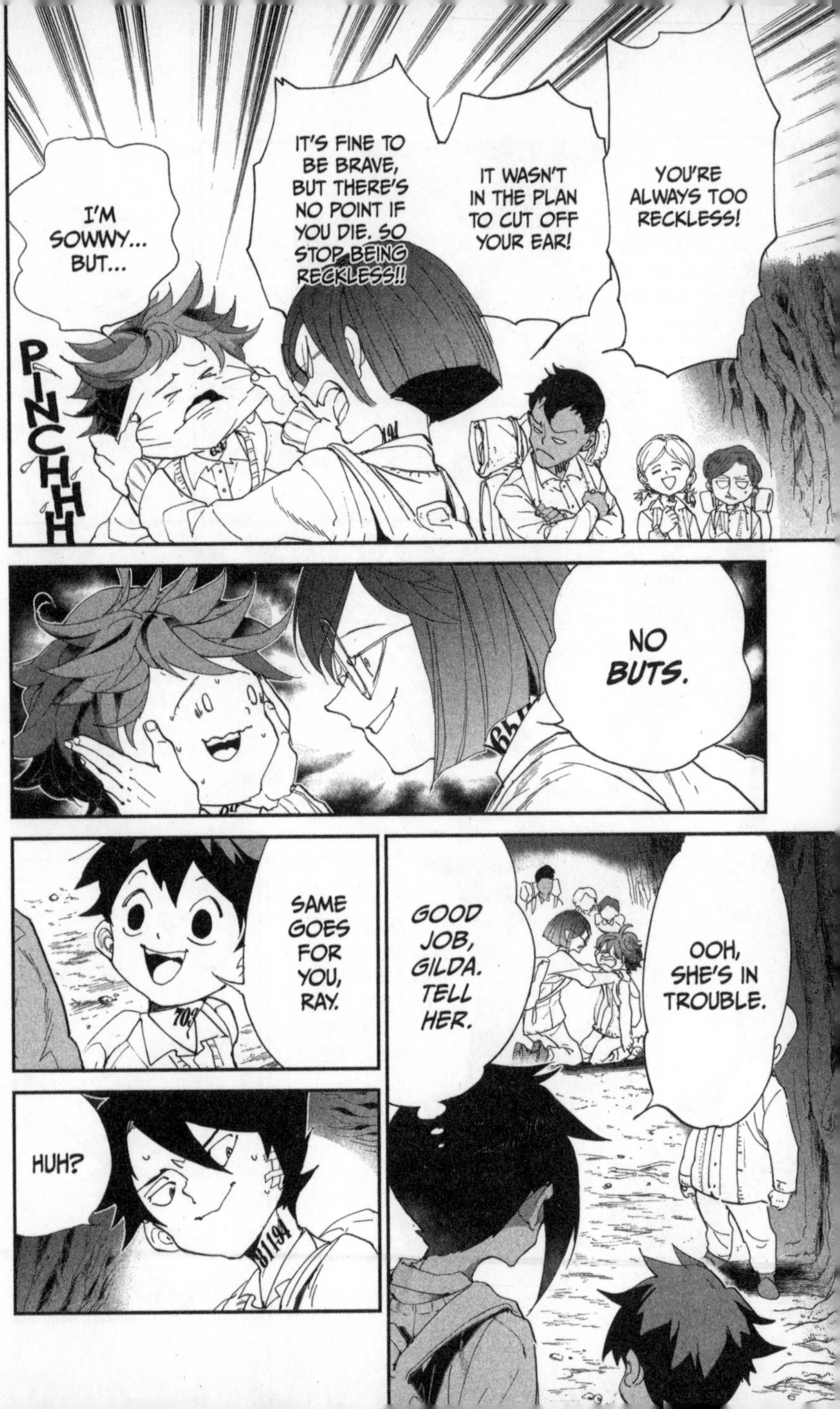
YOU'RE ALWAYS TOO RECKLESS!
IT WASN'T IN THE PLAN TO CUT OFF YOUR EAR!
IT'S FINE TO BE BRAVE, BUT THERE'S NO POINT IF YOU DIE. SO STOP BEING RECKLESS!!
I'M SOWWY... BUT...
PINCHHH
NO BUTS.
OOH, SHE'S IN TROUBLE.
GOOD JOB, GILDA. TELL HER.
SAME GOES FOR YOU, RAY.
HUH?

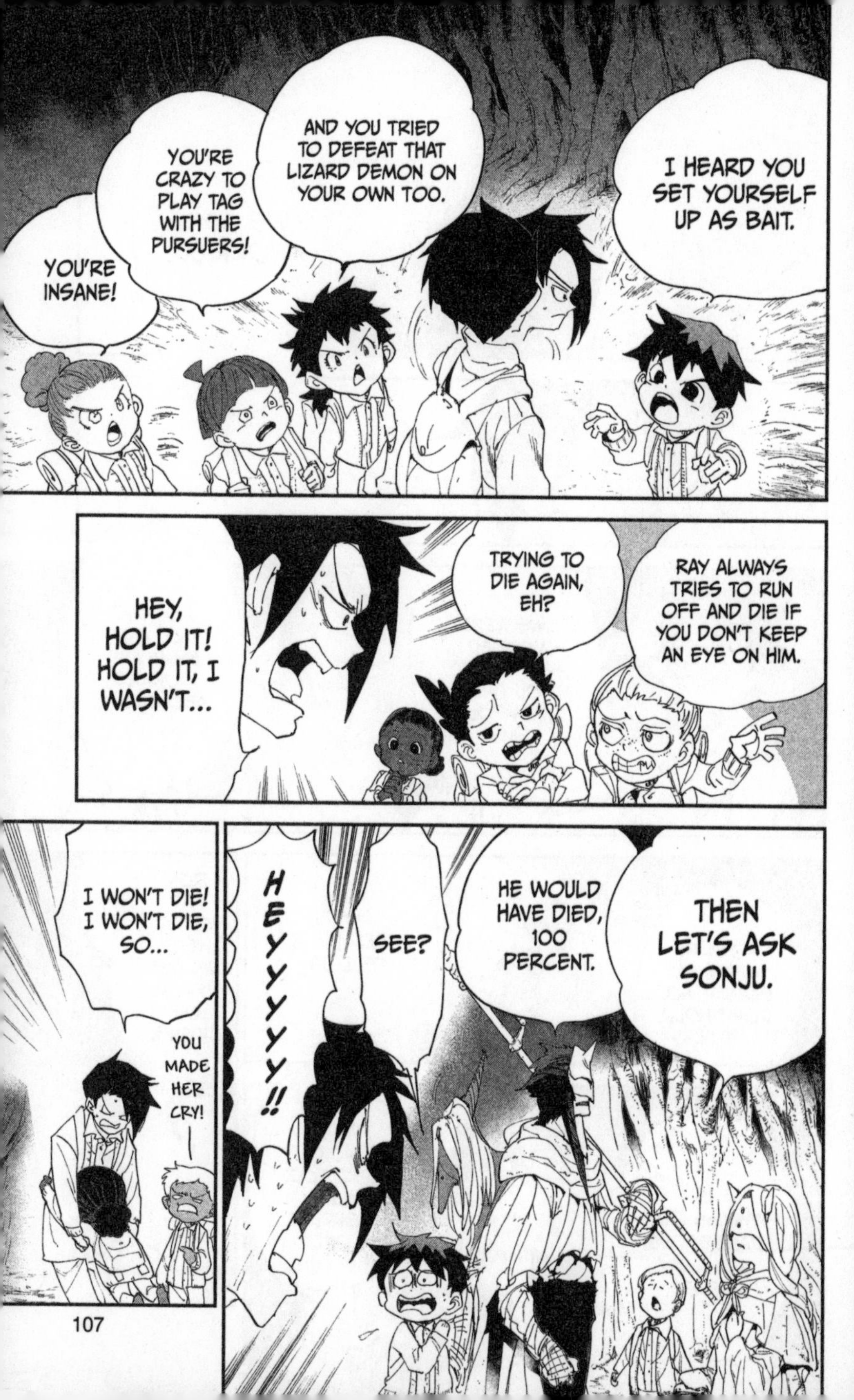
I HEARD YOU SET YOURSELF UP AS BAIT.
AND YOU TRIED TO DEFEAT THAT LIZARD DEMON ON YOUR OWN TOO.
YOU'RE CRAZY TO PLAY TAG WITH THE PURSUERS!
YOU'RE INSANE!
RAY ALWAYS TRIES TO RUN OFF AND DIE IF YOU DON'T KEEP AN EYE ON HIM.
TRYING TO DIE AGAIN, EH?
HEY, HOLD IT! HOLD IT, I WASN'T...
THEN LET'S ASK SONJU.
HE WOULD HAVE DIED, 100 PERCENT.
SEE?
HEYYYYYY!!
I WON'T DIE! I WON'T DIE, SO...
YOU MADE HER CRY!

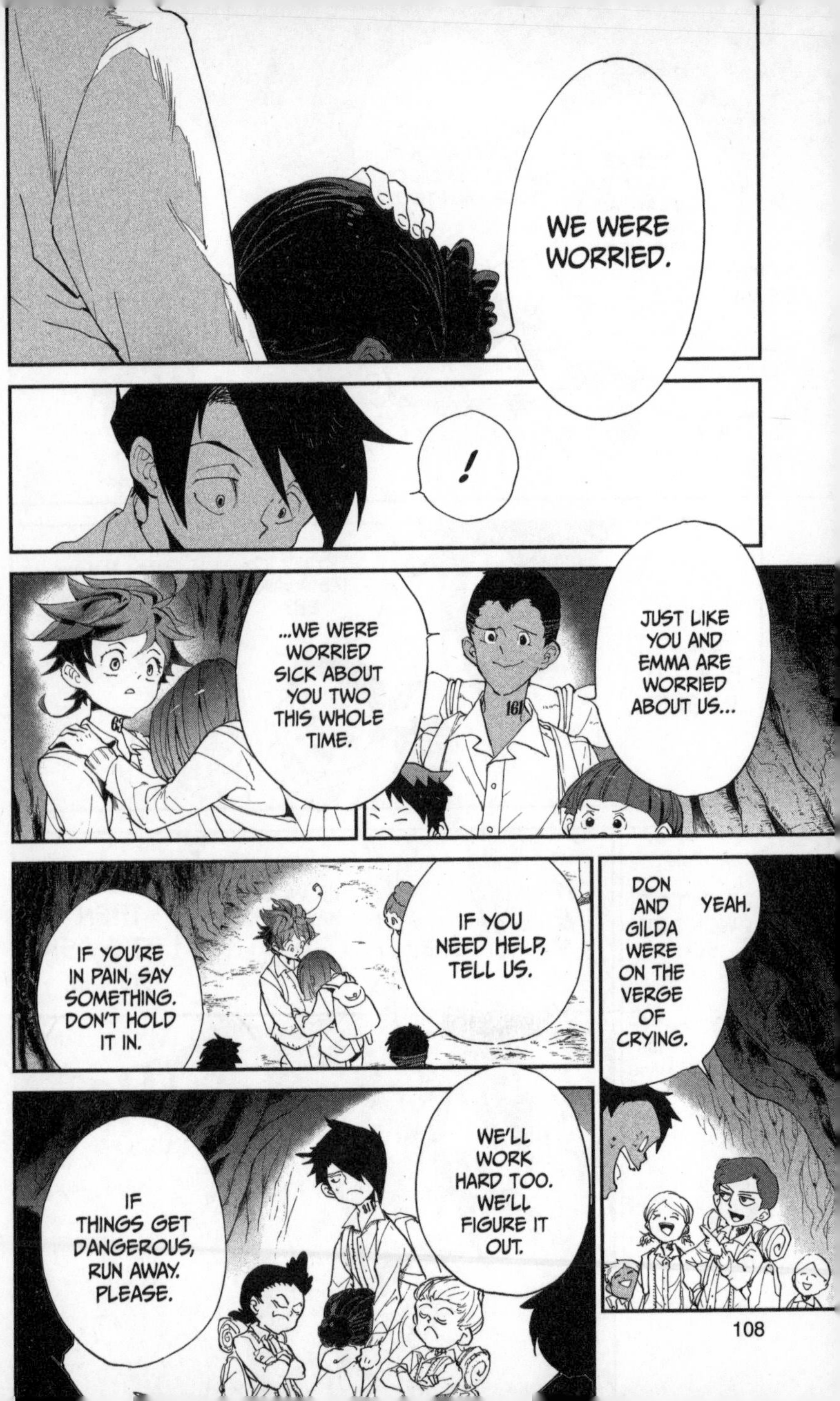
WE WERE WORRIED.
!
JUST LIKE YOU AND EMMA ARE WORRIED ABOUT US...
...WE WERE WORRIED SICK ABOUT YOU TWO THIS WHOLE TIME.
YEAH.
DON AND GILDA WERE ON THE VERGE OF CRYING.
IF YOU NEED HELP, TELL US.
IF YOU'RE IN PAIN, SAY SOMETHING. DON'T HOLD IT IN.
WE'LL WORK HARD TOO. WE'LL FIGURE IT OUT.
IF THINGS GET DANGEROUS, RUN AWAY. PLEASE.

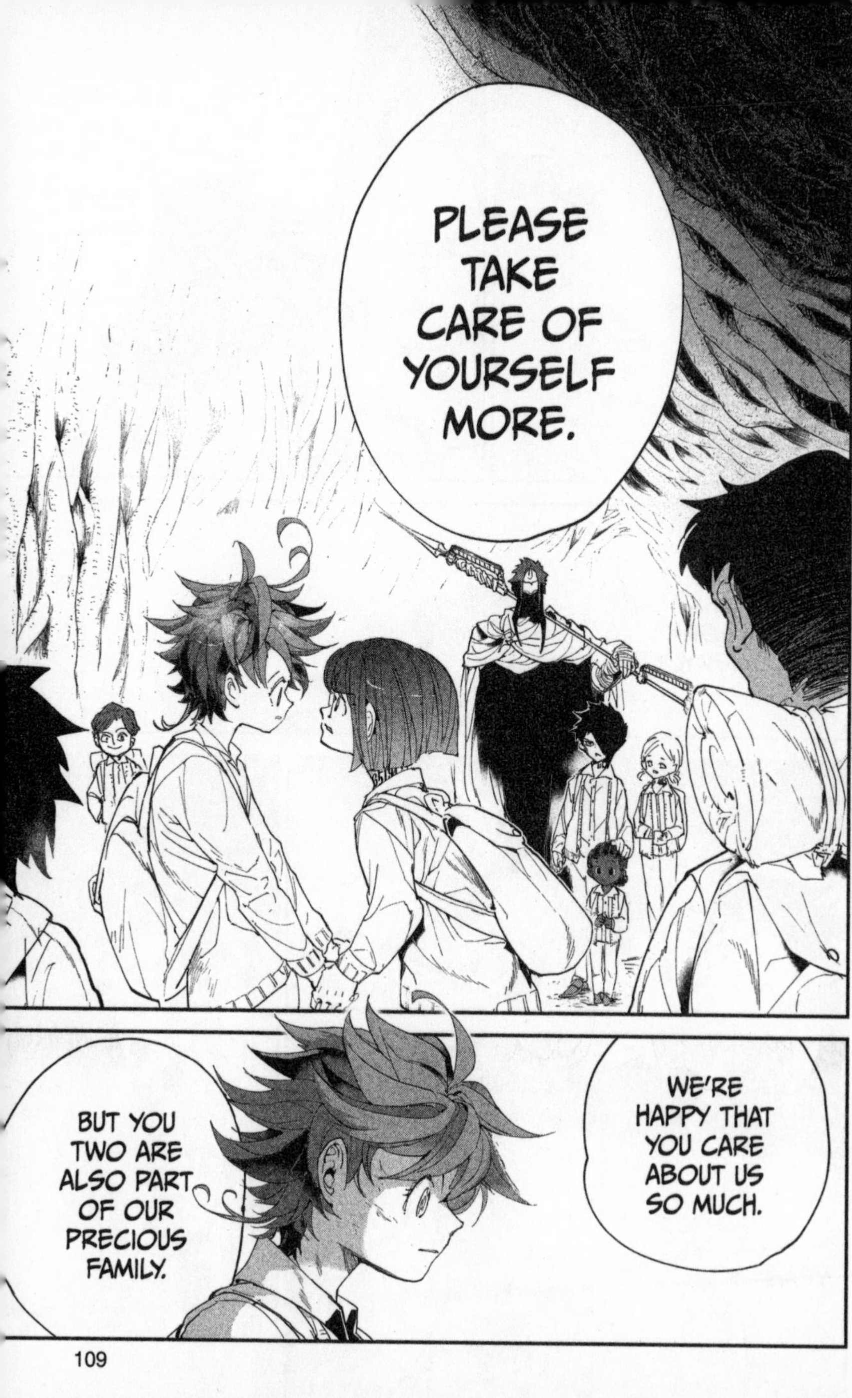
PLEASE TAKE CARE OF YOURSELF MORE.
WE'RE HAPPY THAT YOU CARE ABOUT US SO MUCH.
BUT YOU TWO ARE ALSO PART OF OUR PRECIOUS FAMILY.

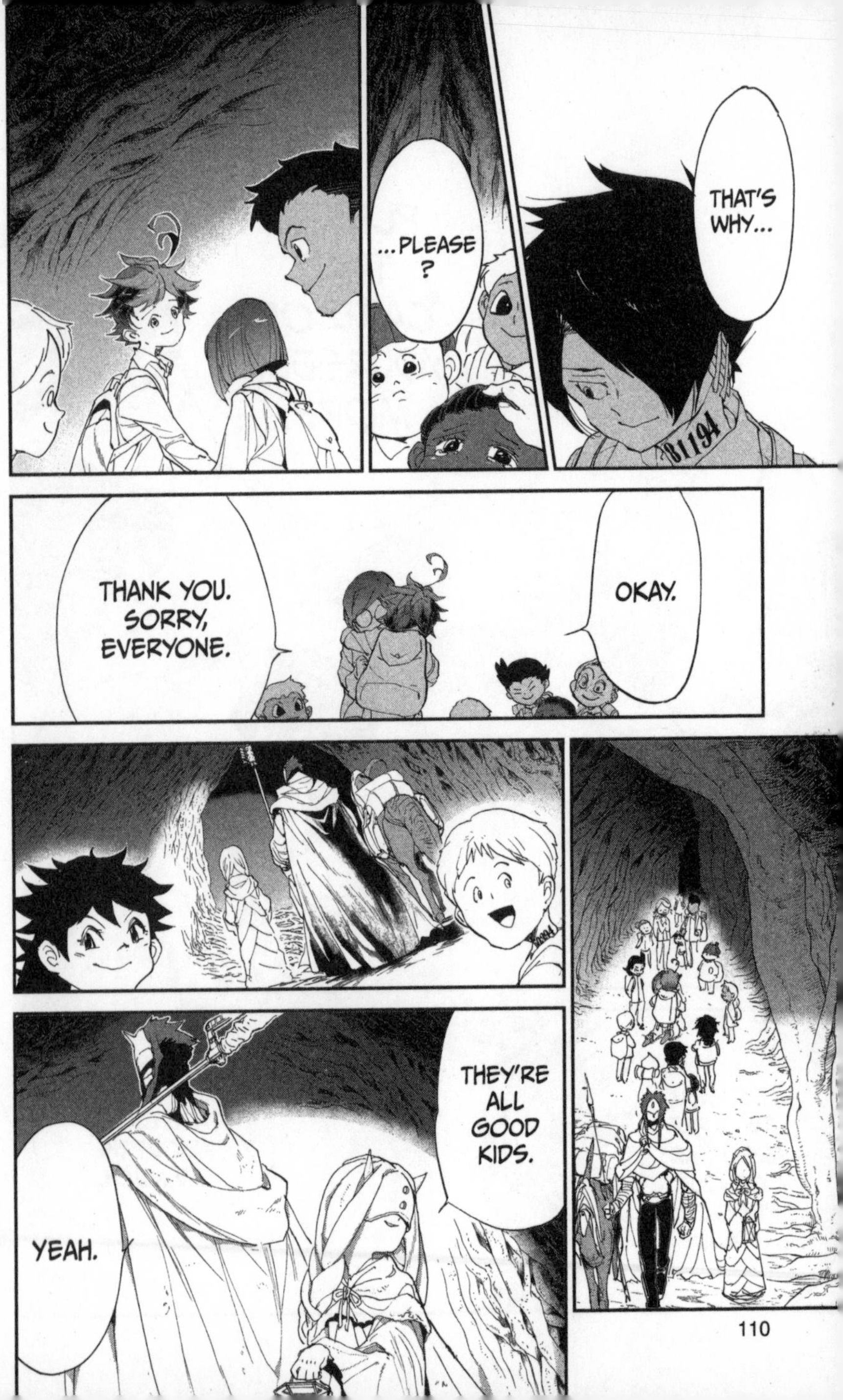
THAT'S WHY...
...PLEASE?
OKAY.
THANK YOU. SORRY, EVERYONE.
THEY'RE ALL GOOD KIDS.
YEAH.

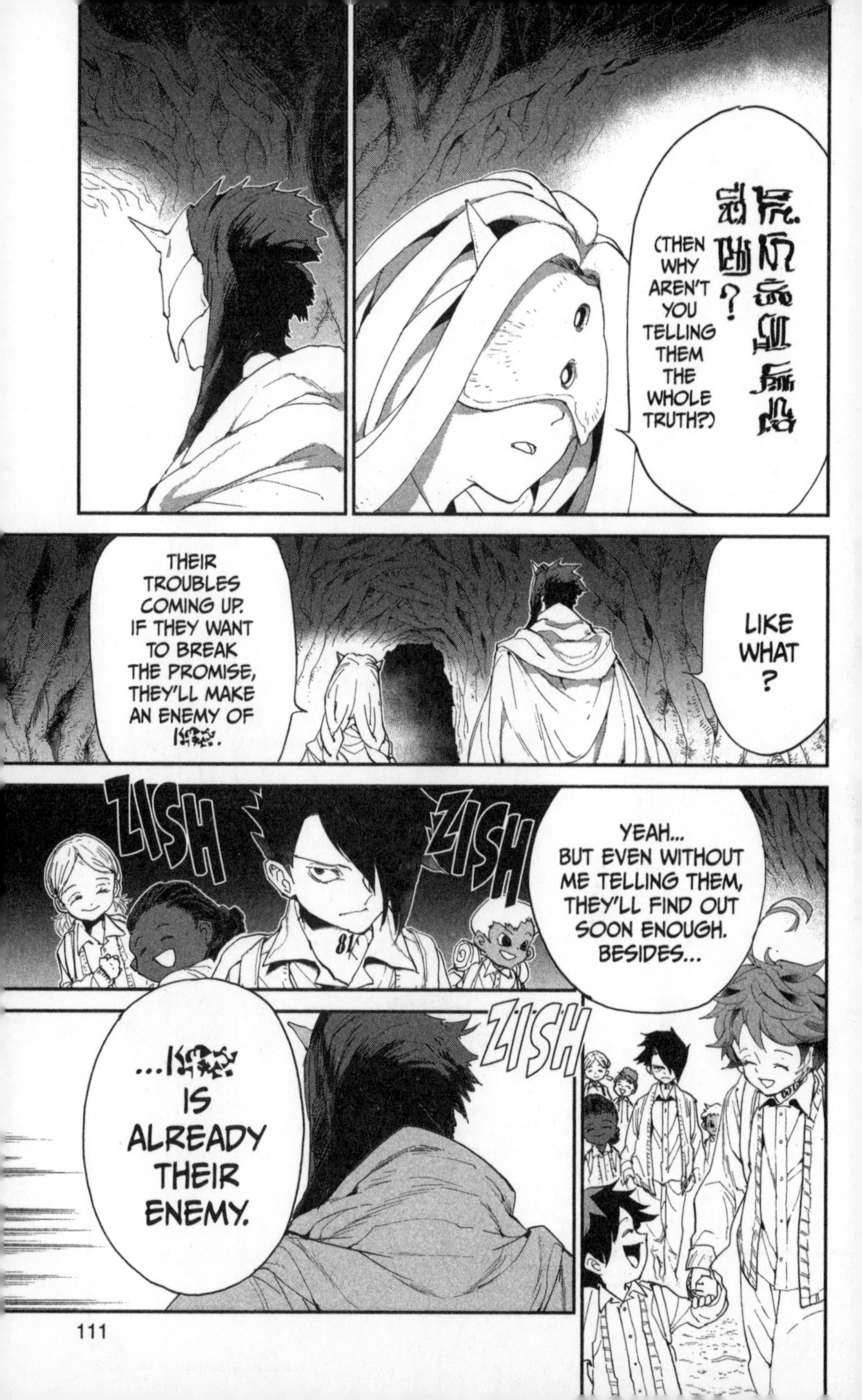
(THEN WHY AREN'T YOU TELLING THEM THE WHOLE TRUTH?)
LIKE WHAT?
THEIR TROUBLES COMING UP. IF THEY WANT TO BREAK THE PROMISE, THEY'LL MAKE AN ENEMY OF
YEAH... BUT EVEN WITHOUT ME TELLING THEM, THEY'LL FIND OUT SOON ENOUGH. BESIDES...
ZISH
ZISH
ZISH
... IS ALREADY THEIR ENEMY.

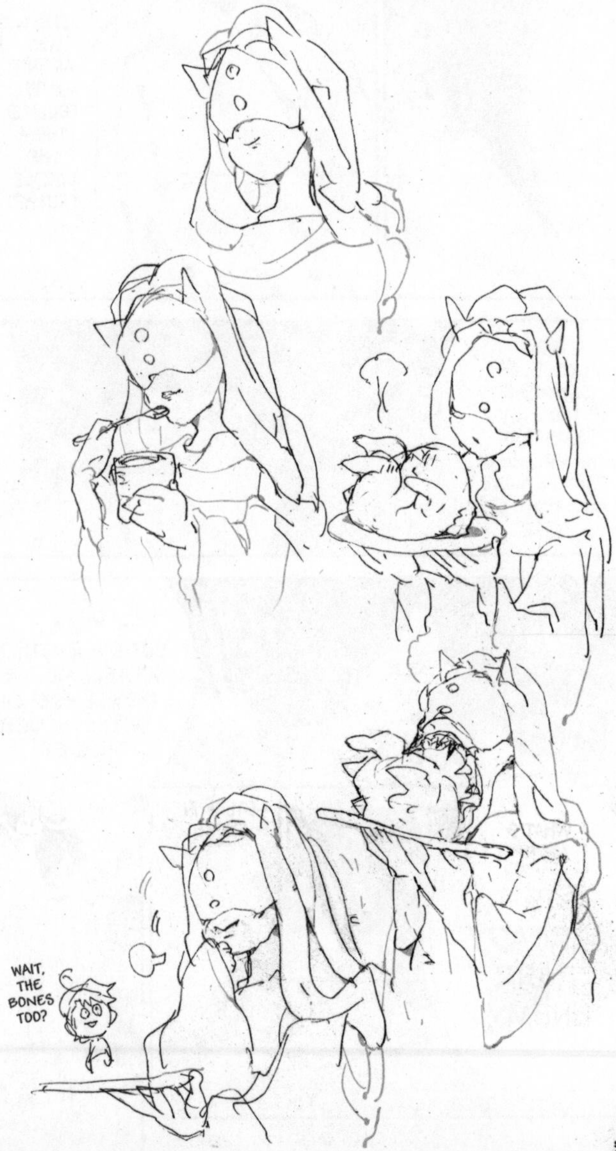
WAIT, THE BONES TOO?

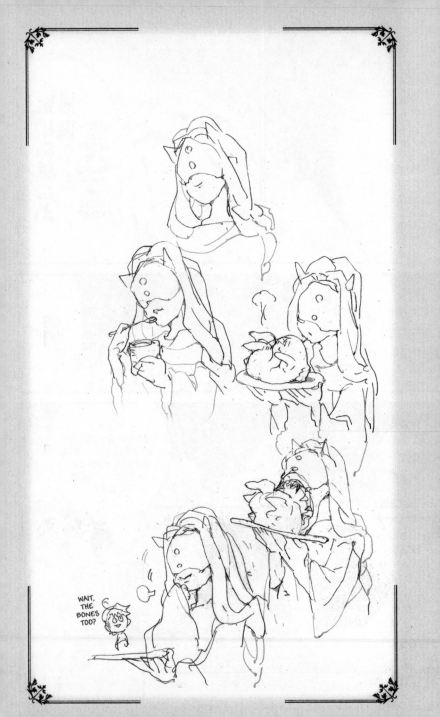

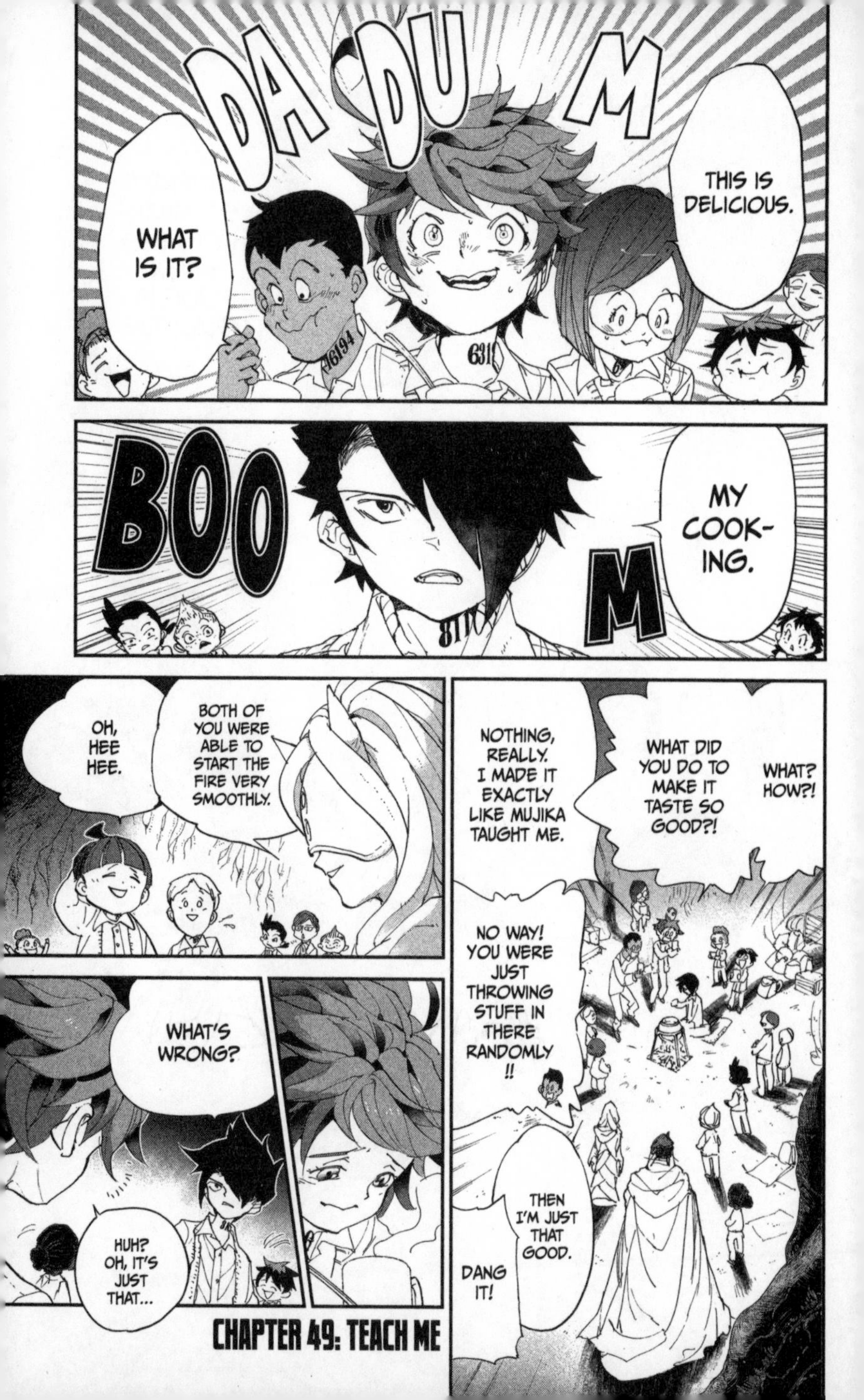
DA DU M
THIS IS DELICIOUS.
WHAT IS IT?
BOOM
MY COOKING.
WHAT? HOW?!
WHAT DID YOU DO TO MAKE IT TASTE SO GOOD?!
NOTHING, REALLY. I MADE IT EXACTLY LIKE MUJIKA TAUGHT ME.
NO WAY! YOU WERE JUST THROWING STUFF IN THERE RANDOMLY!!
THEN I'M JUST THAT GOOD.
DANG IT!
BOTH OF YOU WERE ABLE TO START THE FIRE VERY SMOOTHLY.
OH, HEE HEE.
WHAT'S WRONG?
HUH? OH, IT'S JUST THAT...

CHAPTER 49: TEACH ME

CHAPTER 49: TEACH ME
...THERE'S SO MUCH HAPPINESS WHEN FOOD IS DELICIOUS.

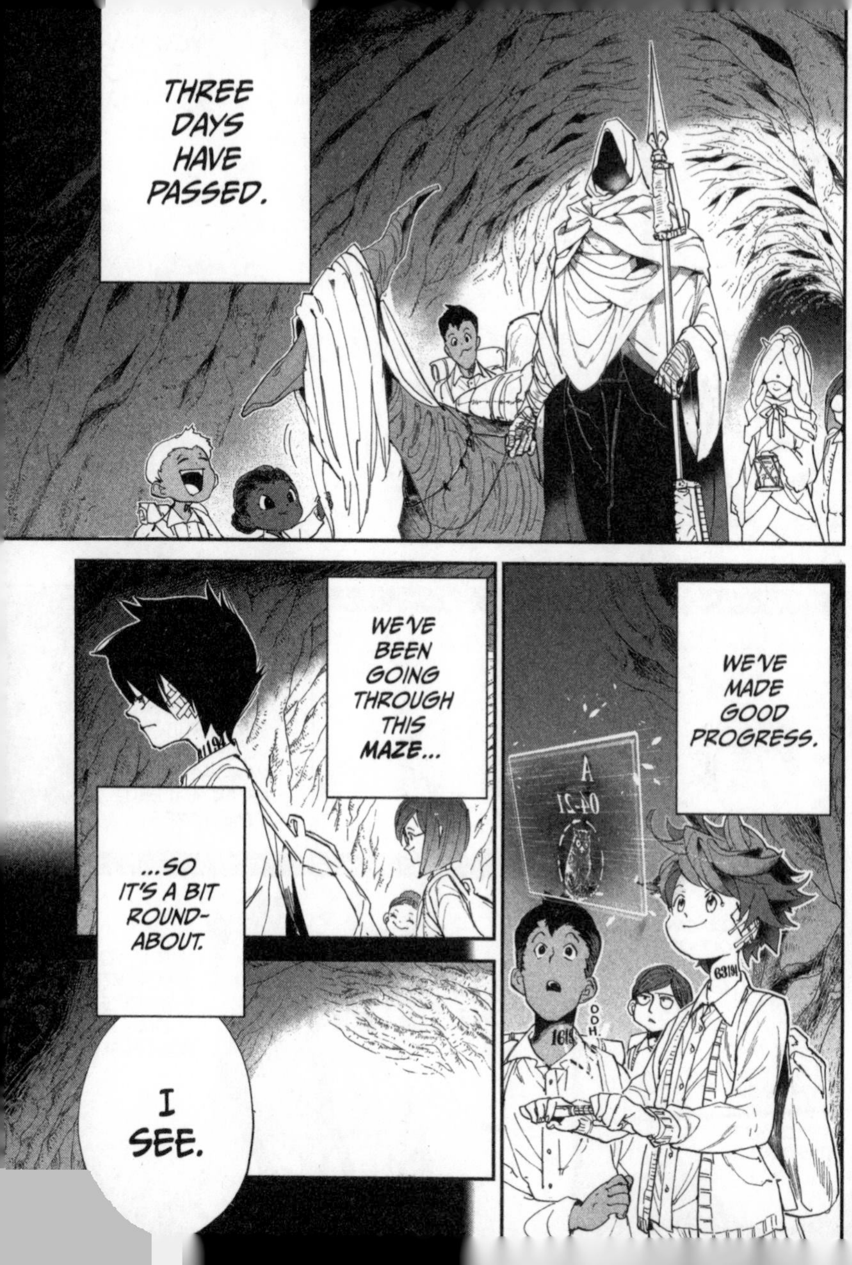
THREE DAYS HAVE PASSED.
WE'VE MADE GOOD PROGRESS.
OOH.
WE'VE BEEN GOING THROUGH THIS MAZE...
...SO IT'S A BIT ROUND-ABOUT.
I SEE.

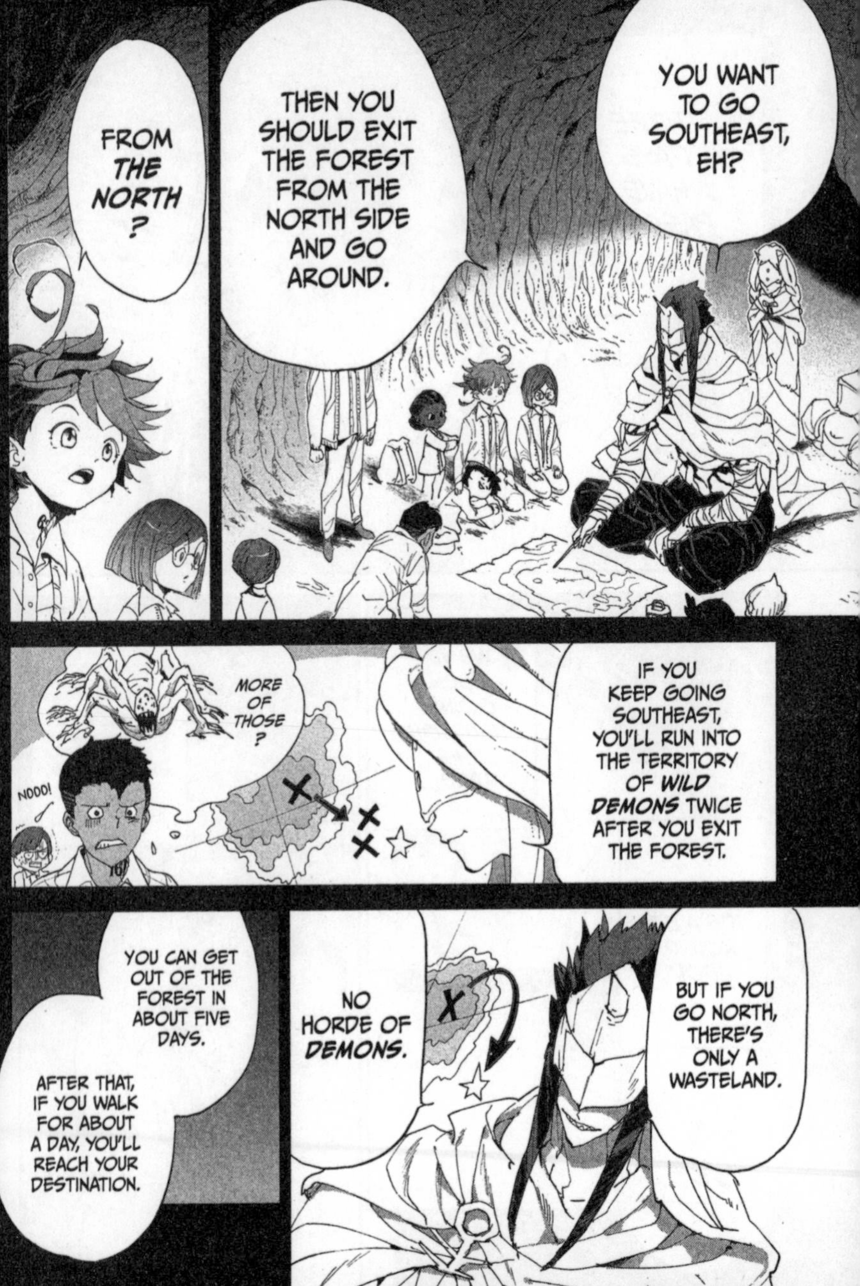
YOU WANT TO GO SOUTHEAST, EH?
THEN YOU SHOULD EXIT THE FOREST FROM THE NORTH SIDE AND GO AROUND.
FROM *THE NORTH* ?
IF YOU KEEP GOING SOUTHEAST, YOU'LL RUN INTO THE TERRITORY OF ***WILD DEMONS*** TWICE AFTER YOU EXIT THE FOREST.
MORE OF THOSE ?
NOOO!
BUT IF YOU GO NORTH, THERE'S ONLY A WASTELAND.
NO HORDE OF ***DEMONS.***
YOU CAN GET OUT OF THE FOREST IN ABOUT FIVE DAYS.
AFTER THAT, IF YOU WALK FOR ABOUT A DAY, YOU'LL REACH YOUR DESTINATION.

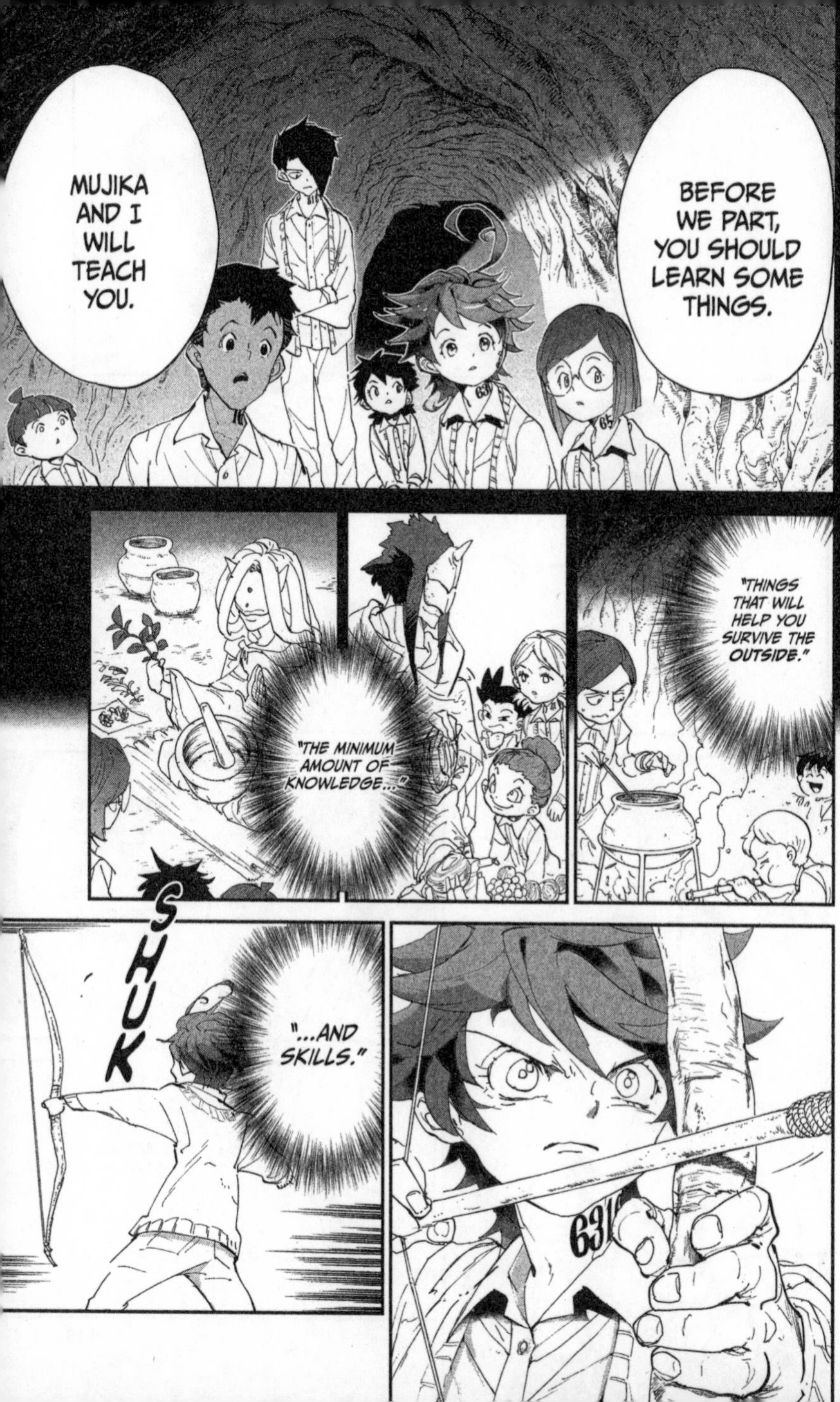
BEFORE WE PART, YOU SHOULD LEARN SOME THINGS.
MUJIKA AND I WILL TEACH YOU.
"THINGS THAT WILL HELP YOU SURVIVE THE OUTSIDE."
"THE MINIMUM AMOUNT OF KNOWLEDGE..."
"...AND SKILLS."
SHUK

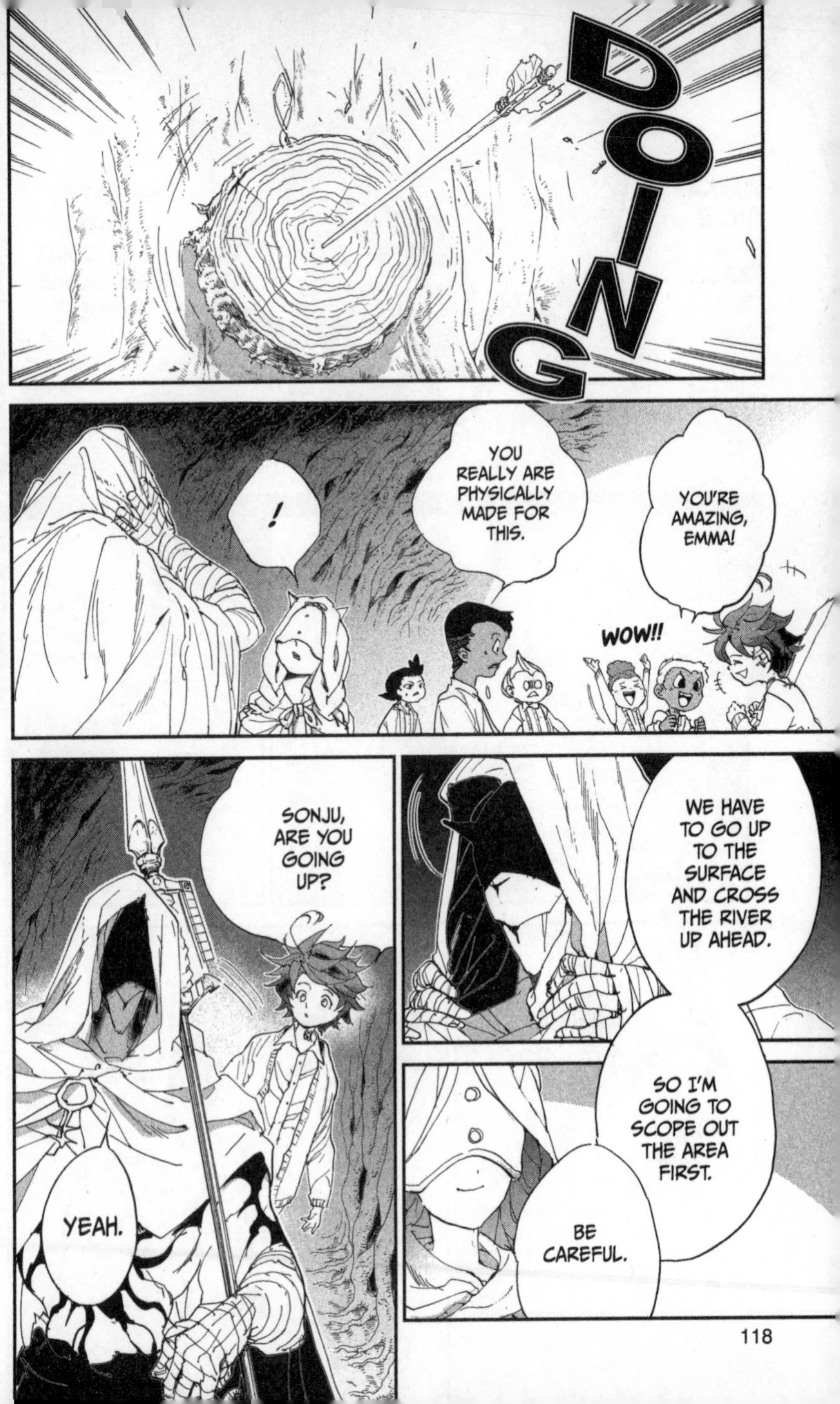
DOING
YOU'RE AMAZING, EMMA!
WOW!!
YOU REALLY ARE PHYSICALLY MADE FOR THIS.
!
WE HAVE TO GO UP TO THE SURFACE AND CROSS THE RIVER UP AHEAD.
SO I'M GOING TO SCOPE OUT THE AREA FIRST.
BE CAREFUL.
SONJU, ARE YOU GOING UP?
YEAH.

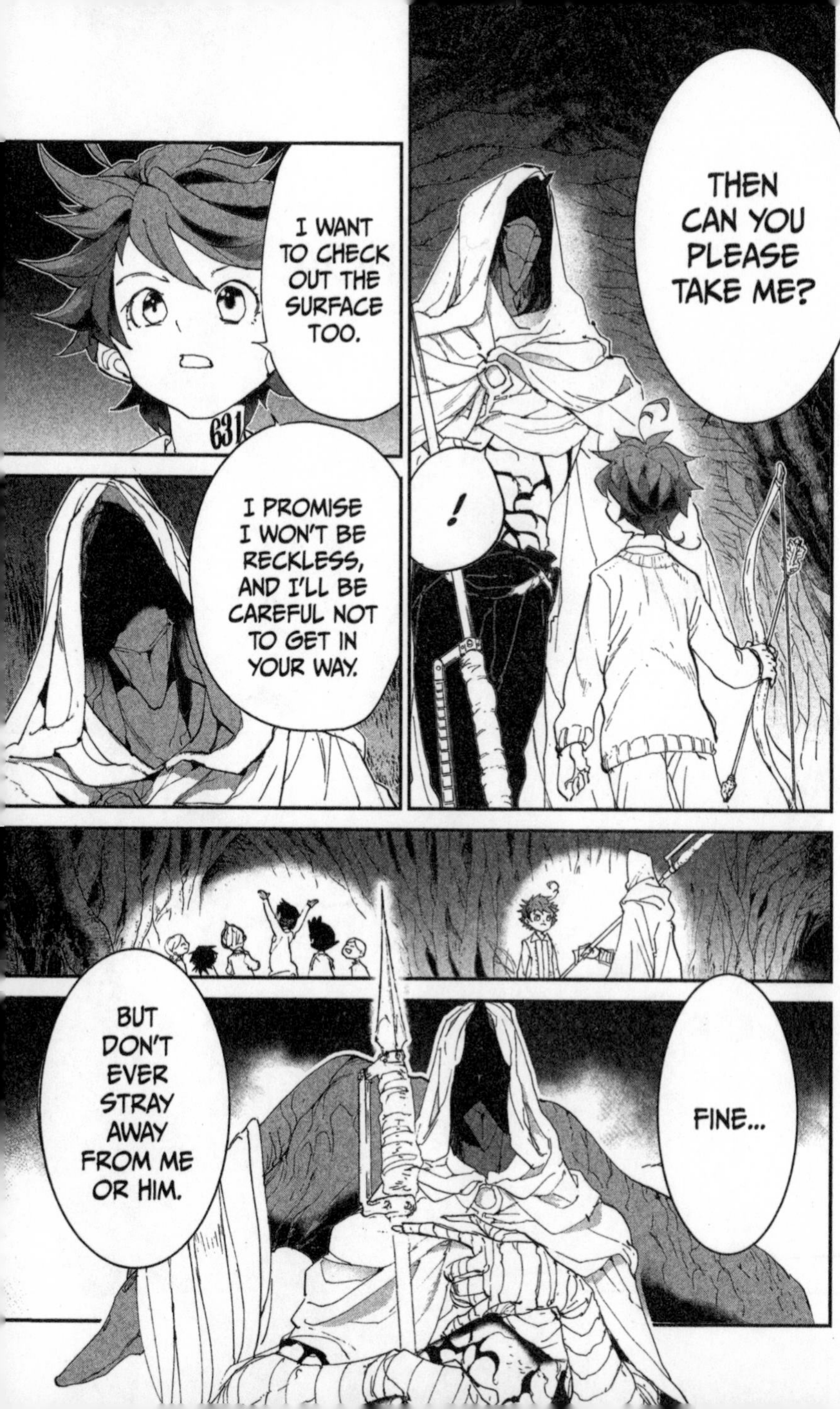
THEN CAN YOU PLEASE TAKE ME?
!
I WANT TO CHECK OUT THE SURFACE TOO.
631
I PROMISE I WON'T BE RECKLESS, AND I'LL BE CAREFUL NOT TO GET IN YOUR WAY.
FINE...
BUT DON'T EVER STRAY AWAY FROM ME OR HIM.

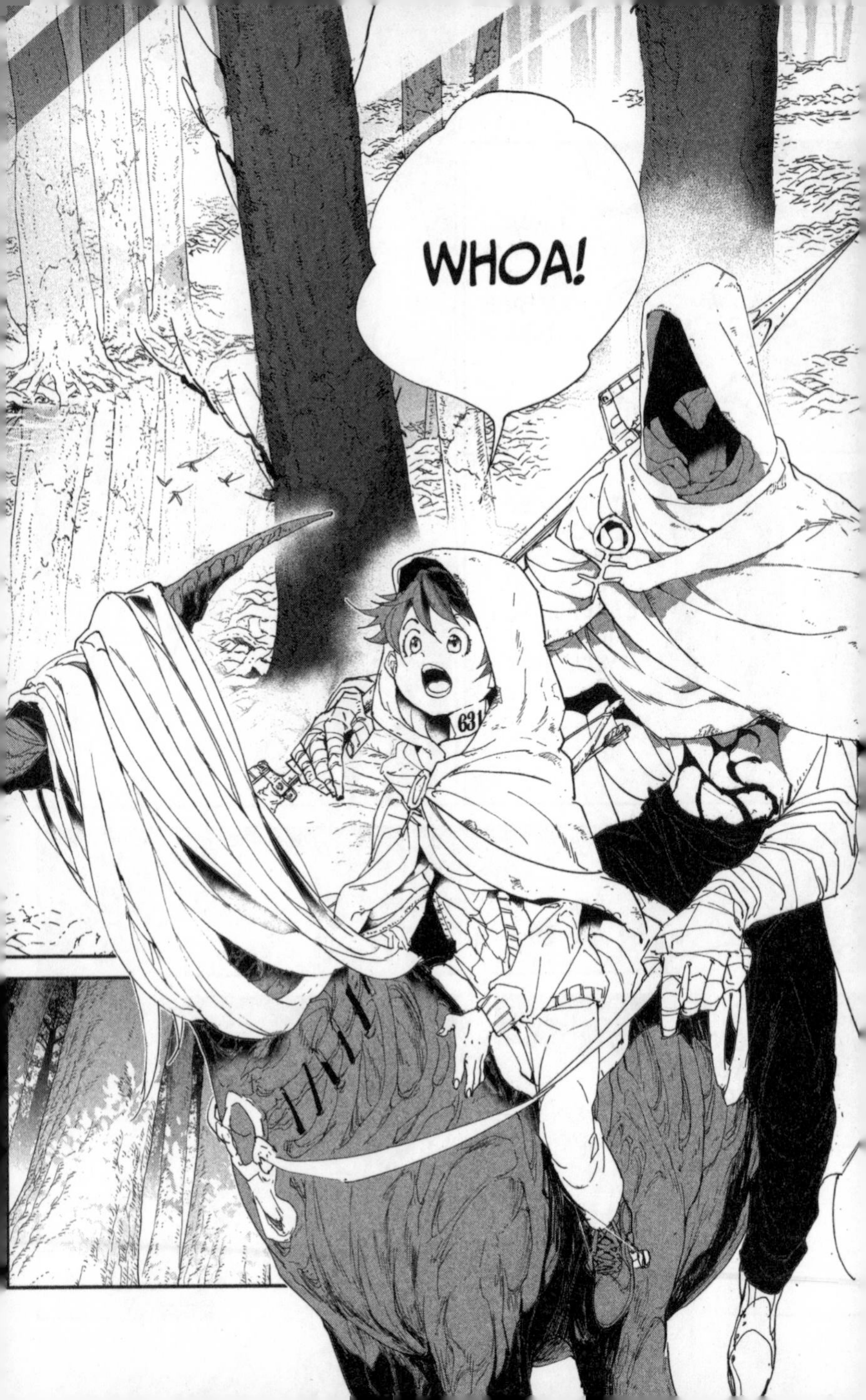
WHOA!
631

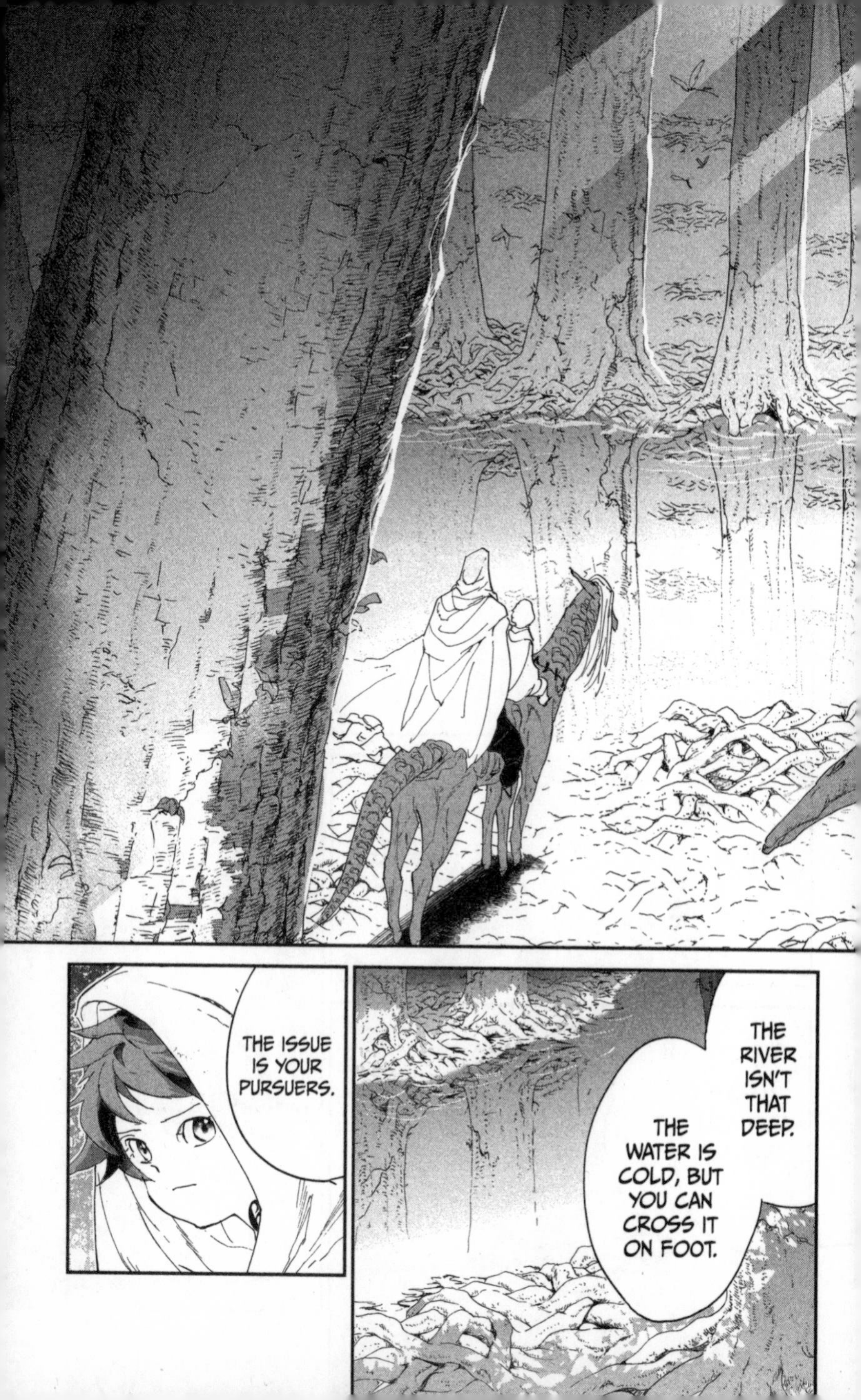
THE RIVER ISN'T THAT DEEP.
THE WATER IS COLD, BUT YOU CAN CROSS IT ON FOOT.
THE ISSUE IS YOUR PURSUERS.

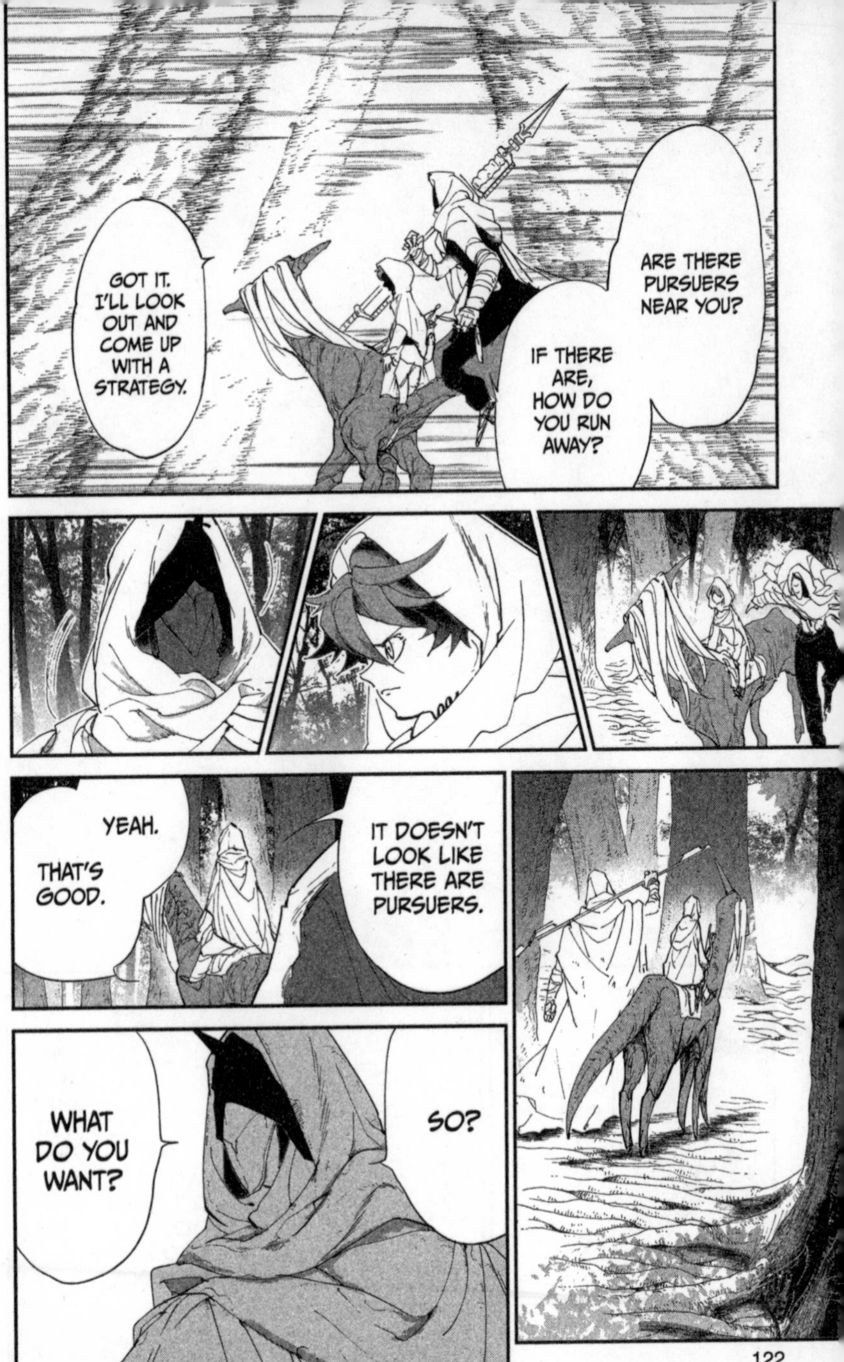
ARE THERE PURSUERS NEAR YOU?
IF THERE ARE, HOW DO YOU RUN AWAY?
GOT IT. I'LL LOOK OUT AND COME UP WITH A STRATEGY.
IT DOESN'T LOOK LIKE THERE ARE PURSUERS.
YEAH.
THAT'S GOOD.
SO?
WHAT DO YOU WANT?

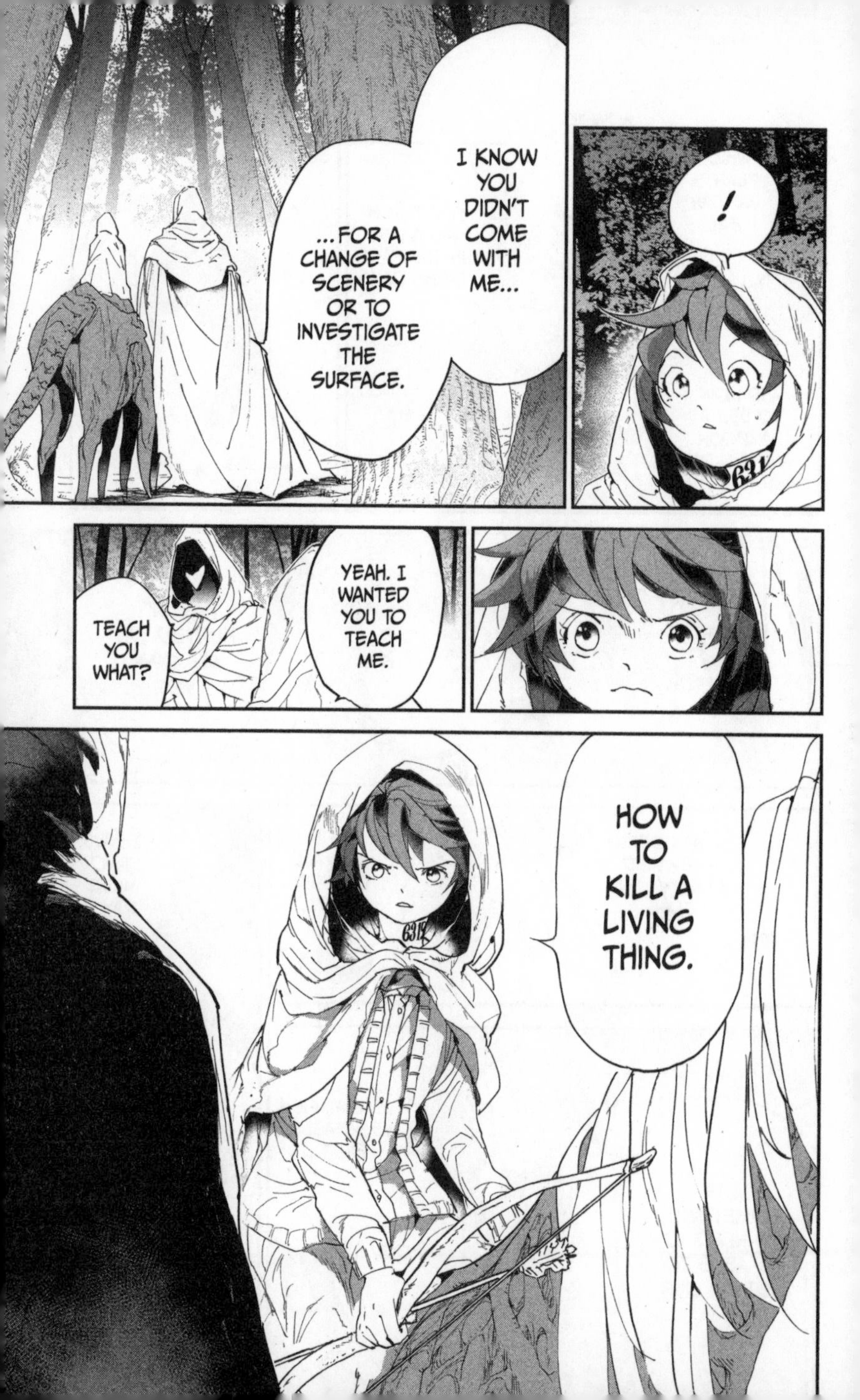
!
I KNOW YOU DIDN'T COME WITH ME...
...FOR A CHANGE OF SCENERY OR TO INVESTIGATE THE SURFACE.
YEAH. I WANTED YOU TO TEACH ME.
TEACH YOU WHAT?
HOW TO KILL A LIVING THING.

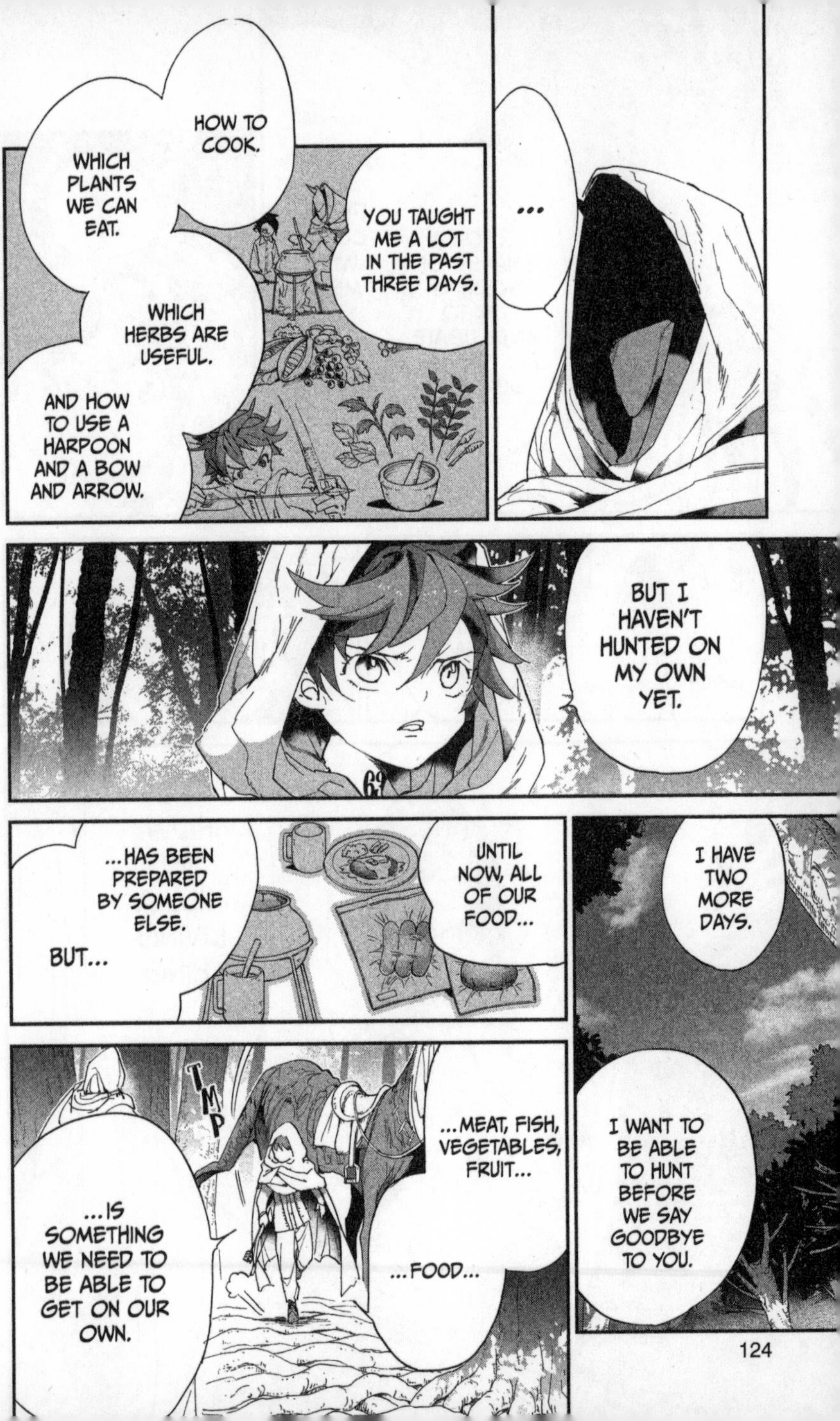
...
YOU TAUGHT ME A LOT IN THE PAST THREE DAYS.
HOW TO COOK.
WHICH PLANTS WE CAN EAT.
WHICH HERBS ARE USEFUL.
AND HOW TO USE A HARPOON AND A BOW AND ARROW.
BUT I HAVEN'T HUNTED ON MY OWN YET.
I HAVE TWO MORE DAYS.
I WANT TO BE ABLE TO HUNT BEFORE WE SAY GOODBYE TO YOU.
UNTIL NOW, ALL OF OUR FOOD...
...HAS BEEN PREPARED BY SOMEONE ELSE.
BUT...
TMP
...MEAT, FISH, VEGETABLES, FRUIT...
...FOOD...
...IS SOMETHING WE NEED TO BE ABLE TO GET ON OUR OWN.

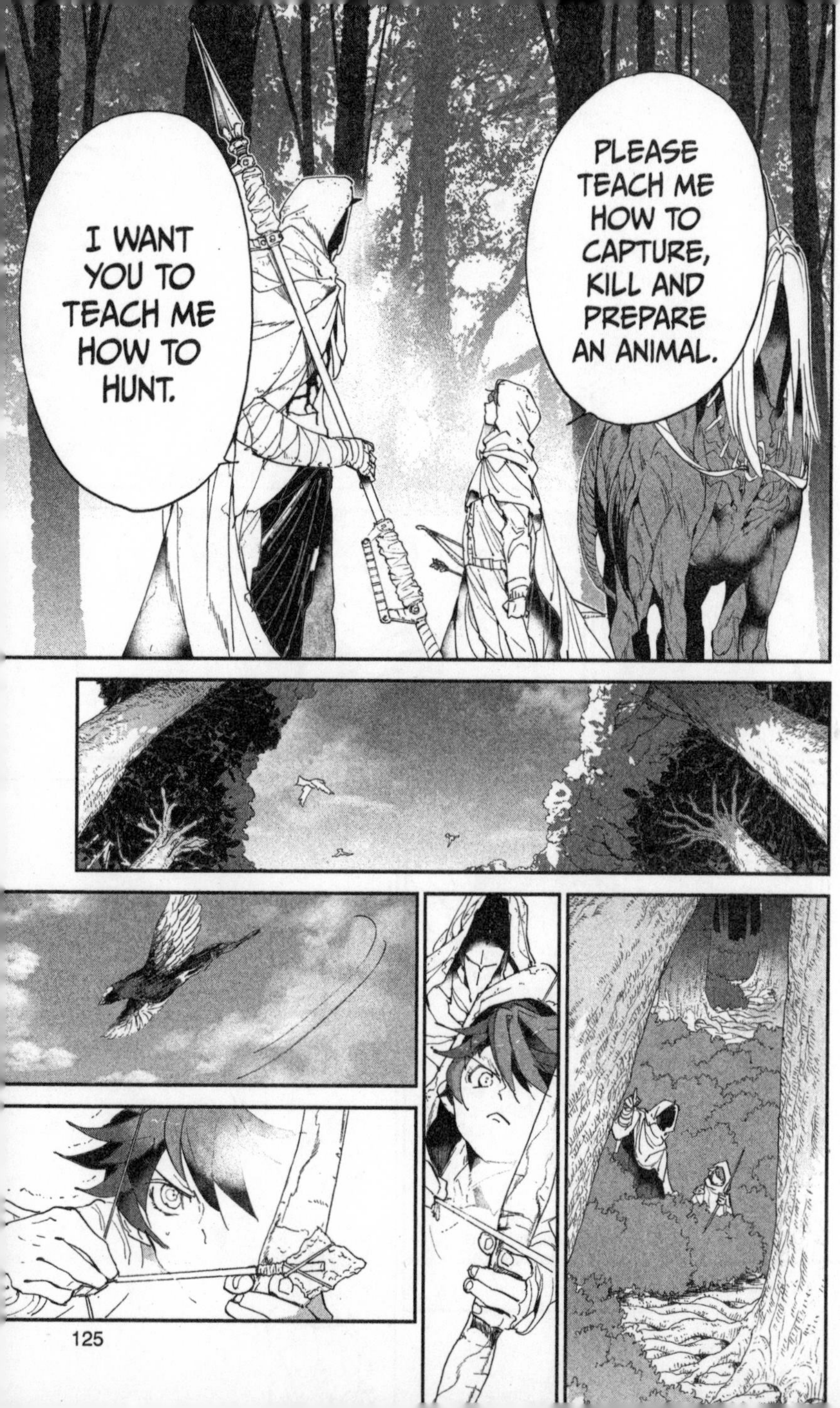
PLEASE TEACH ME HOW TO CAPTURE, KILL AND PREPARE AN ANIMAL.
I WANT YOU TO TEACH ME HOW TO HUNT.

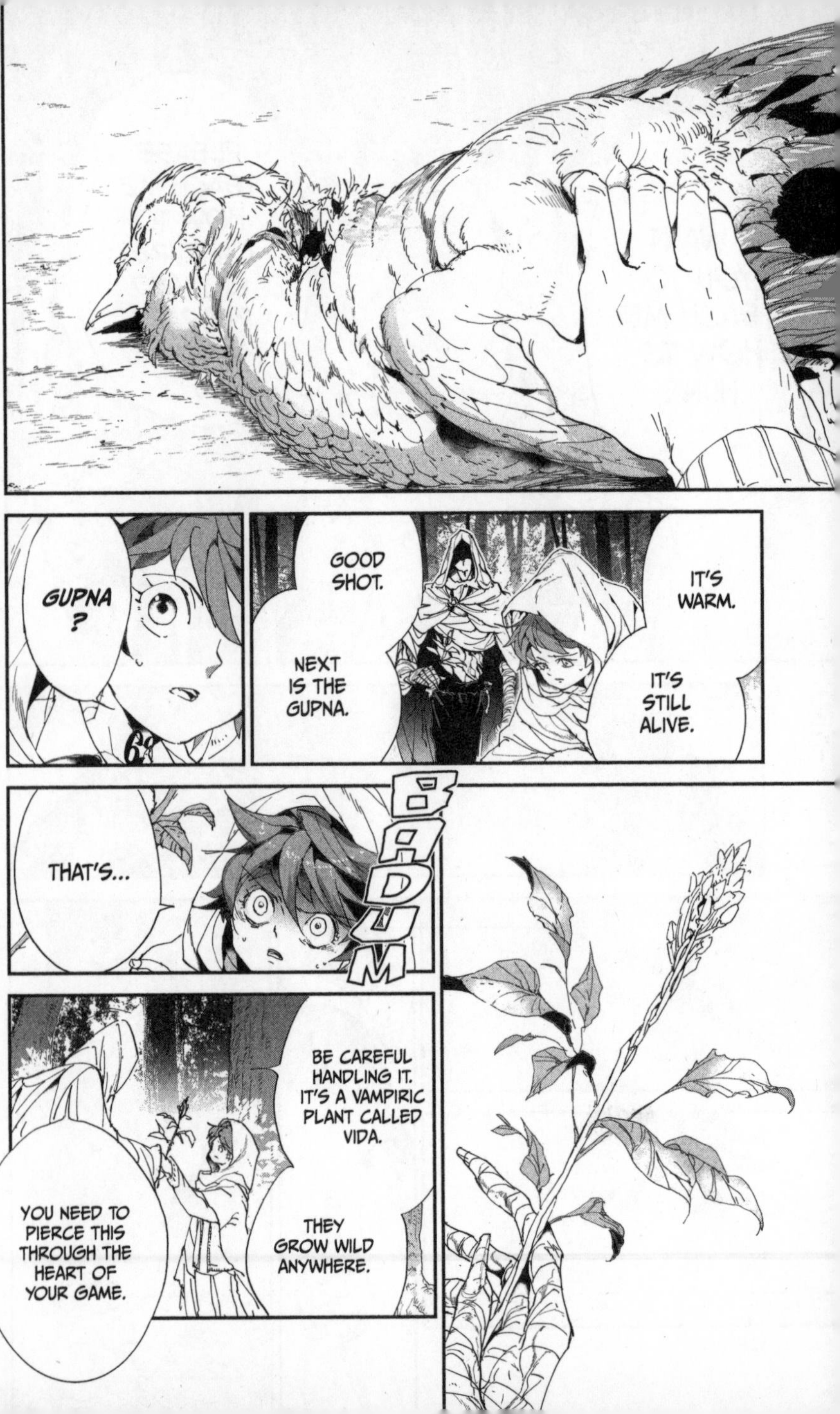
IT'S WARM.
IT'S STILL ALIVE.
GOOD SHOT.
NEXT IS THE GUPNA.
GUPNA?
BADUM
THAT'S...
BE CAREFUL HANDLING IT. IT'S A VAMPIRIC PLANT CALLED VIDA.
THEY GROW WILD ANYWHERE.
YOU NEED TO PIERCE THIS THROUGH THE HEART OF YOUR GAME.

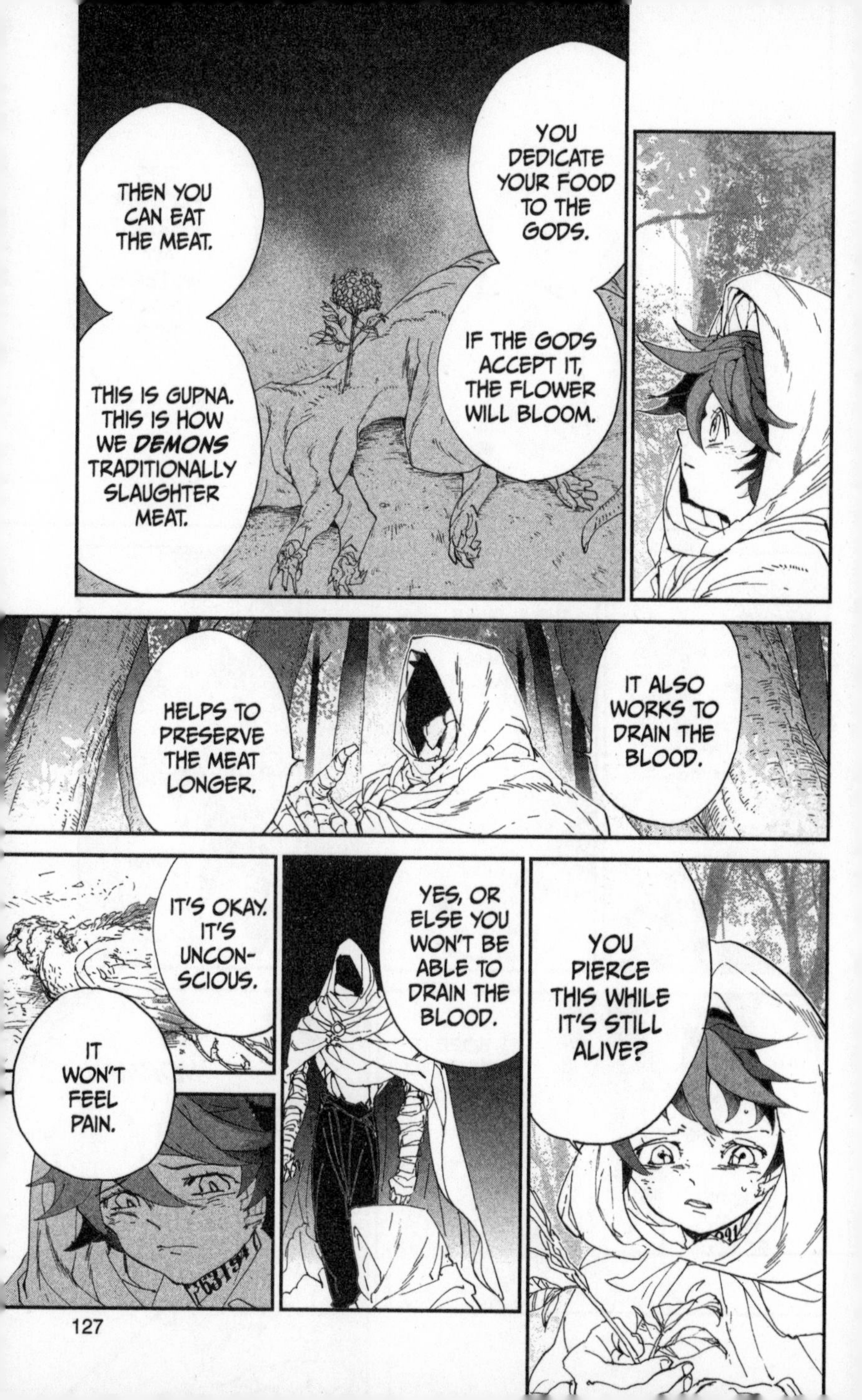
YOU DEDICATE YOUR FOOD TO THE GODS.
IF THE GODS ACCEPT IT, THE FLOWER WILL BLOOM.
THEN YOU CAN EAT THE MEAT.
THIS IS GUPNA. THIS IS HOW WE *DEMONS* TRADITIONALLY SLAUGHTER MEAT.
IT ALSO WORKS TO DRAIN THE BLOOD.
HELPS TO PRESERVE THE MEAT LONGER.
YOU PIERCE THIS WHILE IT'S STILL ALIVE?
YES, OR ELSE YOU WON'T BE ABLE TO DRAIN THE BLOOD.
IT'S OKAY. IT'S UNCON-SCIOUS.
IT WON'T FEEL PAIN.

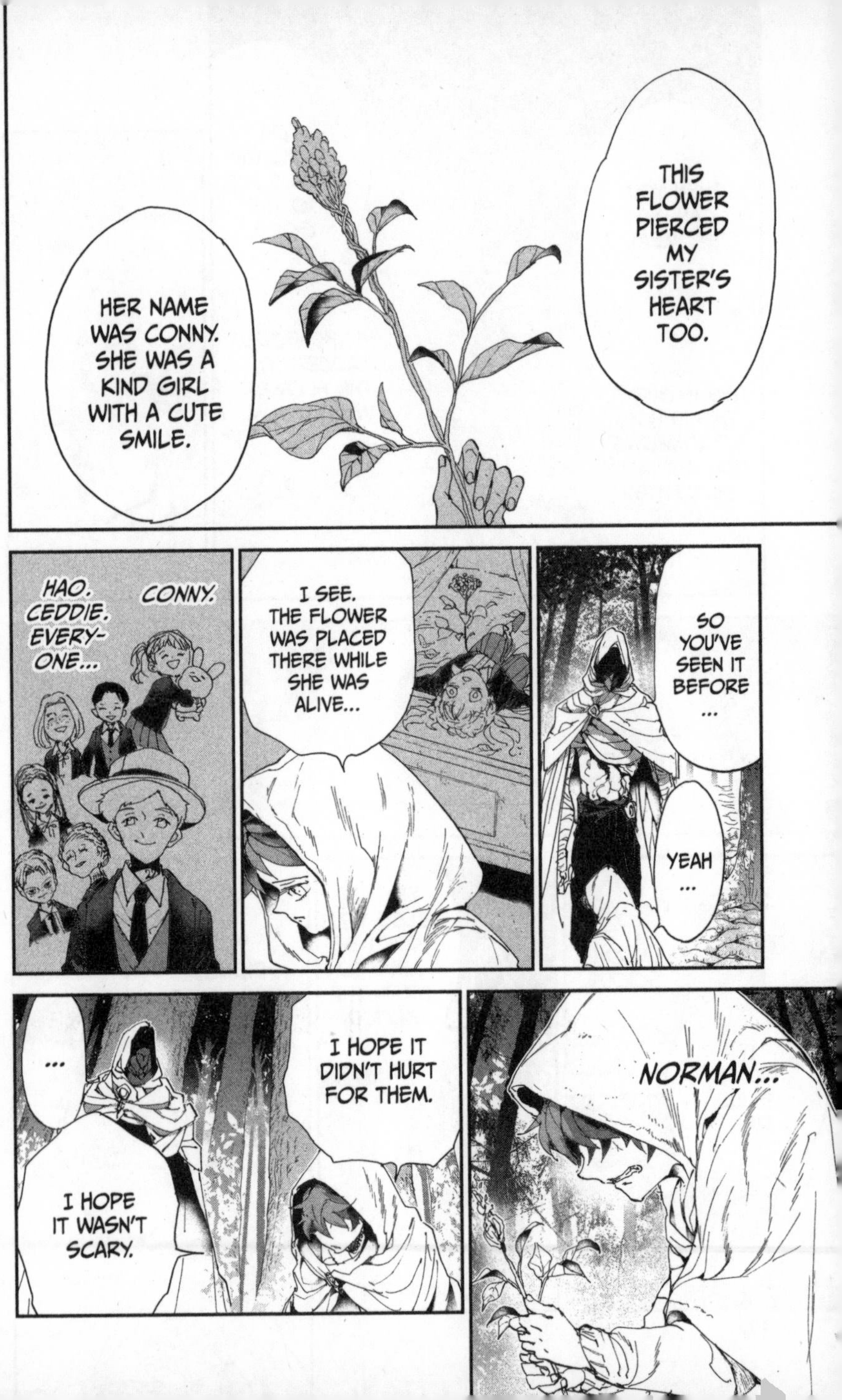
THIS FLOWER PIERCED MY SISTER'S HEART TOO.
HER NAME WAS CONNY. SHE WAS A KIND GIRL WITH A CUTE SMILE.
SO YOU'VE SEEN IT BEFORE ...
YEAH ...
I SEE. THE FLOWER WAS PLACED THERE WHILE SHE WAS ALIVE...
CONNY.
HAO. CEDDIE. EVERY-ONE...
NORMAN...
I HOPE IT DIDN'T HURT FOR THEM.
...
I HOPE IT WASN'T SCARY.

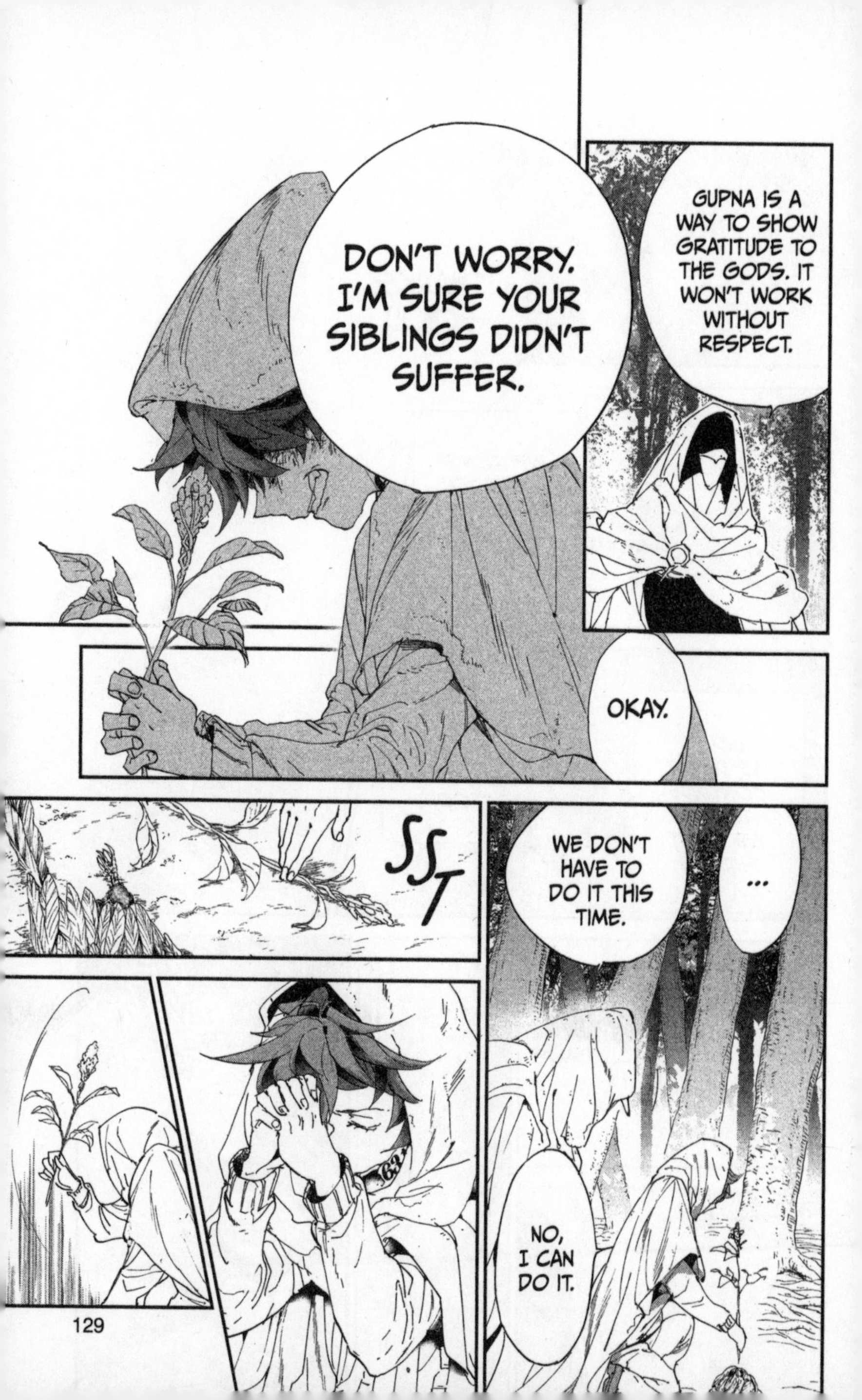
GUPNA IS A WAY TO SHOW GRATITUDE TO THE GODS. IT WON'T WORK WITHOUT RESPECT.
DON'T WORRY. I'M SURE YOUR SIBLINGS DIDN'T SUFFER.
OKAY.
...
WE DON'T HAVE TO DO IT THIS TIME.
NO, I CAN DO IT.
SST

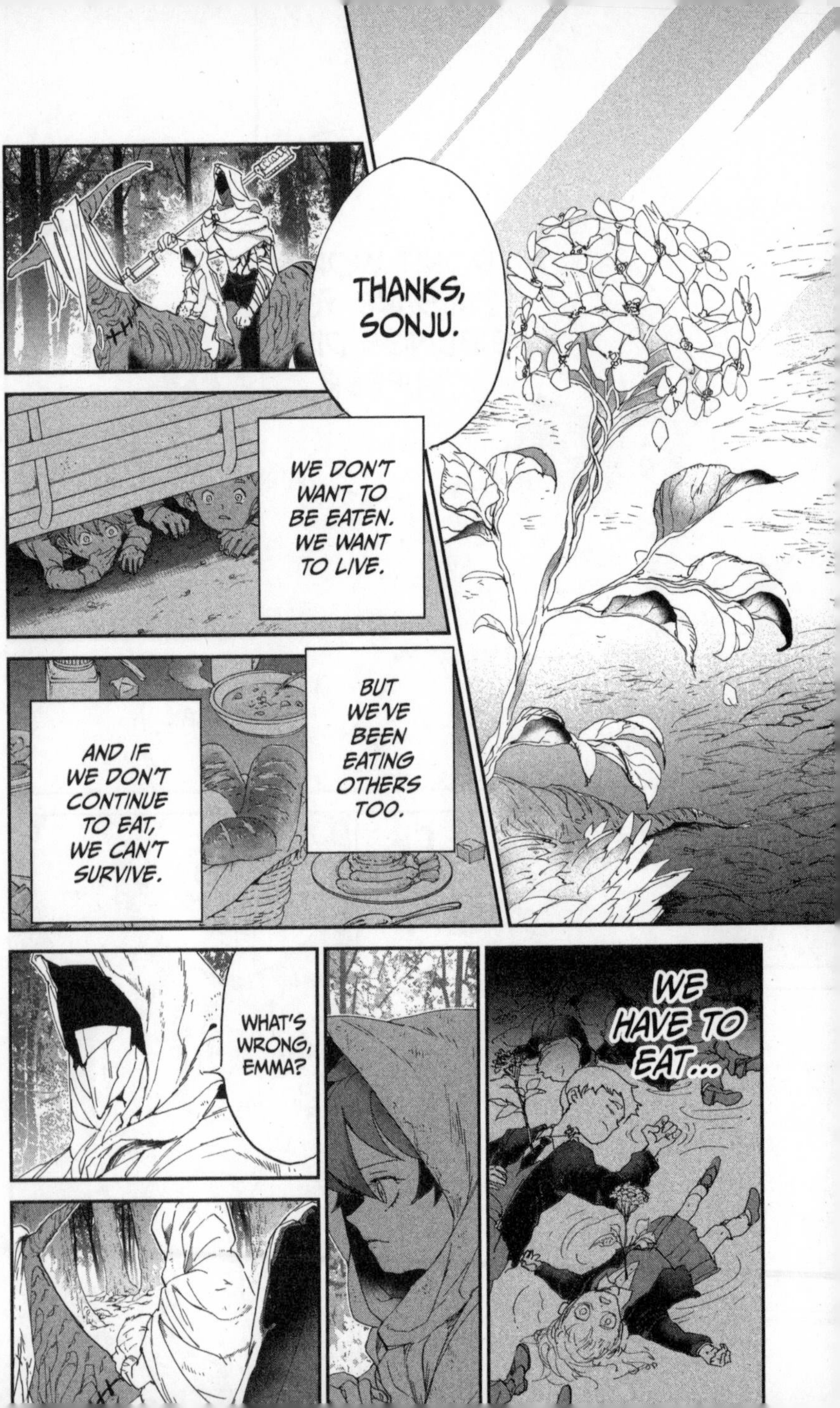
THANKS, SONJU.
WE DON'T WANT TO BE EATEN. WE WANT TO LIVE.
BUT WE'VE BEEN EATING OTHERS TOO.
AND IF WE DON'T CONTINUE TO EAT, WE CAN'T SURVIVE.
WE HAVE TO EAT...
WHAT'S WRONG, EMMA?

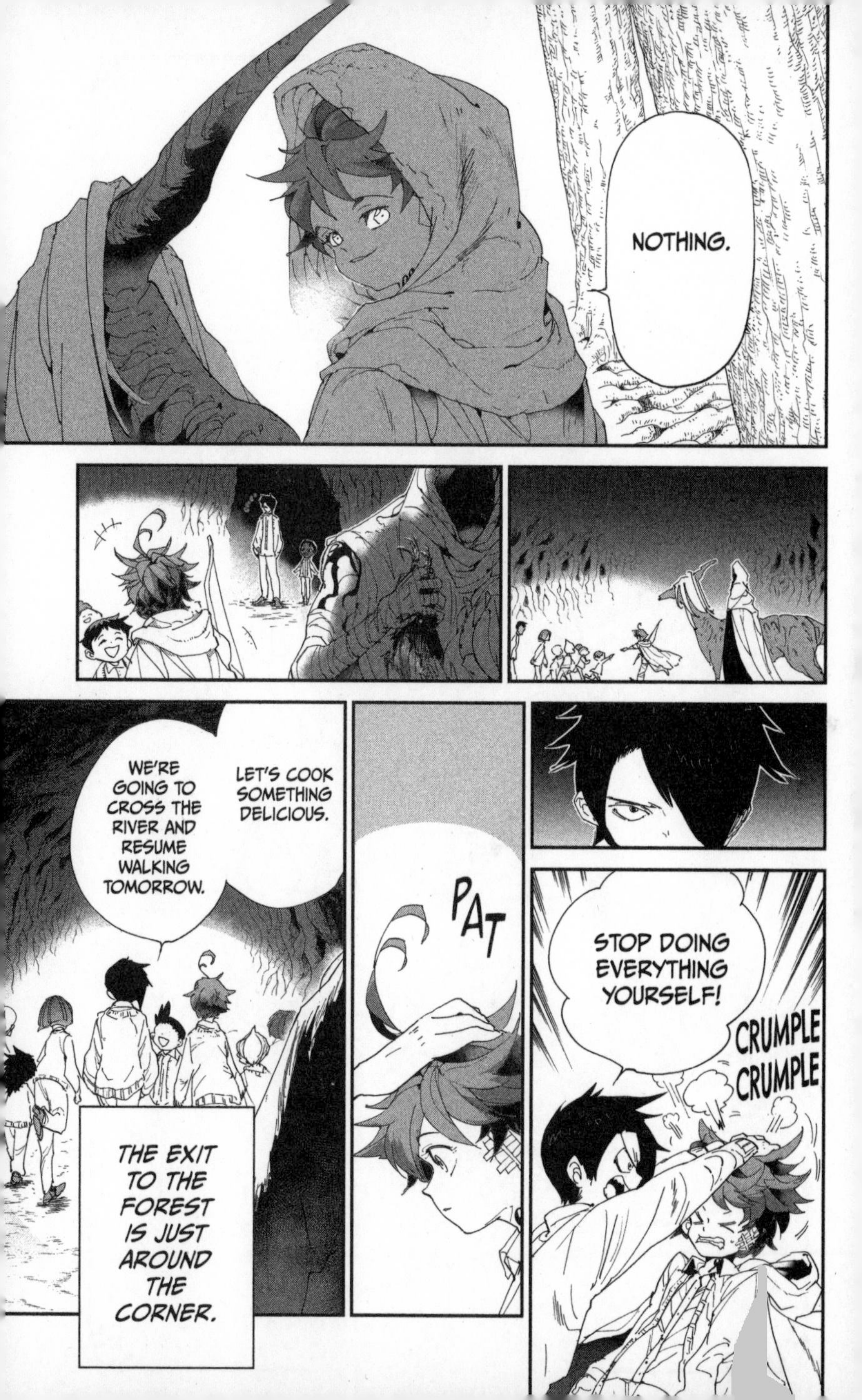
NOTHING.
STOP DOING EVERYTHING YOURSELF!
CRUMPLE CRUMPLE
PAT
LET'S COOK SOMETHING DELICIOUS.
WE'RE GOING TO CROSS THE RIVER AND RESUME WALKING TOMORROW.
THE EXIT TO THE FOREST IS JUST AROUND THE CORNER.

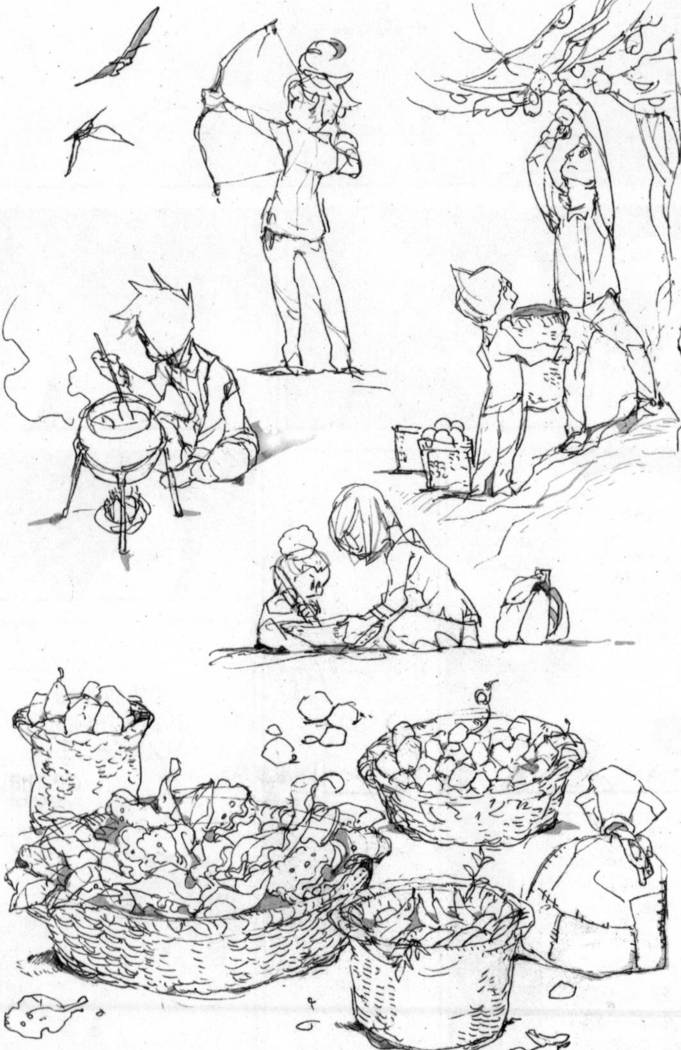

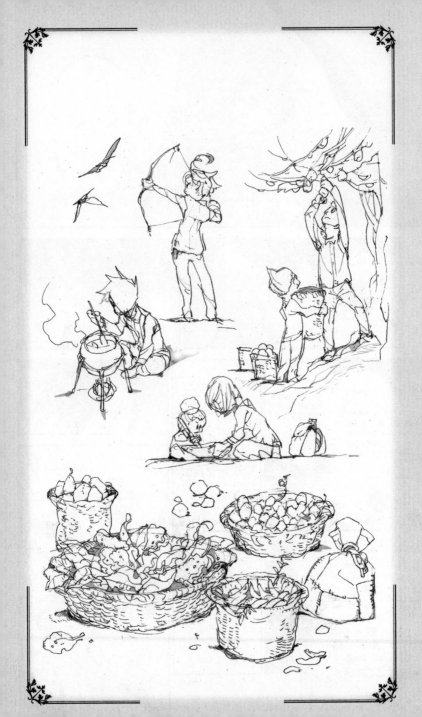

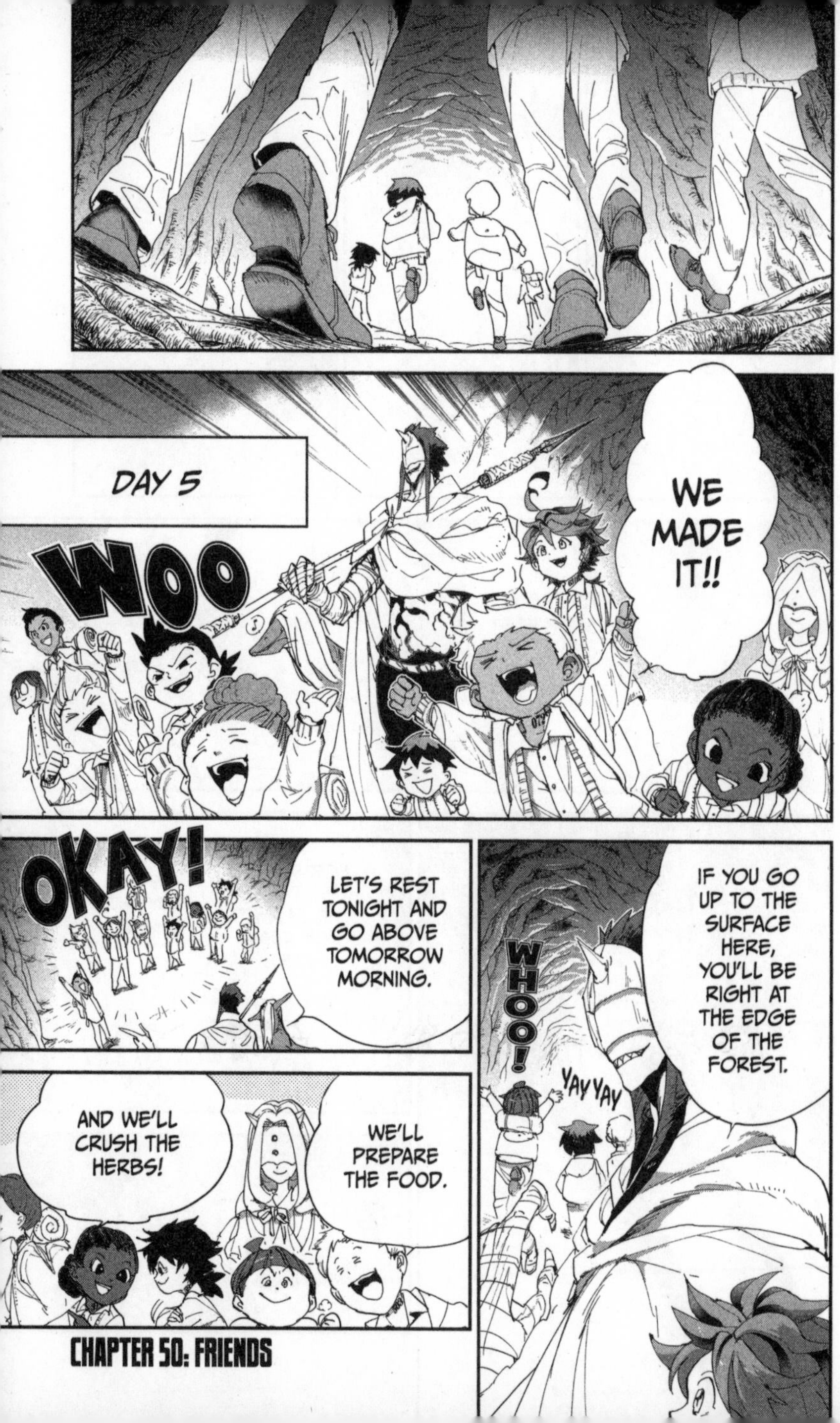
WE MADE IT!!
DAY 5
WOO
IF YOU GO UP TO THE SURFACE HERE, YOU'LL BE RIGHT AT THE EDGE OF THE FOREST.
WHOOO!
YAY YAY
LET'S REST TONIGHT AND GO ABOVE TOMORROW MORNING.
OKAY!
WE'LL PREPARE THE FOOD.
AND WE'LL CRUSH THE HERBS!

CHAPTER 50: FRIENDS

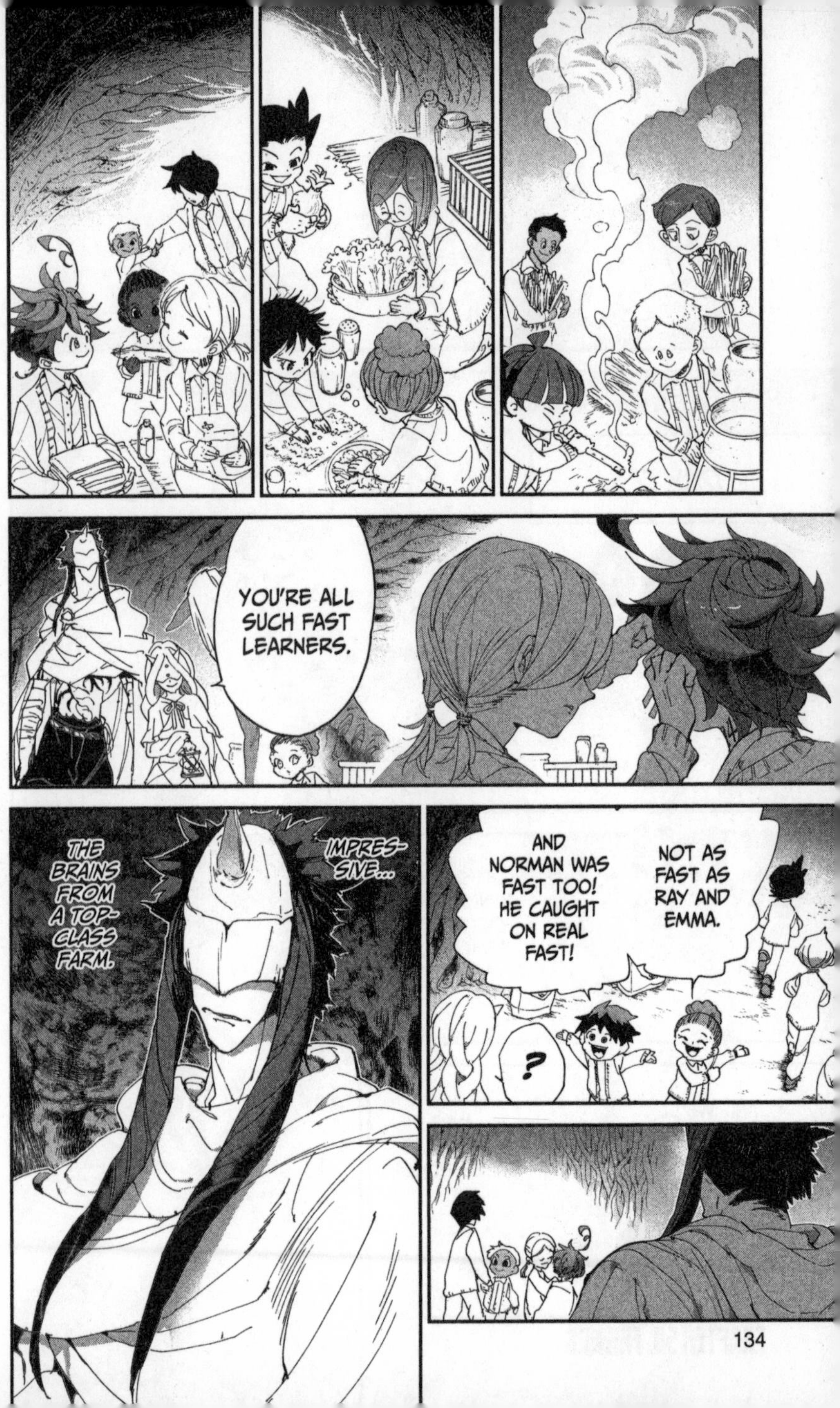
YOU'RE ALL SUCH FAST LEARNERS.
NOT AS FAST AS RAY AND EMMA.
AND NORMAN WAS FAST TOO! HE CAUGHT ON REAL FAST!
?
IMPRES-SIVE...
THE BRAINS FROM A TOP-CLASS FARM.

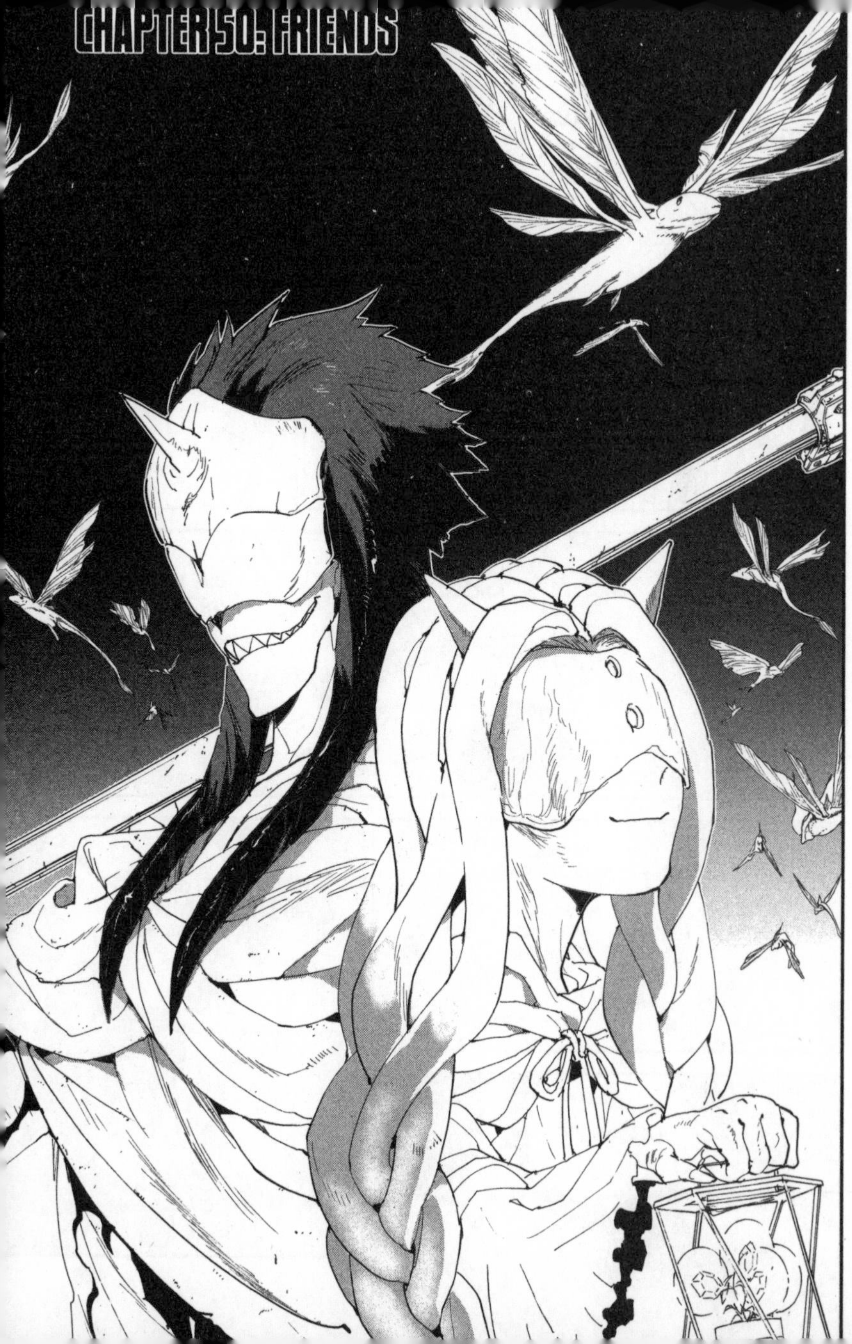
CHAPTER 50: FRIENDS

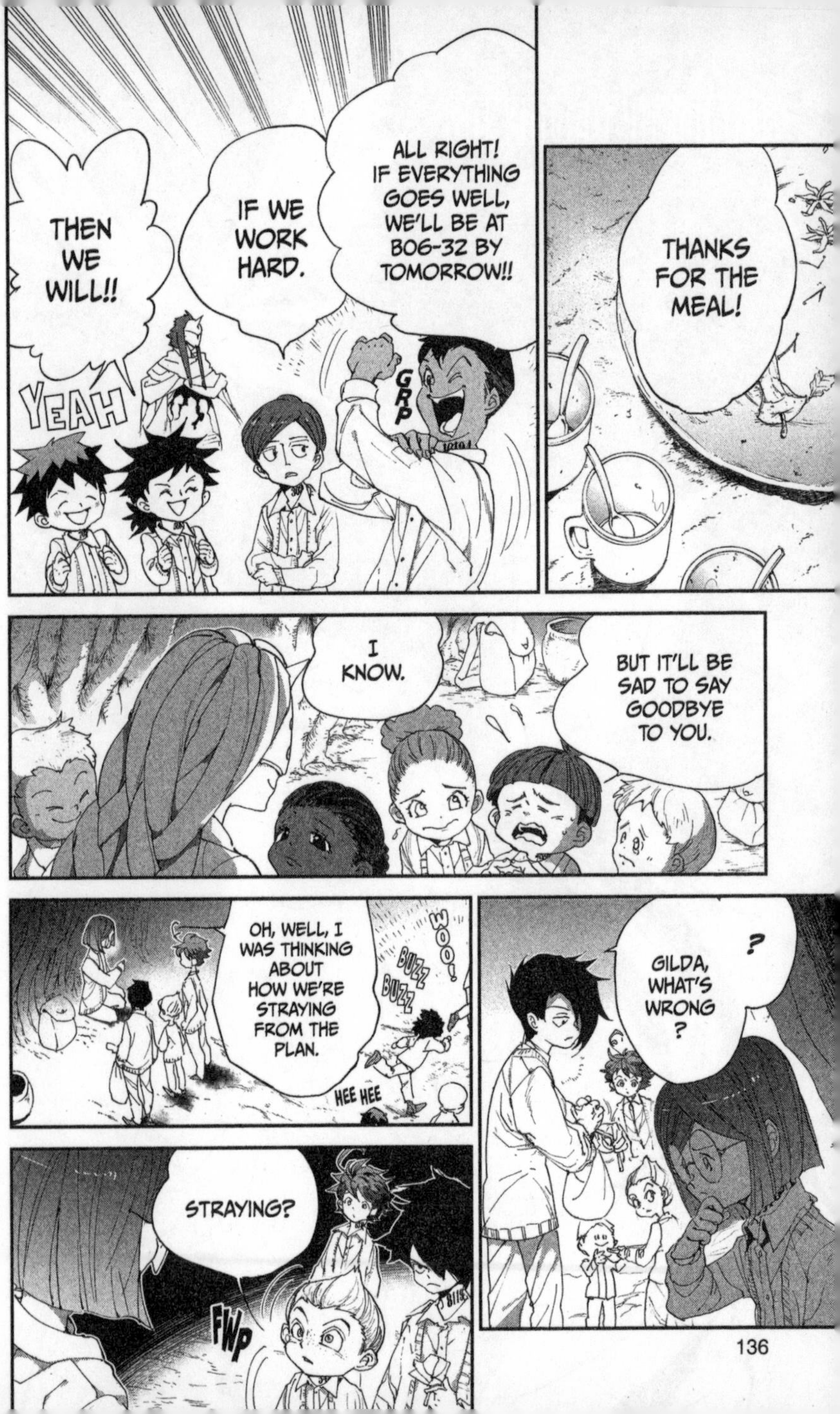
THANKS FOR THE MEAL!
ALL RIGHT! IF EVERYTHING GOES WELL, WE'LL BE AT B06-32 BY TOMORROW!!
GRP
IF WE WORK HARD.
THEN WE WILL!!
YEAH
BUT IT'LL BE SAD TO SAY GOODBYE TO YOU.
I KNOW.
?
GILDA, WHAT'S WRONG?
WOO!
OH, WELL, I WAS THINKING ABOUT HOW WE'RE STRAYING FROM THE PLAN.
BUZZ BUZZ
HEE HEE
STRAYING?
FWP

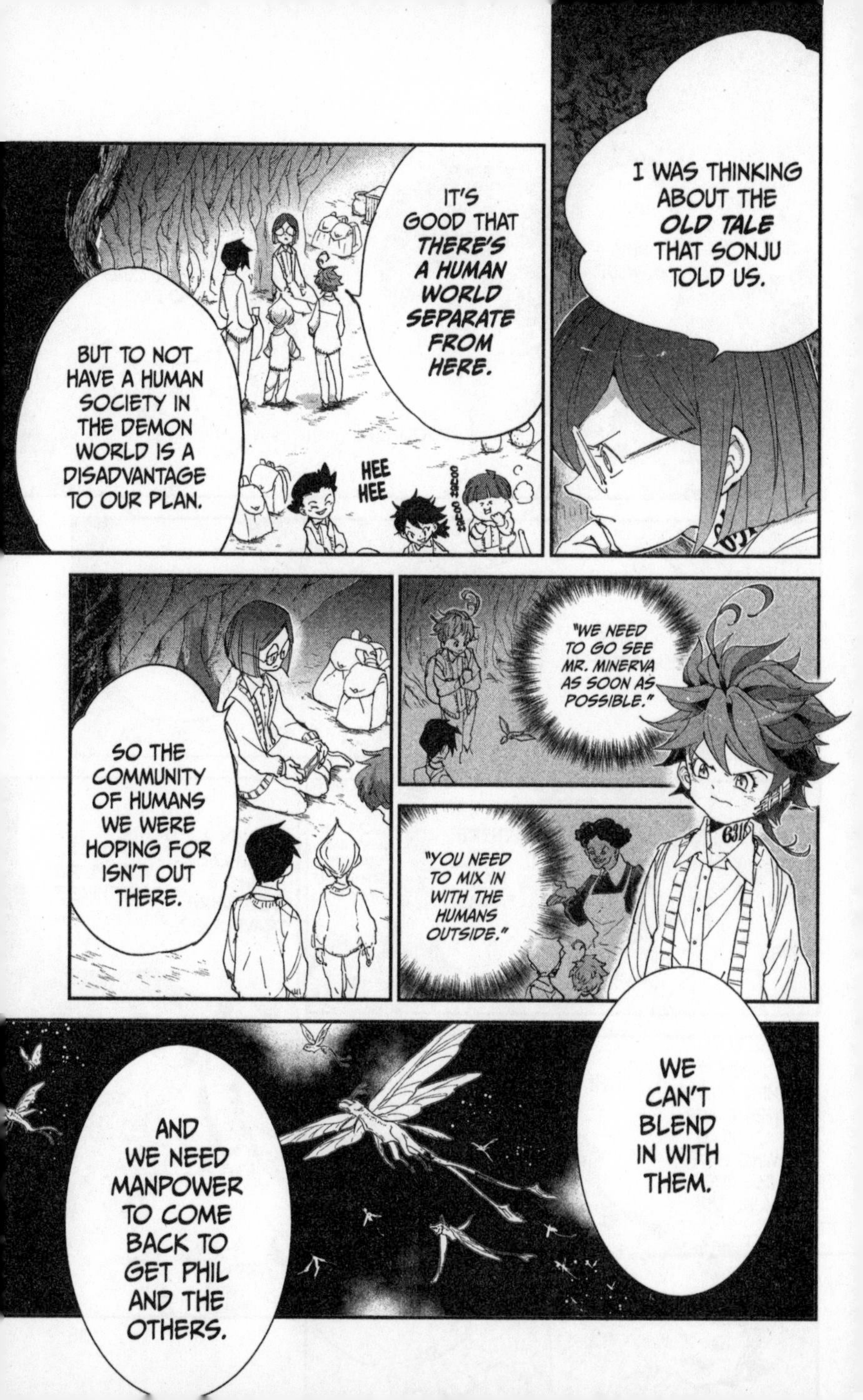
I WAS THINKING ABOUT THE *OLD TALE* THAT SONJU TOLD US.
IT'S GOOD THAT *THERE'S A HUMAN WORLD SEPARATE FROM HERE.*
BUT TO NOT HAVE A HUMAN SOCIETY IN THE DEMON WORLD IS A DISADVANTAGE TO OUR PLAN.
HEE HEE
"WE NEED TO GO SEE MR. MINERVA AS SOON AS POSSIBLE."
"YOU NEED TO MIX IN WITH THE HUMANS OUTSIDE."
SO THE COMMUNITY OF HUMANS WE WERE HOPING FOR ISN'T OUT THERE.
WE CAN'T BLEND IN WITH THEM.
AND WE NEED MANPOWER TO COME BACK TO GET PHIL AND THE OTHERS.

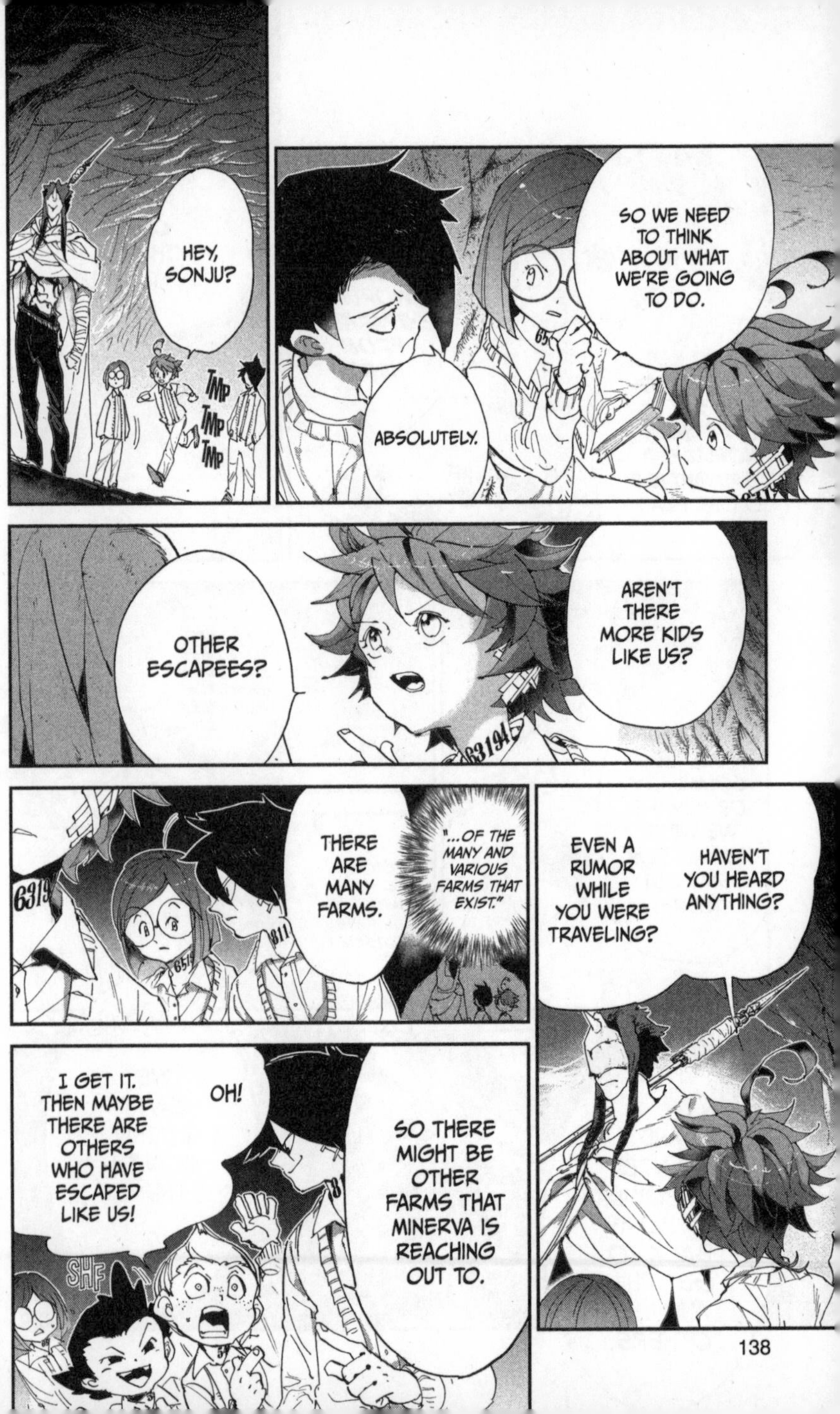
SO WE NEED TO THINK ABOUT WHAT WE'RE GOING TO DO.
ABSOLUTELY.
HEY, SONJU?
TMP
TMP
TMP
AREN'T THERE MORE KIDS LIKE US?
OTHER ESCAPEES?
HAVEN'T YOU HEARD ANYTHING?
EVEN A RUMOR WHILE YOU WERE TRAVELING?
"...OF THE MANY AND VARIOUS FARMS THAT EXIST."
THERE ARE MANY FARMS.
SO THERE MIGHT BE OTHER FARMS THAT MINERVA IS REACHING OUT TO.
OH!
I GET IT. THEN MAYBE THERE ARE OTHERS WHO HAVE ESCAPED LIKE US!
SHF

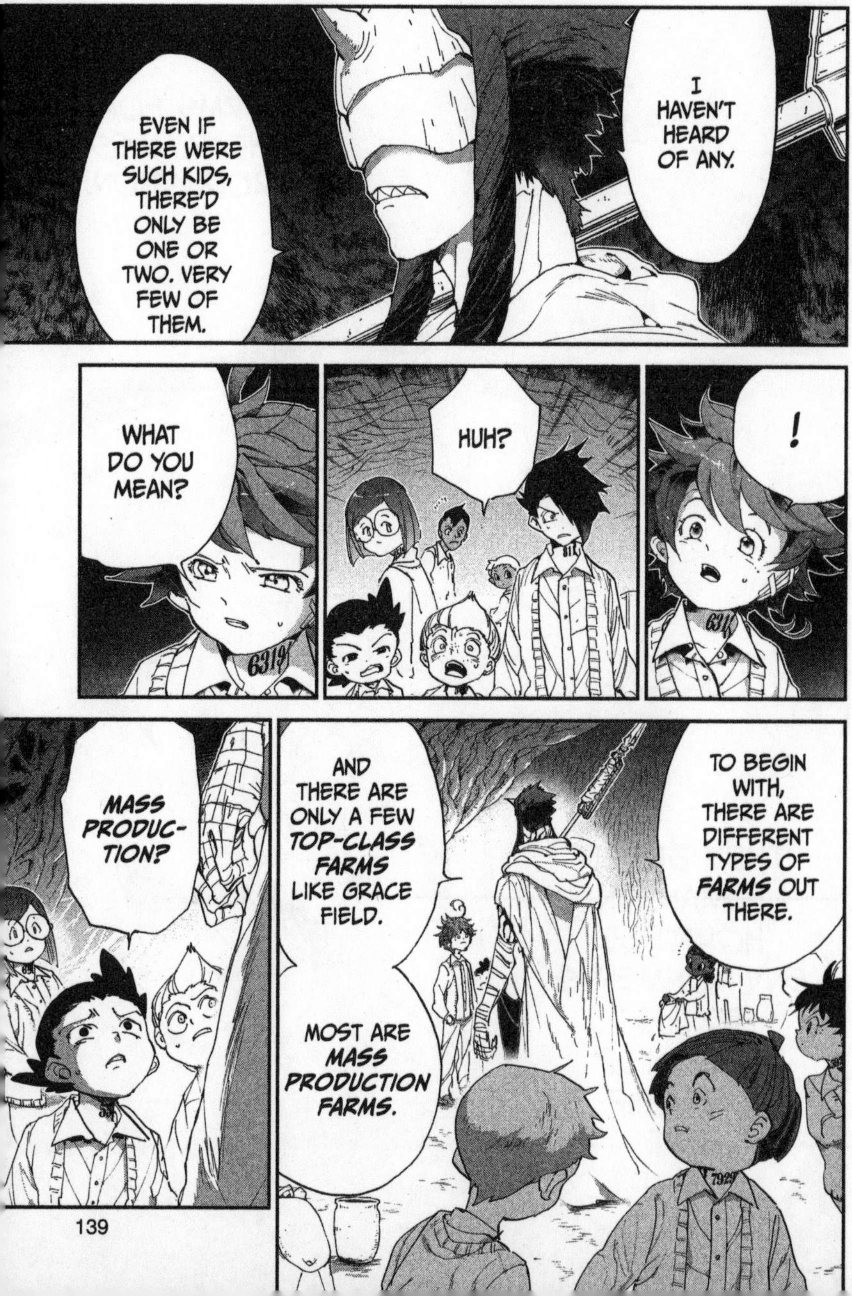
I HAVEN'T HEARD OF ANY.
EVEN IF THERE WERE SUCH KIDS, THERE'D ONLY BE ONE OR TWO. VERY FEW OF THEM.
!
HUH?
WHAT DO YOU MEAN?
TO BEGIN WITH, THERE ARE DIFFERENT TYPES OF *FARMS* OUT THERE.
AND THERE ARE ONLY A FEW *TOP-CLASS FARMS* LIKE GRACE FIELD.
MOST ARE *MASS PRODUCTION FARMS.*
MASS PRODUC-TION?

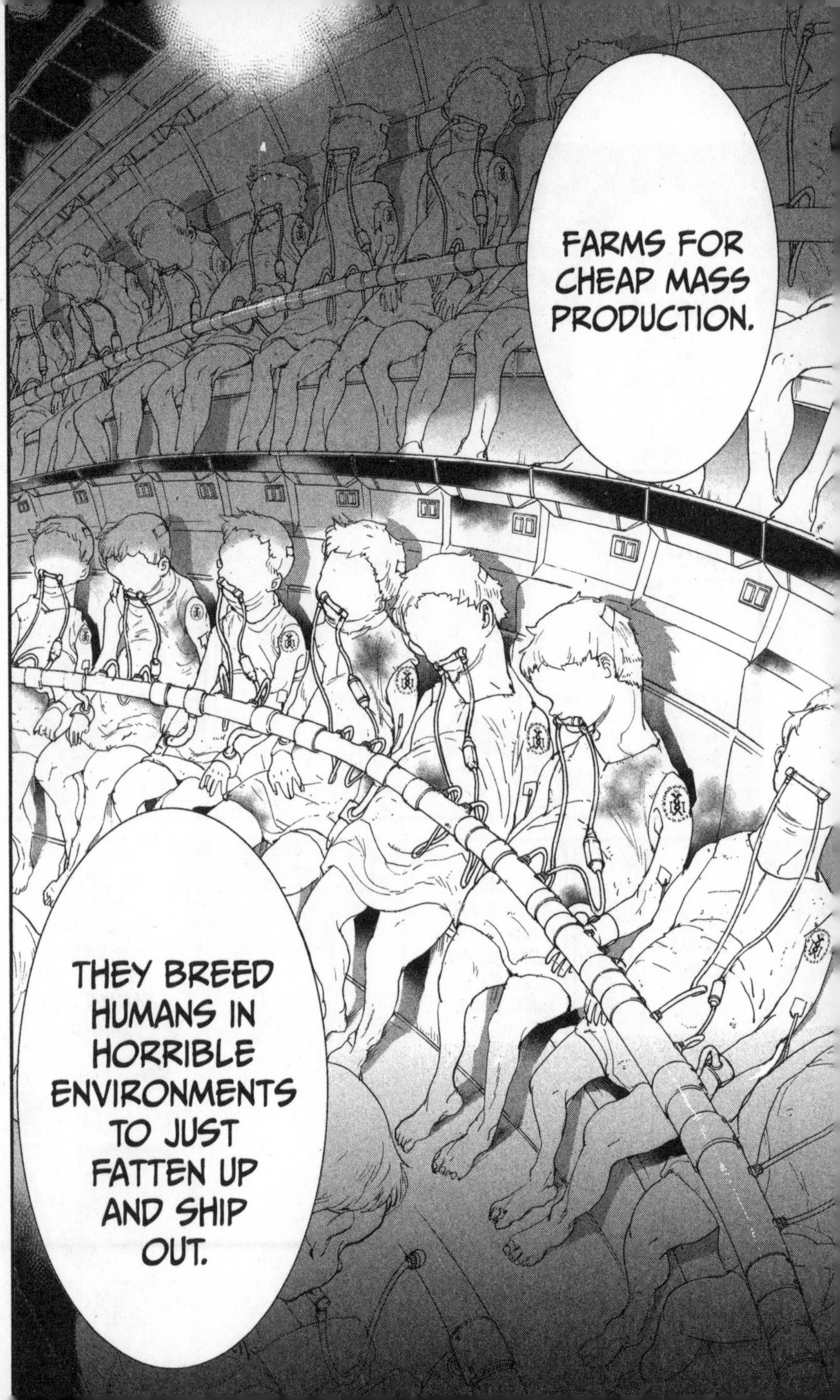
FARMS FOR CHEAP MASS PRODUCTION.
THEY BREED HUMANS IN HORRIBLE ENVIRONMENTS TO JUST FATTEN UP AND SHIP OUT.

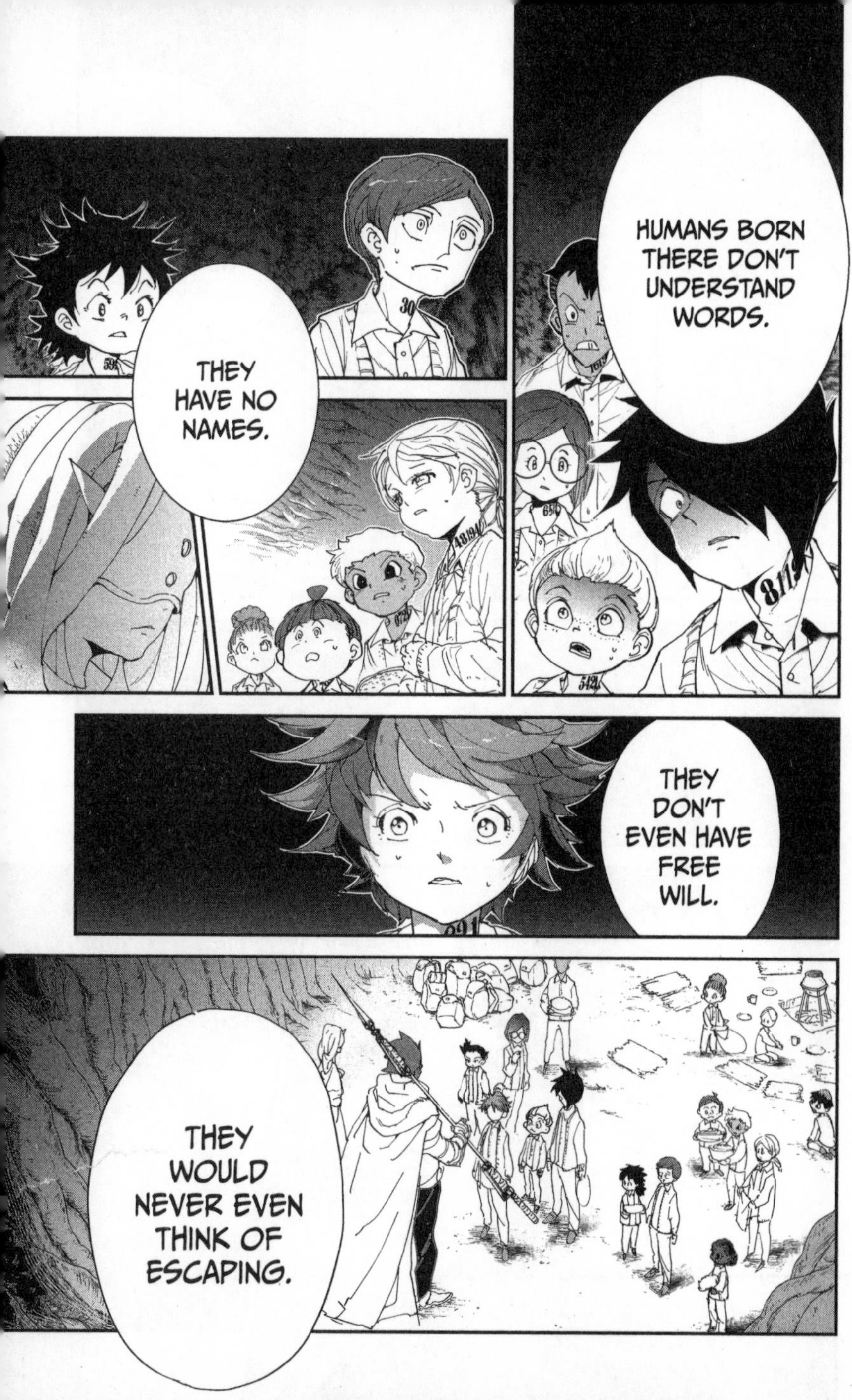
HUMANS BORN THERE DON'T UNDERSTAND WORDS.
THEY HAVE NO NAMES.
THEY DON'T EVEN HAVE FREE WILL.
THEY WOULD NEVER EVEN THINK OF ESCAPING.

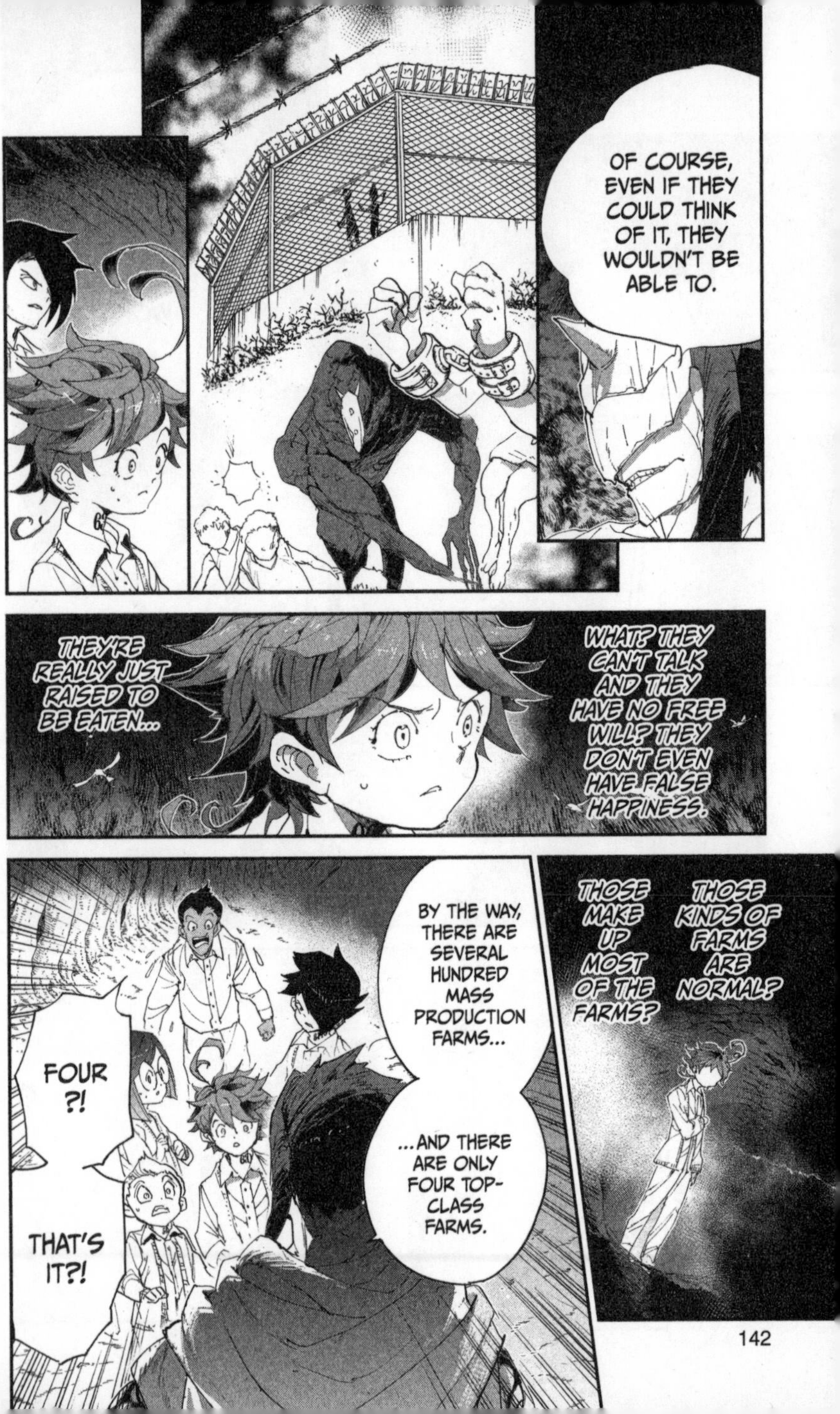
OF COURSE, EVEN IF THEY COULD THINK OF IT, THEY WOULDN'T BE ABLE TO.
WHAT? THEY CAN'T TALK AND THEY HAVE NO FREE WILL? THEY DON'T EVEN HAVE FALSE HAPPINESS.
THEY'RE REALLY JUST RAISED TO BE EATEN...
THOSE KINDS OF FARMS ARE NORMAL?
THOSE MAKE UP MOST OF THE FARMS?
BY THE WAY, THERE ARE SEVERAL HUNDRED MASS PRODUCTION FARMS...
...AND THERE ARE ONLY FOUR TOP-CLASS FARMS.
FOUR ?!
THAT'S IT?!

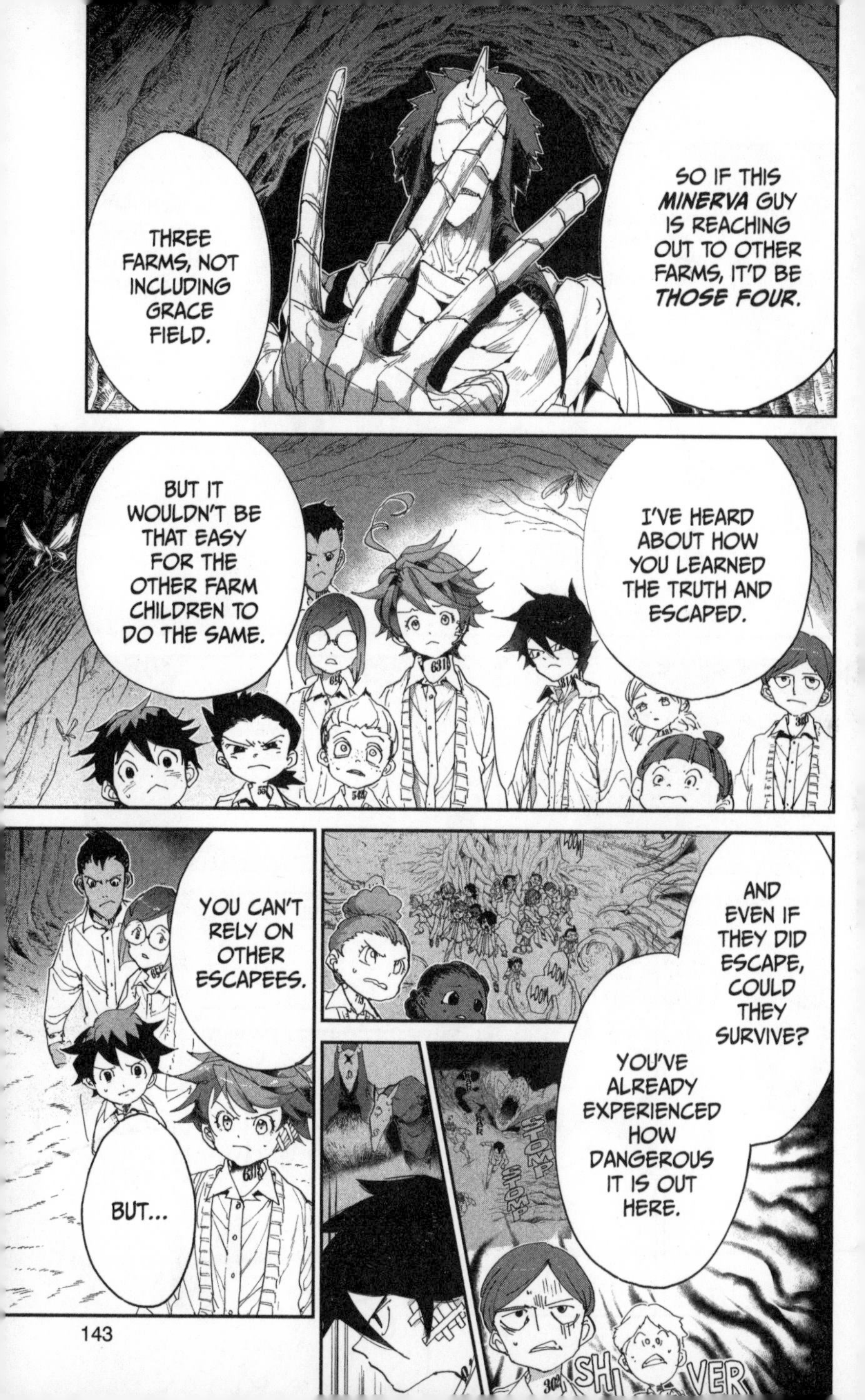

SO IF THIS *MINERVA* GUY IS REACHING OUT TO OTHER FARMS, IT'D BE *THOSE FOUR*.
THREE FARMS, NOT INCLUDING GRACE FIELD.
I'VE HEARD ABOUT HOW YOU LEARNED THE TRUTH AND ESCAPED.
BUT IT WOULDN'T BE THAT EASY FOR THE OTHER FARM CHILDREN TO DO THE SAME.
LOOM
LOOM
LOOM
AND EVEN IF THEY DID ESCAPE, COULD THEY SURVIVE?
YOU'VE ALREADY EXPERIENCED HOW DANGEROUS IT IS OUT HERE.
STOMP
STOMP
SHIVER
YOU CAN'T RELY ON OTHER ESCAPEES.
BUT...

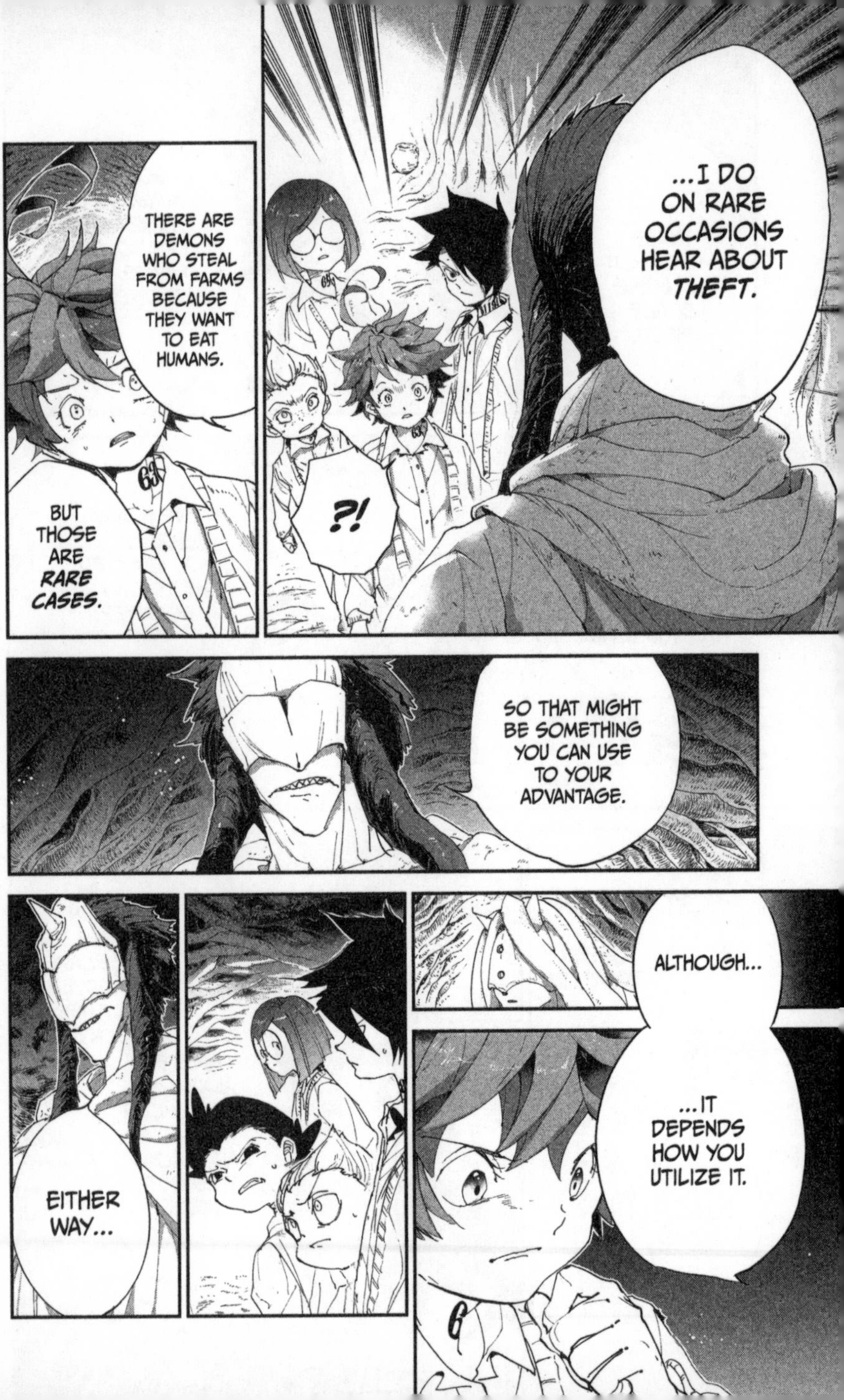
...I DO ON RARE OCCASIONS HEAR ABOUT *THEFT*.
?!
THERE ARE DEMONS WHO STEAL FROM FARMS BECAUSE THEY WANT TO EAT HUMANS.
BUT THOSE ARE *RARE CASES*.
SO THAT MIGHT BE SOMETHING YOU CAN USE TO YOUR ADVANTAGE.
ALTHOUGH...
...IT DEPENDS HOW YOU UTILIZE IT.
EITHER WAY...

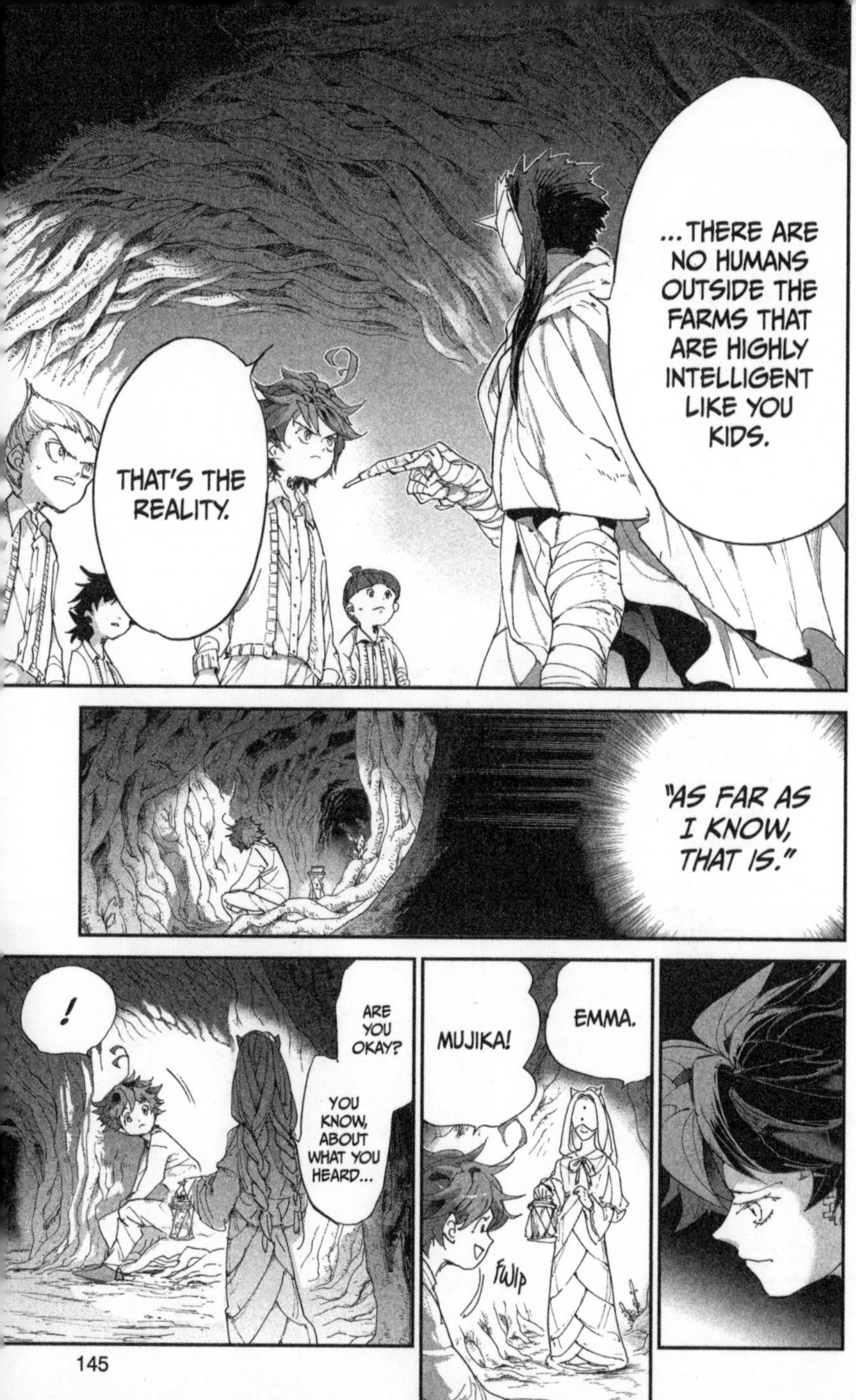

...THERE ARE NO HUMANS OUTSIDE THE FARMS THAT ARE HIGHLY INTELLIGENT LIKE YOU KIDS.
THAT'S THE REALITY.
"AS FAR AS I KNOW, THAT IS."
EMMA.
MUJIKA!
FWIP
ARE YOU OKAY?
YOU KNOW, ABOUT WHAT YOU HEARD...
!

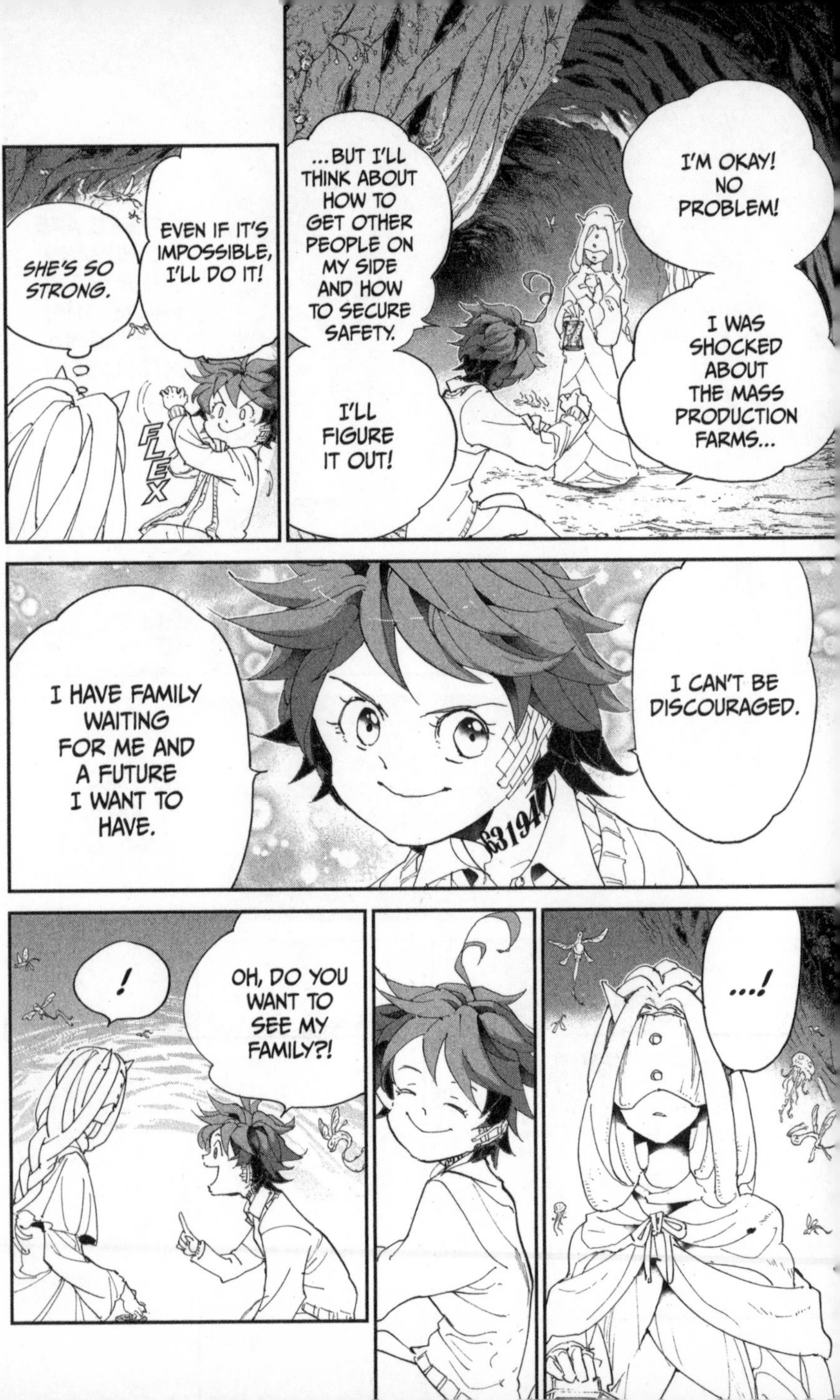
I'M OKAY! NO PROBLEM!
I WAS SHOCKED ABOUT THE MASS PRODUCTION FARMS...
...BUT I'LL THINK ABOUT HOW TO GET OTHER PEOPLE ON MY SIDE AND HOW TO SECURE SAFETY.
I'LL FIGURE IT OUT!
EVEN IF IT'S IMPOSSIBLE, I'LL DO IT!
FLEX
SHE'S SO STRONG.
I CAN'T BE DISCOURAGED.
I HAVE FAMILY WAITING FOR ME AND A FUTURE I WANT TO HAVE.
...!
OH, DO YOU WANT TO SEE MY FAMILY?!
!

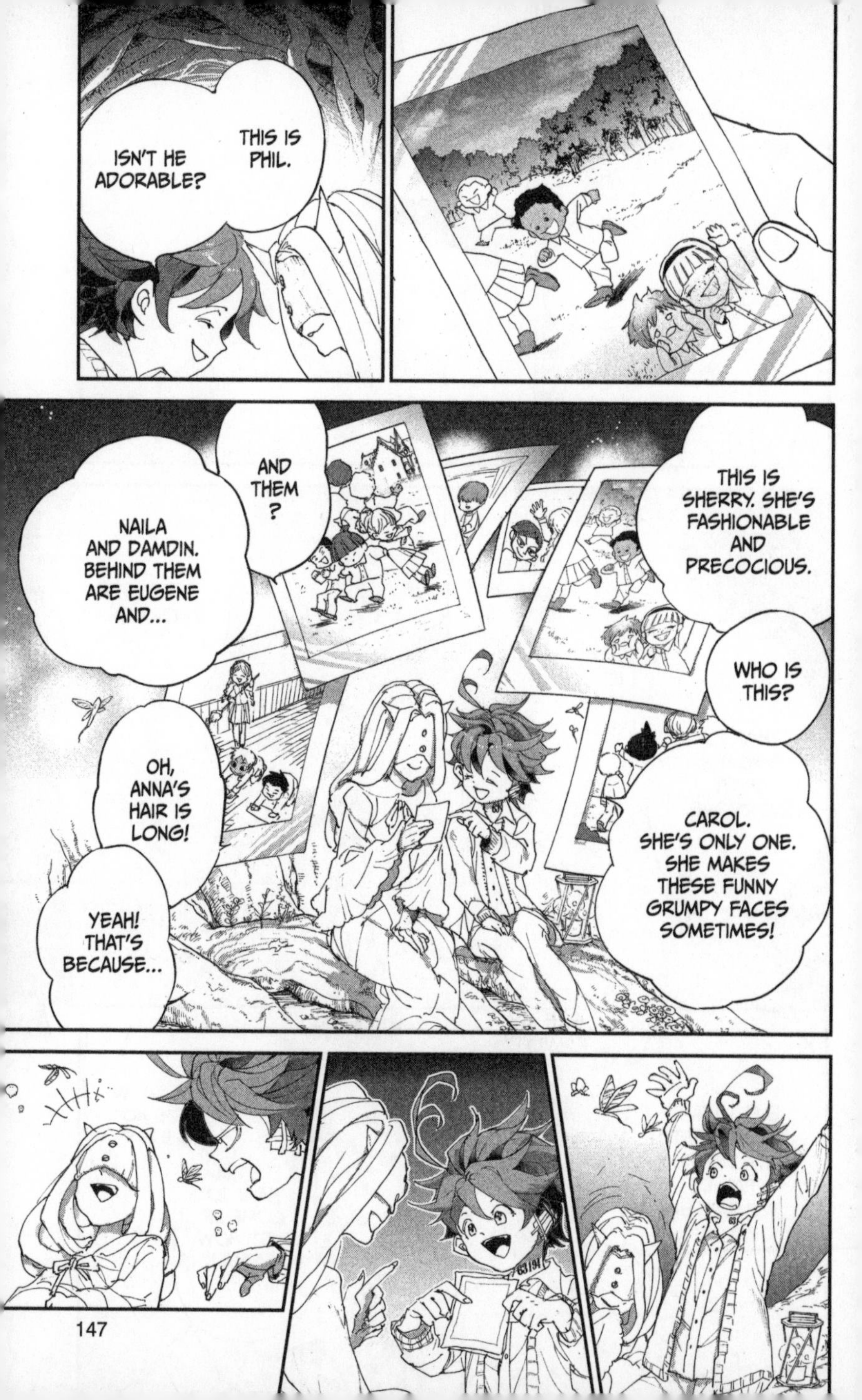
THIS IS PHIL.
ISN'T HE ADORABLE?
THIS IS SHERRY. SHE'S FASHIONABLE AND PRECOCIOUS.
AND THEM?
NAILA AND DAMDIN. BEHIND THEM ARE EUGENE AND...
WHO IS THIS?
CAROL. SHE'S ONLY ONE. SHE MAKES THESE FUNNY GRUMPY FACES SOMETIMES!
OH, ANNA'S HAIR IS LONG!
YEAH! THAT'S BECAUSE...

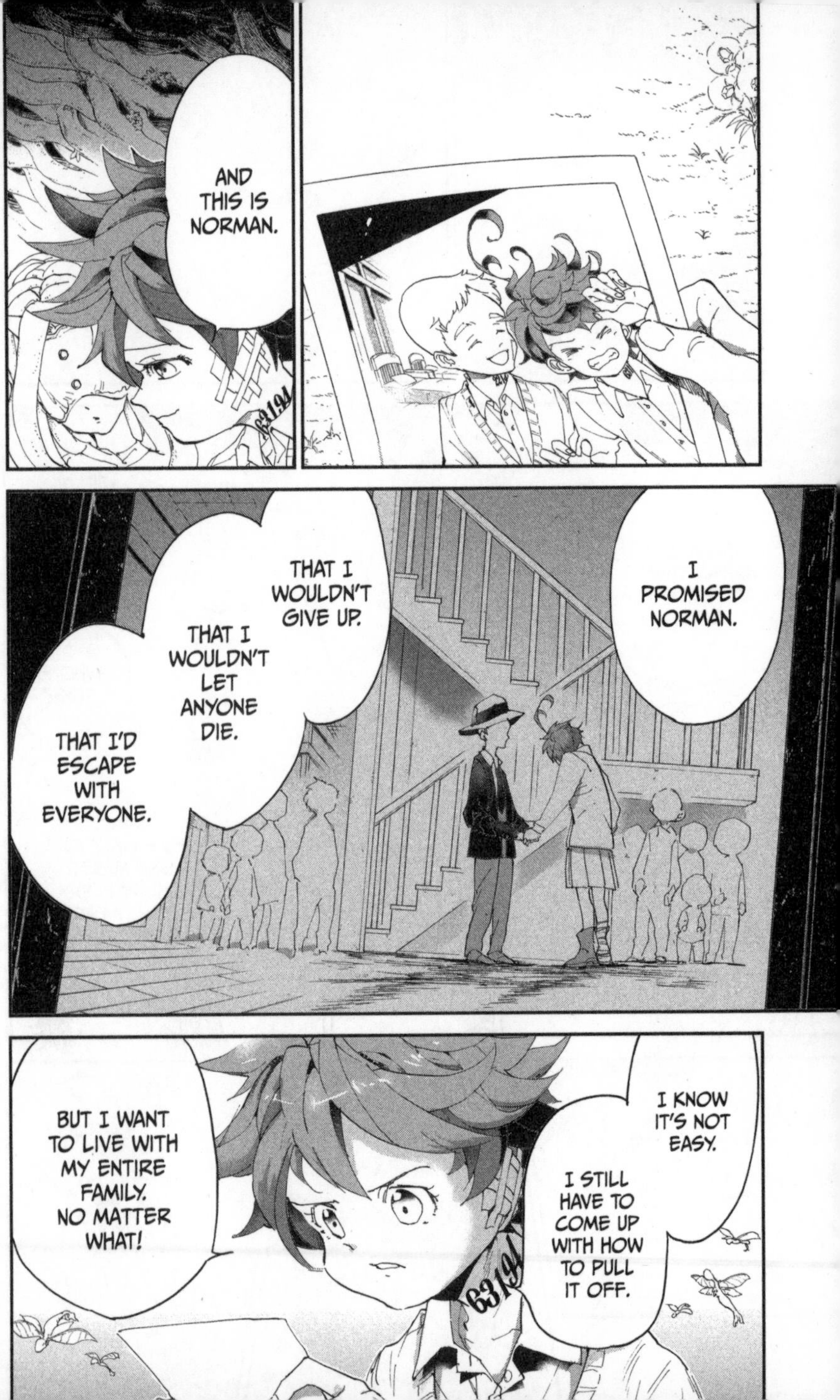
AND THIS IS NORMAN.
I PROMISED NORMAN.
THAT I WOULDN'T GIVE UP.
THAT I WOULDN'T LET ANYONE DIE.
THAT I'D ESCAPE WITH EVERYONE.
I KNOW IT'S NOT EASY.
I STILL HAVE TO COME UP WITH HOW TO PULL IT OFF.
BUT I WANT TO LIVE WITH MY ENTIRE FAMILY. NO MATTER WHAT!

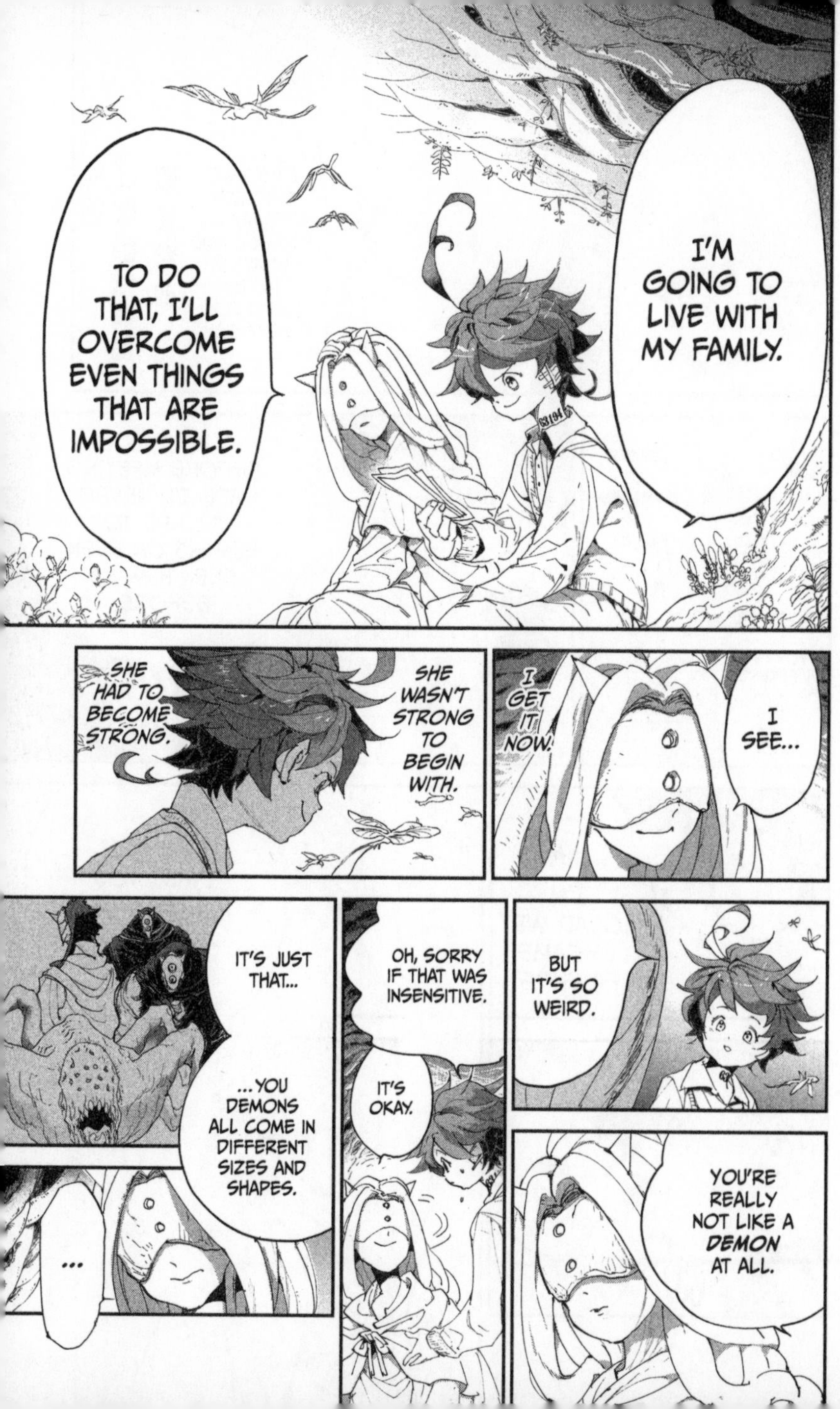

I'M GOING TO LIVE WITH MY FAMILY.
TO DO THAT, I'LL OVERCOME EVEN THINGS THAT ARE IMPOSSIBLE.
I SEE...
I GET IT NOW.
SHE WASN'T STRONG TO BEGIN WITH.
SHE HAD TO BECOME STRONG.
BUT IT'S SO WEIRD.
YOU'RE REALLY NOT LIKE A *DEMON* AT ALL.
OH, SORRY IF THAT WAS INSENSITIVE.
IT'S OKAY.
IT'S JUST THAT...
...YOU DEMONS ALL COME IN DIFFERENT SIZES AND SHAPES.
...

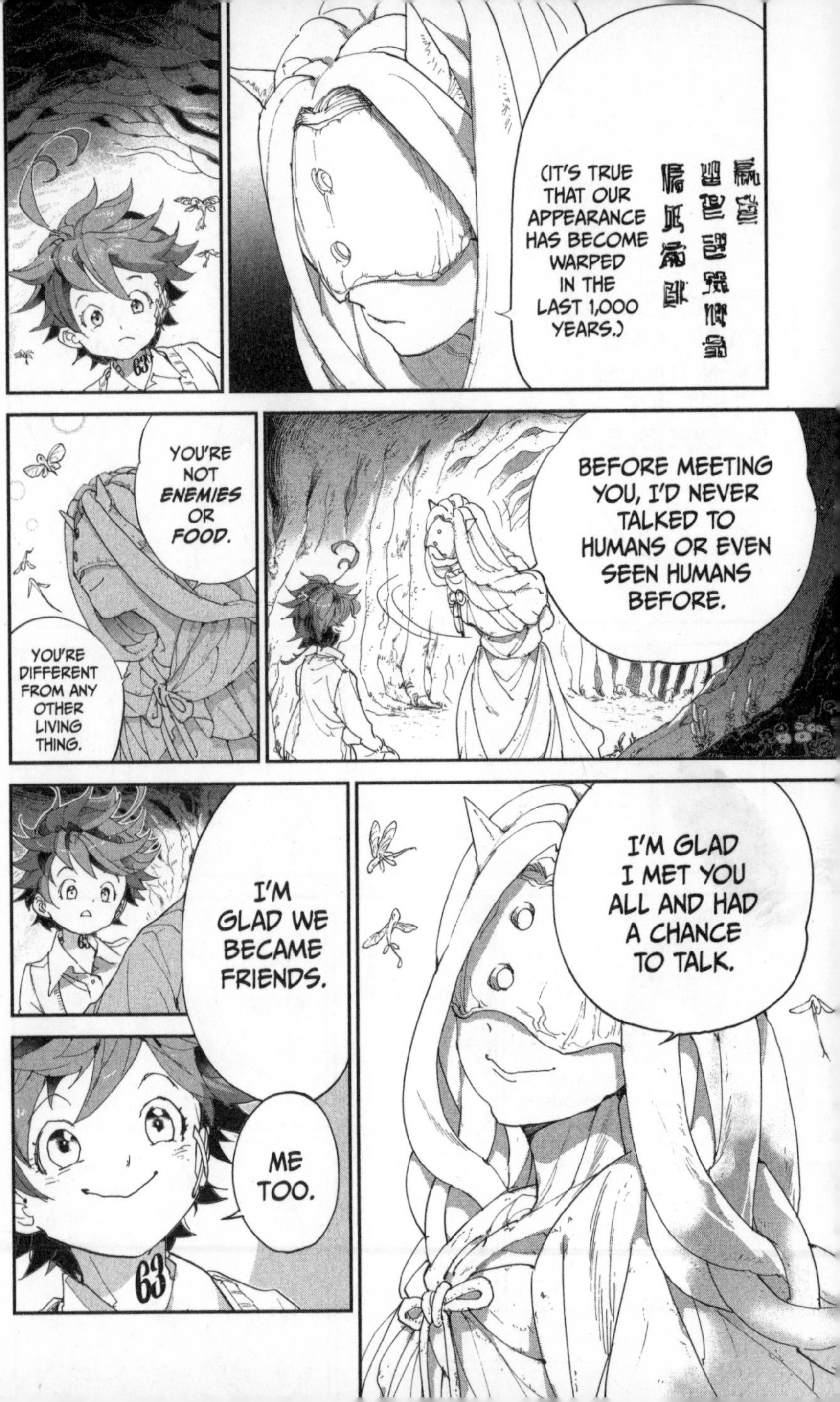
(IT'S TRUE THAT OUR APPEARANCE HAS BECOME WARPED IN THE LAST 1,000 YEARS.)
BEFORE MEETING YOU, I'D NEVER TALKED TO HUMANS OR EVEN SEEN HUMANS BEFORE.
YOU'RE NOT *ENEMIES* OR *FOOD*.
YOU'RE DIFFERENT FROM ANY OTHER LIVING THING.
I'M GLAD I MET YOU ALL AND HAD A CHANCE TO TALK.
I'M GLAD WE BECAME FRIENDS.
ME TOO.

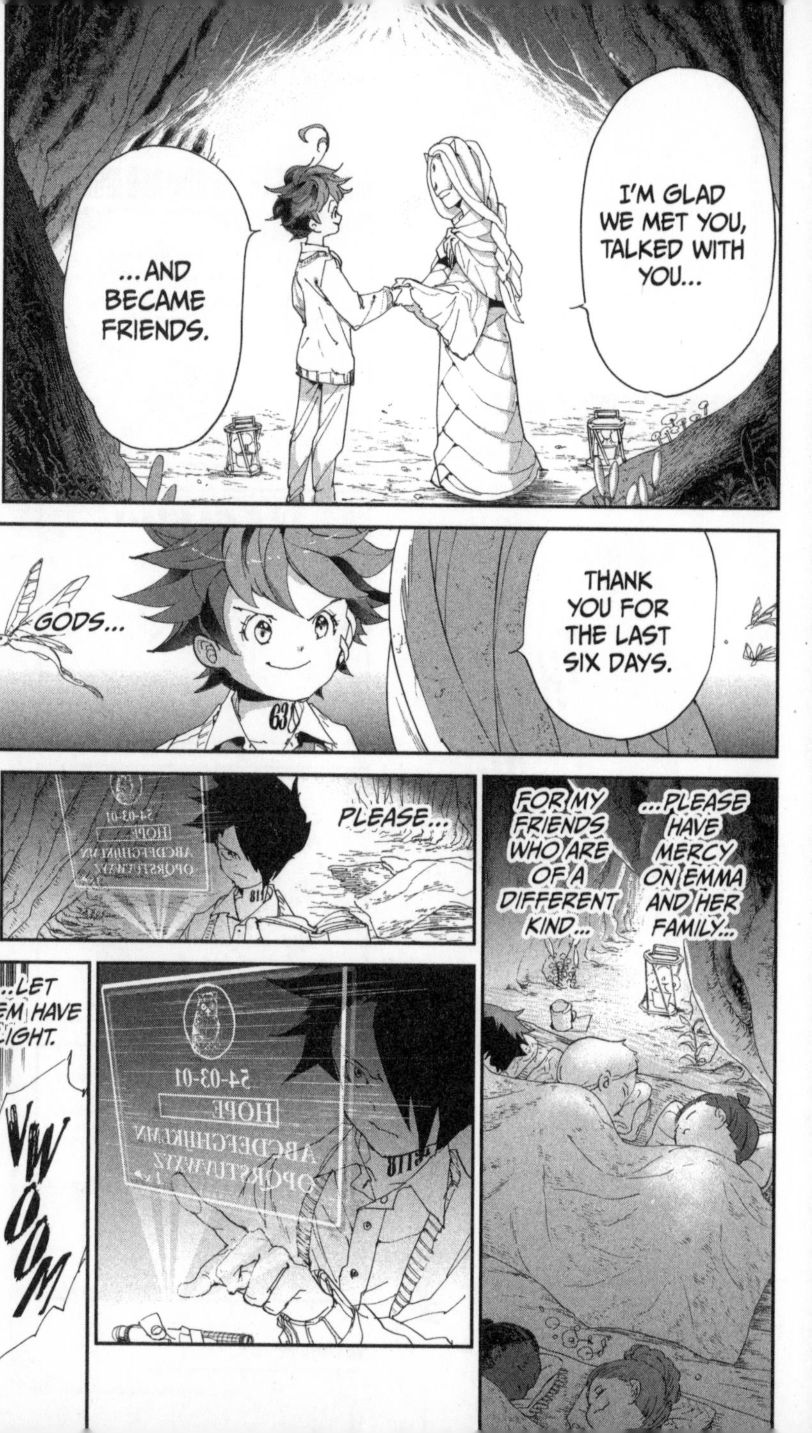
I'M GLAD WE MET YOU, TALKED WITH YOU...
...AND BECAME FRIENDS.
THANK YOU FOR THE LAST SIX DAYS.
GODS...
...PLEASE HAVE MERCY ON EMMA AND HER FAMILY...
FOR MY FRIENDS WHO ARE OF A DIFFERENT KIND...
PLEASE...
...LET THEM HAVE LIGHT.
VWOOM

SIDE STORY 4-2

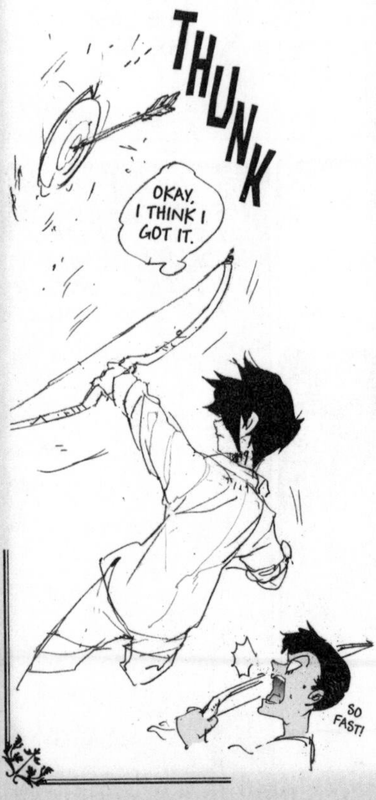
THUNK
OKAY, I THINK I GOT IT.
SO FAST!

NORMAN WITH THE BOW AND ARROWS

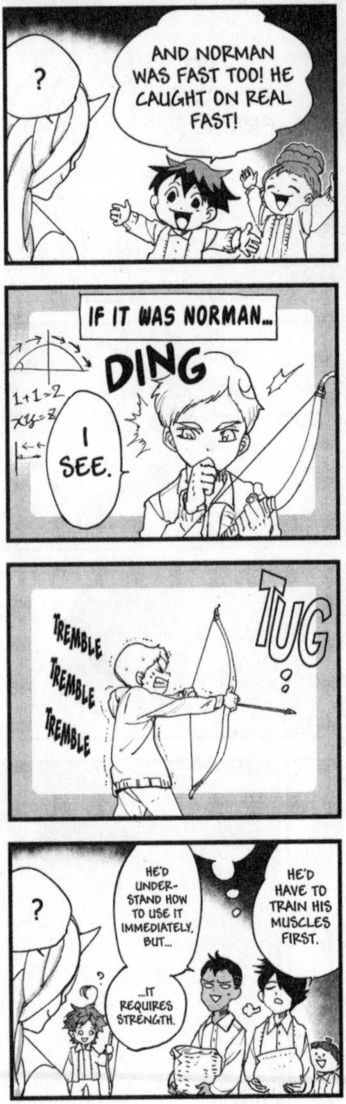
AND NORMAN WAS FAST TOO! HE CAUGHT ON REAL FAST!
?
IF IT WAS NORMAN...
DING
I SEE.
1+1=2
TUG
TREMBLE
TREMBLE
TREMBLE
HE'D HAVE TO TRAIN HIS MUSCLES FIRST.
HE'D UNDER-STAND HOW TO USE IT IMMEDIATELY, BUT...
...IT REQUIRES STRENGTH.
?
?

SIDE STORY 4 -FIN-

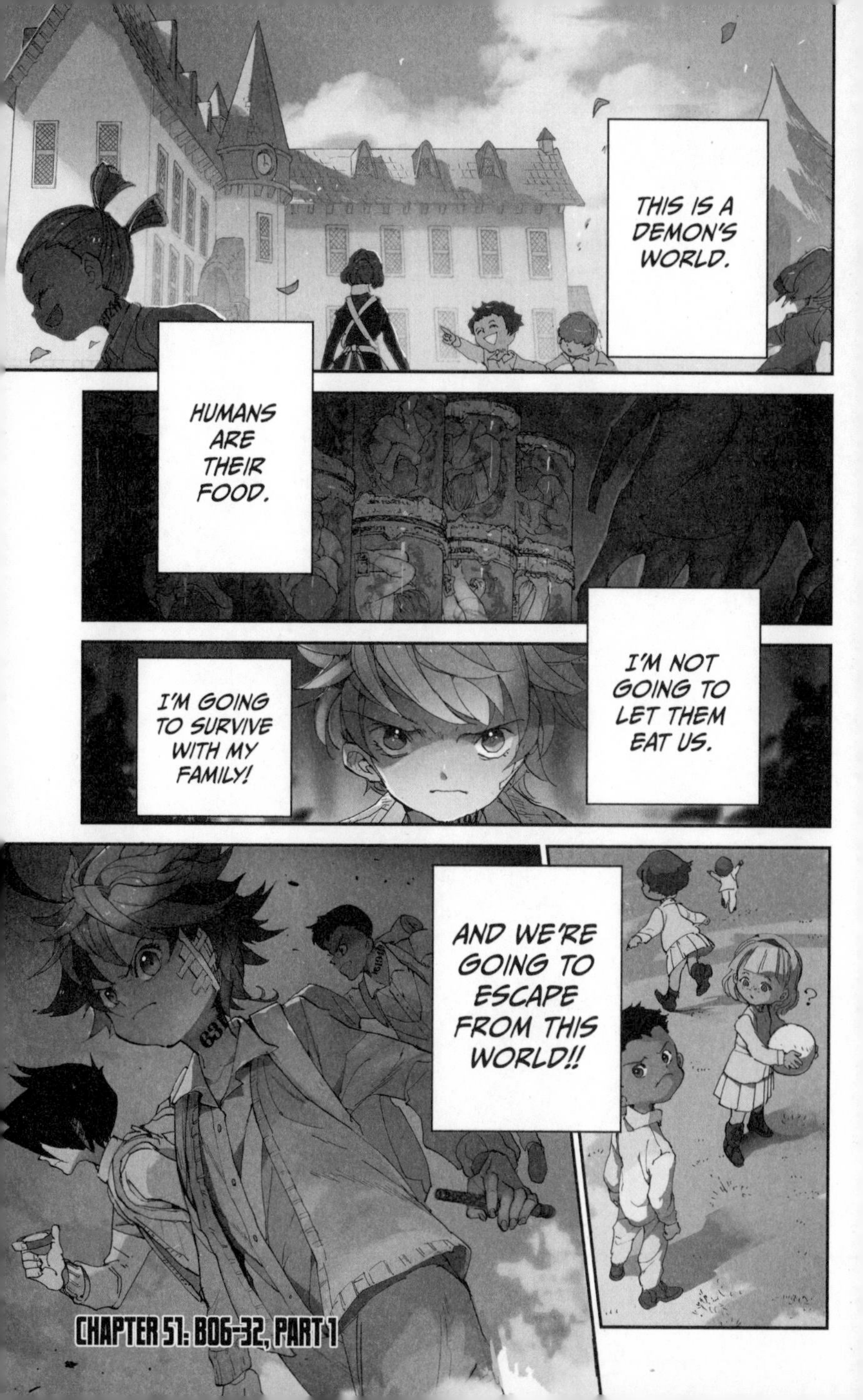
THIS IS A DEMON'S WORLD.
HUMANS ARE THEIR FOOD.
I'M NOT GOING TO LET THEM EAT US.
I'M GOING TO SURVIVE WITH MY FAMILY!
AND WE'RE GOING TO ESCAPE FROM THIS WORLD!!
CHAPTER 51: B06-32, PART 1

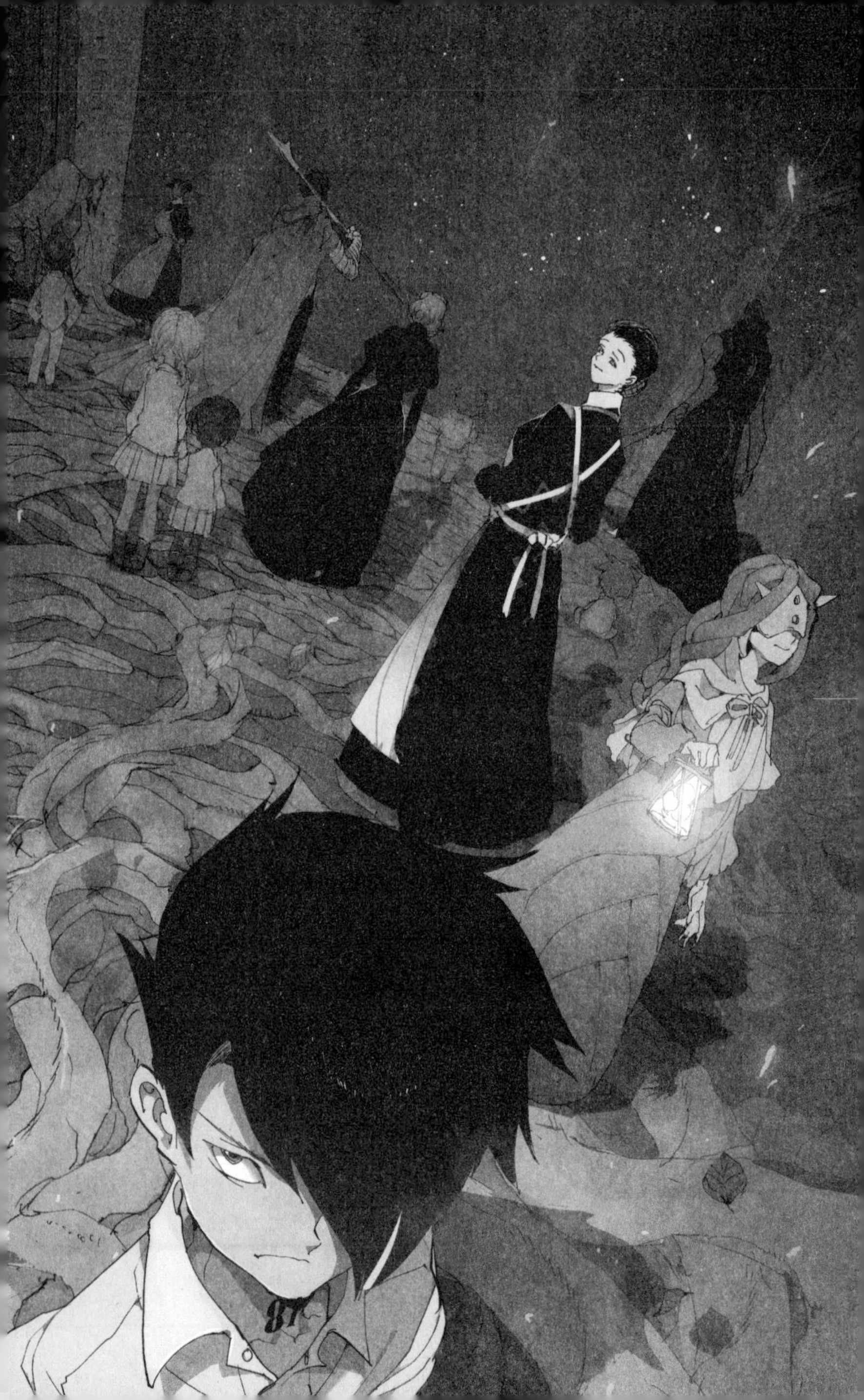

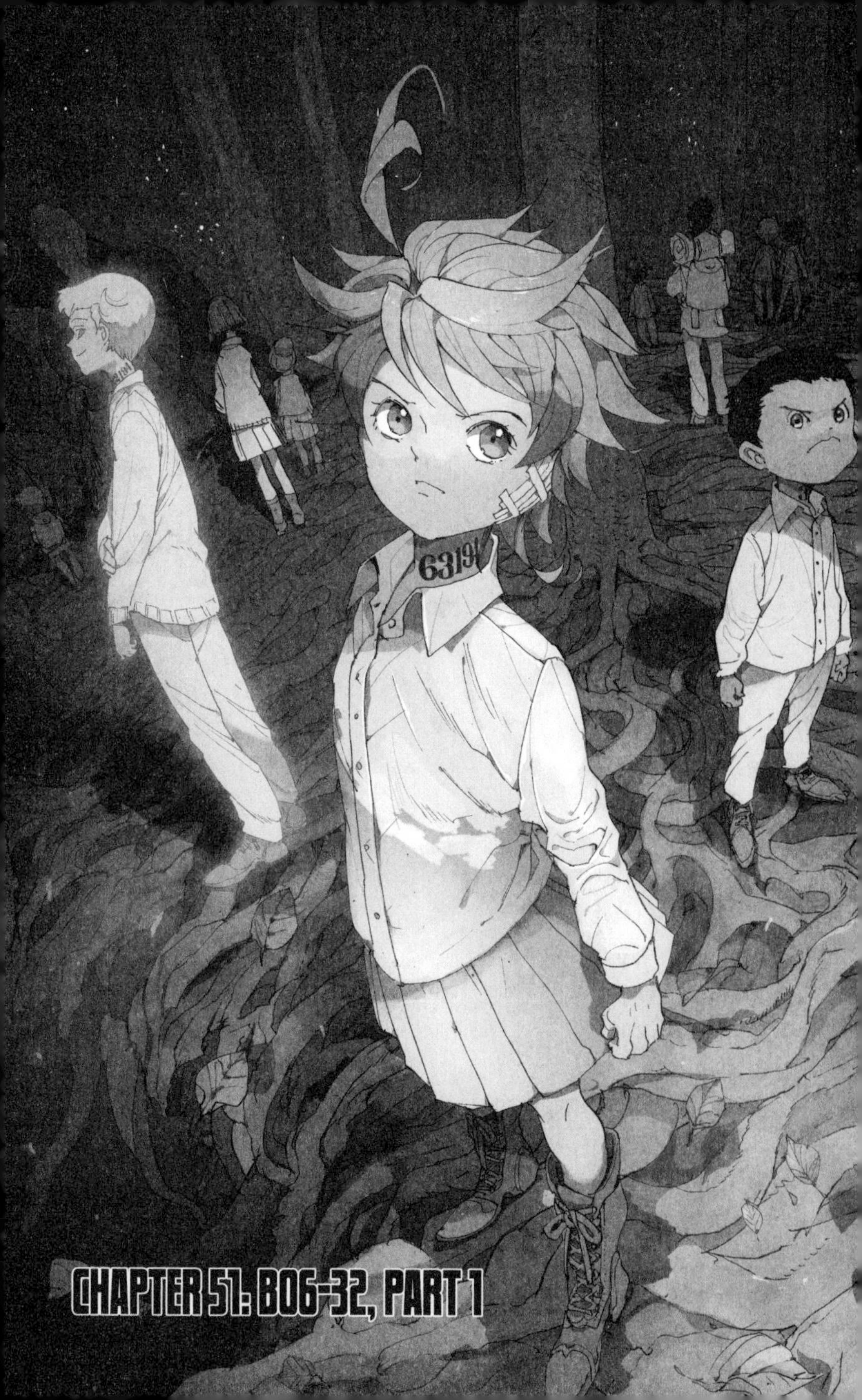
63194

CHAPTER 51: B06-32, PART 1

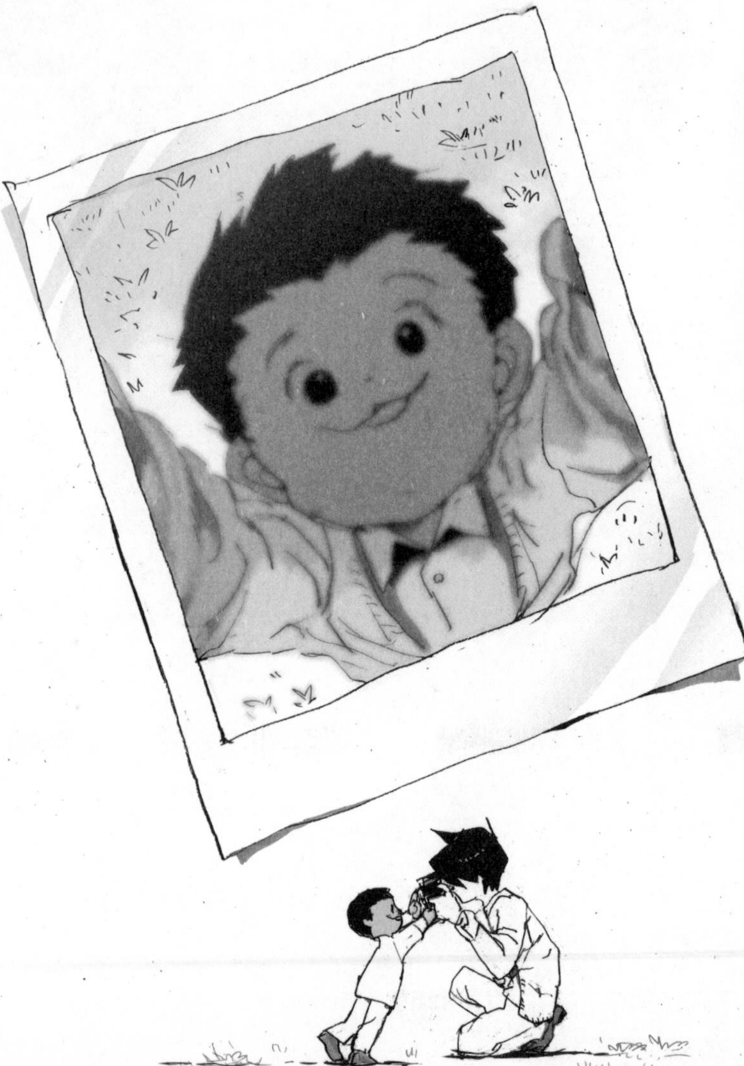

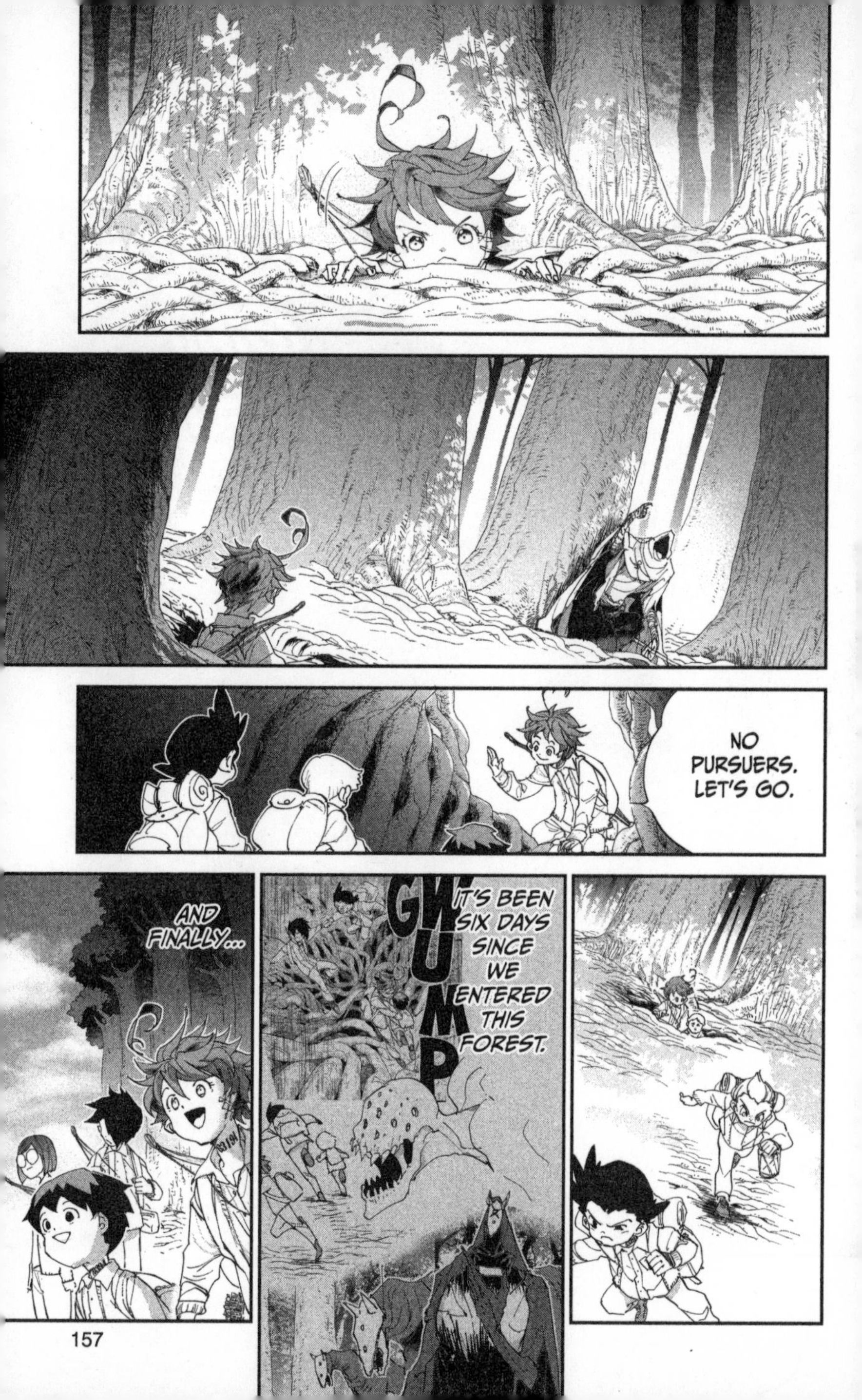
NO PURSUERS. LET'S GO.
IT'S BEEN SIX DAYS SINCE WE ENTERED THIS FOREST.
GWUMP
AND FINALLY...

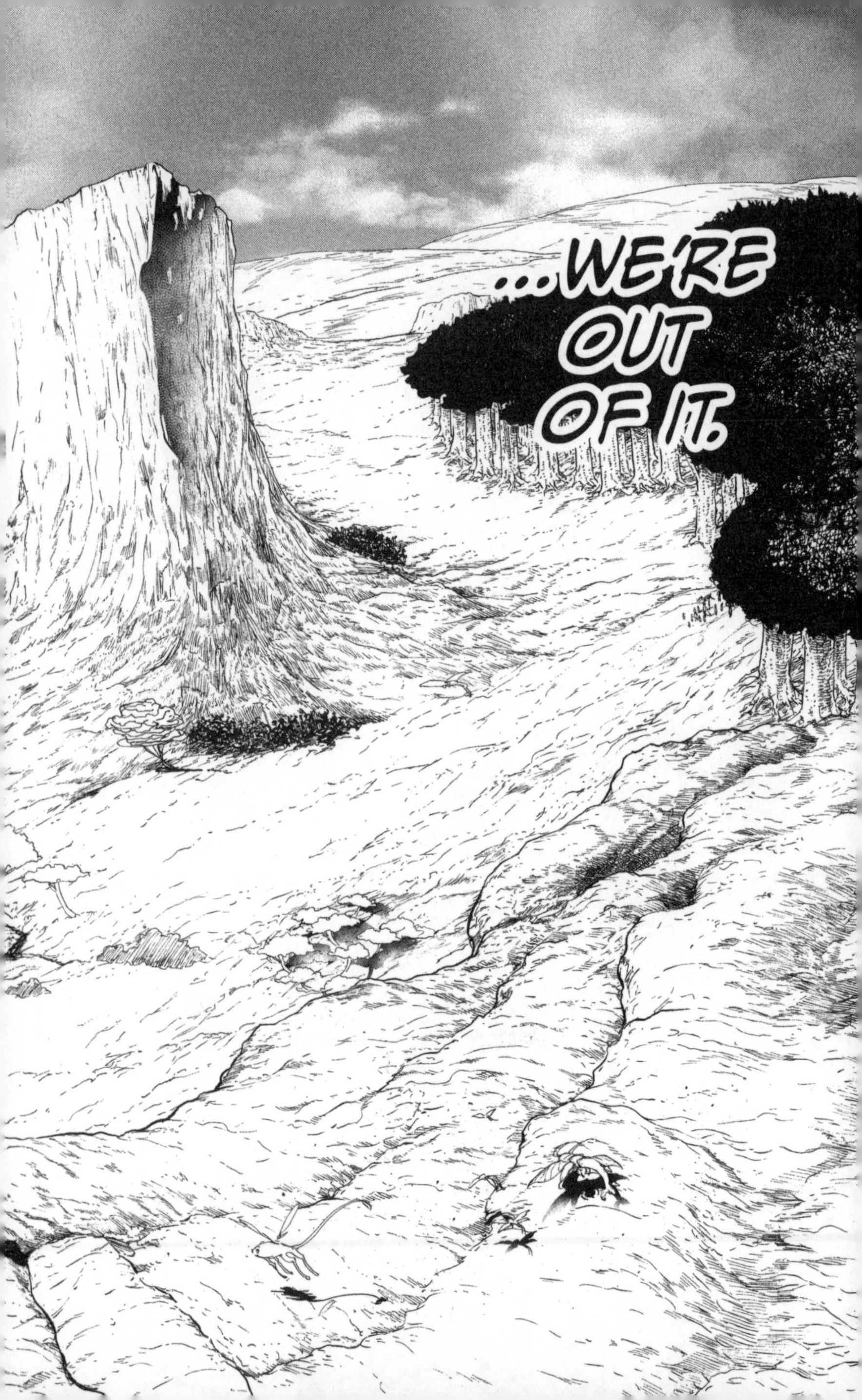
...WE'RE OUT OF IT.

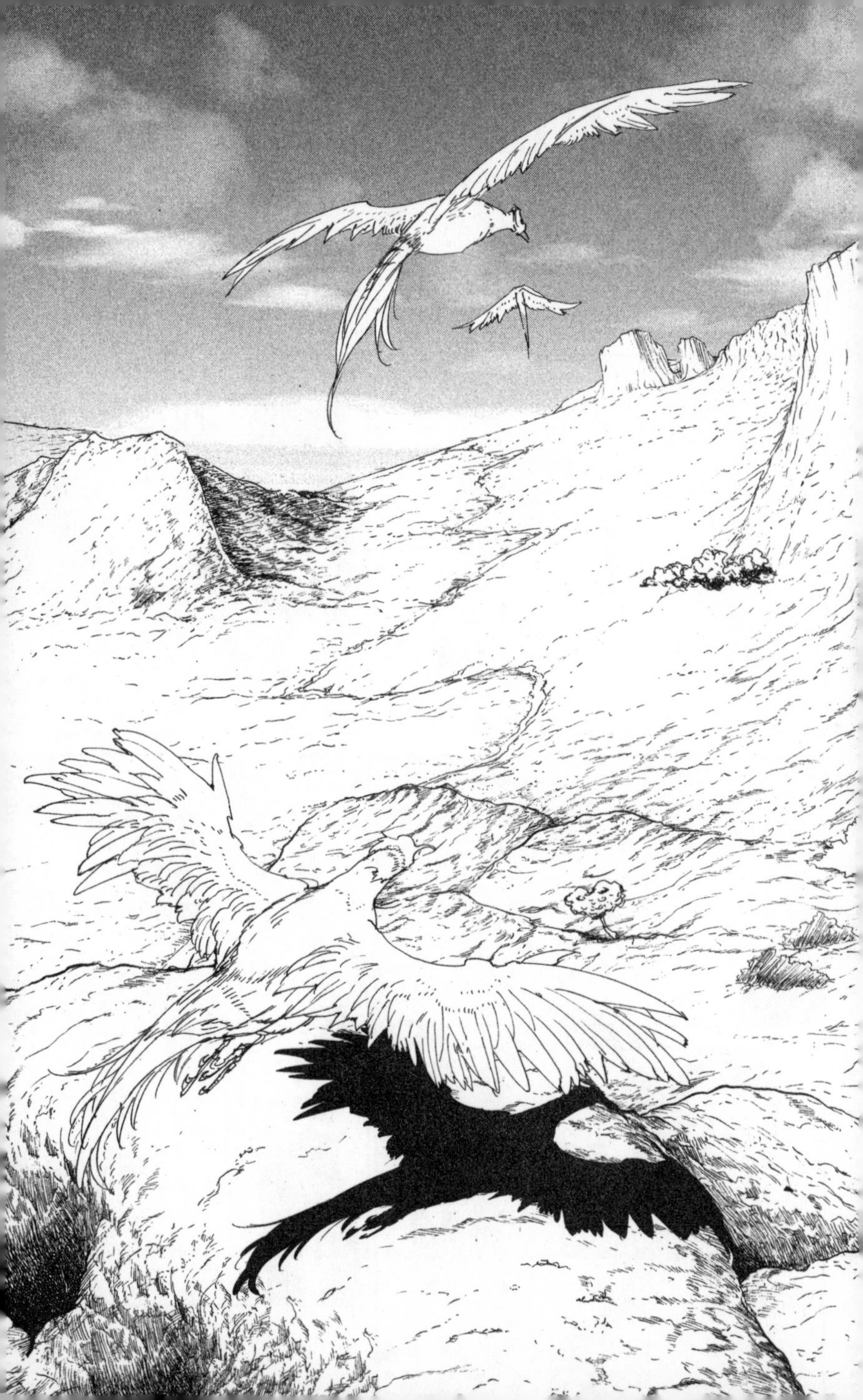

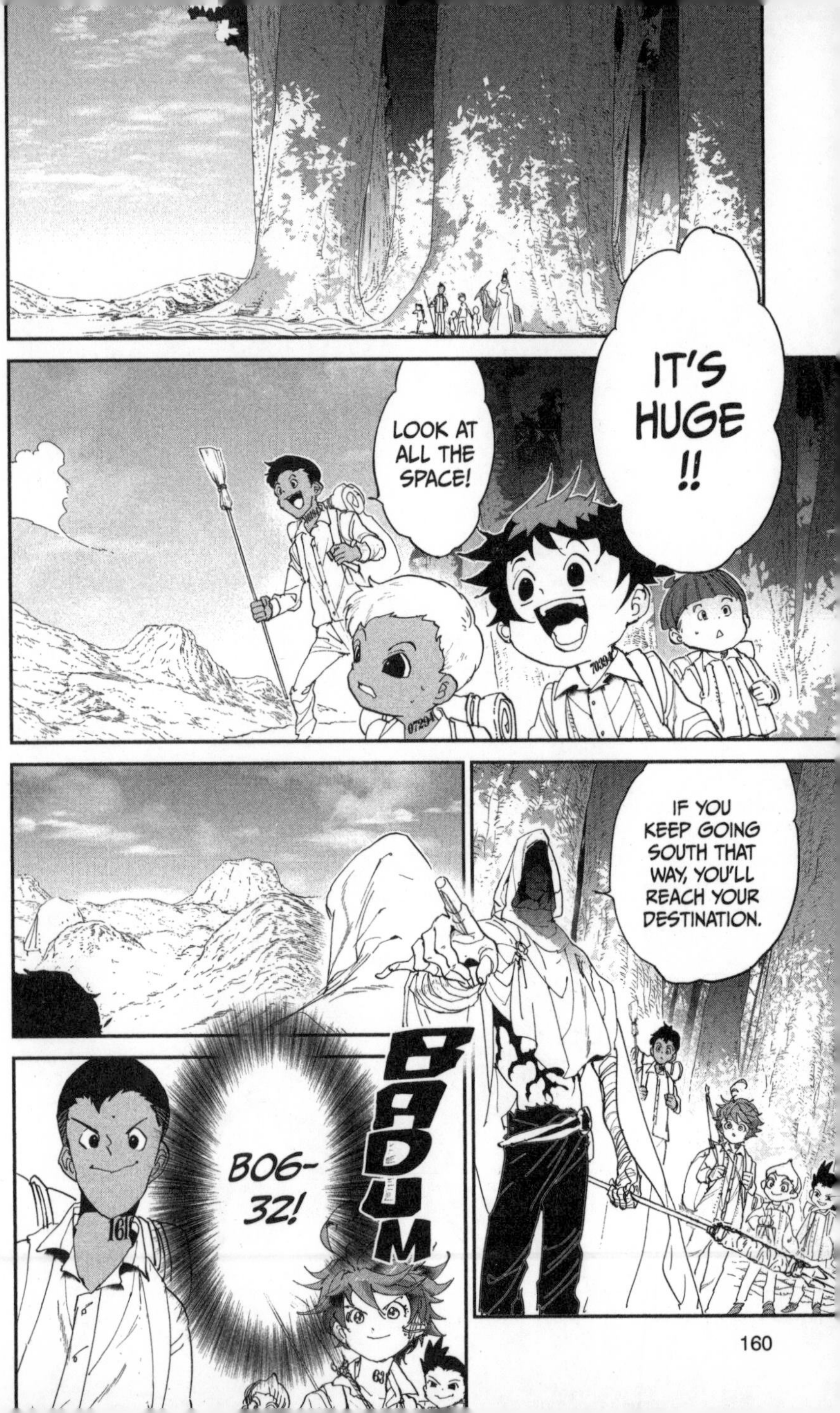
IT'S HUGE!!
LOOK AT ALL THE SPACE!
IF YOU KEEP GOING SOUTH THAT WAY, YOU'LL REACH YOUR DESTINATION.
BADUM
BOG-32!

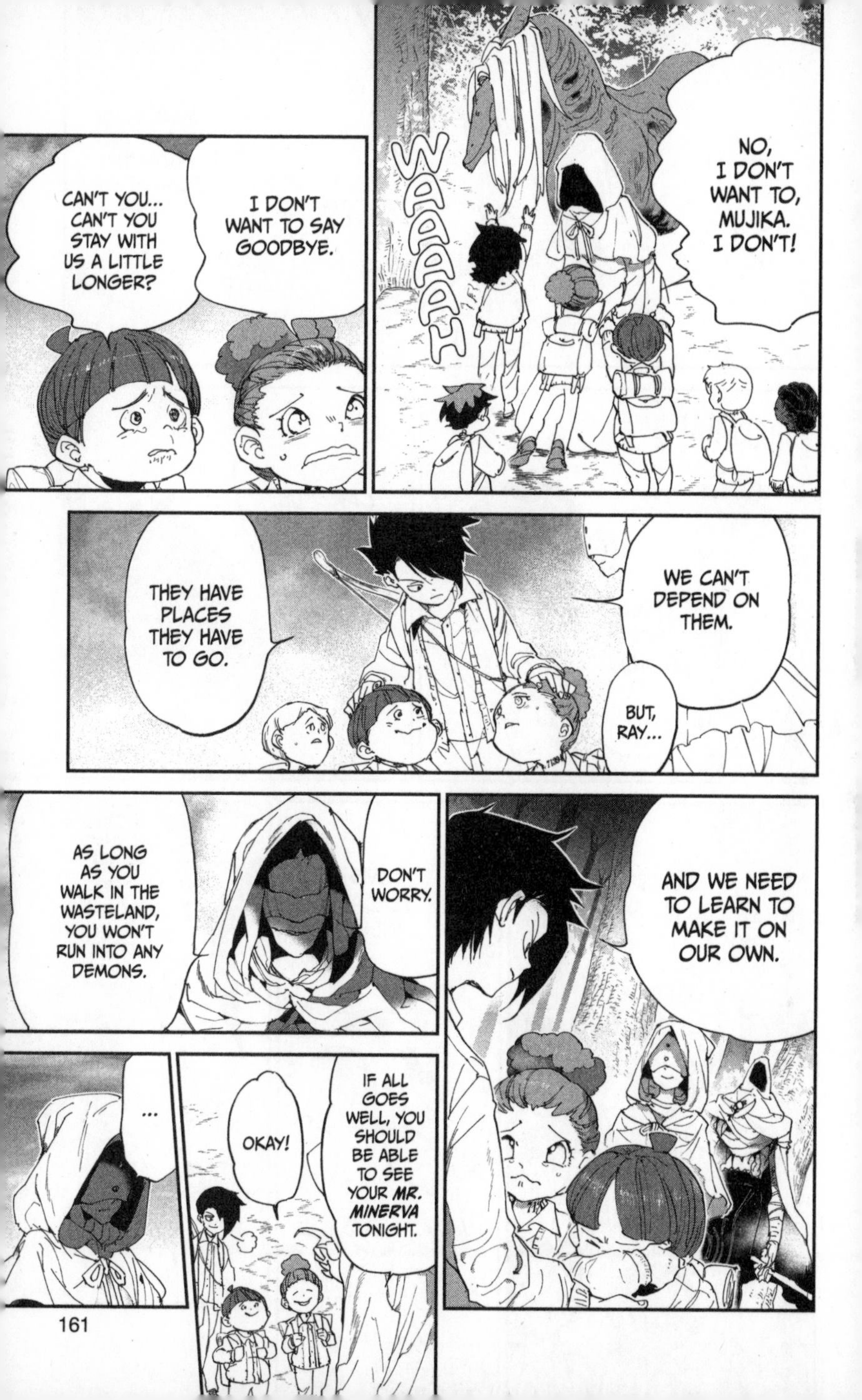
WAAAAAH
NO, I DON'T WANT TO, MUJIKA. I DON'T!
I DON'T WANT TO SAY GOODBYE.
CAN'T YOU... CAN'T YOU STAY WITH US A LITTLE LONGER?
BUT, RAY...
THEY HAVE PLACES THEY HAVE TO GO.
WE CAN'T DEPEND ON THEM.
AND WE NEED TO LEARN TO MAKE IT ON OUR OWN.
DON'T WORRY.
AS LONG AS YOU WALK IN THE WASTELAND, YOU WON'T RUN INTO ANY DEMONS.
IF ALL GOES WELL, YOU SHOULD BE ABLE TO SEE YOUR *MR. MINERVA* TONIGHT.
OKAY!
...

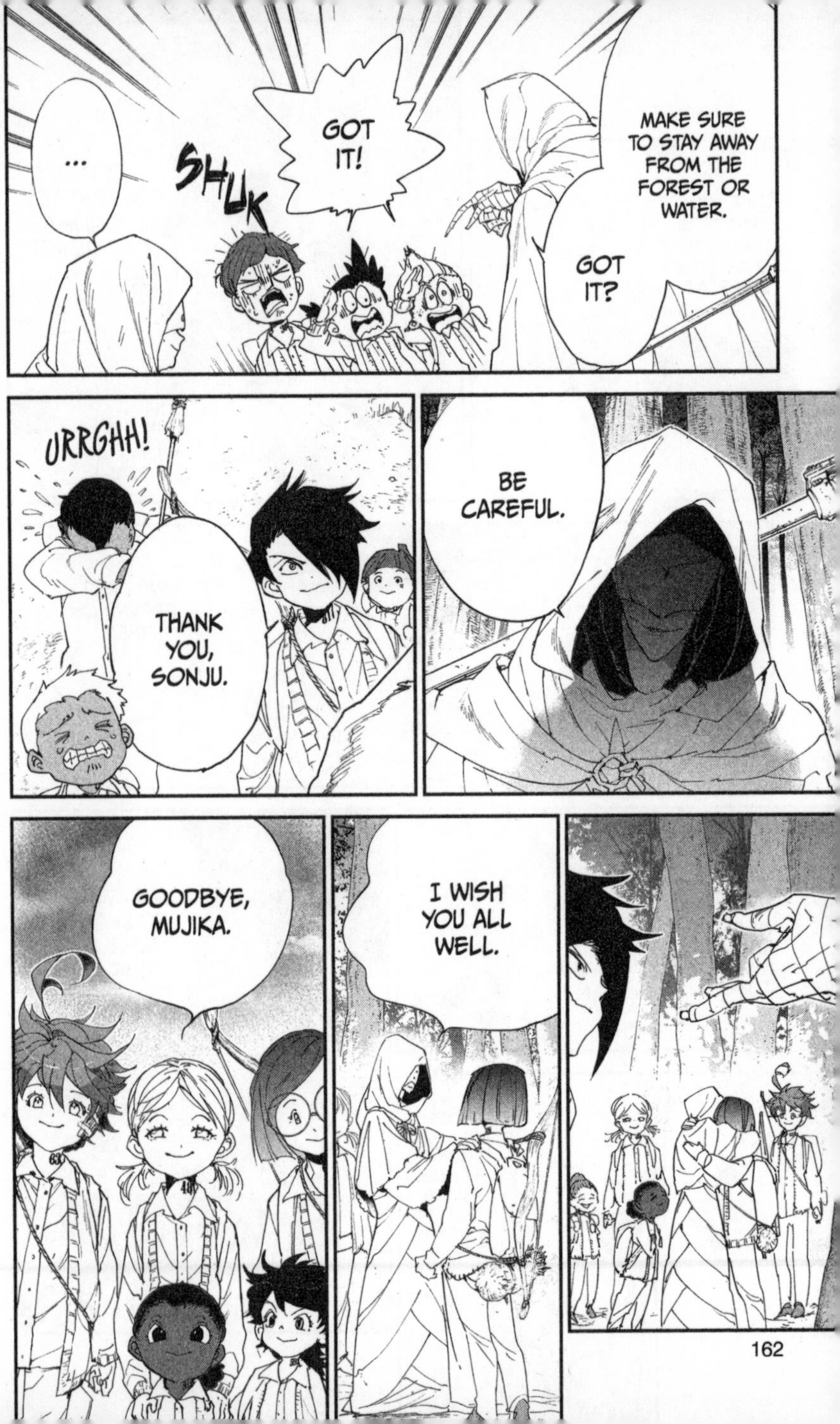
MAKE SURE TO STAY AWAY FROM THE FOREST OR WATER.
GOT IT?
GOT IT!
SHUK
...
BE CAREFUL.
URRGHH!
THANK YOU, SONJU.
I WISH YOU ALL WELL.
GOODBYE, MUJIKA.

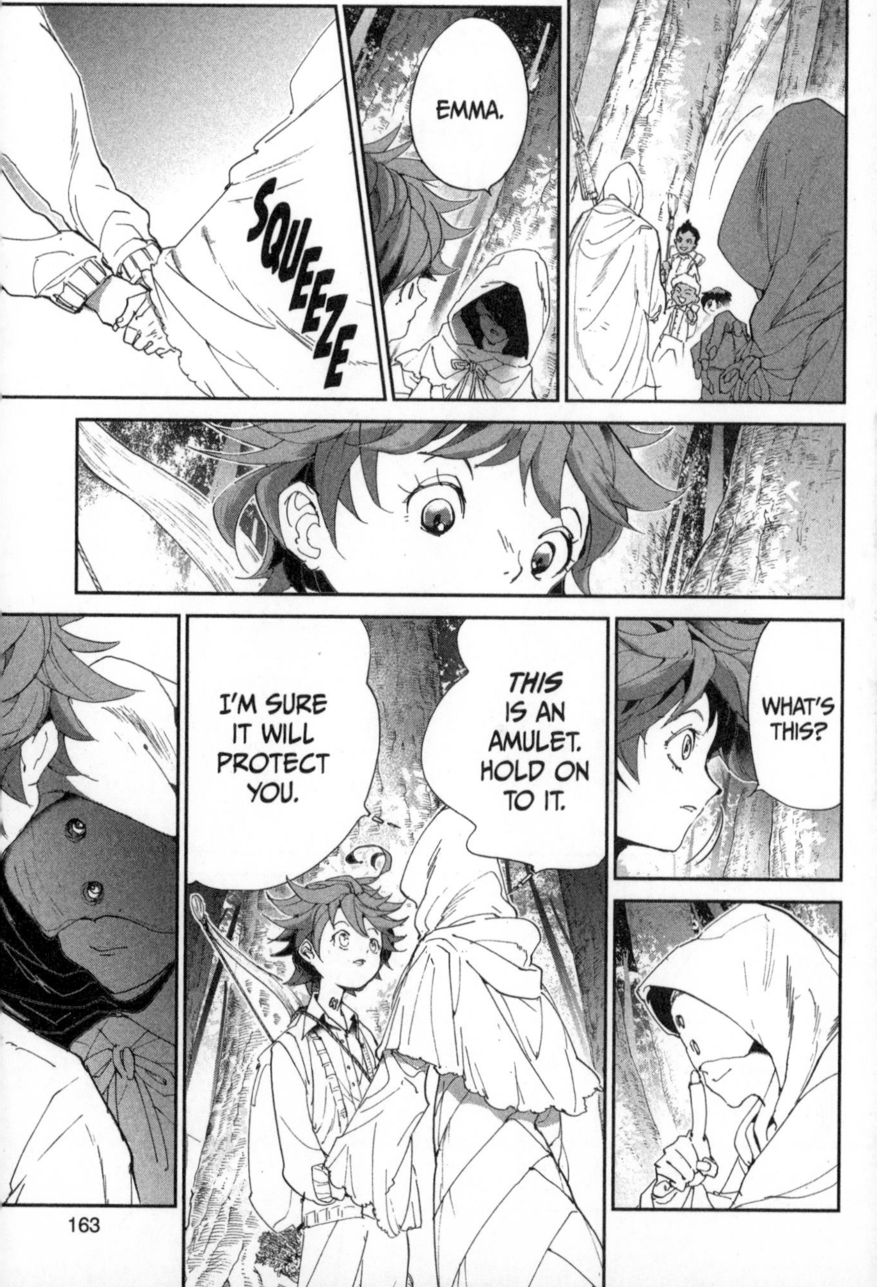
EMMA.
SQUEEZE
WHAT'S THIS?
THIS IS AN AMULET. HOLD ON TO IT.
I'M SURE IT WILL PROTECT YOU.

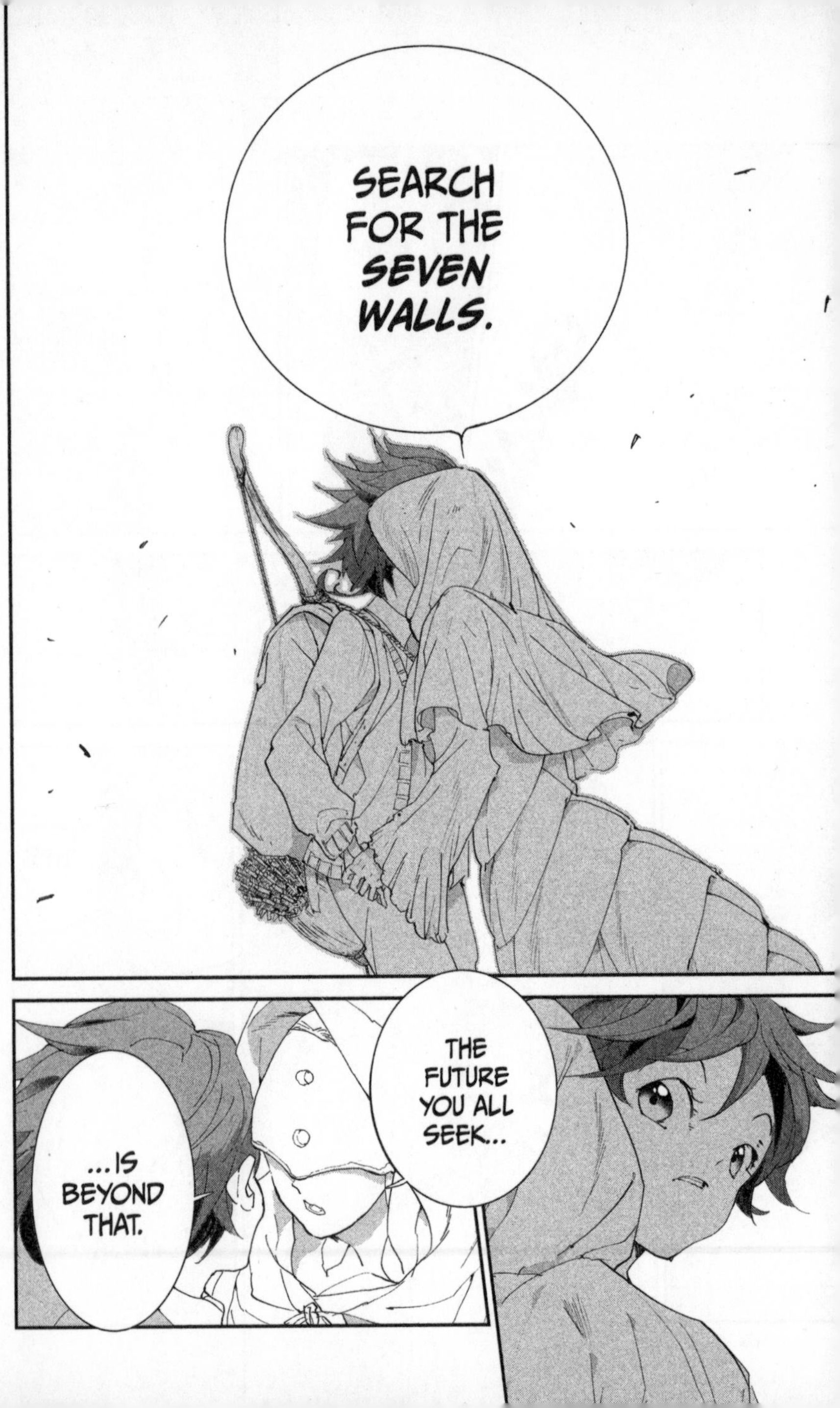
SEARCH FOR THE SEVEN WALLS.
THE FUTURE YOU ALL SEEK...
...IS BEYOND THAT.

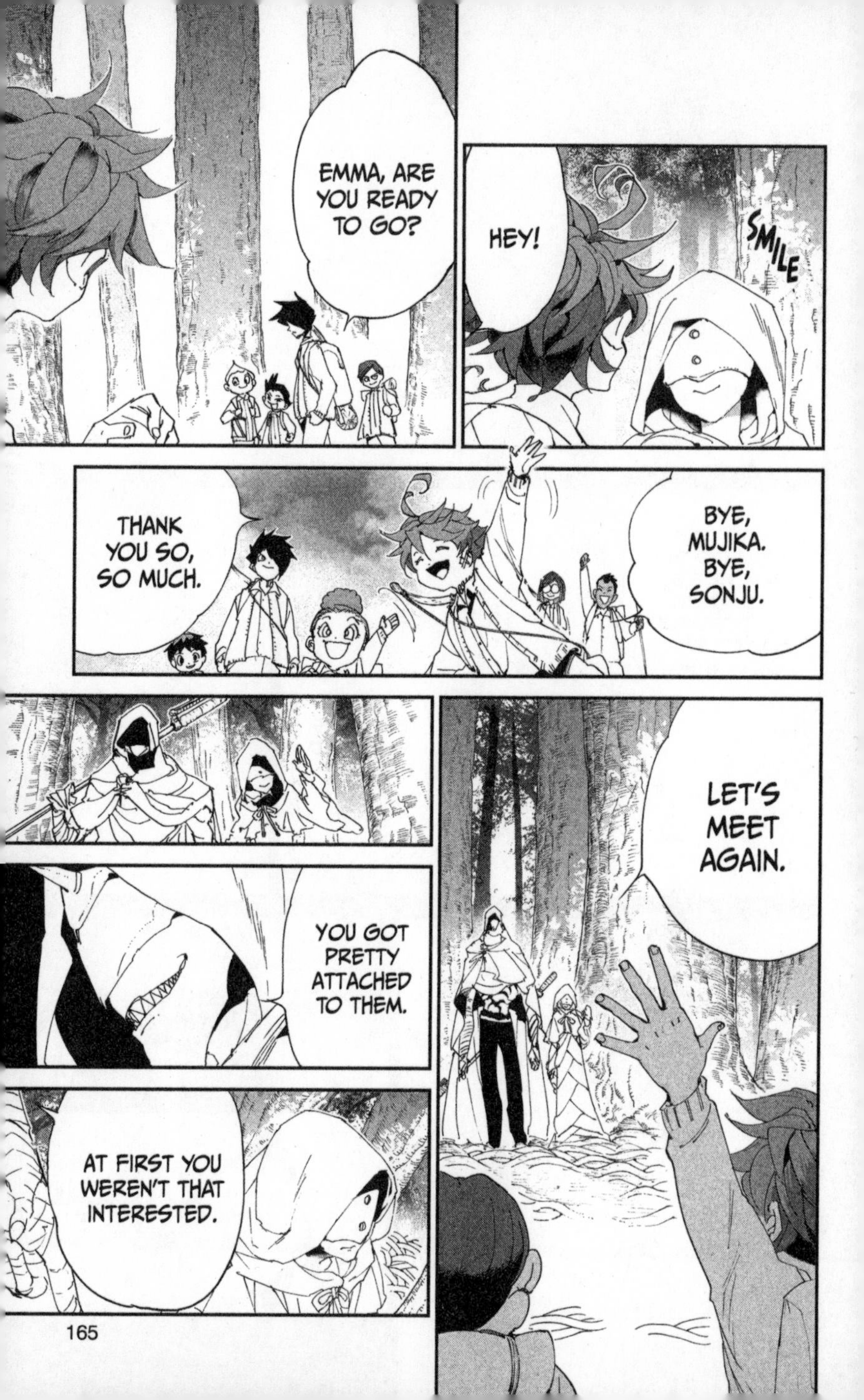
HEY!
SMILE
EMMA, ARE YOU READY TO GO?
BYE, MUJIKA. BYE, SONJU.
THANK YOU SO, SO MUCH.
LET'S MEET AGAIN.
YOU GOT PRETTY ATTACHED TO THEM.
AT FIRST YOU WEREN'T THAT INTERESTED.

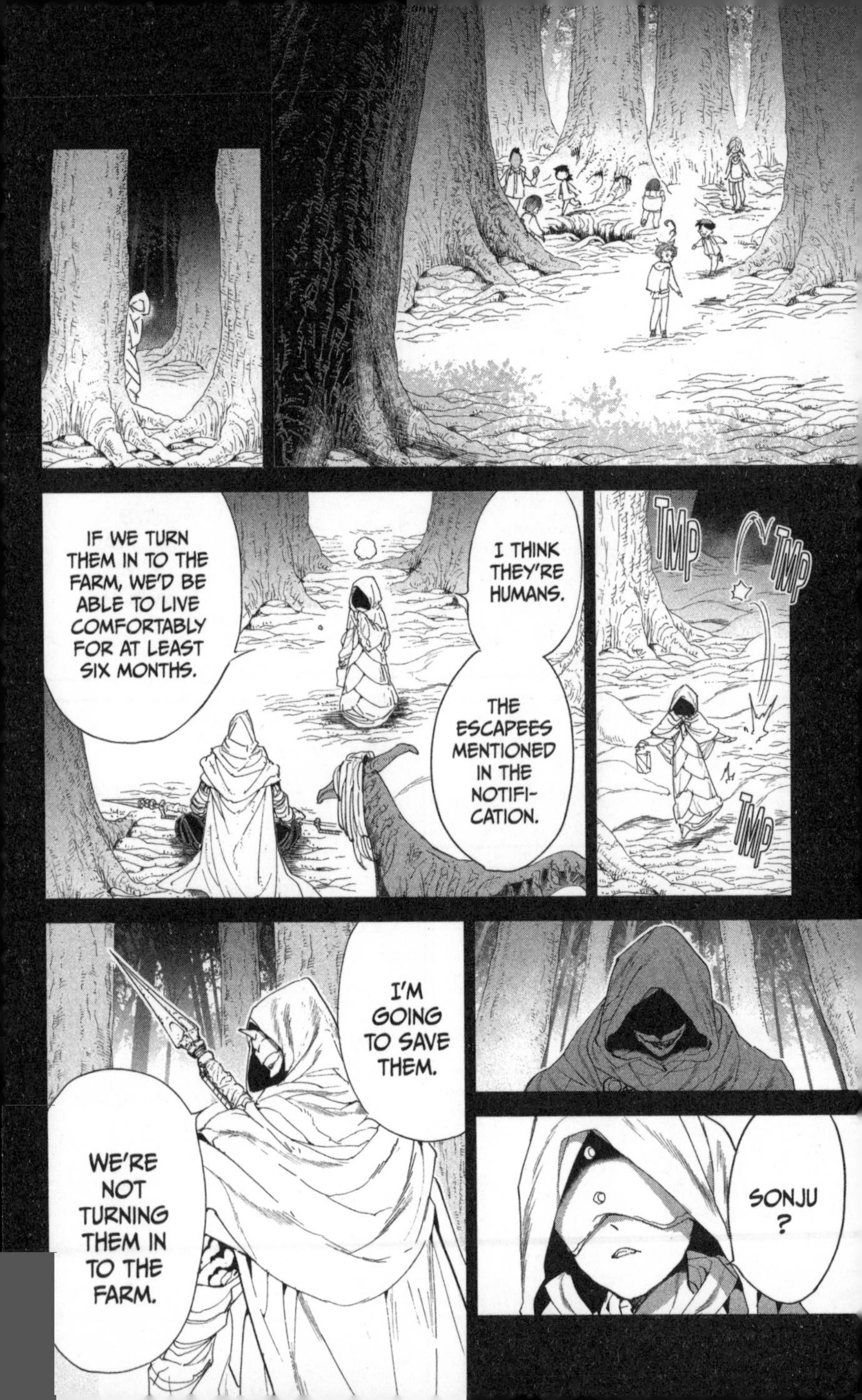
TMP
TMP
TMP
I THINK THEY'RE HUMANS.
THE ESCAPEES MENTIONED IN THE NOTIFI-CATION.
IF WE TURN THEM IN TO THE FARM, WE'D BE ABLE TO LIVE COMFORTABLY FOR AT LEAST SIX MONTHS.
SONJU?
I'M GOING TO SAVE THEM.
WE'RE NOT TURNING THEM IN TO THE FARM.

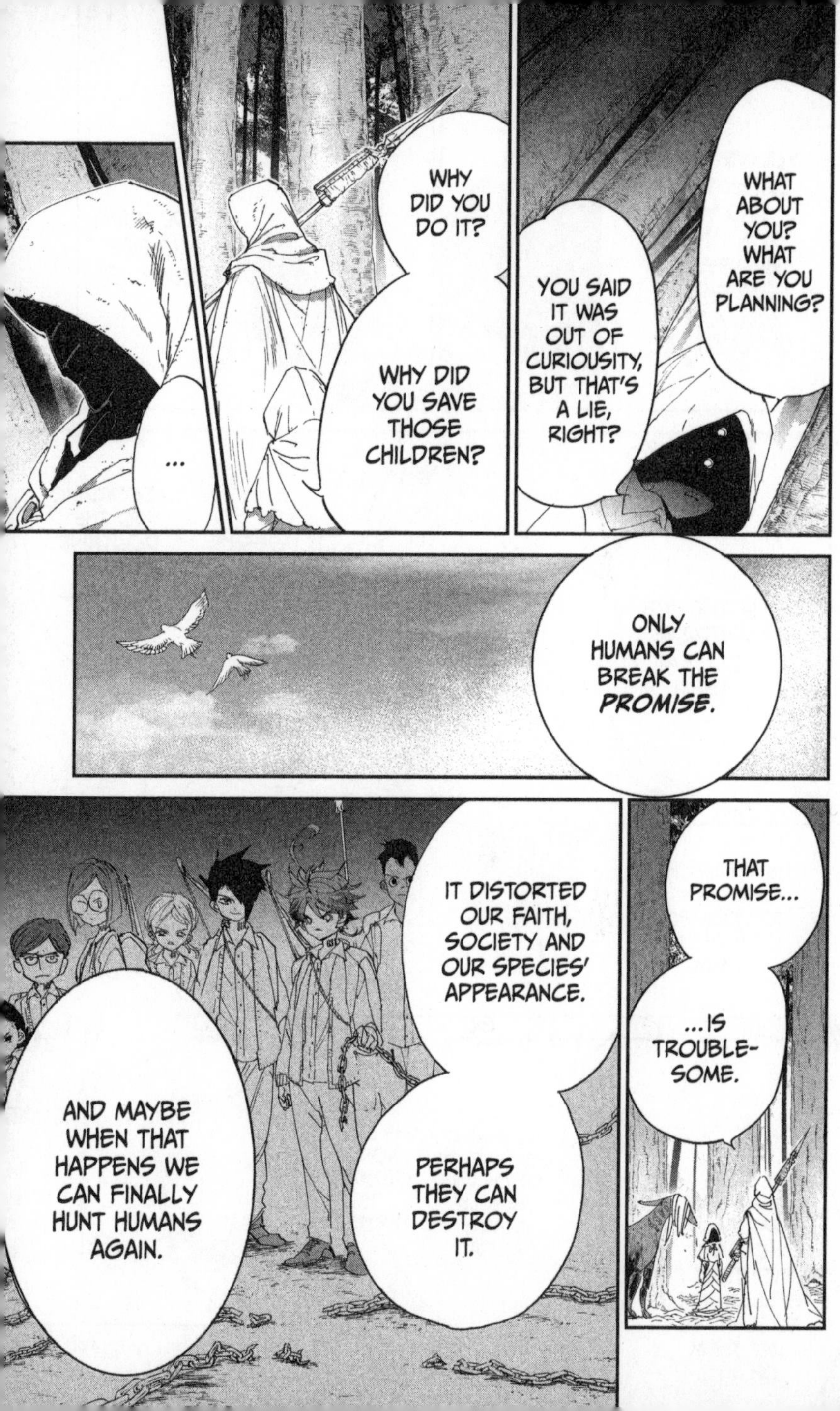
WHAT ABOUT YOU? WHAT ARE YOU PLANNING?
YOU SAID IT WAS OUT OF CURIOUSITY, BUT THAT'S A LIE, RIGHT?
WHY DID YOU DO IT?
WHY DID YOU SAVE THOSE CHILDREN?
...
ONLY HUMANS CAN BREAK THE *PROMISE.*
THAT PROMISE...
...IS TROUBLE-SOME.
IT DISTORTED OUR FAITH, SOCIETY AND OUR SPECIES' APPEARANCE.
PERHAPS THEY CAN DESTROY IT.
AND MAYBE WHEN THAT HAPPENS WE CAN FINALLY HUNT HUMANS AGAIN.

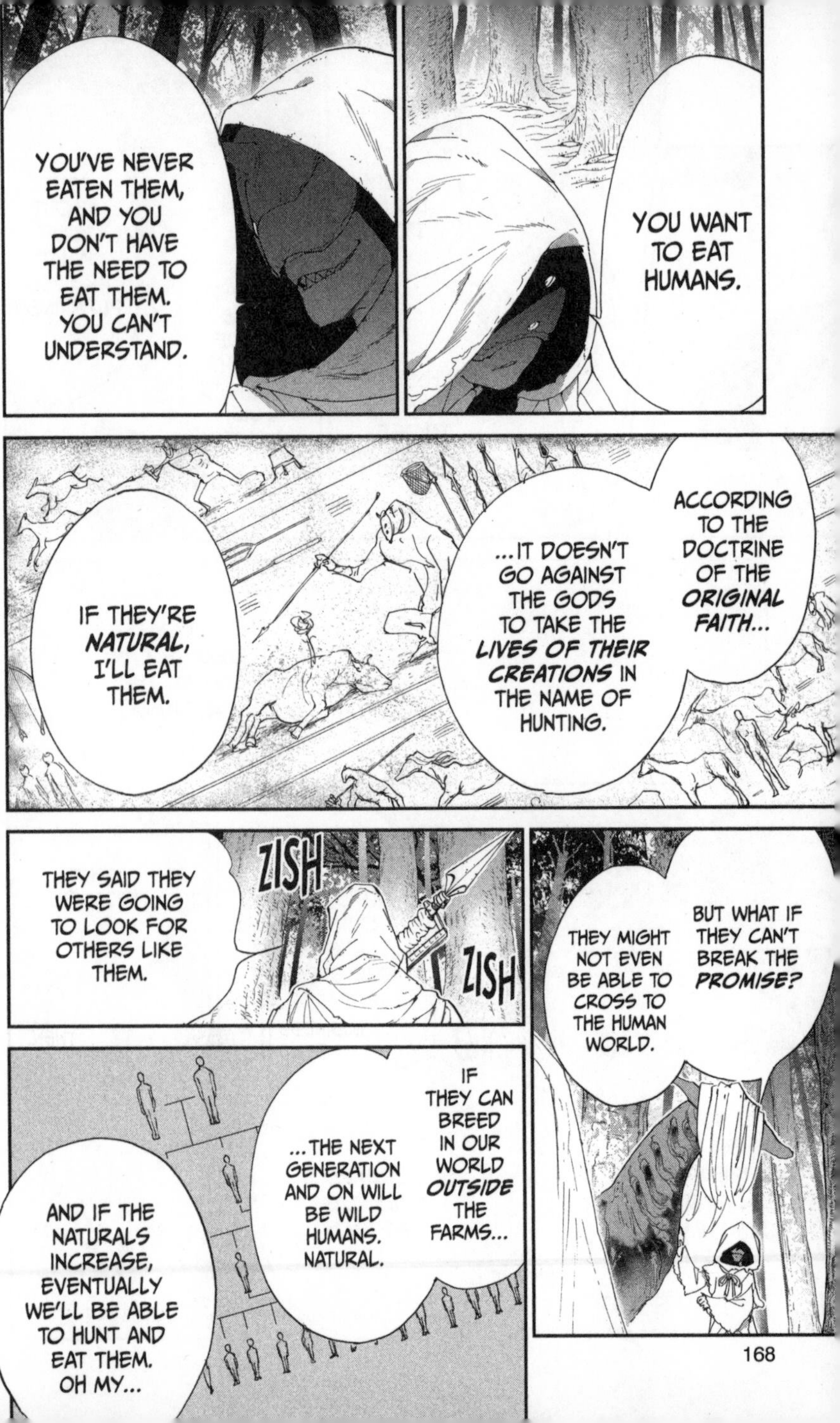
YOU WANT TO EAT HUMANS.
YOU'VE NEVER EATEN THEM, AND YOU DON'T HAVE THE NEED TO EAT THEM. YOU CAN'T UNDERSTAND.
ACCORDING TO THE DOCTRINE OF THE *ORIGINAL FAITH*...
...IT DOESN'T GO AGAINST THE GODS TO TAKE THE *LIVES OF THEIR CREATIONS* IN THE NAME OF HUNTING.
IF THEY'RE *NATURAL*, I'LL EAT THEM.
BUT WHAT IF THEY CAN'T BREAK THE *PROMISE?*
THEY MIGHT NOT EVEN BE ABLE TO CROSS TO THE HUMAN WORLD.
ZISH
THEY SAID THEY WERE GOING TO LOOK FOR OTHERS LIKE THEM.
ZISH
IF THEY CAN BREED IN OUR WORLD *OUTSIDE* THE FARMS...
...THE NEXT GENERATION AND ON WILL BE WILD HUMANS. NATURAL.
AND IF THE NATURALS INCREASE, EVENTUALLY WE'LL BE ABLE TO HUNT AND EAT THEM. OH MY...

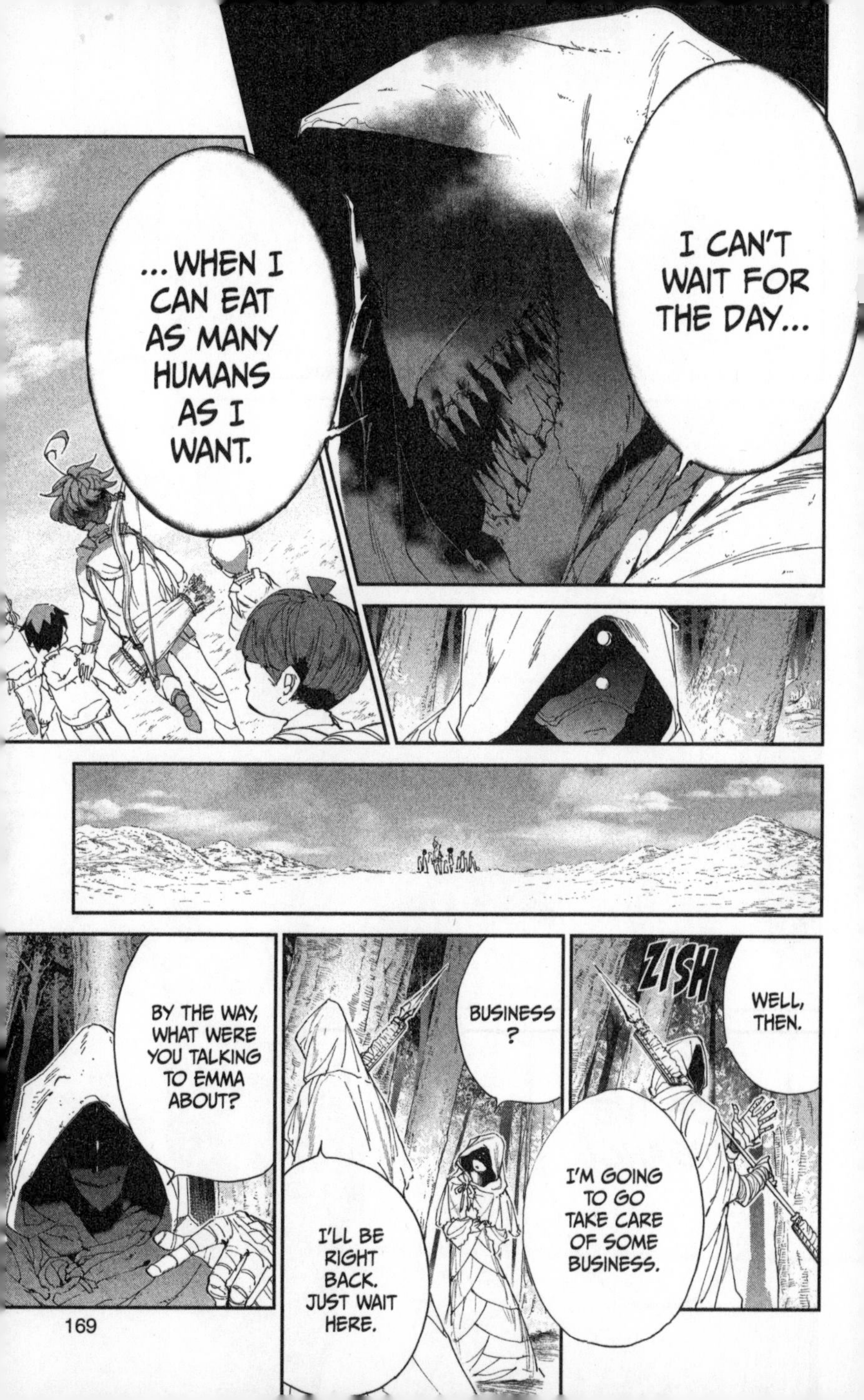
I CAN'T WAIT FOR THE DAY...
...WHEN I CAN EAT AS MANY HUMANS AS I WANT.
ZISH
WELL, THEN.
I'M GOING TO GO TAKE CARE OF SOME BUSINESS.
BUSINESS?
I'LL BE RIGHT BACK. JUST WAIT HERE.
BY THE WAY, WHAT WERE YOU TALKING TO EMMA ABOUT?

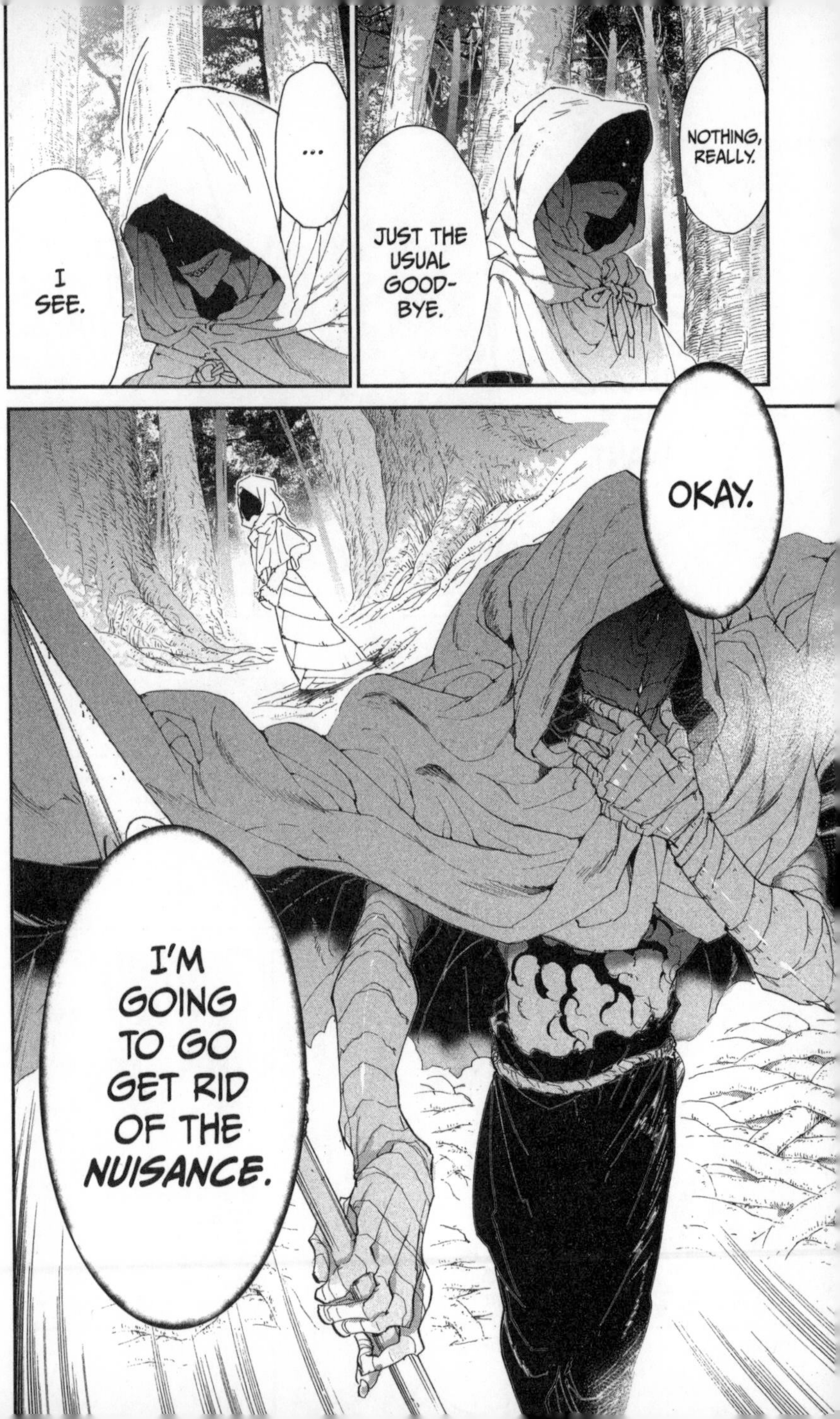
NOTHING, REALLY.
JUST THE USUAL GOOD-BYE.
...
I SEE.
OKAY.
I'M GOING TO GO GET RID OF THE *NUISANCE*.

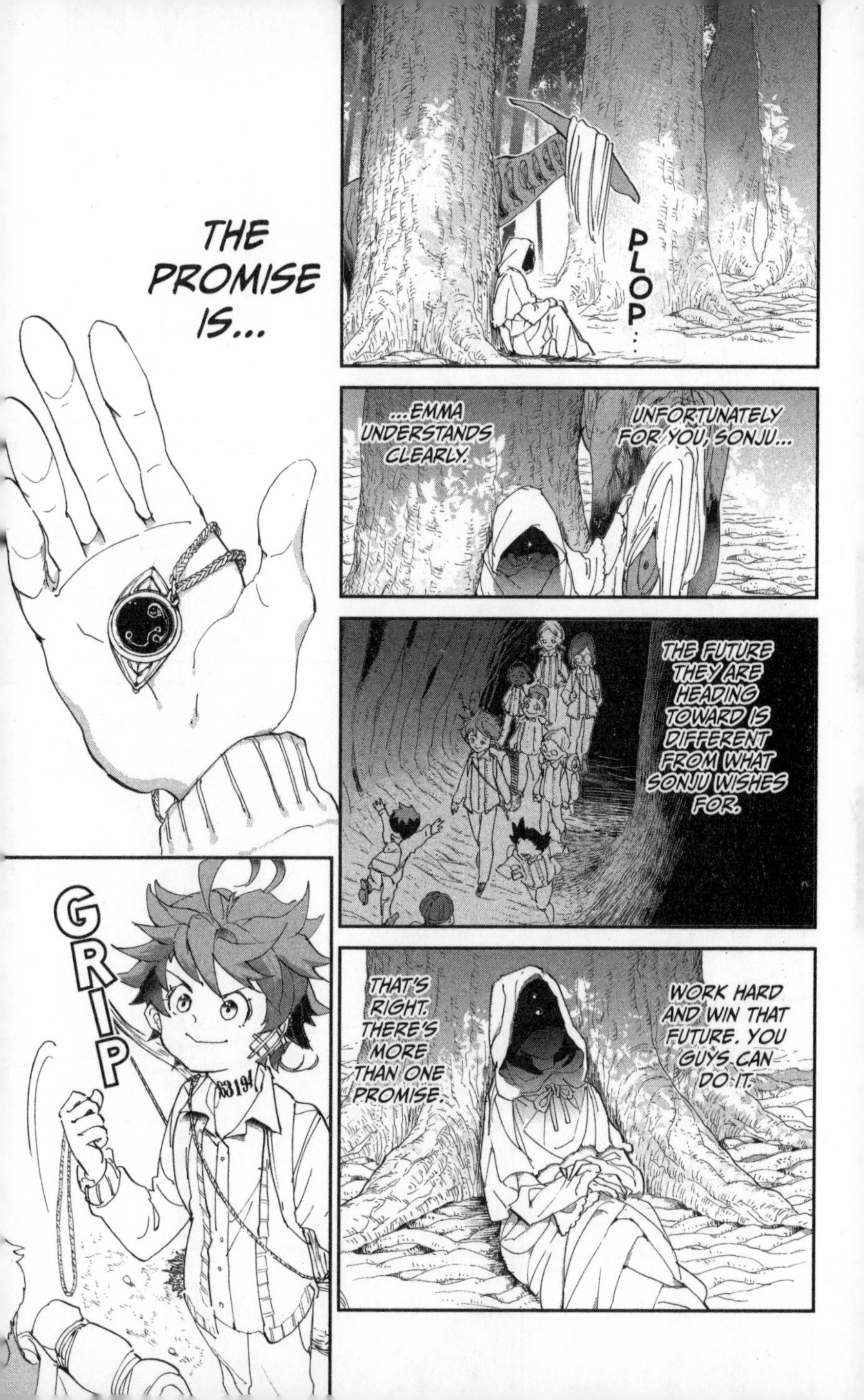
PLOP...
UNFORTUNATELY FOR YOU, SONJU...
...EMMA UNDERSTANDS CLEARLY.
THE FUTURE THEY ARE HEADING TOWARD IS DIFFERENT FROM WHAT SONJU WISHES FOR.
WORK HARD AND WIN THAT FUTURE. YOU GUYS CAN DO IT.
THAT'S RIGHT. THERE'S MORE THAN ONE PROMISE.
THE PROMISE IS...
GRIP
63194

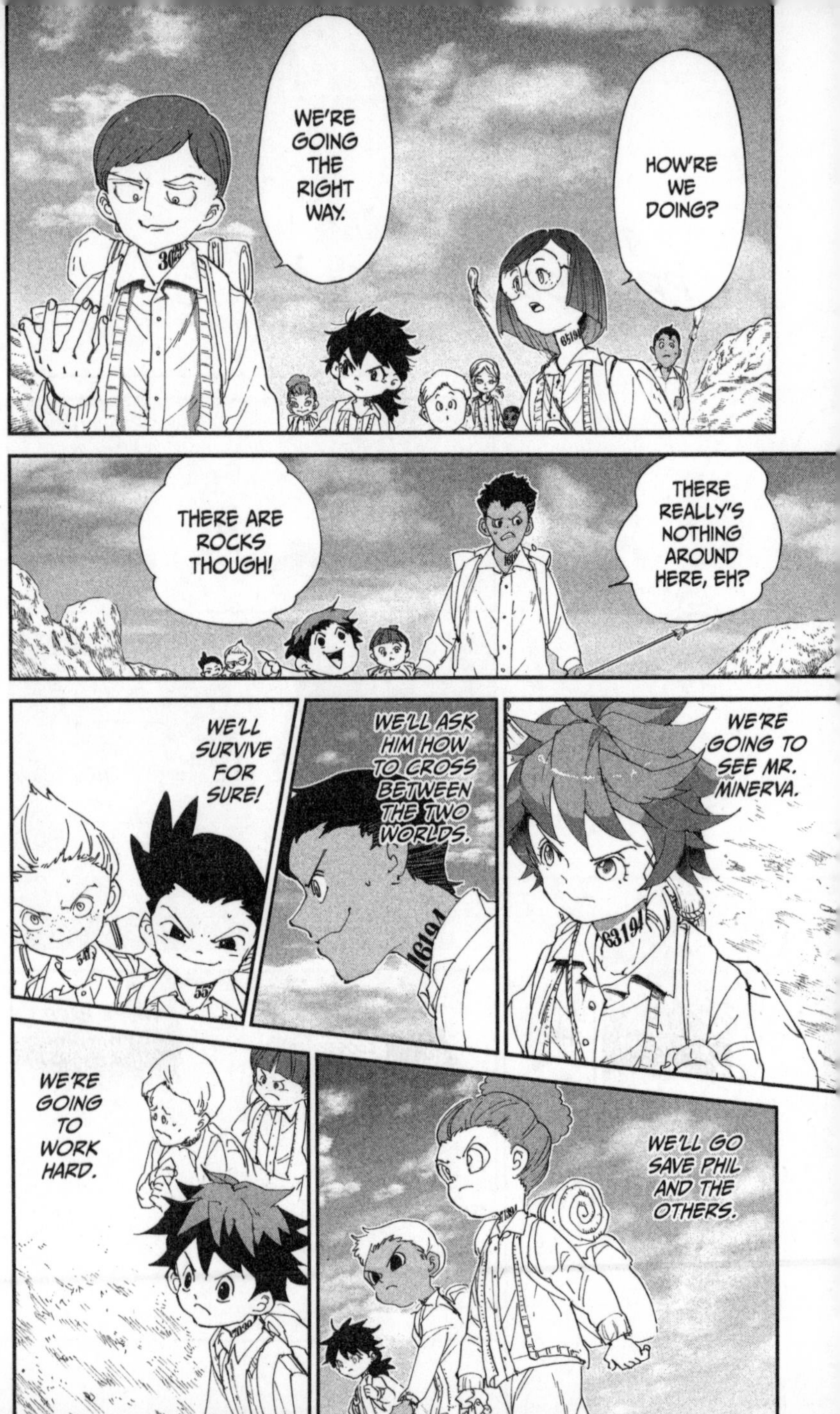
HOW'RE WE DOING?
WE'RE GOING THE RIGHT WAY.
THERE REALLY'S NOTHING AROUND HERE, EH?
THERE ARE ROCKS THOUGH!
WE'RE GOING TO SEE MR. MINERVA.
WE'LL ASK HIM HOW TO CROSS BETWEEN THE TWO WORLDS.
WE'LL SURVIVE FOR SURE!
WE'LL GO SAVE PHIL AND THE OTHERS.
WE'RE GOING TO WORK HARD.

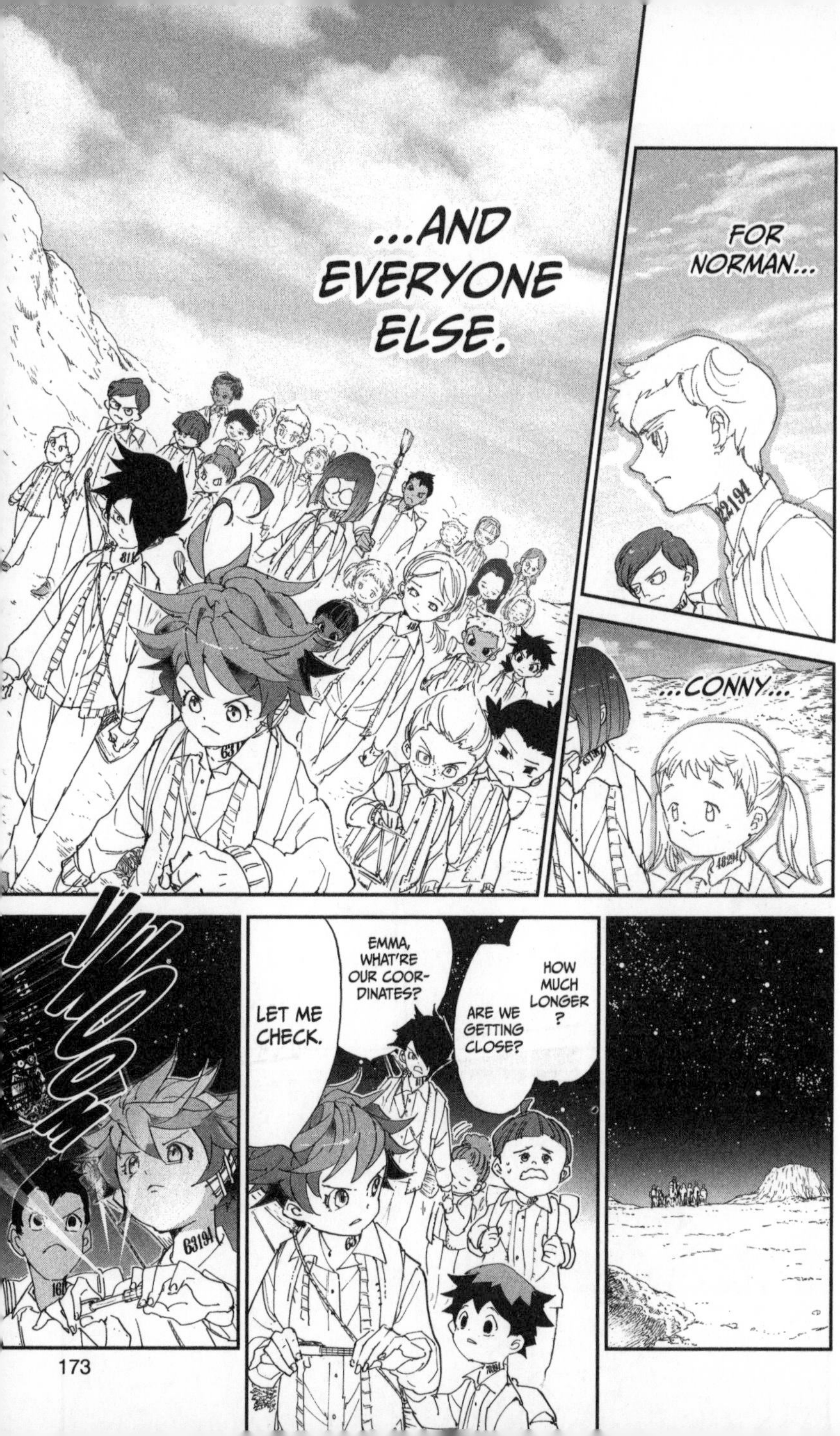
FOR NORMAN...
...CONNY...
...AND EVERYONE ELSE.
HOW MUCH LONGER?
ARE WE GETTING CLOSE?
EMMA, WHAT'RE OUR COOR-DINATES?
LET ME CHECK.
VWOOM

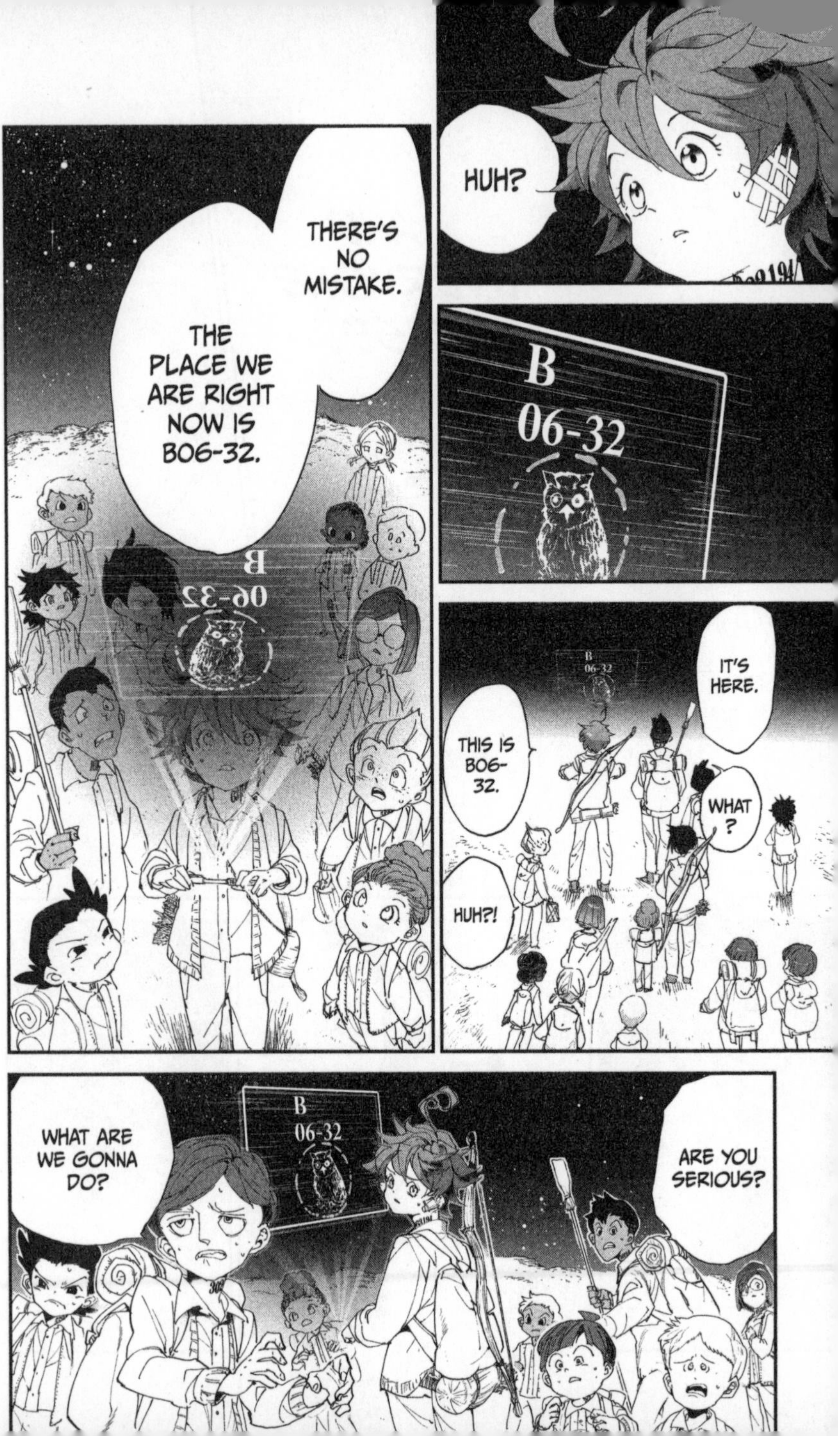
HUH?
B
06-32
IT'S HERE.
THIS IS B06-32.
WHAT?
HUH?!
THERE'S NO MISTAKE.
THE PLACE WE ARE RIGHT NOW IS B06-32.
ARE YOU SERIOUS?
WHAT ARE WE GONNA DO?

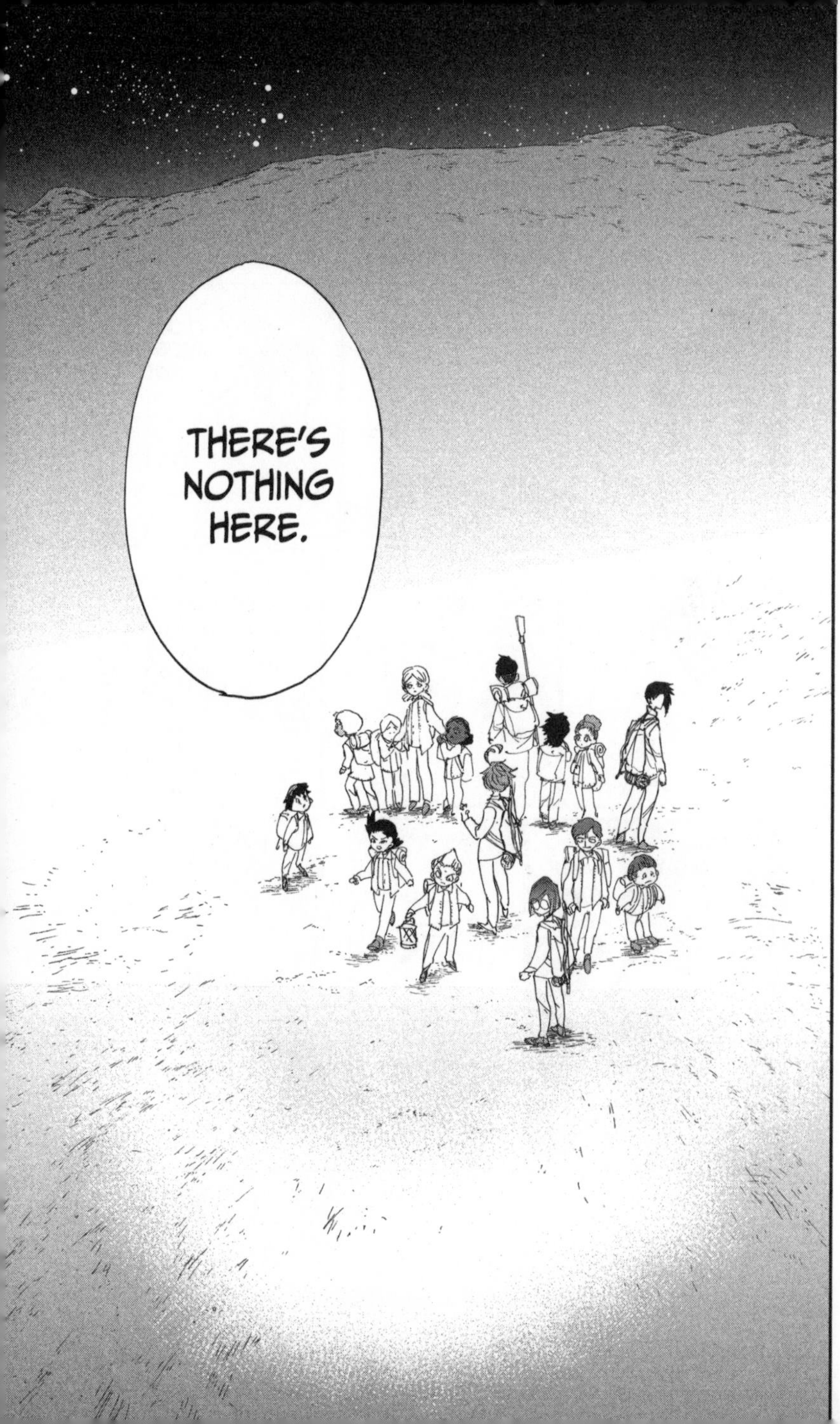
THERE'S NOTHING HERE.

ORIGINAL STREAMER

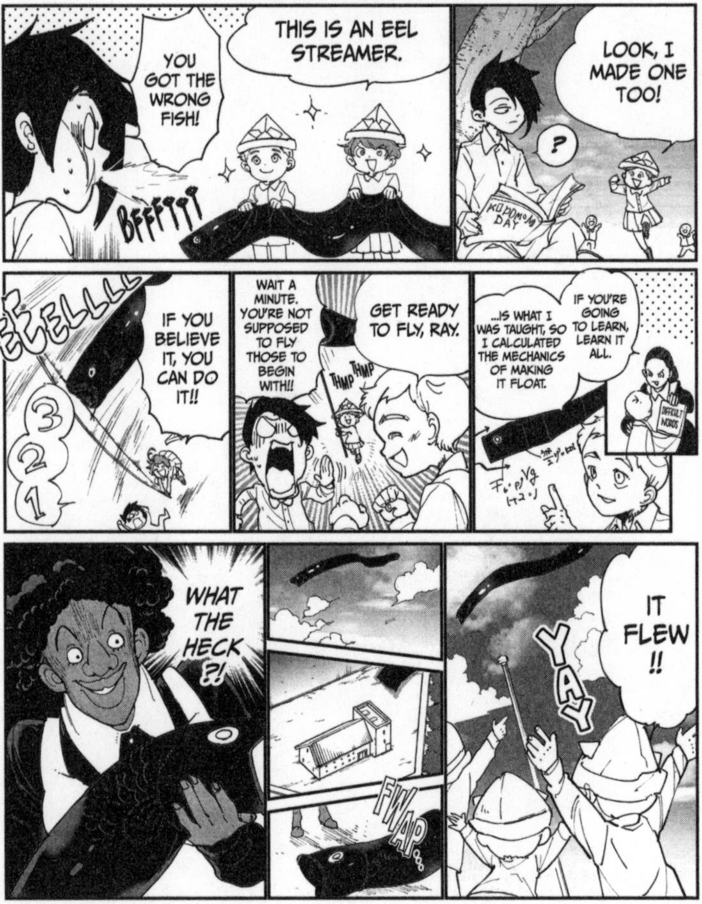
LOOK, I MADE ONE TOO!
?
THIS IS AN EEL STREAMER.
YOU GOT THE WRONG FISH!
BFFFFT
IF YOU'RE GOING TO LEARN, LEARN IT ALL.
DIFFICULT WORDS
...IS WHAT I WAS TAUGHT, SO I CALCULATED THE MECHANICS OF MAKING IT FLOAT.
GET READY TO FLY, RAY.
THMP THMP
WAIT A MINUTE. YOU'RE NOT SUPPOSED TO FLY THOSE TO BEGIN WITH!!
IF YOU BELIEVE IT, YOU CAN DO IT!!
EEELLLL
3
2
1
IT FLEW!!
YAY
FWAP
WHAT THE HECK?!

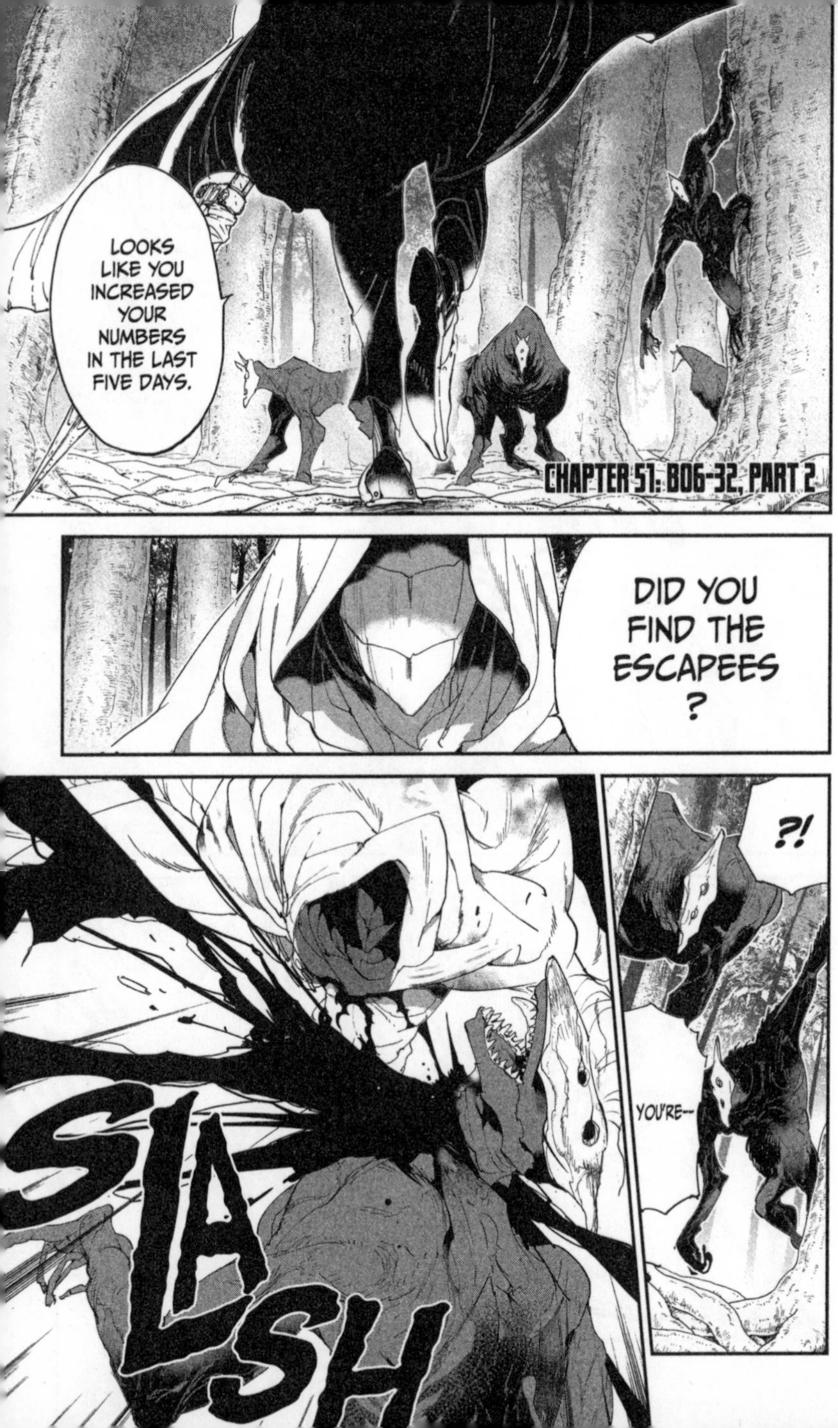
LOOKS LIKE YOU INCREASED YOUR NUMBERS IN THE LAST FIVE DAYS.
CHAPTER 51: B06-32, PART 2
DID YOU FIND THE ESCAPEES?
?!
YOU'RE--
SLASH

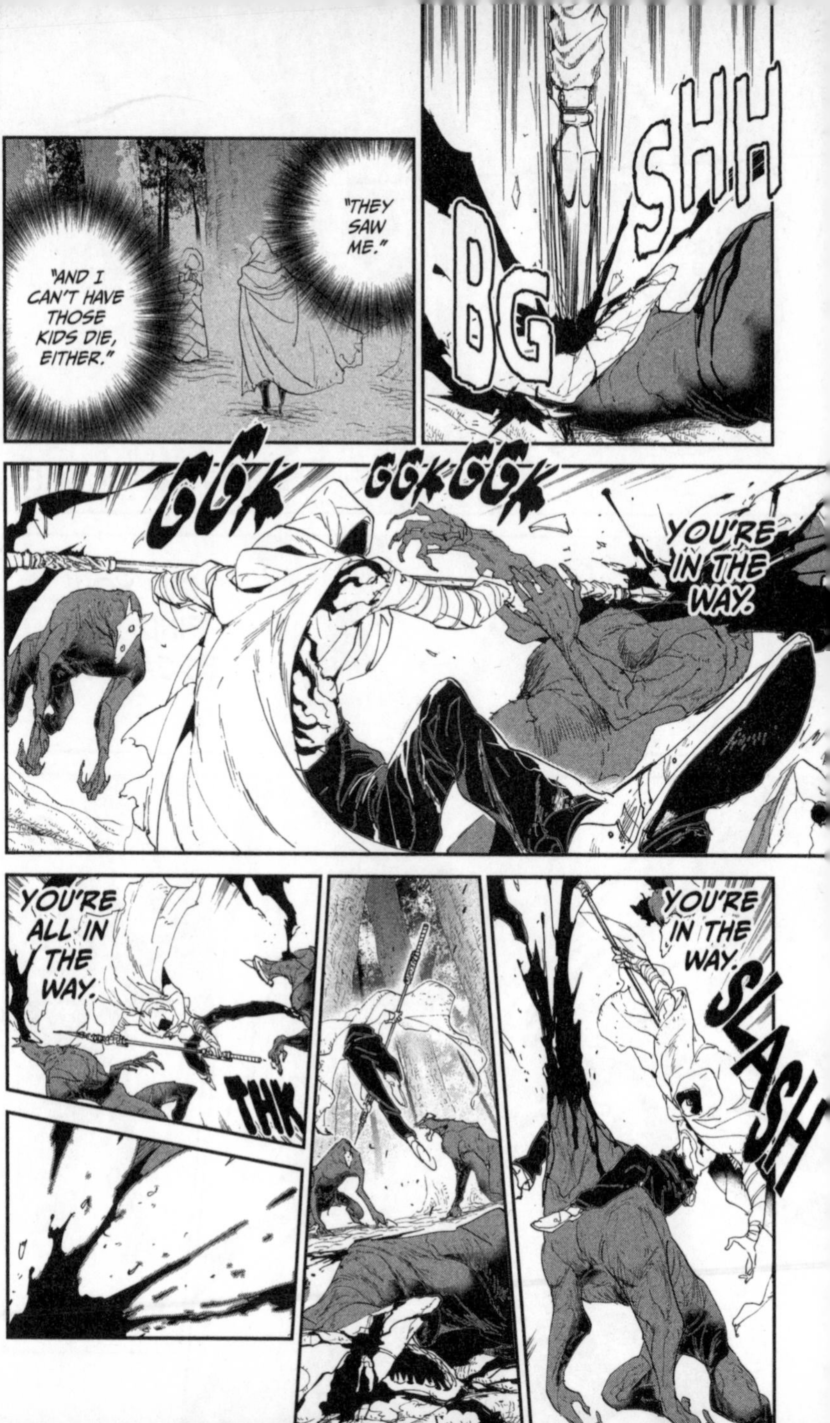
SHH
BG
"THEY SAW ME."
"AND I CAN'T HAVE THOSE KIDS DIE, EITHER."
GGK GGK
GGK
YOU'RE IN THE WAY.
YOU'RE IN THE WAY.
SLASH
YOU'RE ALL IN THE WAY.
THK

[redacted]

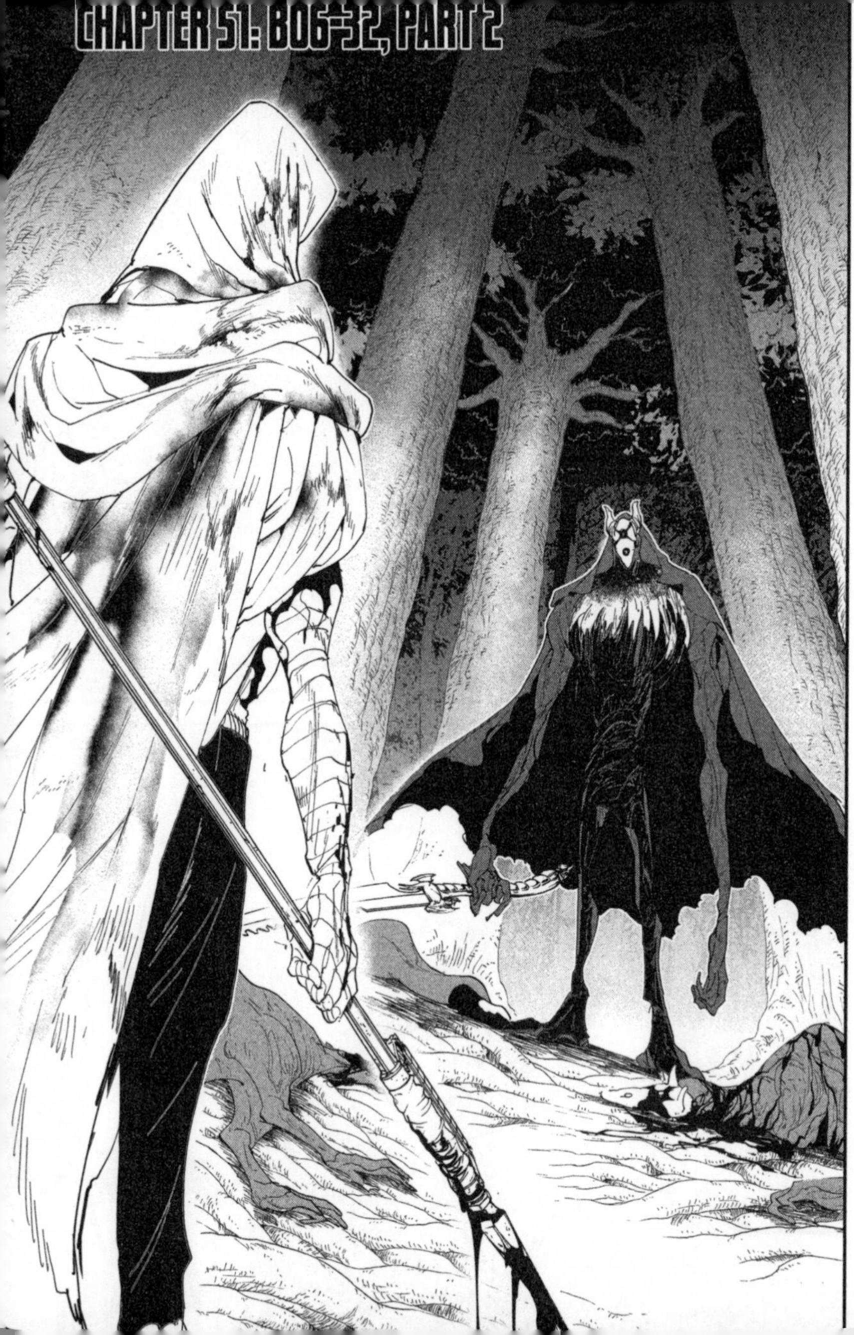

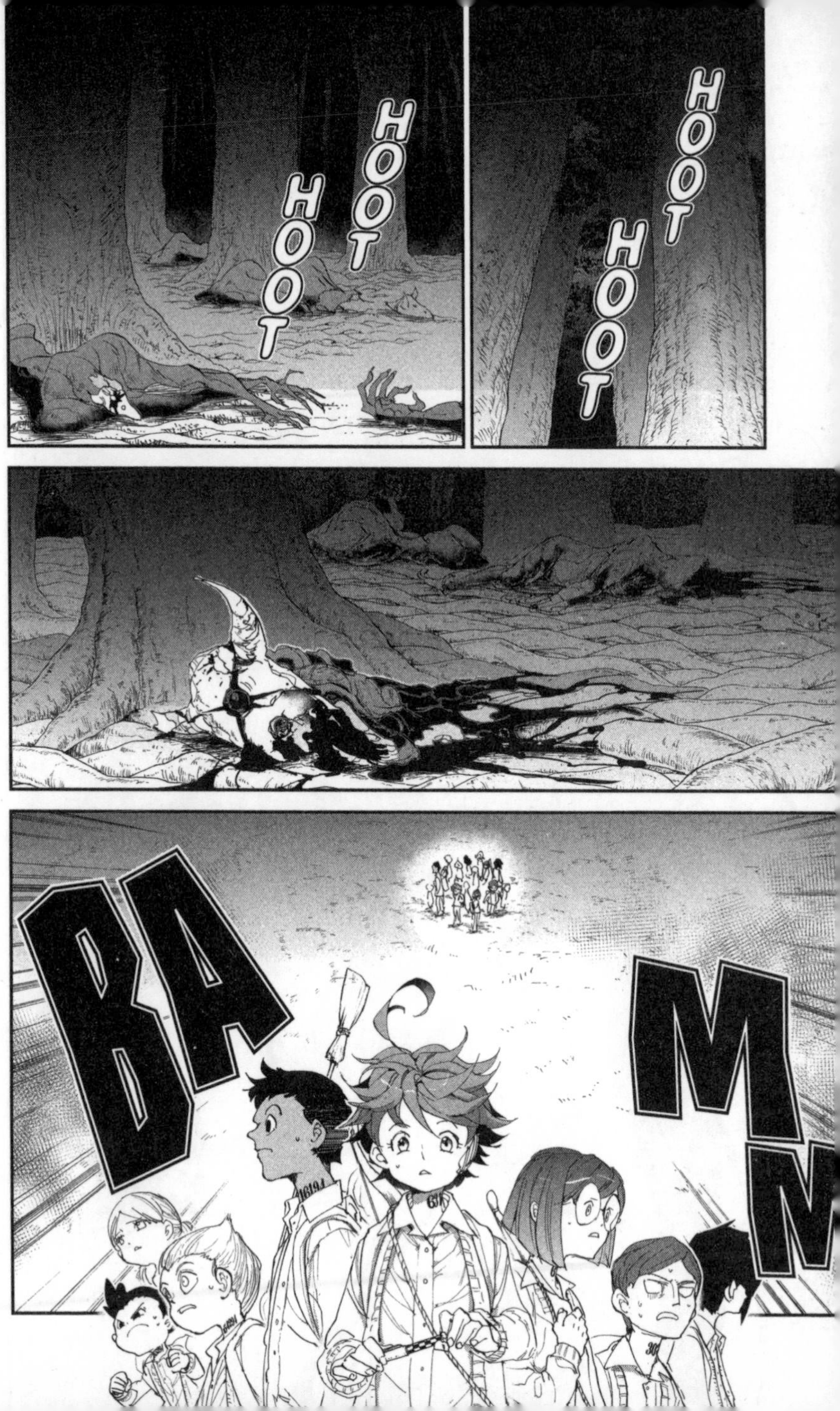
HOOT
HOOT
HOOT
HOOT
BAMN

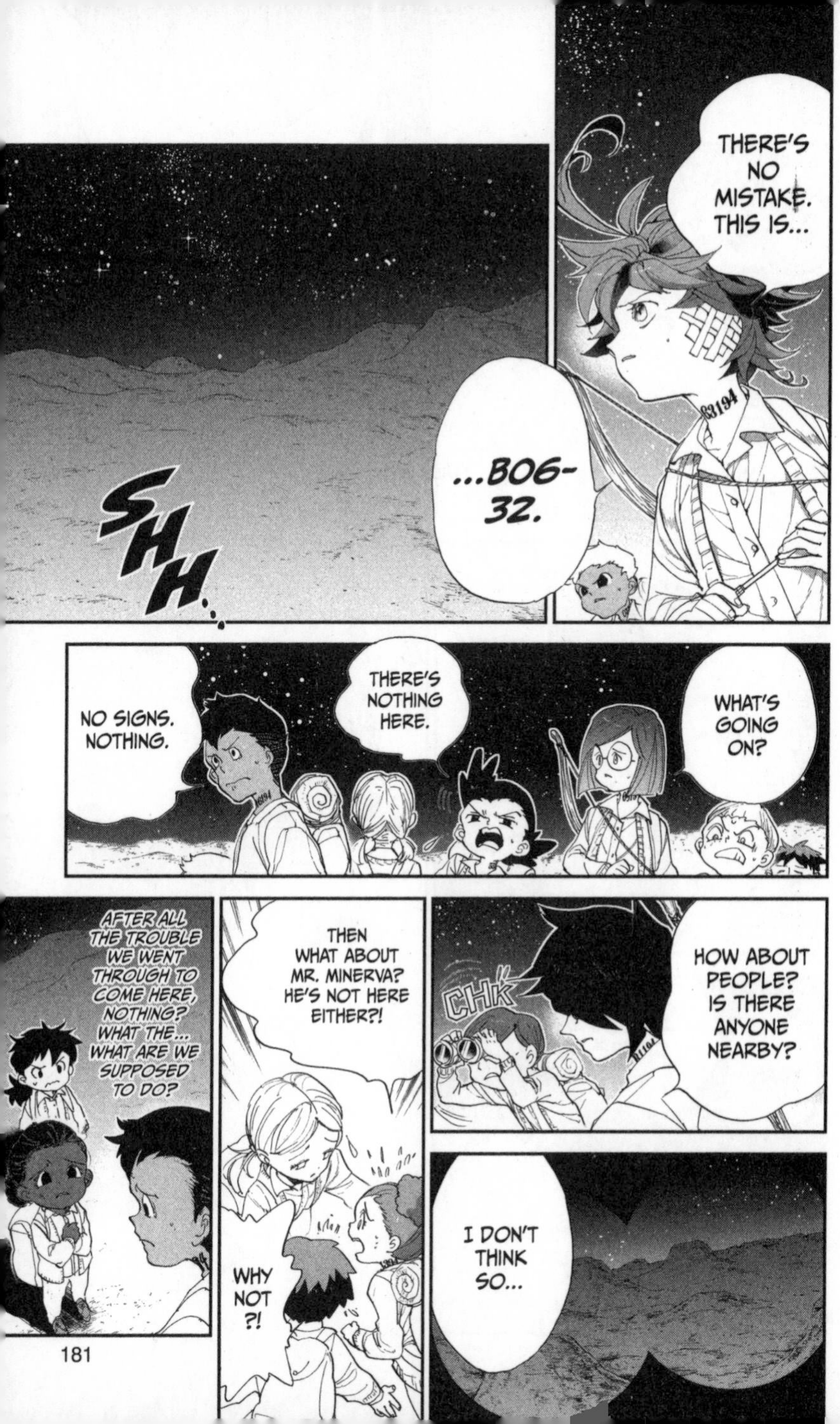
THERE'S NO MISTAKE. THIS IS...
...B06-32.
SHH...
WHAT'S GOING ON?
THERE'S NOTHING HERE.
NO SIGNS. NOTHING.
CHK
HOW ABOUT PEOPLE? IS THERE ANYONE NEARBY?
I DON'T THINK SO...
THEN WHAT ABOUT MR. MINERVA? HE'S NOT HERE EITHER?!
WHY NOT?!
AFTER ALL THE TROUBLE WE WENT THROUGH TO COME HERE, NOTHING? WHAT THE... WHAT ARE WE SUPPOSED TO DO?

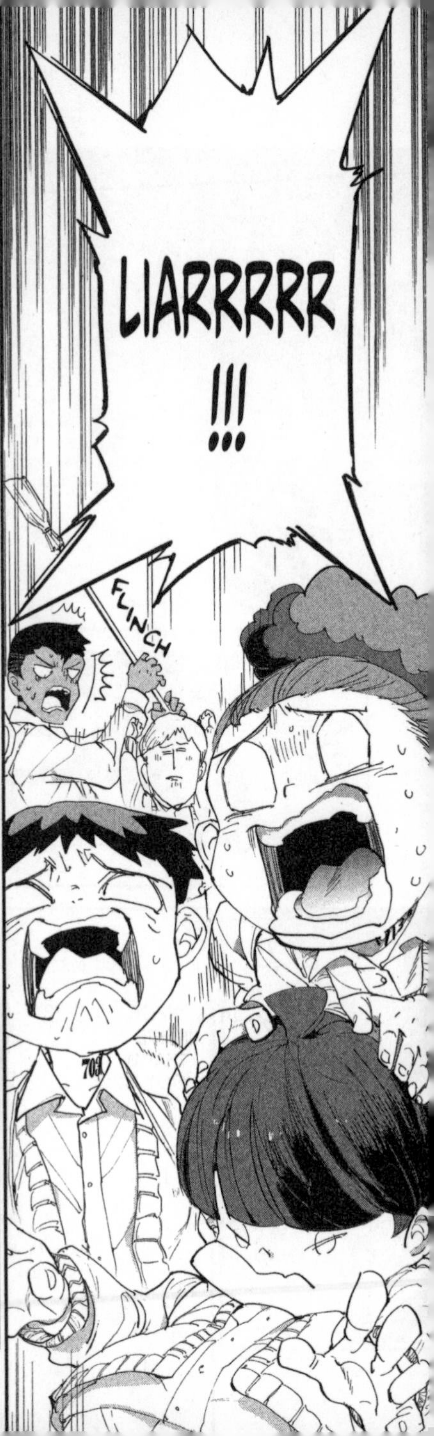
LIARRRRR!!!
FLINCH

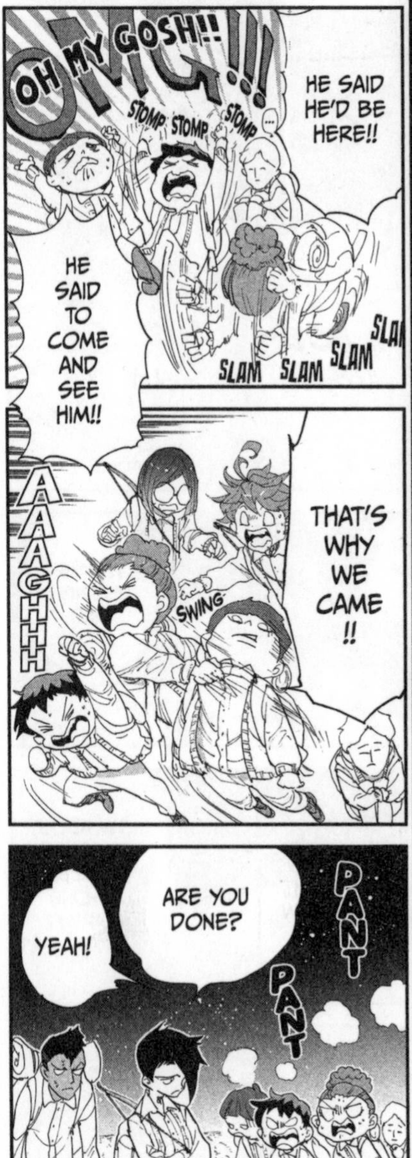
HE SAID HE'D BE HERE!!
OH MY GOSH!!
OMG!!!
STOMP STOMP STOMP
...
HE SAID TO COME AND SEE HIM!!
SLAM SLAM SLAM SLAM
THAT'S WHY WE CAME!!
SWING
AAAAGHHHH
PANT PANT
ARE YOU DONE?
YEAH!

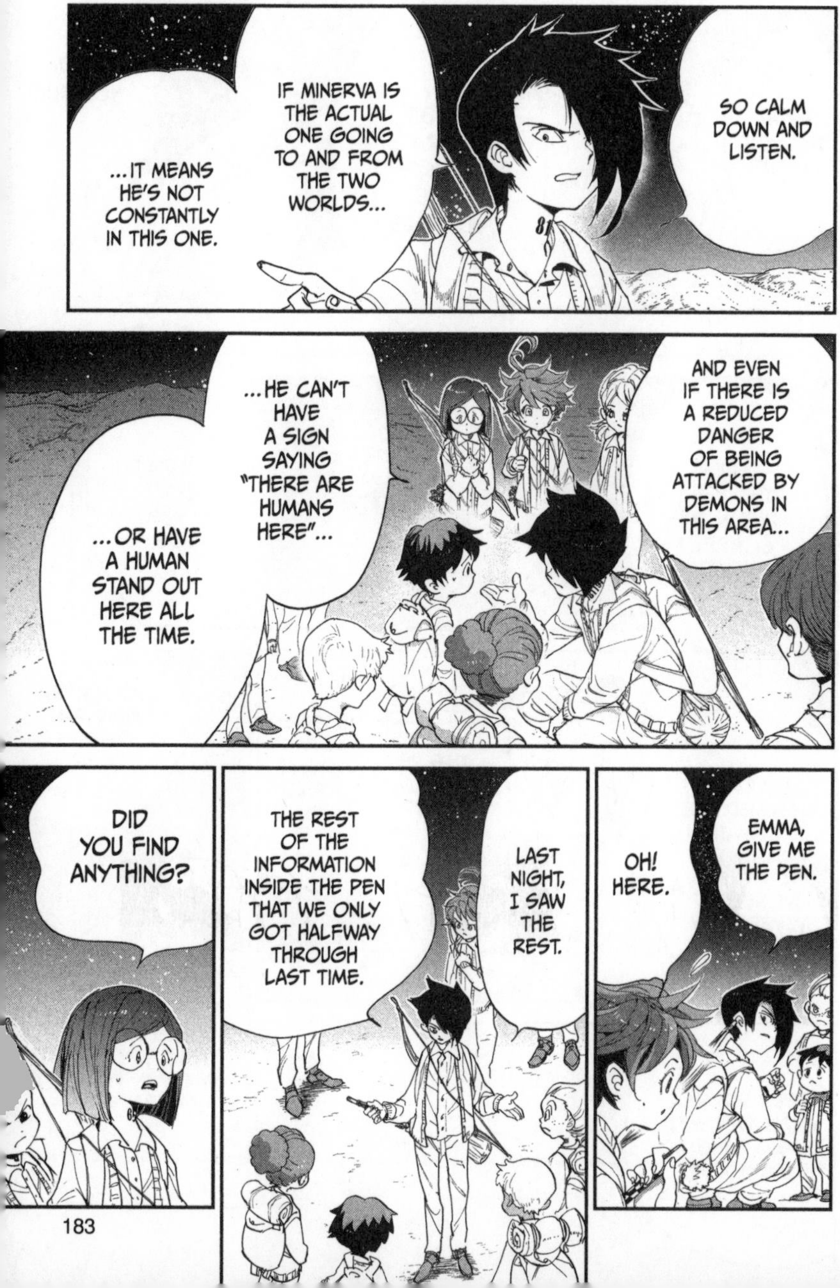
SO CALM DOWN AND LISTEN.
IF MINERVA IS THE ACTUAL ONE GOING TO AND FROM THE TWO WORLDS...
...IT MEANS HE'S NOT CONSTANTLY IN THIS ONE.
AND EVEN IF THERE IS A REDUCED DANGER OF BEING ATTACKED BY DEMONS IN THIS AREA...
...HE CAN'T HAVE A SIGN SAYING "THERE ARE HUMANS HERE"...
...OR HAVE A HUMAN STAND OUT HERE ALL THE TIME.
EMMA, GIVE ME THE PEN.
OH! HERE.
LAST NIGHT, I SAW THE REST.
THE REST OF THE INFORMATION INSIDE THE PEN THAT WE ONLY GOT HALFWAY THROUGH LAST TIME.
DID YOU FIND ANYTHING?

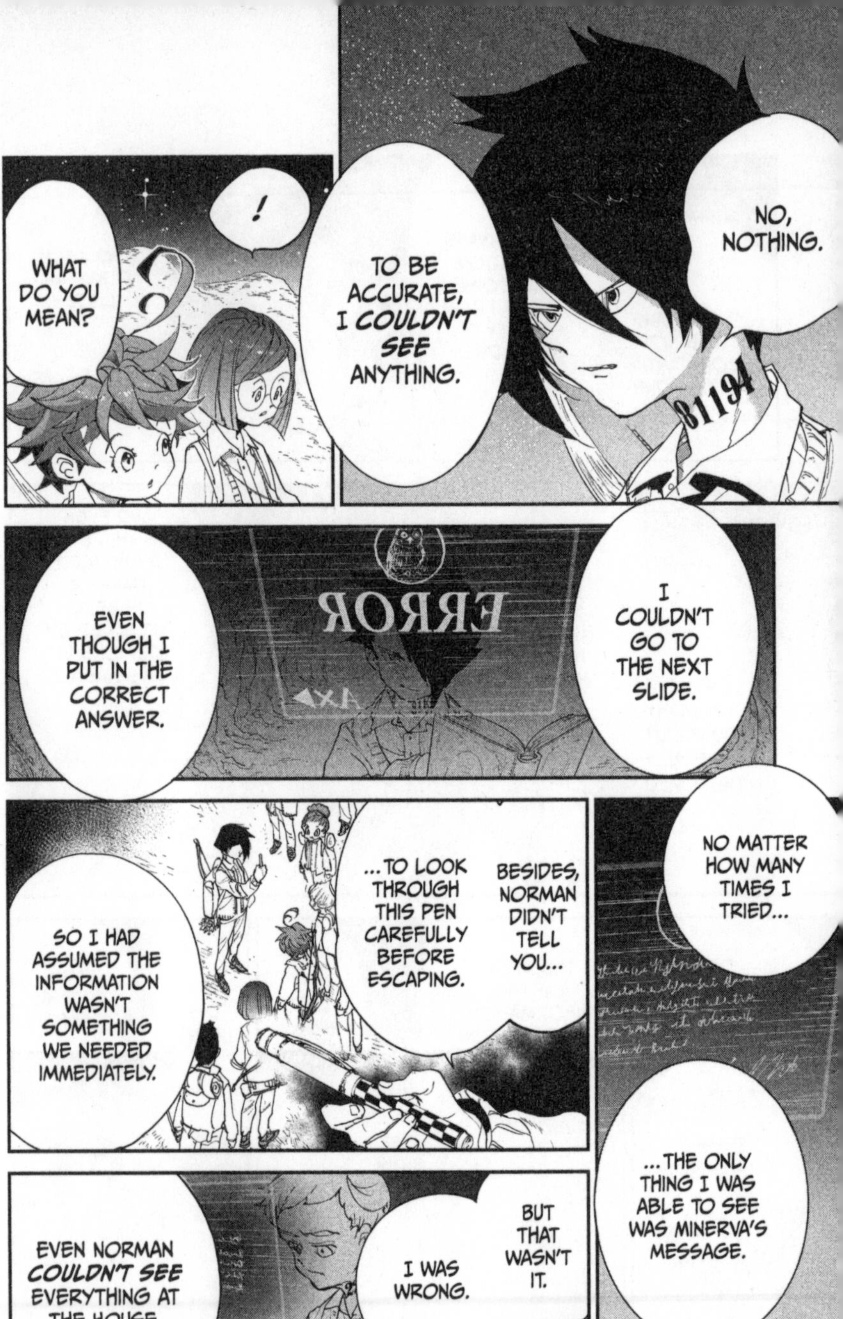

NO, NOTHING.
TO BE ACCURATE, I COULDN'T SEE ANYTHING.
!
WHAT DO YOU MEAN?
I COULDN'T GO TO THE NEXT SLIDE.
ERROR
EVEN THOUGH I PUT IN THE CORRECT ANSWER.
NO MATTER HOW MANY TIMES I TRIED...
...THE ONLY THING I WAS ABLE TO SEE WAS MINERVA'S MESSAGE.
BESIDES, NORMAN DIDN'T TELL YOU...
...TO LOOK THROUGH THIS PEN CAREFULLY BEFORE ESCAPING.
SO I HAD ASSUMED THE INFORMATION WASN'T SOMETHING WE NEEDED IMMEDIATELY.
BUT THAT WASN'T IT.
I WAS WRONG.
EVEN NORMAN COULDN'T SEE EVERYTHING AT THE HOUSE.

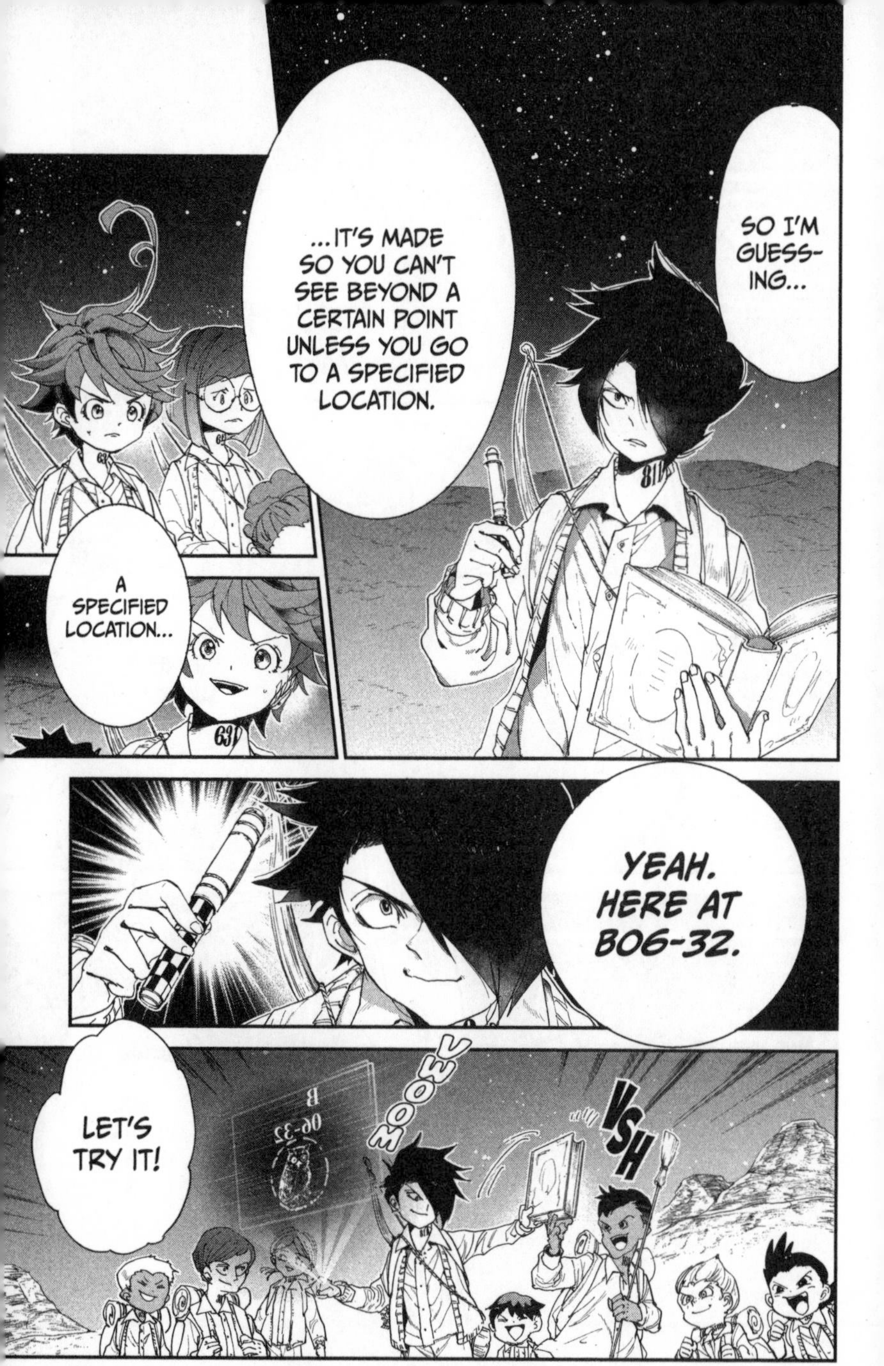
SO I'M GUESS-ING...
...IT'S MADE SO YOU CAN'T SEE BEYOND A CERTAIN POINT UNLESS YOU GO TO A SPECIFIED LOCATION.
A SPECIFIED LOCATION...
YEAH. HERE AT B06-32.
VSH
VWOOM
LET'S TRY IT!

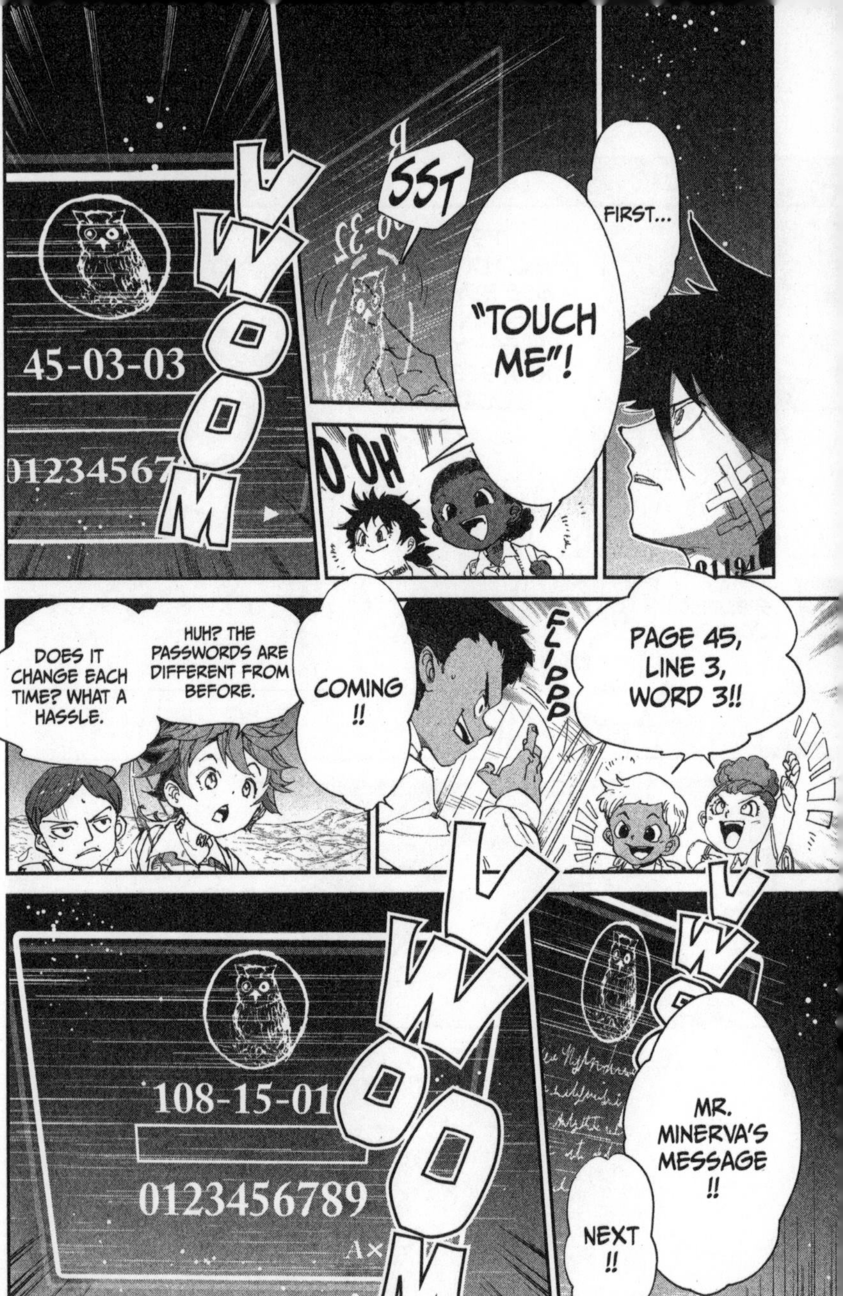
FIRST...
"TOUCH ME"!
SST
OOH
VWOOM
45-03-03
01234567
PAGE 45, LINE 3, WORD 3!!
FLIPPP
COMING!!
HUH? THE PASSWORDS ARE DIFFERENT FROM BEFORE.
DOES IT CHANGE EACH TIME? WHAT A HASSLE.
MR. MINERVA'S MESSAGE!!
NEXT!!
VWOOM
108-15-01
0123456789

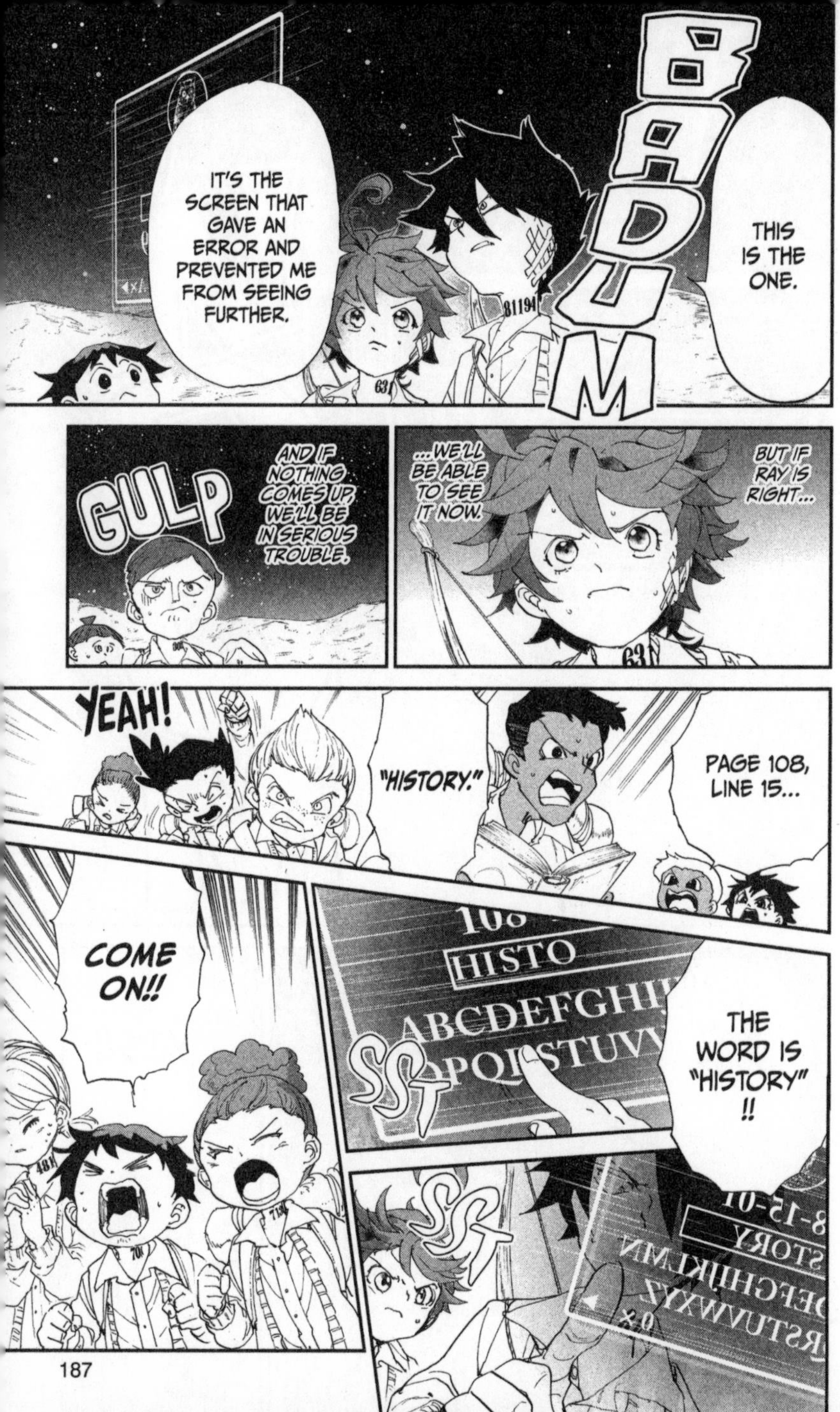
THIS IS THE ONE.
BADUM
IT'S THE SCREEN THAT GAVE AN ERROR AND PREVENTED ME FROM SEEING FURTHER.
BUT IF RAY IS RIGHT...
...WE'LL BE ABLE TO SEE IT NOW.
AND IF NOTHING COMES UP, WE'LL BE IN SERIOUS TROUBLE.
GULP
PAGE 108, LINE 15...
"HISTORY."
YEAH!
THE WORD IS "HISTORY" !!
HISTO
SST
COME ON!!
SST

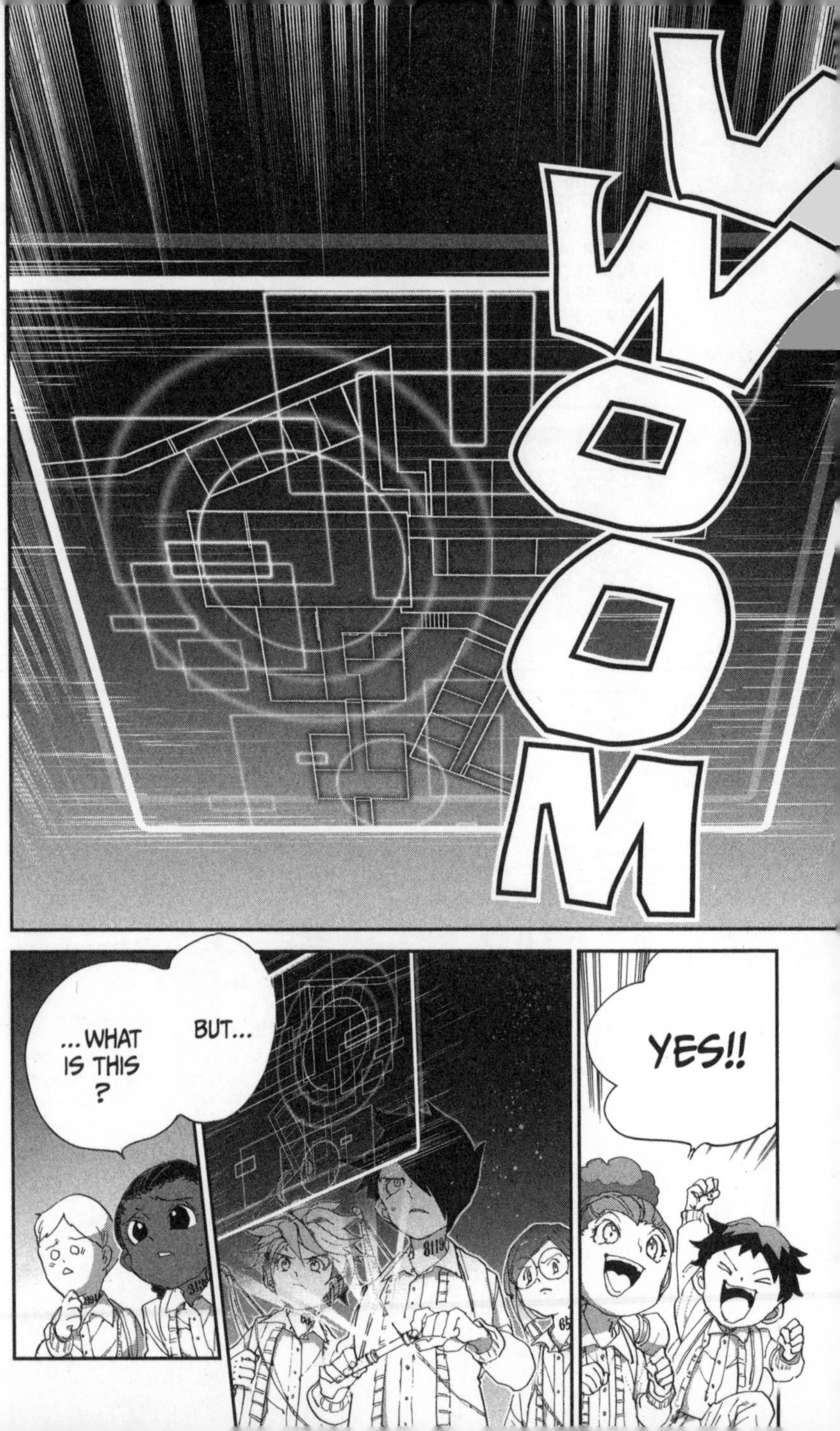
WOOM
YES!!
BUT...
...WHAT IS THIS ?

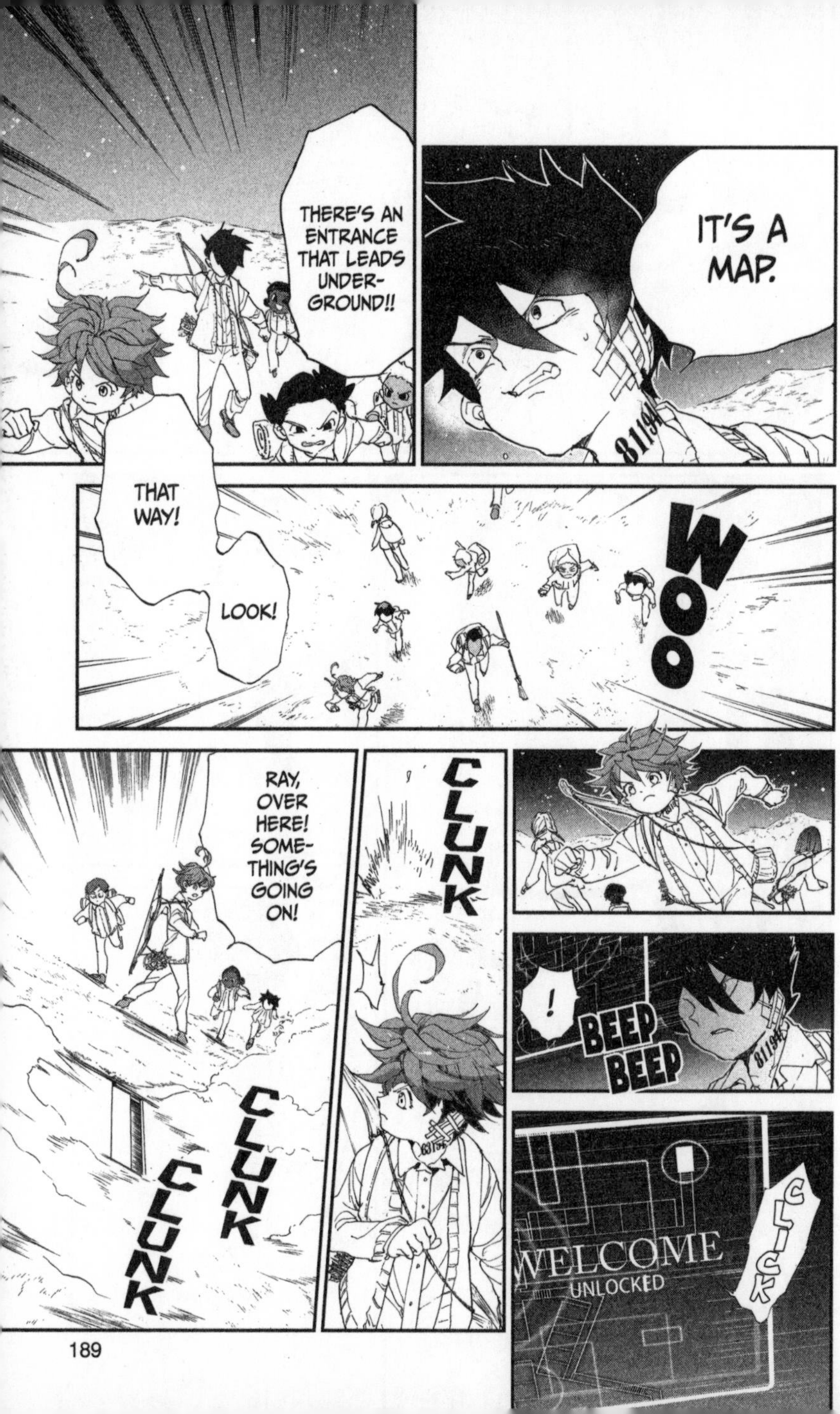
IT'S A MAP.
THERE'S AN ENTRANCE THAT LEADS UNDER-GROUND!!
THAT WAY!
WOO
LOOK!
!
BEEP BEEP
CLICK
WELCOME
UNLOCKED
CLUNK
RAY, OVER HERE! SOME-THING'S GOING ON!
CLUNK
CLUNK

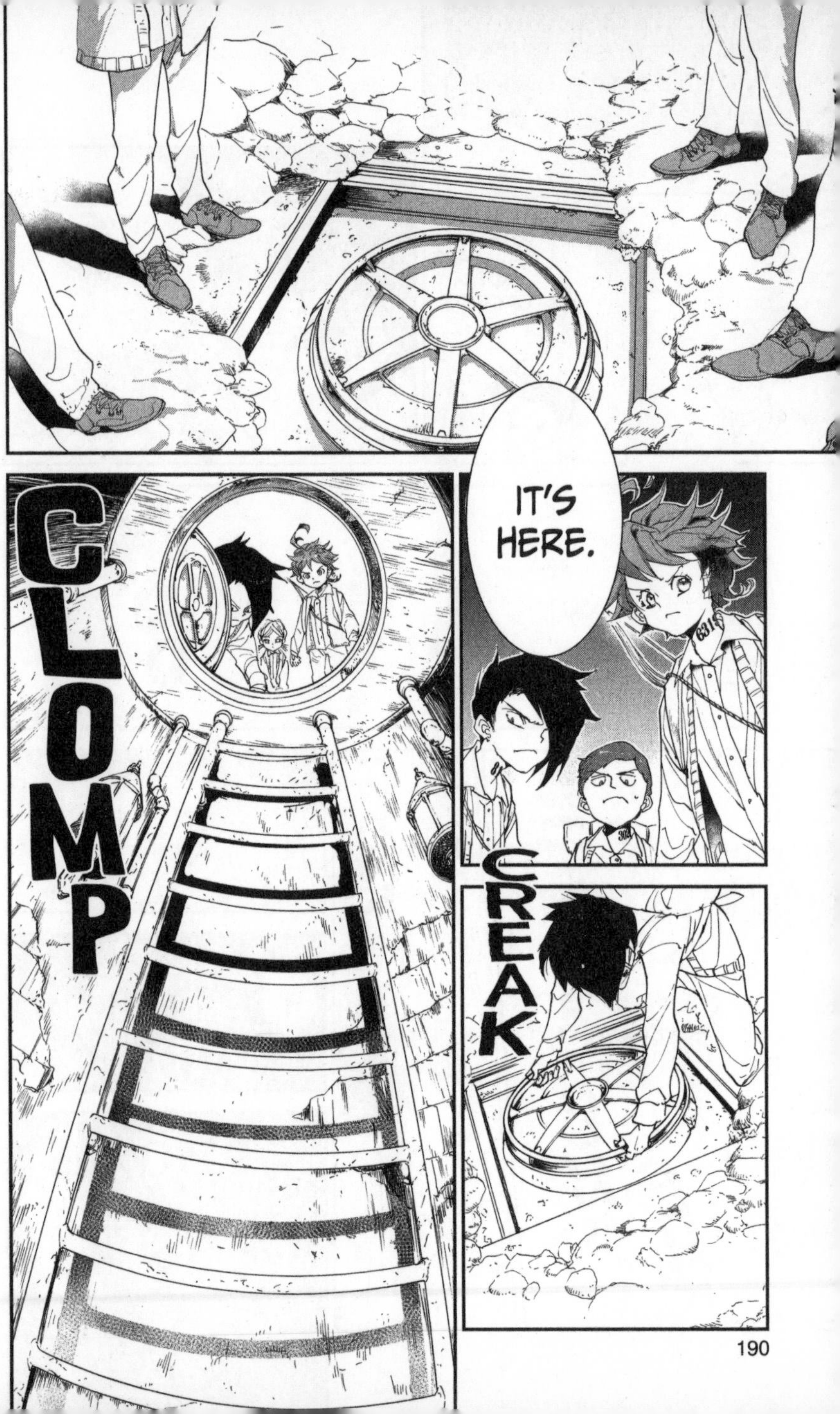
IT'S HERE.
CREAK
CLOMP

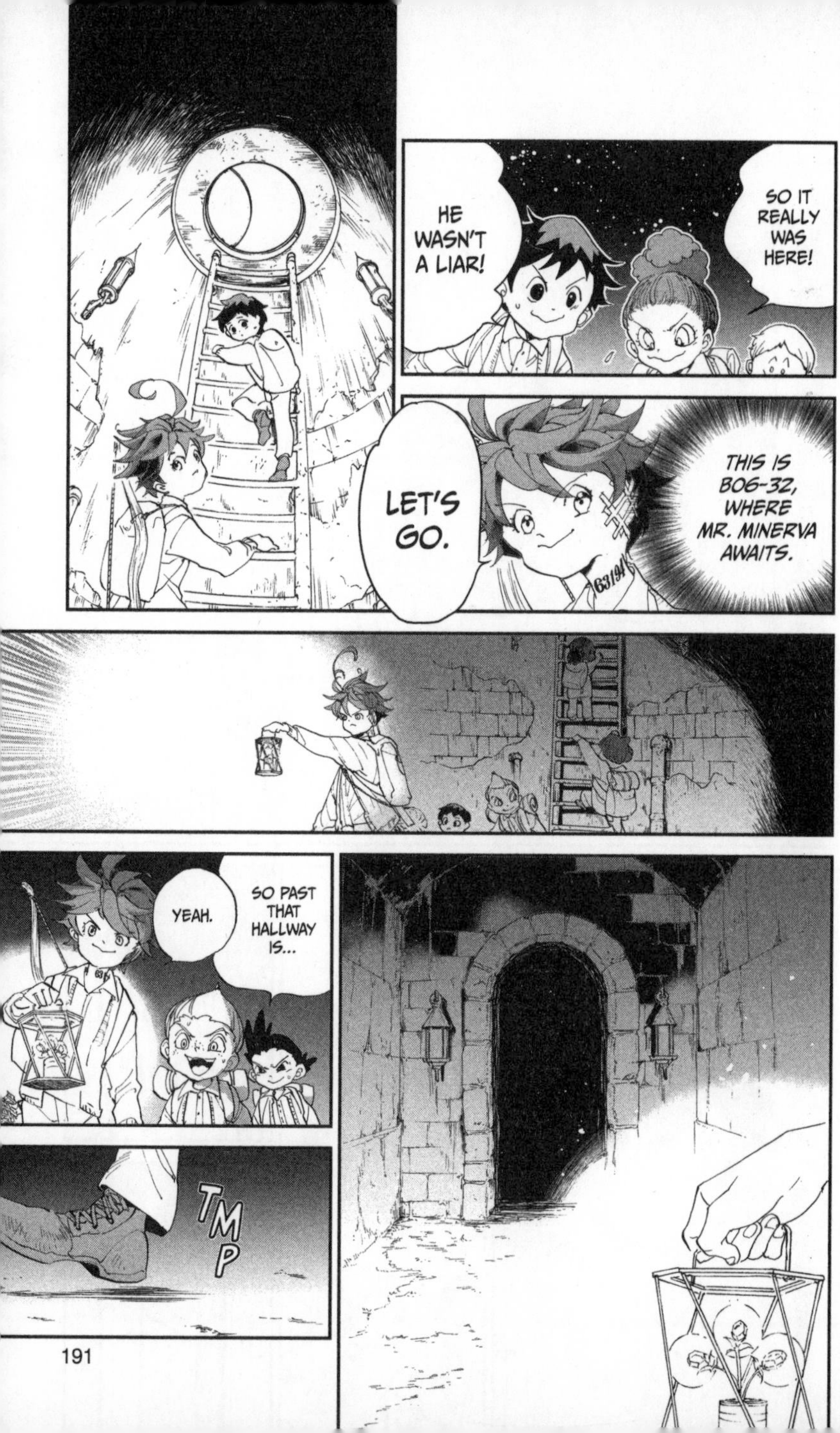
SO IT REALLY WAS HERE!
HE WASN'T A LIAR!
THIS IS B06-32, WHERE MR. MINERVA AWAITS.
LET'S GO.
63194
SO PAST THAT HALLWAY IS...
YEAH.
TMP

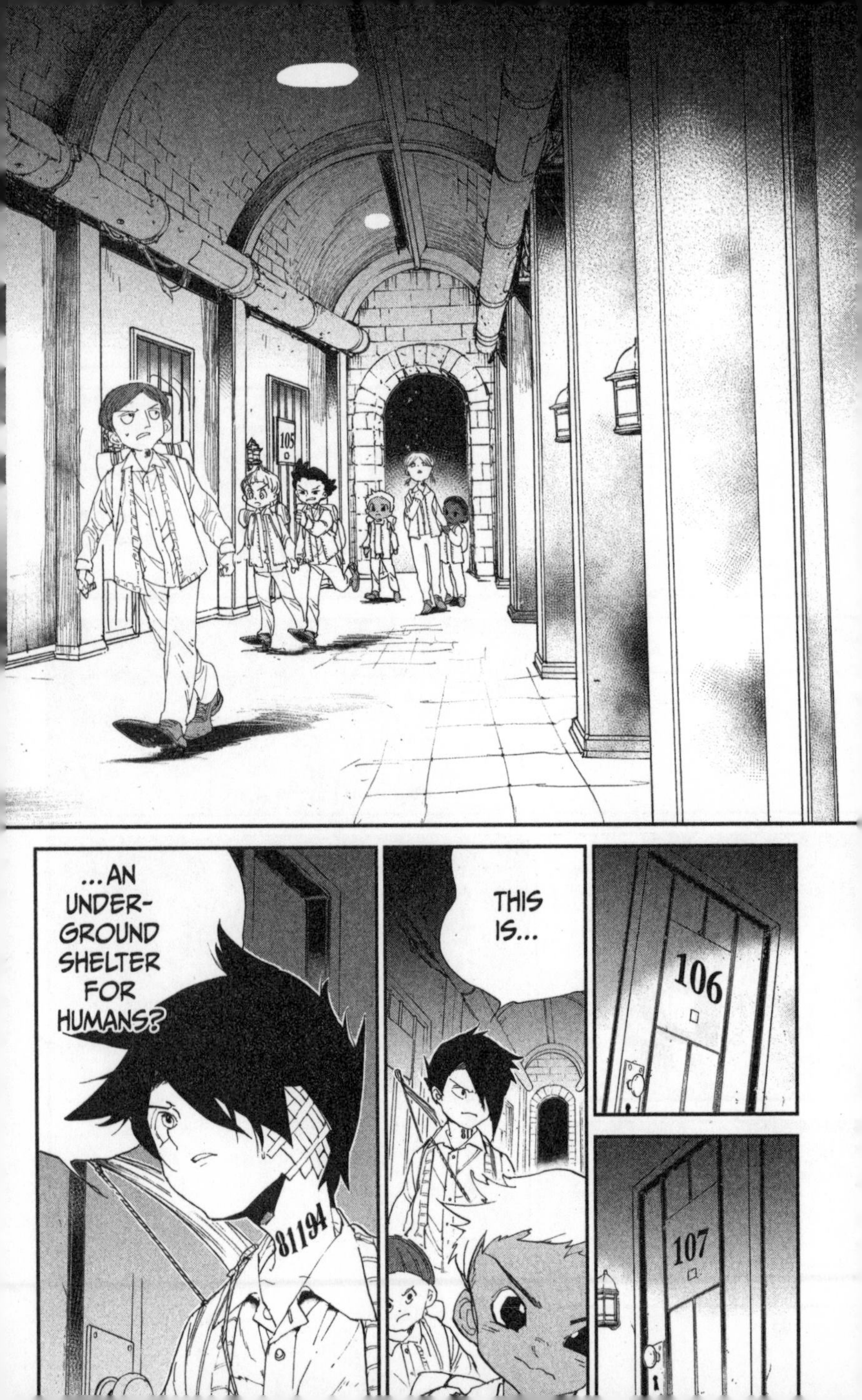
105
106
107
THIS IS...
...AN UNDER-GROUND SHELTER FOR HUMANS?
81194

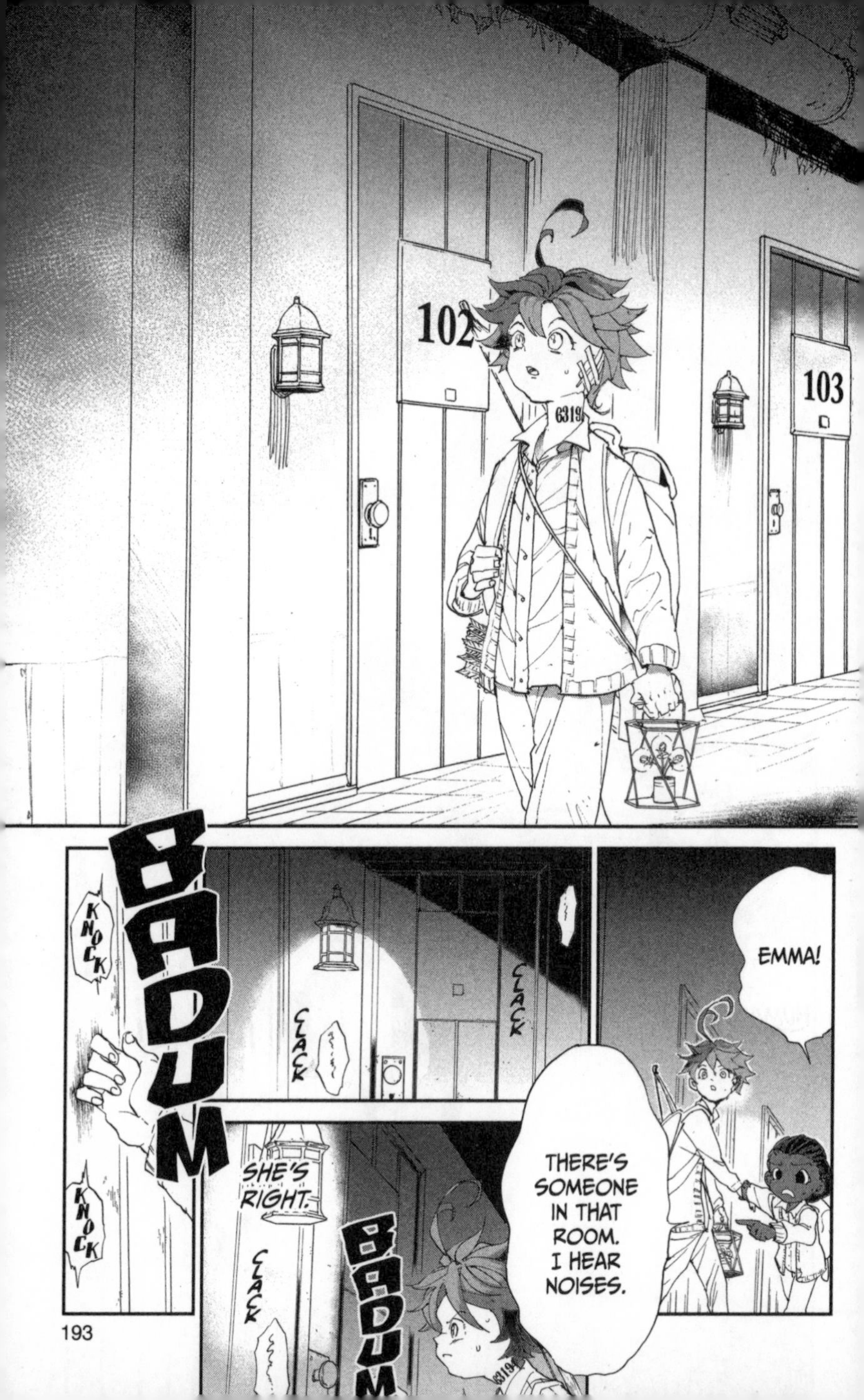
102
6319
103
EMMA!
THERE'S SOMEONE IN THAT ROOM. I HEAR NOISES.
CLACK
CLACK
BADUM
KNOCK
SHE'S RIGHT.
CLACK
BADUM
KNOCK
6319

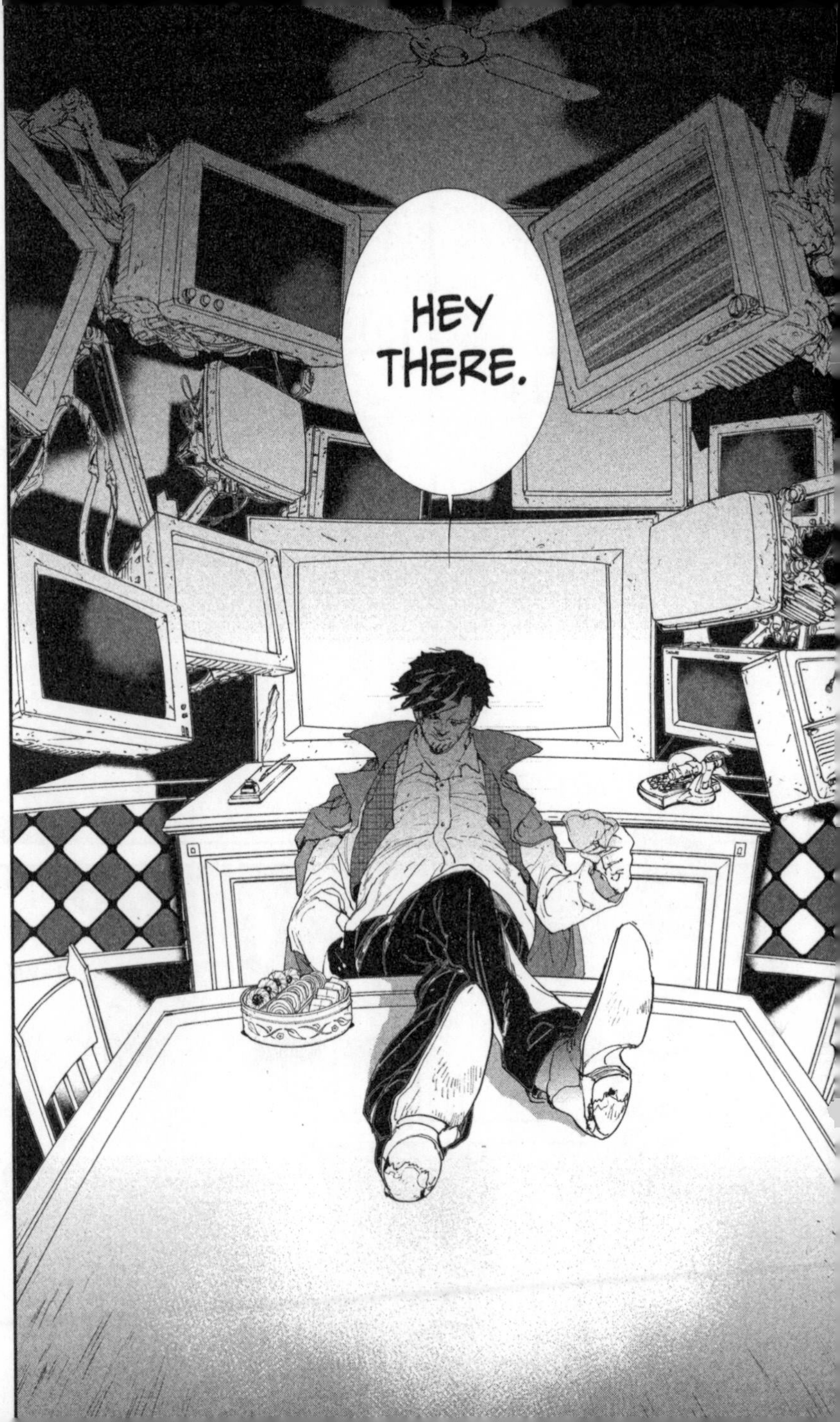
HEY THERE.

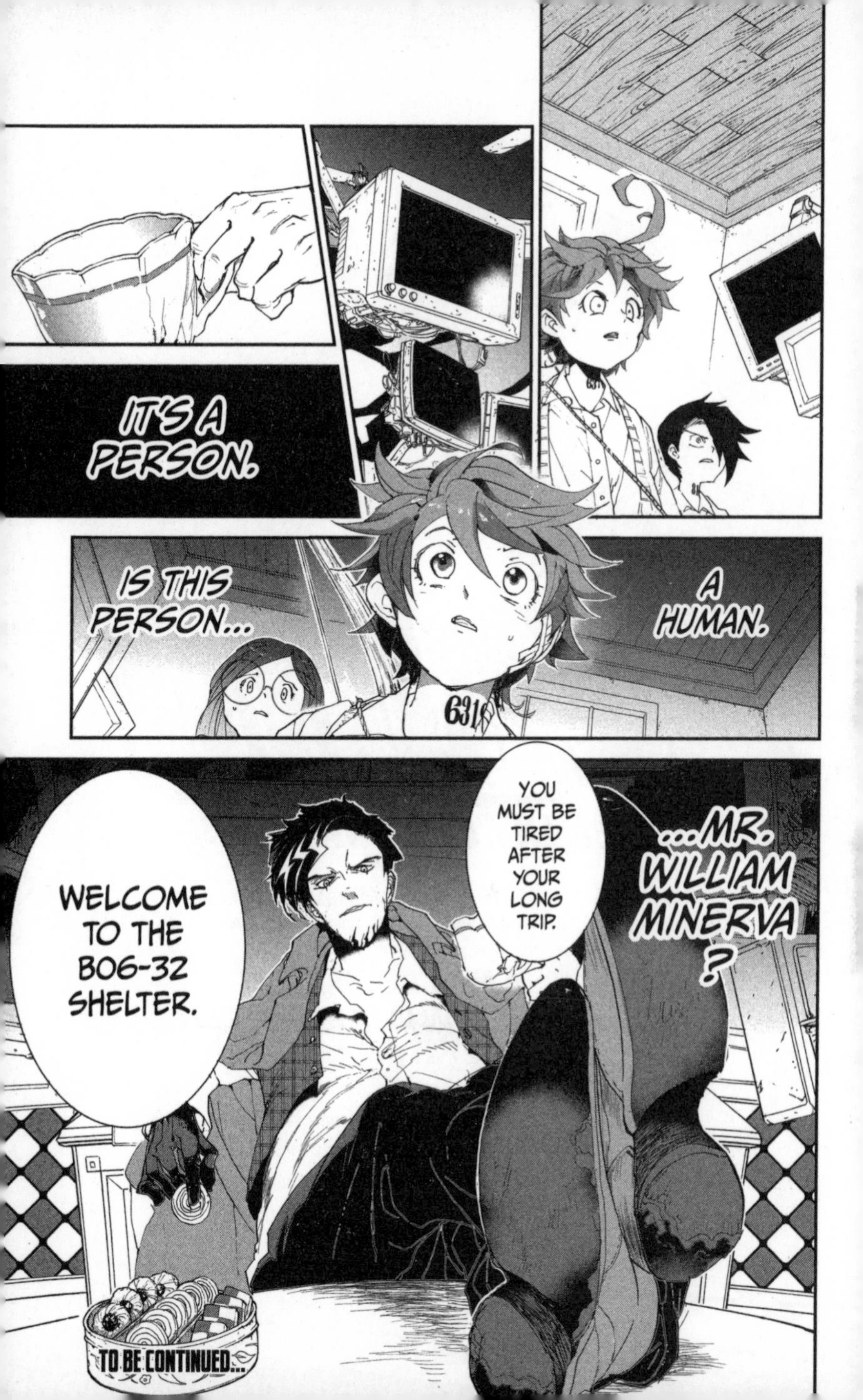
IT'S A PERSON.
IS THIS PERSON...
A HUMAN.
...MR. WILLIAM MINERVA?
YOU MUST BE TIRED AFTER YOUR LONG TRIP.
WELCOME TO THE B06-32 SHELTER.
TO BE CONTINUED...

BORUTO
=NARUTO NEXT GENERATIONS=

CREATOR/SUPERVISOR **Masashi Kishimoto**
ART BY **Mikio Ikemoto** SCRIPT BY **Ukyo Kodachi**

A NEW GENERATION OF NINJA IS HERE!

Naruto was a young shinobi with an incorrigible knack for mischief. He achieved his dream to become the greatest ninja in his village, and now his face sits atop the Hokage monument. But this is not his story... A new generation of ninja is ready to take the stage, led by Naruto's own son, Boruto!

Black ✳ Clover

STORY & ART BY YŪKI TABATA

Asta is a young boy who dreams of becoming the greatest mage in the kingdom. Only one problem—he can't use any magic! Luckily for Asta, he receives the incredibly rare five-leaf clover grimoire that gives him the power of anti-magic. Can someone who can't use magic really become the Wizard King? One thing's for sure—Asta will never give up!

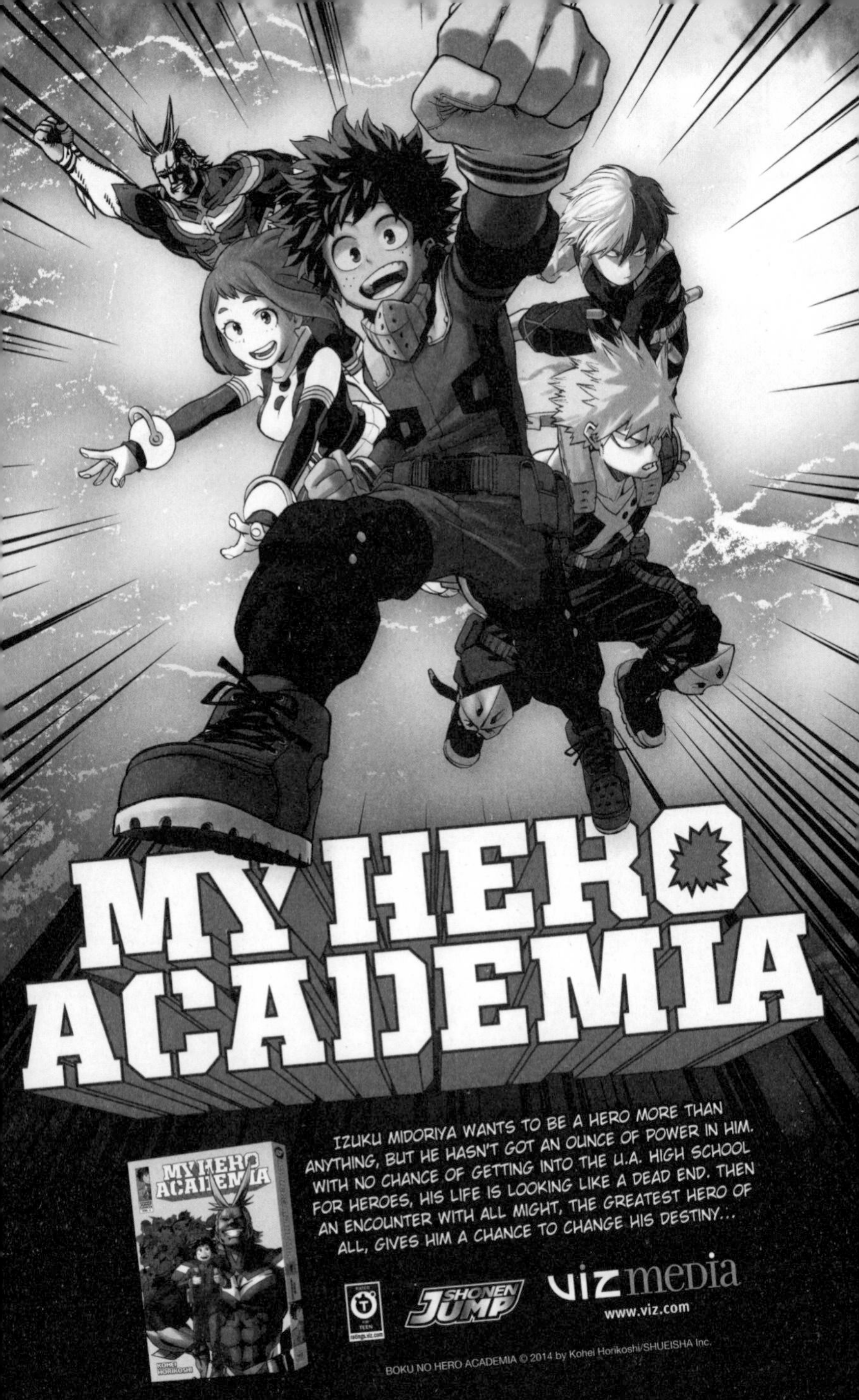

MY HERO ACADEMIA

IZUKU MIDORIYA WANTS TO BE A HERO MORE THAN ANYTHING, BUT HE HASN'T GOT AN OUNCE OF POWER IN HIM. WITH NO CHANCE OF GETTING INTO THE U.A. HIGH SCHOOL FOR HEROES, HIS LIFE IS LOOKING LIKE A DEAD END. THEN AN ENCOUNTER WITH ALL MIGHT, THE GREATEST HERO OF ALL, GIVES HIM A CHANCE TO CHANGE HIS DESTINY...

SHONEN JUMP   VIZ media
www.viz.com

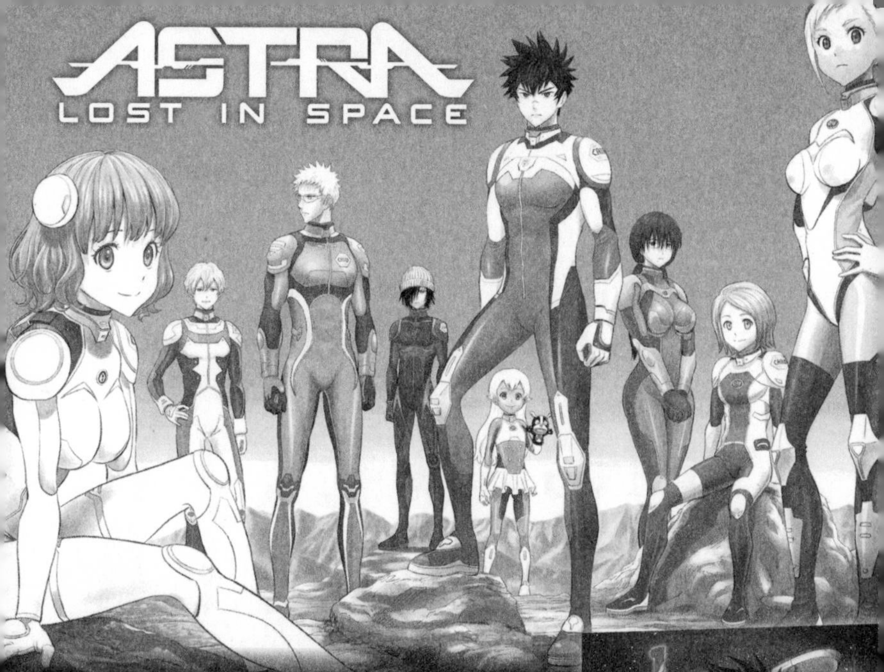

ASTRA
LOST IN SPACE

CAN EIGHT TEENAGERS FIND THEIR WAY HOME FROM 5,000 LIGHT-YEARS AWAY?

It's the year 2063, and interstellar space travel has become the norm. Eight students from Caird High School and one child set out on a routine planet camp excursion. While there, the students are mysteriously transported 5,000 light-years away to the middle of nowhere! Will they ever make it back home?!

YOU'RE READING THE **WRONG WAY!**

The Promised Neverland reads from right to left, starting in the upper-right corner. Japanese is read from right to left, meaning that action, sound effects and word-balloon order are completely reversed from English order.